American English File

Third Edition

5

Christina Latham-Koenig
Clive Oxenden
Jerry Lambert

Paul Seligson and Clive Oxenden
are the original co-authors of
English File 1 and *English File 2*

OXFORD
UNIVERSITY PRESS

Contents

Course overview

American English File
THIRD Edition

Welcome to **American English File Third Edition**. This is how to use the Student Book, Online Practice, and the Workbook in and out of class.

Student Book

All the language and skills you need to improve your English, with Grammar, Vocabulary, Pronunciation, and skills work in every File.

Use your Student Book in class with your teacher.

Workbook

Grammar, Vocabulary, and Pronunciation practice for every lesson.

Use your Workbook for homework or for self-study to practice language and to check your progress.

Go to americanenglishfileonline.com and use the code on your Access Card to log into the Online Practice.

ACTIVITIES **AUDIO** **VIDEO** **RESOURCES**

ONLINE

LOOK AGAIN

- Review the language from every lesson.
- Watch the video and listen to all the class audio as many times as you like.

PRACTICE

- Improve your skills with extra Reading, Writing, Listening, and Speaking practice.
- Use the interactive video to practice Colloquial English.

CHECK YOUR PROGRESS

- Test yourself on the language from the File and get instant feedback.
- Try a Challenge activity.

SOUND BANK

- Use the Sound Bank video to practice and improve your pronunciation of English sounds.

Online Practice

Look again at Student Book language you want to review or that you missed in class, do extra *Practice* activities, and *Check your progress* on what you learned so far.

Use the Online Practice to learn outside the classroom and get instant feedback on your progress.

americanenglishfileonline.com

1A Self-portrait

G *have*: auxiliary or main verb? **V** personality **P** using a dictionary

1 LISTENING

a Look at a painting by Frida Kahlo and answer the questions with a partner, giving your reasons.

1 Do you know anything about Frida Kahlo? Which person do you think is her in the painting?
2 Do you think the painting is finished? Why (not)?
3 Who do you think the people in the "cloud" are, and why do you think they are arranged in that way?
4 What do you think the unborn child in the middle represents?
5 Who do you think the three people with blank faces in the bottom right-hand corner might be?

b 🔊 1.2 Listen to an audio guide about the painting and check your answers to **a**. Then match the people below to numbers 1–9 in the diagram.

☐ Frida
☐ her maternal grandparents Antonio and Isabel
☐ her parents Matilde and Guillermo
☐ *1* her paternal grandparents

☐ her niece Isolda
☐ her nephew Antonio
☐ her sister Matilde
☐ her sister Adriana
☐ her sister Cristina

c 🔊 1.3 Listen to Part 1 again, about Frida. Complete Frida's biography.

Frida Kahlo

She was born in ¹_____ in ²_____ . She was the ³_____ of ⁴_____ daughters. She caught ⁵_____ as a child, and when she was ⁶_____ years old, she was in a terrible accident when a ⁷_____ crashed into a ⁸_____ . She had previously wanted to study ⁹_____ , but after the accident she decided to ¹⁰_____ instead. Frida started work on this painting in ¹¹_____ , but never ¹²_____ it. She died in ¹³_____ at the age of ¹⁴_____ .

d 🔊 1.4 Listen to Part 2 again, about the painting. Answer the questions.

1 What is the significance of the position of the unborn child?
2 Where was her father's family from?
3 Where was her mother's family from?
4 What do we learn from the painting about her parents' marriage?
5 What was Frida's relationship like with her sister Cristina?

e Talk to a partner.

1 What do you think of the painting?
2 Do you have any photos of your family that you particularly like or dislike? Why?
3 Imagine that your family has been painted in the same way. Draw a quick sketch and tell your partner about the people.

2 SPEAKING

a Work in small groups. Choose one of the sets of questions below and answer them.

- Do you have any ancestors from a different country? Who were they? Where did they come from? When did they come to live in your country?
- Who are you closest to in your family? Why do you get along with them so well? Is there anyone you don't get along with?
- Who are you most like in your family? Are there any family traits (appearance or personality) that members of your family share?

b You are going to discuss the statements below. First decide individually if you agree (**A**), half-agree (**HA**), or disagree (**D**) with the statements. Think of reasons and examples to support your opinion.

> You have to love your family, but you don't have to like them.
>
> Your "family" is the group of people who care about you, not necessarily your blood relatives.
>
> It's better to be an only child than to have brothers and sisters.
>
> Your parents raised you, so it's your responsibility to take care of them when they're old.
>
> When children are young it's better for one parent not to work and to look after them.
>
> The only person who should be allowed to criticize your family is you.
>
> You should always defend members of your family for posting controversial opinions on social media, even if you don't agree with them.

c 🔊 1.5 Listen to the expressions in the box. Which words carry extra stress for emphasis? Listen again and repeat the phrases, copying the rhythm and intonation.

🔍 **Expressions for agreeing and disagreeing**

agreeing
1 *I totally agree.*
2 *That's what I think, too.*
3 *Absolutely!*

half-agreeing
4 *I see your point, but…*
5 *I see what you mean, but…*
6 *I agree up to a point, but…*

disagreeing
7 *I completely disagree.*
8 *I don't agree at all.*
9 *I don't think you're right.*

Some English speakers don't feel comfortable using strong expressions of disagreement, e.g., *I completely disagree*, so they try to soften the fact that they disagree by half-agreeing or by using expressions such as *I'm not sure I agree with you*, *I'm afraid I really don't agree with you*, *I don't really think you're right*.

---

d Have a short discussion about the topics in **b**. Use language from **c** to agree, half-agree, or disagree with the other people in your group, and say why.

3 GRAMMAR *have*: auxiliary or main verb?

a With a partner, look at the groups of sentences 1–4. Answer the three questions for each group.

- Are all the options possible?
- Is there any difference in meaning or register?
- Is *have* a main verb or an auxiliary verb?

1	I **haven't got** time | I **don't have** time	to see my family often.
2	I**'ve been making** lots of food. I**'ve made** lots of food.	We're having a family dinner tonight.
3	**Have we got to** **Do we have to**	dress up for the party, or is it just family?
4	I**'ve had** a portrait **painted** I**'ve painted** a portrait	of our children.

b 🌐 p.142 **Grammar Bank 1A** Learn more about *have*, and practice it.

c With a partner, for each of the sentences below say if it's true for you or not, and why.

- I can't stand having my photo taken, and I'd hate to have my portrait painted.
- I have lots of friends online, but I only have a few close friends that I see regularly face-to-face.
- I've never wanted to leave home. I really like living with my family.
- I'm the most competitive person in my family. Whenever I play a sport or game, I always have to win.
- I've got to try to get out more. I think I spend too much time at home.
- I have a few possessions that are really important to me and that I would hate to lose.
- I've been arguing a lot with my family recently.

🔵 **Go online** to review the lesson

4 VOCABULARY personality

a Look at the adjectives that describe personality below. With a partner, say if you consider them to be positive or negative qualities, and why. Would you use any of them to describe yourself?

> affectionate assertive bossy curious easygoing loyal moody outgoing rebellious reliable sensible sensitive stubborn

b **V** p.162 **Vocabulary Bank** Personality

5 PRONUNCIATION using a dictionary

a Underline the stressed syllable in the words below.

1 con|sci|en|tious
2 de|ter|mined
3 thor|ough
4 ea|sy|go|ing
5 stea|dy
6 spon|ta|ne|ous

b Look at the pink letters in each word. Match them to the sound pictures below.

c ◀) 1.9 Listen and check your answers to **a** and **b**.

> **🔍 Checking pronunciation in a dictionary**
>
> All good dictionaries, whether paper or online, give the pronunciation of a word in phonetics, with a stress mark (') to show the stressed syllable. Online dictionaries also have an icon you can click on to hear the words, many giving both American and British pronunciation.
>
> > **needy** adjective NAmE /'nidi/(◀)); BrE /'nidi/ (◀))
> > (of people) not confident, and needing a lot of love and emotional support from other people
> > She is shy and **needy**.

d Look at the phonetics for some more adjectives of personality. With a partner, figure out how they are pronounced and spelled, and say what they mean if you know. Check with a dictionary.

> 1 /'æŋkʃəs/ 2 /'laɪvli/ 3 /'noʊzi/ 4 /'soʊʃəbl/ 5 /'stɪndʒi/

e Do you usually use a paper dictionary or an online one? What do you think are its main advantages?

6 READING

a To what extent do you think the following are good ways of predicting personality types?
- online quizzes
- personality tests
- your handwriting
- your astrological sign

b You are going to take a well-known personality test. Before you start, look at the following painting for 30 seconds. Write down what you see. You will need this when you take the test.

> **LEXIS IN CONTEXT**
>
> **🔍 Looking up phrasal verbs and idioms in a dictionary**
>
> **Phrasal verbs** PHR V
>
> Phrasal verbs are listed in alphabetical order after the entry for the verbs.
>
> If the object (somebody or something) is shown **between** the two parts, e.g., *put something off*, this means the phrasal verb is separable, and the object can go between the verb and the particle **or** after the particle. If the object is shown **after** the particle, e.g., *look for something*, it means the verb and the particle cannot be separated.
>
> **Idioms** IDM
>
> You can usually find the definition of an idiom under one of its "main" words (nouns, verbs, adverbs, or adjectives, but NOT prepositions and articles), e.g., the definition of *catch your eye* will be given under *catch* or *eye*.
>
> After some very common verbs, e.g., *be*, *get*, and adjectives, e.g., *good*, *bad*, the idioms are usually under the entries for the next "main" word, e.g., *be a good sport* comes under *sport*.

c With a partner, look at the test *What's your personality?* Read the questions and possible answers. Try to figure out the meaning of the highlighted phrasal verbs and idioms, but don't look them up yet.

d Use a dictionary to check the meaning of the highlighted phrases.

e Now take the test. For each question, decide which answer best describes you and circle it.

WHAT'S YOUR PERSONALITY?

A PLANNER OR SPONTANEOUS

1 Are you...?
   a a perfectionist who hates leaving things unfinished
   b someone who hates being under pressure and tends to over-prepare
   c a little disorganized and forgetful
   d someone who puts things off until the last minute

2 Imagine you have bought a piece of furniture that requires assembly (e.g., a wardrobe or a cabinet). Which of these are you more likely to do?
   a Check that you have all the items and the tools you need before you start.
   b Carefully read the instructions and follow them to the letter.
   c Quickly read through the instructions to get the basic idea of what you have to do.
   d Start assembling it right away. Check the instructions only if you get stuck.

3 Before you go on vacation, which of these do you do?
   a Plan every detail of your vacation.
   b Put together a rough itinerary, but make sure you leave yourself plenty of free time.
   c Get an idea of what kinds of things you can do, but not make a decision until you get there.
   d Book the vacation at the last minute and plan hardly anything in advance.

B FACTS OR IDEAS

4 Which option best describes what you wrote about the painting in b on p.8?
   a It's basically a list of what appears in the picture.
   b It tells the story of what's happening in the picture.
   c It tries to explain what the picture means.
   d It's a lot of ideas that the picture made you think of.

5 You need to give a friend directions to your house. Do you...?
   a write down a list of detailed directions
   b send a link to a website that provides directions
   c give rough directions
   d draw a simple map showing only the basic directions

6 When you go shopping at the supermarket, do you...?
   a always go down the same aisles in the same order
   b carefully check prices and compare products
   c buy whatever catches your eye
   d go around a different way each time, according to what you want to buy

C HEADS OR HEARTS

7 If an argument starts when you are with friends, do you...?
   a face it head on and say what you think
   b try to find a solution yourself
   c try to keep everyone happy
   d do anything to avoid hurting people's feelings

8 Imagine you had the choice between two apartments to rent. Would you...?
   a write down what your ideal apartment would be like and then see which one was the most similar
   b make a list of the pros and cons of each one
   c just go with your gut feeling
   d consider carefully how each apartment would affect other members of your family

9 Imagine a friend of yours started going out with someone new, and they asked you for your opinion. If you really didn't like the person, would you...?
   a tell them exactly what you thought
   b be honest, but as tactful as possible
   c try to avoid answering the question directly
   d tell a "white lie"

D EXTROVERT OR INTROVERT

10 You are out with a group of friends. Do you...?
   a say hardly anything
   b say a little less than most people
   c talk a lot
   d do nearly all the talking

11 When you meet a new group of people, do you...?
   a try to stay with people you already know
   b have to think hard about how to keep the conversation going
   c try to get to know as many people as possible
   d just try to enjoy yourself

12 If the phone rings while you are in the middle of something, do you...?
   a ignore it and continue with what you're doing
   b answer it quickly, but say you'll call back
   c have a conversation, but make sure you keep it short
   d welcome the interruption and enjoy a nice long chat

From www.bbc.co.uk/science

f Now find out which type you are for each section.

   A more a and b = **PLANNER**
      more c and d = **SPONTANEOUS**
   B more a and b = **FACTS**
      more c and d = **IDEAS**
   C more a and b = **HEAD**
      more c and d = **HEART**
   D more a and b = **INTROVERT**
      more c and d = **EXTROVERT**

g **Communication** What's your personality? p.106. Find out which category you fit into and read the description of your personality. Compare with your partner. How accurate were the descriptions of your personalities?

Go online to review the lesson

> Whenever you are asked if you can do a job, tell 'em, "Certainly I can." Then get busy and find out how to do it.
> *Theodore Roosevelt, US President 1901–1909*

G discourse markers (1): linkers **V** work **P** the rhythm of spoken English

1 READING & SPEAKING

a Think about people you know who either absolutely hate or really love their jobs. What do they do? Why do they feel that way? How do you know how they feel?

b *The Guardian* runs a weekly series called *What I'm really thinking*, where people in different jobs or situations reveal their true feelings. Look at the three jobs in the articles. With a partner, say which person you think said the following, and why.

1 Although it is not my place to judge, I get frustrated sometimes.
2 I'm aware that I'm a novelty.
3 Your expressions and bodies reveal far more than you know.

c Read the articles and check. Reading between the lines, do you think on the whole they like or dislike their jobs?

d Read the articles again and answer **A**, **B**, or **C**. Who…?

1 ▢ implies that he / she doesn't care how people feel about his / her looks / physical appearance
2 ▢ says people seem to think he / she can't see them
3 ▢ uses his / her job to figure out any problems he / she might be experiencing in his / her life outside of work
4 ▢ has to ask one particular question, to which it is not always easy to get the answer
5 ▢ would like the opportunity to give feedback on the people he / she works with
6 ▢ notices a physical change in him / herself when he / she is working
7 ▢ describes a moment when he / she really loves the job
8 ▢ realizes he / she is a role model
9 ▢ tries to empathize with the people he / she speaks to

LEXIS IN CONTEXT

e Look at the highlighted phrasal verbs and idioms and guess the meaning of the ones you don't know from the context. Then match them to the definitions 1–7.

1 _____ IDM defend myself
2 _____ IDM makes me very upset
3 _____ PHR V move or make progress at the same rate as somebody / something
4 _____ IDM (*informal*) reasonable, acceptable
5 _____ IDM not understood the most important fact
6 _____ IDM vitally important
7 _____ IDM can't think what to do or say

What I'm really thinking

A | THE FEMALE BOXING COACH

Apparently, I don't look like a boxer. I get told that a lot. I've lost count of the number of times people have exclaimed, "What if you mess up your nose?" and, "What if your mess up your face?" They've missed the point: I'm not a model, so what does it matter if my nose isn't straight? And anyway, boxing means more to me than that: it's my structure and my sanity. Cheaper than therapy, that's what we say. Injuries are part of the game, but I've been lucky so far.

As the only girl who spars in my gym, I'm aware that I'm a novelty. I've always been a tomboy, though, so it doesn't bother me to train with the blokes. Some men don't like to spar with a woman, and that's fair enough. But mostly they get used to it.

When I'm not in the mood and consider giving up, I think about the children I help teach. There are a couple of young girls coming up who are really good and I want to be an example. Every time I hold my own in the ring, I challenge someone's expectations a little bit, and I'm proud of myself for that.

B | THE UNIVERSITY LECTURER

I look at the 23 of you in the room—a small group this year—and wonder if you're even aware of me as I teach. Might it be that because you're not talking directly to me, you forget to adjust the expressions on your faces? Or is it that you imagine, in a crowd, you are somehow invisible? Your expressions and bodies reveal far more than you know—sneering, eye-rolling, yawning, you can barely stay awake sometimes.

Your indifference bears no relation to my hours of preparation. The university asks you to comment, anonymously, on the quality of my teaching. I would like the chance to comment on the quality of your listening. When you are really disengaged and disconnected, I see hands reach for phones in bags. You connect, but it's usually to someone outside this room. Sometimes you even pass notes, giggle, and whisper.

Yet I also see you when you laugh at my jokes. When you are concentrating hard, I can almost hear your minds working. Some of you take notes so intensively, fighting to keep up with my words, as if it's life or death if you miss something.
I see your faces light up when you want to say something, the eagerness to comment, to take part. You are relaxed, smiling, enjoying the moment of understanding. We connect. Now I see you and you see me.

C | THE EMERGENCY OPERATOR

The hardest part of my job is also the simplest—getting the address. Often when someone calls, they go blank. Or in the case of a road accident, they don't know exactly where they are. But the most important element is the address because that's what brings the ambulance. I have to ask for it twice, which infuriates people.

It still surprises me to hear my voice during a call. It changes, becoming deeper, almost authoritative. I have to take control of the situation. I suppose that's why I wear a uniform. I have a script, but I refuse to be a robot; hearing people at their most vulnerable makes me add to it. When the caller is hysterical, telling them, "I'm going to help you" and "I know you're frightened" calms them down. But it breaks my heart when they're in pain or their loved one is dying; I have to take a "stress break" after harrowing calls.

Although it is not my place to judge, I get frustrated sometimes. The man who rang because his toothpaste was burning his mouth; the mother whose baby was afraid of a fly. Don't they realize they're taking up precious time when a life-or-death situation may be needing help? But the moment I call them time-wasters is the moment I should quit my job.

Glossary

mess up physically hurt somebody, especially by hitting them

bloke (NAmE man) an informal term to describe a man

emergency operator a professional who answers incoming calls for police, fire, and emergency assistance

f Look at some extracts from other *What I'm really thinking* articles. Match them to the jobs in the list. What do they imply that the people (sometimes) feel about their jobs?

| beauty counter manager ☐ | dentist ☐ | driving instructor ☐ |
| IT support worker ☐ | pizza delivery person ☐ | taxi driver ☐ |

1 Sometimes what I do is painful, and I'm not a sadist.
2 I don't expect to chat, but sometimes my cab becomes a mobile confessional.
3 Men are risk-takers. They go too fast and don't like being told what to do.
4 I'd like some respect—people who answer the door while they're on the phone really bug me, as do the ones who take a long time to find the money.
5 It's a cliché, but "Did you turn it on and off again?" is the first thing that comes to my mind every single time someone calls.
6 I work in an industry that convinces people to part with their cash in pursuit of a perfection that does not exist. I am betraying my sisterhood.

g Of all the jobs mentioned in the articles and extracts, which one(s)…?
• would you never do under any circumstances
• might you consider doing if you desperately needed the money
• would you actually like to do

2 VOCABULARY work

a Look at three sentences from the articles and complete the missing words.

1 Every time I hold my own in the ring, I c_____ someone's expectations a little bit, and I'm proud of myself for that.
2 It changes, becoming deeper, almost a_____.
3 But the moment I call them time-wasters is the moment I should qu_____ my job.

b ⓥ p.163 **Vocabulary Bank** Work

c Complete sentences 1–5 with words or phrases from the list. Then write five sentences for your partner to complete with the other five words.

| apply for | be fired | be laid off | clock out |
| perks | quit | rewarding | skills | tedious | unpaid |

1 Can we leave whenever we like or do we have to _____ at a certain time?
2 Nursing is often described as a _____ job, even though it may be badly paid.
3 The company has decided that around 20% of its workforce will have to _____ until the economic situation improves.
4 The only _____ required for this position are a good level of English and the ability to drive.
5 If you are prepared to do _____ work, there are several volunteer organizations that are looking for people.

Go online to review the lesson

3 SPEAKING & LISTENING

a Since 2001, the *Sunday Times* has been running an annual survey to find the 100 best companies to work for. Look at the criteria that they use to assess the companies and complete them with the headings.

Fair deal
Giving something back
Leadership
~~My company~~
My manager
My team
Personal growth
Well-being

1 *My company* : how staff feel about the organization they work for as opposed to the people they work with

2 _____ : how staff feel about the pressures of work and the balance between their work and home duties

3 _____ : how much companies are thought by their staff to contribute to the local community and society

4 _____ : to what extent staff feel they are stretched and challenged by their job

5 _____ : how staff feel towards their immediate boss

6 _____ : how employees feel about the head of the company and its senior managers

7 _____ : how staff feel about their immediate colleagues

8 _____ : how happy the workforce is with their pay and benefits

b Which three criteria do you think are the most important when judging a company you are thinking of working for?

c Now look at the photos and read about Skyscanner, a travel comparison website, one of the top-rated companies in the *Sunday Times* survey. Does it sound like a company you would like to work for? Why (not)?

Skyscanner

Who are they?

AS A KEEN SKIER who regularly escaped to the slopes, math graduate Gareth Williams became frustrated with the tedious process of searching through a multitude of airline and travel-agency websites to find the cheapest flights. So he and two university friends set about creating a single website that could collect, collate, and compare prices for every commercial flight in the world. Launched in Edinburgh in 2001, Skyscanner, which also provides instant online comparisons for hotels and car rentals, gets more than 60 million visitors a month and now operates worldwide—it also has offices in Singapore, Beijing, Miami, and Barcelona. No organization offers as many opportunities to learn and grow as this one does, say its employees. Skyscanner perks include a paid day off to do a social activity, and home-country working, where people who aren't native to the UK can spend up to three weeks a year working in their country of origin. As the staff represent more than 35 different nationalities, this is a particularly popular benefit.

d ◑ 1.13 Listen to an interview with a Skyscanner employee. What is her position in the company? How positive is she about the company and her job on a scale of 1–5 (5 = very positive)? What makes you think so?

> **Glossary**
> **PR** Public Relations

e Listen again and answer the questions.

1 How long has she been at Skyscanner?
2 Why did she apply for a job there?
3 Where did she go the day after the interview?
4 What three benefits does she mention about working for Skyscanner?
5 Which benefit does she value most highly and why?
6 What challenge does she say that the company faces?

LEXIS IN CONTEXT

f ◑ 1.14 Listen to the phrases in context. What do you think the highlighted words and phrases mean?

1 …**somewhere** that was kind of travel-focused…
2 …it very quickly becomes the norm for someone who works here…
3 …maybe **that's** the plan, maybe that's the ploy that they've gone with!
4 …**it's** a very casual thing…you're in charge, you're the … you're the one who knows your workload…
5 …so I think at some point **that** will be something that becomes more of an issue…I'm pretty confident that Skyscanner will be able to tackle that…

g What do you think of Skyscanner after listening to the interview? Are you more or less attracted to working there?

4 GRAMMAR discourse markers (1): linkers

> …it very quickly becomes the norm for someone who works here, all these amazing benefits we have, _____ when you talk to someone else in another company, you suddenly think "Wow, we're so lucky."

a Look at the extract from the interview. What do you think the missing word is? What kind of clause does it introduce?

b With a partner, put two linkers from the list into each column.

> as   consequently   despite   due to   even though
> in order to   so as to   therefore

a result	a reason	a purpose	a contrast
so	because	to	but

c **G** p.143 **Grammar Bank 1B** Learn more about linkers, and practice them.

5 PRONUNCIATION the rhythm of spoken English

> 🔍 **Fine-tuning your pronunciation: the rhythm of English**
> In spoken English, words with two or more syllables have one main stressed syllable. In sentences, some words have stronger stress and other words are weaker. This pattern of strong and weak stress gives English its rhythm. Stressed words in a sentence are usually **content words**, e.g., nouns, verbs, adjectives, and adverbs. Unstressed words tend to be **function words** and include auxiliary verbs, prepositions, conjunctions, determiners, and possessive adjectives.

a ◑ 1.15 Listen and repeat the sentences. Try to copy the rhythm as exactly as possible.

> **Boston** transpor**ta**tion **workers** were on **strike yesterday**.
> As a **result**, it **took people twice** as **long** to **get** to **work**.

b ◑ 1.16 Listen and write down the beginnings of eight sentences. Compare with a partner, and then decide how you think the sentences might continue.

c ◑ 1.17 Now listen and complete the sentences. Are they similar to what you predicted? Practice saying them with a natural rhythm.

6 WRITING

W p.114 **Writing** A job application Analyze a model email and write a cover email applying for a job at a festival.

Go online to review the lesson

Colloquial English Work and family

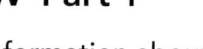
discourse markers | musical families

1 ▶ THE INTERVIEW Part 1

a Read the biographical information about Eliza Carthy. Have you ever heard any English, Scottish, or Irish folk music?

Eliza Carthy is a folk musician known both for singing and playing the violin. She is the daughter of singer / guitarist Martin Carthy and singer Norma Waterson, who are also folk musicians. In addition to her solo work, she has played and sung with several groups, including as lead vocalist with Blue Murder. She has been nominated twice for the Mercury Music Prize for album of the year and has won seven BBC Folk Awards. In 2010, she released an album of collaborations with her mother, entitled *Gift*. A reviewer wrote: "The gift in question here…is a handing of talent from generation to generation."

b ◀》1.18 Watch or listen to Part 1 of the interview. What is her overwhelming memory of her childhood?

c Now listen again. What does she say about…?

1 her father in the 50s and 60s
2 The Watersons
3 her mother's grandmother
4 her mother's uncle and father
5 *The Spinning Wheel*
6 the farm where she was brought up
7 her parents' friends

Glossary
Bob Dylan (b.1941) an American singer-songwriter, who has influenced popular music and culture for more than five decades
Paul Simon (b.1941) an American singer-songwriter, at one time half of the duo Simon and Garfunkel
Hull a city in Yorkshire, England
travelers / gypsies people who traditionally travel around and live in trailers
banjo a musical instrument like a guitar, with a long neck, a round body, and four or more strings
The Spinning Wheel an Irish ballad written in the mid-1800s

▶ Part 2

a ◀》1.19 Now watch or listen to Part 2. What do you think Eliza Carthy was like as a child? What do you find out about her as a mother?

b Listen again and answer the questions.

1 Did Eliza Carthy originally want to become a musician?
2 Why did her mother retire?
3 How old was she at her first public performance?
4 How much did she sing during the concert?
5 How has she reorganized her life because of having her own children?
6 What does she feel she's lacking right now?

Glossary
the Fylde an area in western Lancashire, England
Fleetwood a town in the Fylde
the Marine Hall a venue in Fleetwood

▶ Part 3

a ◀》1.20 Now watch or listen to Part 3. How has Eliza Carthy's family influenced her approach to music?

b Listen again. Mark the sentences **T** (true) or **F** (false). Correct the false sentences.

1 Eliza Carthy thinks the reason she doesn't like working alone is because of being brought up surrounded by people.
2 Right now she has a 30-piece band.
3 Her father understands that working with family members is different.
4 Her father was a blood relation in the group The Watersons.
5 Eliza Carthy's daughter Florence plays three musical instruments and also sings well.
6 She thinks there's a close link between foreign languages and singing.
7 Her younger daughter Isabella is not yet interested in music.
8 She would rather her children didn't become touring musicians.

Glossary
Twinkle, Twinkle a well-known children's song (*Twinkle, twinkle little star, How I wonder what you are…*)

2 LOOKING AT LANGUAGE

🔍 **Discourse markers**
Eliza Carthy uses several discourse markers when she speaks, that is, adverbs (e.g., *so, anyway*) or adverbial expressions (e.g., *in fact, after all*) that connect and organize language, and help you to follow what she is saying.

a 🔊 **1.21** Watch or listen to some extracts from the interview and fill in the blanks with one or two words.

1 "and they were also instrumental in the beginning of the 60s folk revival, the formation of the folk clubs, and the, the beginning of, _____, the professional music scene that I work on now."

2 **Interviewer:** "And were your parents both from musical families?"
Eliza: "Um, _____, both sides of my family are musical…"

3 "My mum retired in 1966…65…66 from professional touring to raise me. _____ _____, the road is a difficult place…"

4 "But yes, _____ I just—the first song they started up singing, tugged on his leg…"

5 **Interviewer:** "Has having children yourself changed your approach to your career?"
Eliza: "Uh, yes, _____ a _____, yes, _____ a _____, it has."

6 "The Watersons was a brother and two sisters, and he joined that, and _____ _____ he was married to my mum, but he wasn't related to her."

7 "And Isabella, my youngest as well, she's really, she's really showing interest in it, I love it when they do that. _____ _____ whether or not I'd want them to be touring musicians…"

8 "But, you know, I think the—I think the world is changing _____, I don't know how many touring musicians there are going to be in the world in 20 years…"

b How do the discourse markers affect the meaning of what Eliza says in each extract?

3 ▶ ON THE STREET

a 🔊 **1.22** Watch or listen to five people talking about their family trees. Who mentions foreign ancestors? Where were they from?

| Sarah | Kent | Alison | Marylin | Hannah |
| *American* | *American* | *English* | *American* | *American* |

b Watch or listen again. Who (**S, K, A, M,** or **H**)…?

☐ has an ancestor who died in a famous disaster
☐ has a family member who was adopted
☐ has tried unsuccessfully to contact some distant relatives
☐ has used ancestry.com to research their family tree
☐ thinks their ancestors worked on the land

c 🔊 **1.23** Watch or listen and complete the Colloquial English phrases. What do you think they mean?

1 "Uh, I actually know _____ _____ _____ about my family tree on my dad's side…"

2 "Um, 'cause I think they were farmers, I'm not _____ _____…"

3 "Um, I know a _____ _____ because, um, my dad's done some research…"

4 "Um, well, _____ _____, it's precisely those relatives…"

5 "…but it doesn't _____ _____ _____ than that and that's only on my dad's side."

> **Glossary**
> **The Mayflower** a ship that sailed from Plymouth, England to what is now the US, in 1620.
> **Cornwall** a county in southwestern England

4 SPEAKING

Answer the questions with a partner or in small groups.

- How much do you know about your family tree? Have you ever researched it?
- Is there anyone in your family that you'd like to know more about?
- Do you know anyone who works in a family business? How well do the relationships work?
- Would you like to work with your parents or with your siblings? Why (not)?
- Do you think it's easier or more difficult for the children of successful parents to be successful themselves?

🖱️ **Go online** to watch the video, review the lesson, and check your progress

Changing language

> Americans who travel abroad for the first time are often shocked to discover that many foreign people still speak in foreign languages.
> *Dave Barry, US writer*

G pronouns   **V** learning languages   **P** sound–spelling relationships; understanding accents

1 SPELLING

a ◀)) **2.1** A recent survey found the ten most commonly mispelled words in English. Listen to sentences 1–10 and complete the missing words. How many did you spell correctly? What do many of the words have in common?

1 He always _____ to his father as "my old man."

2 I like all vegetables except _____ .

3 The food was _____ , but no more than that.

4 I think taking the dog with us is an _____ complication.

5 There was a _____ of opinion that the article should not be published.

6 It was a very strange _____ .

7 Please don't _____ me by wearing that hat!

8 During your driver's test you will be asked to perform some standard _____ .

9 We'll _____ be there by seven.

10 They married in 2016, but _____ two years later.

b ◀)) **2.2** Now listen to the following poem. Find nine spelling mistakes of a different kind. What is the message of the poem?

> I have a spelling checker
>
> It came with my PC
>
> It plainly marks for my revue
>
> Mistakes I cannot sea
>
> I've run this poem threw it
>
> I'm sure your pleased to no
>
> It's letter-perfect in it's weigh
>
> My checker tolled me sew

2 READING & SPEAKING

a With a partner, decide how to pronounce the following words. Do you know what they all mean?

ghost   gnome   know   moon   blood   mice   debt   movable   rhubarb

b Read the review on p.17 of *Spell It Out,* a book about the story of English spelling. What do you learn about the spelling and pronunciation of the words in **a**?

LEXIS IN CONTEXT

🔍 **Making sense of whole phrases**
Even when you understand the individual words in a text, you may still have problems understanding the meaning. When you read, focus on whole phrases or sentences, and refer to the surrounding context to figure out what the writer is saying.

c Read the review again and look at phrases 1–6 in context. In pairs, say what you think the reviewer means.

1 he was bewildered by the random nature of English spelling (lines 10–11)

2 Fashion and snobbery have played as big a part in spelling as they have in other parts of English life. (lines 25–26)

3 scribes looked to Latin for guidance (line 28)

4 For a long time, there was no stigma attached to variant spellings. (line 32)

5 Even today, spelling is more fluid than we might think. (line 39)

6 the internet is the ultimate spelling democracy (line 41)

d Answer the questions in small groups.

1 How do you think the reviewer feels towards students of English? Do you agree?

2 What modern example does she give of the damaging effects of bad spelling?

3 Are there any words in your language that people have particular problems spelling? Why (not)?

4 Do you think good spelling matters?

Have you ever wondered why *ghost* is spelled with an *h*? Why isn't it "gost" or "goast" to rhyme with "most" or "toast"? Other words that begin with a hard *g*, such as "golf," don't have an *h*. The answer, according to David Crystal's entertaining *Spell It Out*, is a result of the whim of a Flemish compositor, a man whose job it was in the late 15th century to arrange type for printing. His English wasn't good, and, like many non-native speakers, he was bewildered by the random nature of English spelling. So when he saw the word "gost" (spelled "gheest" in Flemish), he decided to spell it the Flemish way, with an *h*.

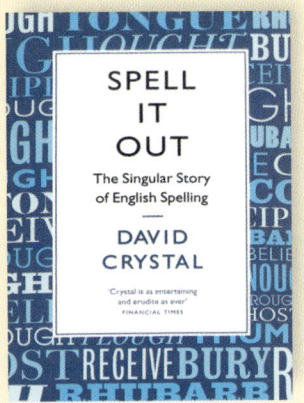

SPELL IT OUT
The Singular Story of English Spelling
DAVID CRYSTAL
'Crystal is as entertaining and erudite as ever'
FINANCIAL TIMES

The Flemish *h* in *ghost* is one of Crystal's many examples that show that the development of English spelling has been both random and unsystematic. The original monks who tried to write down Anglo-Saxon English in a Latin alphabet, he says, did a pretty good job. Every word was pronounced phonetically—so the *g* in *gnome* would be pronounced, as would the *k* in *know*. But the alphabet they devised didn't have enough letters to represent all the sounds in spoken English and that was where the problems started. Scribes started to double vowels to represent different sounds, such as double *o* for the long /u/ sound in *moon, food*, etc. But then in some words like *blood* and *flood,* the pronunciation changed in the south of England, shortening the vowel, so that now, as Crystal puts it, "these spellings represent the pronunciation of a thousand years ago."

Fashion and snobbery have played as big a part in spelling as they have in other parts of English life. After the Norman invasion, Anglo-Saxon spellings were replaced by French ones: *servis* became *service, mys* became *mice*, for instance. During the Renaissance, scribes looked to Latin for guidance—take the word *debt*. In the 13th century this could be spelled *det, dett, dette,* or *deytt*. But 16th-century writers looked to the Latin word *debitum*, and inserted a silent *b*—linking the word to its Latin counterpart, but making it much harder to spell.

For a long time, there was no stigma attached to variant spellings. Shakespeare famously wrote his name several ways (Shaksper, Shakspere, Shakspeare), but, by the 18th century, an English aristocrat was writing to his son that "orthography...is so absolutely necessary for a man of letters, or a gentleman, that one false spelling may fix a ridicule upon him for the rest of his life." Dan Quayle, the former US vice-president, never recovered from spelling *potato* with an *e* on the end when he corrected a pupil's writing in front of the cameras at a junior school in 1992.

Even today, spelling is more fluid than we might think. *Moveable*, for example—*The Times* style guide keeps the *e*, *The Guardian* prefers *movable*. And online there are no guides—the internet is the ultimate spelling democracy. Take *rhubarb*, with its pesky silent *h*: in 2006 there were just a few hundred instances of *rubarb* in the Google database; they have now passed the million mark. 'If it carries on like this," Crystal notes, "*rubarb* will overtake *rhubarb* as the commonest online spelling... And where the online orthographic world goes in one decade, I suspect the offline world will go in the next."

Reading this book made me thankful that English is my native language; the spelling must make it so fiendishly hard to learn!

By Daisy Goodwin in the Sunday Times

Glossary
Flemish /ˈflɛmɪʃ/ from Flanders, the northern part of present-day Belgium

monk /mʌŋk/ a member of a religious group of men who often live apart from other people in a monastery

scribe /skraɪb/ a person who made copies of written documents before printing was invented

the Norman Invasion the occupation of England in 1066 by the Normans, who came from northern France

orthography /ɔːˈθɒɡrəfi/ (formal) the system of spelling in a language

junior school (NAmE elementary school) a school for children between the ages of 5 and 12

---

3 PRONUNCIATION
sound–spelling relationships

> 🔍 **Learning spelling rules or patterns**
> Although many people think that English pronunciation has no rules, especially regarding sounds and spelling, estimates suggest that around 80% of words are pronounced according to a rule or pattern, e.g., the letter *h* before a vowel is almost always pronounced /h/.

a With a partner, say each group of words aloud. How are the pink letters pronounced? Circle the different word if there is one.

1 /h/ hurt dishonest inherit heart himself
2 /oʊ/ throw elbow lower power grow
3 /aɪ/ compromise despite river write quite
4 /w/ whenever why whose where which
5 /dʒ/ jealous journalist reject job enjoy
6 /tʃ/ challenging achieve chorus catch charge
7 /s/ sense seem sympathetic synonym sure
8 /ɔ/ awful raw flaw drawback law
9 /ɔr/ short corner work ignore reporter
10 /ər/ firm dirty third T-shirt birth

b 🔊 **2.3** Listen and check. What's the pronunciation rule for each spelling? Can you think of any more exceptions?

c Think about the spelling patterns in **a**. How do you think these words are probably pronounced? Check their pronunciation and meaning with your teacher or with a dictionary.

chime   howl   jaw   whirl   worm

4 GRAMMAR pronouns

a 🔊 **2.4** Look at the phonetics for a word that is often mispelled, but never corrected by spell checkers. How is it pronounced? Listen and check.

/ðɛr/

b Now fill in the blanks with three different spellings of the word in **a**.

1 _____ pronoun + contracted verb
2 _____ adverb
3 _____ possessive adjective

c 🅖 **p.144 Grammar Bank 2A** Learn more about pronouns, and practice them.

Go online to review the lesson

a Look at the section headings 1–4 in *Working With Words*. With a partner, say what they mean.

b Do the exercises in *Working With Words*. Then compare with a partner.

Working With Words

1 Collocations

Complete with *say*, *speak*, *talk*, or *tell*.

1 I can _____ three languages fluently: English, French, and German.

2 _____ me the truth. Did you <u>really</u> do this yourself?

3 This situation can't go on. We need to _____.

4 What did you _____? I couldn't hear you because of the noise.

5 Did you _____ Mark about the party next week?

6 Hi. Could I _____ to Maria, please? It's Jennifer.

7 You could learn the basics in, let's _____, six months.

8 Sorry, I can't _____ now. I'm in a meeting.

2 Phrasal verbs

Match the phrasal verbs in 1–5 to their meanings A–E.

1 [ ] I spent a month in Florence and I was able to **pick up** quite a bit of Italian.

2 [ ] I'll need to **brush up** on my Spanish before we go to Mexico. I haven't spoken it since college!

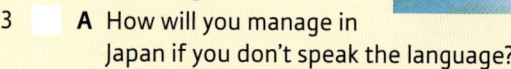

3 [ ] **A** How will you manage in Japan if you don't speak the language?

B I think I'll be able to **get by**. I can speak a little Japanese and most people speak some English.

4 [ ] Your pronunciation is fantastic. You could almost **pass for** a local!

5 [ ] Even though my English is fluent, I found it hard to **take in** what my boss said in the meeting because he spoke so fast.

A be accepted as somebody / something

B to quickly improve a skill, especially when you haven't used it for a long time

C to absorb, understand

D to learn a new skill or language by practicing it rather than being taught

E to manage to live or do a particular thing using the money, knowledge, equipment, etc. that you have

3 Synonyms and register

a Match the words or expressions 1–5 to synonyms A–E.

1 error   A respond to somebody
2 answer somebody B language
3 request somebody to C vocabulary
4 tongue   D mistake
5 lexis   E ask somebody to

b Which word is more formal in each pair?

4 Idioms

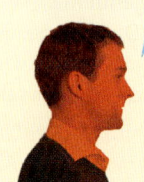

Your father isn't well, is he?

How's your father?

Match sentences 1–5 to A–E.

1 [ ] I think we're talking **at cross purposes**.

2 [ ] The word's **on the tip of my tongue**.

3 [ ] When I talk to my boss, I'm going to **speak my mind**.

4 [ ] I just can't **get my tongue around** this word.

5 [ ] I can't **get my head around** this definition.

A I'm going to tell her my honest feelings.

B It's really hard for me to pronounce.

C It's too complicated and I can't understand it.

D I can't remember it right now, but I'm sure I will soon.

E When you said "lunch on Sunday" I thought you meant this Sunday, not next Sunday.

6 PRONUNCIATION understanding accents

🔍 **Received Pronunciation and General American English**
There are many different native-speaker accents in English. Received Pronunciation, or RP, is defined in the *Concise Oxford English Dictionary* as "the standard accent of English as spoken in the south of England" and General American is defined as "a form of US speech without marked dialectal or regional characteristics". However, only a small percentage of native-speakers have these standard British and American accents, so it is important to be able to understand different ones as well.

a 🔊 **2.5** Listen to six people talking with different native-speaker accents. Can you match any of the accents?

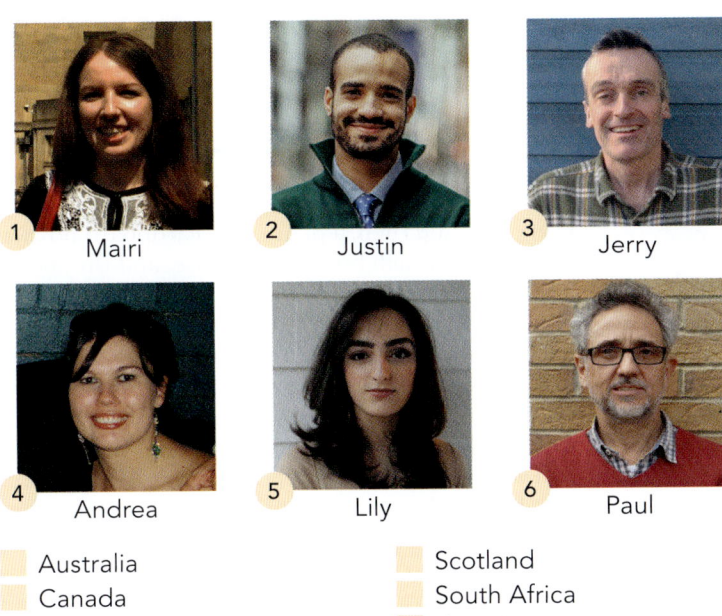

1 Mairi   2 Justin   3 Jerry

4 Andrea   5 Lily   6 Paul

☐ Australia   ☐ Scotland
☐ Canada   ☐ South Africa
☐ England   ☐ the US

b 🔊 **2.6** Listen and check. Are you familiar with any of these accents? Which ones, and why?

7 LISTENING

a You're going to hear Cristina from Romania, who has lived in the US for several years, answering some questions about her experiences of being a non-native speaker of English. Before you listen, check that you understand the words in the glossary.

Glossary
hit it out of the park meet a goal even more than was expected. This expression comes from baseball, when the ball is hit so far that it flies outside of the ballpark or stadium.
slam dunk something that is achieved easily. This expression comes from basketball, when a player jumps above the basket and "dunks" it in the hoop without opposition.

Cristina in Hollywood, California

b Before you listen, answer questions 1–2 with a partner.

1 Do you find it easier to understand native or non-native speakers of English?

2 How do you feel about having your English corrected?

c 🔊 **2.7** Now listen to Cristina. How does she answer the questions? How easy do you find it to understand her accent?

d Listen again. What does she say about…?
- regional US accents
- talking on the phone
- what happens when she's tired

e Answer questions 3–4 with a partner.

3 Do you have any funny or embarrassing stories related to misunderstanding someone?

4 Is there anything you still find difficult about English?

f 🔊 **2.8** Now listen to Cristina. How does she answer the questions?

g Listen again. What does she say about…?
- the word *hideout*
- baseball, basketball, and American football
- the difference between Romanian spelling and English spelling

h Were any of Cristina's answers the same as yours? What else did she say that you identified with?

🔵 **Go online** to review the lesson

> Children begin by loving their parents; after a time they judge them; rarely do they forgive them.
> *Oscar Wilde, Irish dramatist*

G the past: habitual events and specific incidents **V** word building: abstract nouns **P** word stress with suffixes

1 READING

a Imagine that you were going to write your autobiography. Where would you start? What periods of your childhood or specific incidents would you definitely include?

b 🔊 2.9 You're going to read and listen to an extract from *Boy*, the autobiography of author Roald Dahl. Read and listen to Part 1 and answer the questions with a partner.

1 Why did the chocolate bars have numbers stamped underneath them?
2 What do you think was the point of the control bar?
3 What exactly did the boys have to do?
4 Why was it clever of Cadbury's to use the boys?
5 How did they behave when they were sampling the products?

c 🔊 2.10 Now do the same for Part 2.

1 How did Roald Dahl imagine the "inventing room" to be?
2 What would he sometimes imagine himself doing?
3 How did he imagine Mr. Cadbury reacting to his invention?
4 What effect did the testing of the chocolate bars have on Dahl in later life?

LEXIS IN CONTEXT

🔍 **Understanding dramatic language**

A good writer will often use dramatic verbs to make the action in a scene come alive. In this text, Part 1 narrates a sequence of events, but in Part 2 Roald Dahl achieves a more dramatic, imaginative effect, partly through his choice of vocabulary.

d Read Part 2 again carefully. Find more dramatic synonyms for the following verbs.

1 _____ imagine
2 _____ cook
3 _____ create by mixing together
4 _____ take quickly (in one's hand)
5 _____ run quickly
6 _____ jump
7 _____ hit (with the hand)

e What kind of child do you get the impression that Roald Dahl was? When you were a child, what did you use to dream of doing?

Part 1

1 Every now and then, a plain, gray cardboard box was dished out to each boy in our House, and this, believe it or not, was a present from the great chocolate manufacturers Cadbury. Inside the box there were twelve
5 bars of chocolate, all of different shapes, all with different fillings and all with numbers from one to twelve stamped underneath. Eleven of these bars were new inventions from the factory. The twelfth was the "control" bar, one
10 that we all knew well, usually a Cadbury's Coffee Cream bar. Also in the box was a sheet of paper with the numbers one to twelve on it as well as two blank columns, one for giving marks to each chocolate from nought to ten, and the other for comments.
15 All we were required to do in return for this splendid gift was to taste very carefully each bar of chocolate, give it marks, and make an intelligent comment on
20 why we liked or disliked it. It was a clever stunt. Cadbury's were using some of the greatest chocolate-bar experts in the world to test out their new inventions. We
25 were of a sensible age, between thirteen and eighteen, and we knew intimately every chocolate bar in existence, from the Milk Flake to the Lemon Marshmallow. Quite obviously our opinions on anything new would be valuable. All of
30 us entered into this game with great gusto, sitting in our studies and nibbling each bar with the air of connoisseurs, giving our marks and making our comments. "Too subtle for the common palate" was one note that I remember writing down.

Glossary

House many UK boarding schools are divided into "Houses" and each student belongs to one; Houses may compete with one another in sports and other activities
nought (*old-fashioned*) zero or nothing
with great gusto (*old-fashioned*) with enthusiasm and energy

Part 2

⁴⁵ For me the importance of all this was that I began to realize that the large chocolate companies actually did possess inventing rooms and they took their inventing very seriously. I used to picture a long white room like a laboratory, with pots of chocolate and fudge ⁵⁰ and all sorts of other delicious fillings bubbling away on the stoves, while men and women in white coats moved between the bubbling pots, tasting and mixing and concocting their wonderful new inventions. I used to imagine myself working in one of these labs, ⁴⁵ and suddenly I would come up with something so unbearably delicious that I would grab it in my hand and go rushing out of the lab and along the corridor and right into the offices of the great Mr. Cadbury himself. "I've got it, Sir," I would shout, putting the ⁵⁰ chocolate in front of him. "It's fantastic! It's fabulous! It's marvelous! It's irresistible!" Slowly the great man would pick up my newly-invented chocolate and he would take a small bite. He would roll it round his mouth. Then all at once he would leap from his chair ⁵⁵ crying, "You've got it! You've done it! It's a miracle!" He would slap me on the back and shout, "We'll sell it by the million! We'll sweep the world with this one! How on earth did you do it? Your salary is doubled."

It was lovely dreaming those dreams, and I have ⁶⁰ no doubt at all that thirty-five years later, when I was looking for a plot for my second book for children, I remembered those little cardboard boxes and the newly-invented chocolates ⁶⁵ inside them, and I began to write a book called *Charlie and the Chocolate Factory*.

Glossary

fudge /fʌdʒ/ a type of soft, brown candy made from sugar, butter, and milk

2 GRAMMAR the past: habitual events and specific incidents

a Look at the highlighted verbs in Part 2 of the extract from *Boy*. Which ones describe…?

1 specific incidents in the past
2 repeated or habitual actions in the past

b What other verb forms could you use for **1** and **2**?

c **G** p.145 **Grammar Bank 2B** Learn more about verb forms for describing habitual events and specific incidents in the past, and practice them.

3 SPEAKING & WRITING

a 🔊 2.11 Listen to six people talking about their childhoods. What are the different expressions they use to say (approximately) how old they were at the time?

b With a partner, choose two of the topics below and talk about things you habitually did or felt in your childhood.

things I used to be afraid of

my elementary school

places we would go to for family vacations

food and drink I used to love (or hate)

Christmas
being sick
toys and games I used to love

birthdays
nightmares I used to have

When I was little I used to be terrified of the dark, and I'd always sleep with the light on…

c Now take turns choosing one of the topics and talk about a specific incident from your childhood.

I remember the time when we went on our first family vacation in the mountains…

d **W** p.116 **Writing** An article Analyze an online article and write an article about how life has changed over the last 30 years.

🔁 **Go online** to review the lesson

4 VOCABULARY & PRONUNCIATION
word building: abstract nouns; word stress with suffixes

> 🔍 **Abstract nouns**
>
> An abstract noun is one that is used to express an idea, a concept, an experience, or a quality rather than an object, e.g., *childhood* and *fear* are abstract nouns, whereas *bed* and *pants* are not.
>
> Abstract nouns are formed:
> 1 by adding a suffix to nouns, verbs, or adjectives, e.g., *child—child**hood***.
>   nouns can add *-hood*, *-ship*, or *-dom*
>   verbs can add *-ment* or *-tion*
>   adjectives can add *-ness*, *-ity*, or *-dom*
>
> 2 with a new word, e.g., *afraid—fear*.

a Make abstract nouns by adding a suffix to the words below and making any other changes necessary, and write them in the correct columns.

achieve   adult   amaze   aware
bored
    celebrate   curious   disappoint
excite   free   friend   frustrate
generous   happy   imagine   improve
kind   member
    neighbor   partner
possible   relation
      sad   tempt   wise
        sick

1 + -hood	2 + -ship	3 + -dom	4 + -ity

5 + -ness	6 + -(a)tion	7 + -ment

b 🔊 **2.12** Listen to each group and check.

c 🔊 **2.13** Underline the stressed syllable in these words. Listen and check. Which endings often cause a change in stress?

1 a|dult   a|dult|hood
2 ce|le|brate   ce|le|bra|tion
3 cur|i|ous   cur|i|o|si|ty
4 dis|ap|point   dis|ap|point|ment
5 free   free|dom
6 hap|py   hap|pi|ness
7 re|la|tion   re|la|tion|ship

d Now look at the abstract nouns and complete the adjective and verb column.

abstract noun	adjective
1 anger	*angry*
2 shame	_____
3 death	_____
4 danger	_____

abstract noun	verb
5 belief	_____
6 hatred	_____
7 loss	_____
8 memory	_____

e 🔊 **2.14** Listen and check.

> 🔍 **Collocations**
>
> Noticing and recording words that go together, e.g., *a remote possibility*, not *a distant possibility*, will improve the accuracy and fluency of your speaking and writing.

f Complete the highlighted phrases below with an abstract noun from **a** or **d** that collocates in the phrase.

1 I'm writing to express my sympathy for your terrible _____ . John's death was a shock to us all…
2 To my complete _____ , I realized I'd won first prize.
3 I've been seeing my girlfriend for about six months now. It's becoming a serious _____ .
4 There's a strong _____ that I'll be offered the manager's job in the next few weeks.
5 I could smell gas in my kitchen, but the gas company decided there was no immediate _____ .
6 When I heard I'd failed the exam, it was a huge _____ . I'd been expecting to pass.
7 Contrary to popular _____ , for many children, high school is not the happiest of times.
8 My eldest daughter has a very vivid _____ —I think she'll end up becoming a writer.

5 LISTENING

a 🔊 **2.15** Listen to three people talking about their earliest childhood memory and answer the questions for each speaker.

1 How old was he / she?
2 What event was his / her memory of?
3 What emotion(s) did he / she feel?

b What is your earliest memory? Answer questions 1–3 about it with a partner.

c You're going to listen to a radio program about some research that has been done on first memories. Before you listen, discuss the following questions with a partner.

1 How far back in our lives can we usually remember things?
2 Why can't we remember things before that age?
3 What kinds of a) feelings and b) events might people be more likely to remember?
4 Are our first memories mostly visual or of sounds and smells?
5 Why might some people's first memories be unreliable?

d 🔊 **2.16** Listen to what the speaker says and compare your answers. Were you surprised by anything? How reliable do you think your first memory is?

e 🔊 **2.17** Now listen to the speaker talk about psychologist Jean Piaget's first memory. Write down what you think are the key words. Listen again and try to add more detail. Compare your words with a partner and then retell the story together.

6 SPEAKING

a Do you have any childhood memories of the feelings or events below? Do you know roughly how old you were at the time? Choose one feeling and one event to talk about.

feelings

boredom
disappointment
amazement
embarrassment
excitement
pain
shame
frustration
sadness

events

a festival or celebration
a day out
the birth of a brother or sister
getting a wonderful or disappointing present
figuring out how to do something for the first time
the death of a pet

> 🔍 **Talking about memories**
> When we're talking about a memory of the past, we use *remember* (*somebody* or *something*) + verb + -*ing*:
> ...*I remember standing in the back yard*...
> *I remember arriving, and it was dark*...
> *He remembered his nanny fighting the kidnapper.*

b In small groups, tell each other about your memories. Try to use the expressions in the box.

Go online to review the lesson

GRAMMAR

a Complete the sentences with one word.

1 We need to _____ the heater repaired soon, before it starts getting cold.
2 The Chinese economy is growing and _____ a result, the standard of living is rising.
3 We were very late _____ of a traffic accident on the freeway.
4 Everybody seemed to enjoy the barbecue even _____ the weather wasn't very warm.
5 He wore a baggy shirt _____ people wouldn't notice that he'd gained weight.
6 Will the person who left _____ boarding pass at the security check point please go back and get it?
7 If we lived closer to _____ another, we'd probably spend more time together.
8 Sun-mee always seems pretty reserved to me—she never talks about _____ .
9 When I was young, my family _____ spend every summer vacation at the beach.
10 This street looks different from when I was a child. Didn't _____ use to be a candy store on the corner?

b Rewrite the sentences using the **bold** word(s).

1 I need to pay someone to repair my glasses. **have**
   I need _____ .
2 If we buy a dishwasher, it won't be necessary to do the dishes. **have**
   If we buy a dishwasher, _____ .
3 The last time I saw him was in 2016. **seen**
   I _____ 2016.
4 They managed to get here even though the traffic was heavy. **despite**
   They managed to get here _____ .
5 It was foggy, so the flight was canceled. **due**
   The flight _____ .
6 She wore dark glasses so that she wouldn't be recognized. **so as**
   She wore dark glasses _____ .
7 If you learn a few phrases, the local people really appreciate it. **one**
   _____ , the local people really appreciate it.
8 Mai-ting sees Martha once a month. **each**
   Mai-ting and Martha _____ once a month.
9 The children wrapped the present on their own. **by**
   The children wrapped the present _____ .
10 My aunt always used to bake cookies for us. **would**
    My aunt _____ for us.

VOCABULARY

a Complete the missing words.

1 He's a very unadventurous person—he doesn't like ta_____ ri_____ .
2 They suddenly got married on vacation in Las Vegas—they're very **sp**_____ .
3 She never asks for anyone's help. She's completely **se**_____-**su**_____ .
4 He won't listen to me, but he might **ch**_____ his **mi**_____ if you talk to him.
5 My brother wasn't very **sy**_____ when I failed my driver's test—in fact, he just laughed!
6 She was **de**_____ to be a musician even as a girl.
7 She always finds a solution to problems—she's very **re**_____ .
8 He seems tough, but **de**_____ **do**_____ he's quite sensitive.

b Complete the idioms with one word.

1 My kids can be a real _____ **in the neck** when we eat out—they're so picky!
2 My grandfather's always had **a short** _____ . We were scared of him when we were young.
3 He can be a little bad-tempered, but he has **a** _____ **of gold.**
4 My boss is very **down to** _____ ; you can talk to her about anything.
5 I've read the instructions three times, but I still can't **get my** _____ **around** them.
6 What's that actor's name? It's **on the tip of my** _____ !
7 You never have to wonder how Darla feels about current events. She always **speaks her** _____ .

c Circle the right word or phrase.

1 She's been *under / out of* work since the restaurant she worked at suddenly closed.
2 I won't get that job; I don't have the *qualifications / benefits*.
3 He resigned before they could *quit / fire* him.
4 I'm hoping to get *promoted / a raise* to a more senior position.
5 I must have applied *for / to* dozens of jobs.
6 *Job-searching / Job-hunting* can be really demoralizing.
7 Factory work is usually very *monotonous / motivating*.
8 The manager is in charge of 400 *staff members / workforce*.

d Complete the sentences with the noun form of the **bold** word.

1 I wish there were more good restaurants in our _____. **neighbor**
2 There are classes available for people who have a _____ of flying. **afraid**
3 Don't let this misunderstanding get in the way of our _____. **friend**
4 The _____ of his job affected him very badly. **lose**
5 _____ of speech is a basic human right. **free**
6 The news of their engagement caused great _____. **excite**
7 My _____ is getting worse as I get older. **remember**

CAN YOU understand this text?

a Read the article once. What main advantage of learning a second language does it describe?

b Read the article again and mark the sentences **T** (true) or **F** (false).

1 There had been other studies into bilingualism and the brain before Dr. Bak's.
2 Not all the participants in the study spoke a second language when they were young.
3 People who speak more than one language become more confused as they get older.
4 Learning a second language as a child protects the brain more than learning it as an adult.
5 It isn't known whether bilingual speakers suffer from dementia later than those who speak only one language.

c Look at the highlighted words and phrases and figure out their meaning. Check with your teacher or with a dictionary.

▶ CAN YOU understand this movie?

Watch or listen to a short movie on the history of English and mark the sentences T (true) or F (false).

1 English has been changing for more than a thousand years.
2 The Latin-speaking Romans conquered the native Celts in AD 43.
3 The Anglo-Saxons came to Britain from northern France after the Romans left.
4 The Anglo-Saxons rejected the monks who wanted to convert them to Christianity.
5 The arrival of the Vikings gave English about 2,000 new words.
6 King Harold defeated the Vikings and then the Normans in just three weeks.
7 The Normans didn't introduce many French words.
8 Shakespeare gave English as many new words as the Vikings.
9 In the 20th century, British English "borrowed words" from American, but not vice versa.
10 Today there are more native than non-native speakers of English.

Speaking Two Languages May Slow Brain Aging

Just like exercise helps your body stay strong, exercising your mind also keeps your brain sharp. And what better way to do just that than by learning another language?

Indeed new research published in *Annals of Neurology* reveals that people who speak two or more languages—even those who learned the second language as adults—may slow down cognitive decline from aging. In the past, it hasn't been clear whether people improve their brain functions through learning new languages—or whether those with better cognitive abilities to begin with are more likely to be successful at learning another language.

"Our study is the first to examine whether learning a second language impacts cognitive performance later in life while controlling for childhood intelligence," said lead author Dr. Thomas Bak, of the University of Edinburgh. "Our study shows that bilingualism, even when acquired in adulthood, may benefit the aging brain."

For the study, researchers relied on data from 835 native speakers of English who were born and living in the area of Edinburgh, Scotland. The participants were given an intelligence test in 1947 at age 11 and then again in their early 70s, between 2008 and 2010.

Findings indicate that those who spoke two or more languages had significantly better cognitive abilities compared to what would be expected. The strongest effects were seen in general intelligence and reading. The effects were evident no matter when the second language was learned.

After reviewing the study, Dr. Alvaro Pascual-Leone, of the Harvard Medical School in Boston, said in a press release: "This research paves the way for future studies of bilingualism and the prevention of cognitive decline."

Another study of bilingualism in 2013 found that bilingual patients suffer the onset of dementia an average of 4.5 years later than those who speak only one language.

So what are you waiting for? Scientists say pretty much anyone can learn a new language, so no more excuses!

Glossary
cognitive connected with the mental processes of understanding
dementia /dɪˈmenʃə/ a serious mental disorder caused by brain disease or injury that affects the ability to think, remember, and behave normally

3A Don't get mad, get even

G get   **V** phrases with *get*   **P** words and phrases of French origin

1 READING & SPEAKING

a Read the ten top break-up lines from a website. Which one do you think is the least hurtful way of explaining to someone that you want to break up with them?

"It's not you, it's me.

I love you, but I'm not in love with you.

You are like a brother / sister to me.

I think we'd be better off as friends.

I don't love you anymore.

I need some time to be on my own.

You're a fantastic person, but you're too good for me.

I think I'm just too young to settle down.

We're at very different points in our lives now.

I think we rushed into this relationship too fast."

b Now read an article about how a French artist replied to the break-up email from her former partner. What do you think her motivation was?

1 She wanted to humiliate him.
2 She wanted them to get back together.
3 She wanted to help herself get over the breakup.
4 She wanted to make art.

c Choose the right word for 1–10 in the article.

	a	b	c
1	a turned out	b turned off	c turned up
2	a fear	b pain	c joy
3	a getting	b sending	c writing
4	a included	b involved	c covered
5	a instead of	b according to	c because of
6	a praised	b blamed	c ridiculed
7	a married	b arrested	c avoided
8	a get back	b get over	c get rid of
9	a returned	b revived	c replaced
10	a Though	b Because	c Despite

d Read the article again and answer in groups.

1 Why do you think the exhibition was so successful?
2 Do you think Sophie Calle was justified in making the man's email public?
3 How do you think he felt about the exhibition?
4 Do you think men enjoyed it as much as women?
5 What do you think the moral of the story is?

Getting through a breakup

The exhibition *Prenez Soin de Vous* ("Take Care of Yourself") was first a huge success at the Venice Biennale and then at the Bibliothèque Nationale in Paris. It has since toured in Europe and the Americas, and has been published as a book with the same title.

One day, Sophie Calle's cell phone beeped. It was an email from her boyfriend. He was dumping her electronically, adding that it hurt him more than it hurt her. Here is a short extract:

> Whatever happens, you must know that I will never stop loving you in my own way—the way I've loved you ever since I've known you, which will stay part of me, and never die...I wish things had ¹_____ differently. Take care of yourself...

Sophie was heartbroken. But she is one of France's best-known avant-garde artists, specializing in turning private ²_____ into public art, and two days after ³_____ the email, she started a new project:

> I received an email telling me it was over.
> I didn't know how to respond.
> It was almost as if it hadn't been meant for me.
> It ended with the words, "Take care of yourself."
> And so I did.
> I asked 107 women, chosen for their profession or skills, to interpret this letter.
> To analyze it, comment on it, dance it, sing it.
> Dissect it. Exhaust it. Understand it for me.
> Answer for me.
> It was a way of taking the time to break up.
> A way of taking care of myself.

The artist, Sophie Calle

The women Sophie sent the email to ⁴_____ an actress, an editor, an opera singer, a criminologist, a linguist, a lyricist, and her mother. She asked them to read the email and to analyze it or interpret it ⁵_____ their job, while she filmed or photographed the result. Sophie's mother, who clearly knows her well, wrote:

> *You leave, you get left, that's the name of the game, and for you this breakup could be the wellspring of a new piece of art—am I wrong?*

The editor ⁶_____ the boyfriend's grammar, the lyricist wrote a song, and the criminologist had this to say about the email writer:

> He is proud, narcissistic, and egotistical (he says "I" more than 30 times in a letter with 23 sentences). It is possible that he studied literature. He probably prefers jazz to rock. I can imagine him wearing polo-neck sweaters rather than a suit and tie. He must have a small kitchen and cook up tasty little meals. He must have charm, but not be classically handsome. He is an authentic manipulator, perverse, psychologically dangerous, and / or a great writer. To be ⁷_____ at all costs.

It was therapy for Sophie, and she quickly began to ⁸_____ the end of her relationship. "After a month I felt better. There was no suffering. It worked. The project had ⁹_____ the man."

With hindsight, Sophie's ex almost certainly wishes that he had followed his first instinct (*It seems to me it would be better to say what I have to say to you face-to-face*). ¹⁰_____ he isn't named in the exhibition, it's a sure bet that when he dumps his partners in the future, he'll never again say, "Take care of yourself."

2 PRONUNCIATION words and phrases of French origin

a ● 3.1 Look at the extract from the text. How do you pronounce the **bold** word? Listen and check.

> Sophie was heartbroken. But she is one of France's best-known **avant-garde** artists…

🔍 **Fine-tuning your pronunciation: French words used in English**
A number of French words and phrases are commonly used in English, e.g., *café* /ˈkæfeɪ/, *ballet* /bæˈleɪ/, *coup* /ku/. They are usually said in a way that is close to their French pronunciation, so they do not necessarily follow normal English pronunciation patterns.

b Underline a French word or expression in each sentence below. What do you think they mean? Do you use any of them in your language?

1 I made a real faux pas when I mentioned his ex-wife.
2 When we were introduced I had a sense of déjà vu, though I knew we'd never met before.
3 We used to have a secret rendezvous every Thursday at the Museum of Modern Art.
4 She's engaged to a well-known local entrepreneur.
5 I know it's a cliché, but it really was love at first sight.
6 On our anniversary, he always buys me a huge bouquet of flowers!
7 I met Jane's fiancé last night. They're getting married next year.
8 They knew their parents wouldn't want them to get married, so they did it anyway and presented them with a fait accompli.

c ● 3.2 Listen and focus on how the French expressions are pronounced. Then practice saying the sentences.

3 VOCABULARY phrases with *get*

a With a partner, try to remember these expressions with *get* from the article.

1 get _____ at someone (= take revenge on someone)
2 get _____ a breakup (= recover from a breakup with someone)
3 get _____ (*informal*) (= to cause somebody the same amount of trouble or harm as they have caused you)
4 get _____ _____ (= to start a romantic relationship with somebody again, after having finished a previous relationship with the person)

b Ⓥ **p.164 Vocabulary Bank** Phrases with *get*.

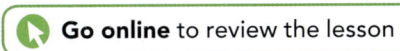 Go online to review the lesson   27

4 SPEAKING & LISTENING

a Have you ever been on a blind date or a date set up by friends? If yes, how did it go? If no, would you consider going on one?

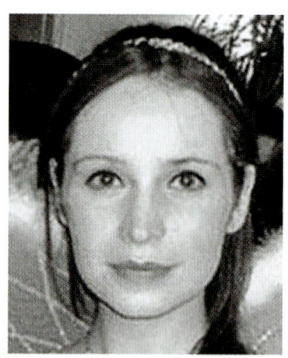 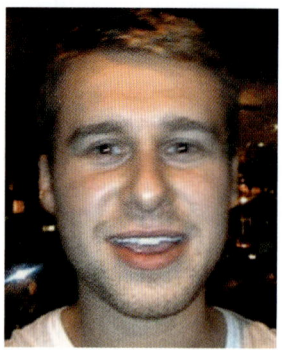

Blind Date

The Guardian has a weekly feature called *Blind Date*, where two readers are matched and a date is organized at a restaurant. Stef and Graham met in London at Miss Q's, an American restaurant with pool tables and a dance floor.

b Read the introduction about Stef and Graham's date. Who do you think said the following—Stef about Graham, or Graham about Stef?

1 First impressions: 'Effortlessly beautiful and unforgivably late.'
2 Table manners: 'Impeccable even though it was burgers.'
3 Best thing about them: 'Really genuine and friendly.'

c **Ⓒ Communication** Blind date **A** p.107 **B** p.111. Check your answers to b and find out what else they said about each other.

d You're going to listen to a radio program about first dates. Before you listen, guess what the missing words are in tips 1–6.

Dos
1 Choose the _____ carefully.
2 Make an effort with your _____ .
3 Be _____ , even if you think the date is going nowhere.

Don'ts
4 Don't forget your _____ .
5 Don't _____ to be anything you're not.
6 Don't make an instant _____ .

e ◗ 3.6 Listen to the program and check. Were your answers exactly the same? If not, did they mean the same thing?

f Listen again. Answer questions 1–6 with a partner.
What do the tips say about…?
1 the best place for a first date
2 looking good
3 lying
4 politeness
5 exaggeration
6 first impressions

g Which do you think are the top two dating tips? Are there any you don't think are important?

LEXIS IN CONTEXT

h ◗ 3.7 Listen to some extracts and complete the phrasal verbs and idioms. What do you think they mean?

1 The advantage of keeping the first date _____ _____ _____ …is that if you don't like each other, you don't have to make it through a seven-course meal together.
2 …if you turn up with unwashed hair, wearing yesterday's clothes, you aren't likely to _____ anyone _____ .
3 Don't tell someone that you'll call and that you can't wait to see them again if you have absolutely no intention of _____ _____ !
4 Turn off your phone, and if the other person is _____ the _____ , remember to say "thank you."
5 It can be very tempting to exaggerate, or to _____ _____ the truth, or just to plain lie…
6 Many of us _____ _____ our _____ about whether we like someone in the first few seconds or minutes of meeting them.
7 Try not to _____ someone _____ right away.
8 If you make a snap decision, you may risk _____ _____ on the love of your life.

5 GRAMMAR *get*

a Look at some sentences from the listening script that contain phrases with *get*. Answer the questions with a partner.

> **A** By **getting your hair done**, say, or wearing something you know you look good in, those kinds of things show that you care.
> **B** Try not to yawn even if you're **getting a little tired**.
> **C** It can be very tempting to exaggerate, or to dress up the truth, or just to plain lie to try to **get your date interested**.

In which phrase…?
1. ☐ does *get* mean *make*
2. ☐ does *get* mean *become*
3. ☐ could you replace *get* with *have* with no change in meaning

b **Ⓖ p.146 Grammar Bank 3A** Learn more about *get*, and practice it.

c Work in pairs. Read the *get* questionnaire and check (✓) eight questions you'd like to ask your partner. Then ask and answer the questions. Explain your answers.

get questionnaire

Are you the kind of person who regularly **gets rid of** old clothes, or do you tend to keep things forever?

Did you use to **get into trouble** a lot when you were a child?

Do you consider yourself a person who usually **gets their own way**? Why (not)?

Do you tend to keep up to date with your work or studies, or do you often **get behind**?

Do you think young drivers **get stopped** by the police more than older drivers? Do you think this is fair?

Have you ever **gotten caught** cheating on an exam? Have you ever cheated on an exam and **gotten away with it**?

Do you think going on vacation together is a good way to really **get to know** people?

How often and where do you usually **get your hair cut**?

If an electrical appliance doesn't work, do you try to figure it out yourself or do you immediately **get an expert to come** and fix it?

If you were able to **get** just **one room in your house redecorated**, which would it be and why?

Do you think women are better than men at **getting presents** for people?

If you were invited to a karaoke evening, would you try to **get out of** going?

If you were supposed to **get a flight** the day after there had been a serious plane crash, would you cancel it?

Is there anyone in your family or group of friends who really **gets on your nerves**?

What kinds of things do / did your parents **get you to do** around the house?

🔵 **Go online** to review the lesson

If you don't know history, then you don't know anything. You are a leaf that doesn't know it is part of a tree.
Michael Crichton, US author

G discourse markers (2): adverbs and adverbial expressions   **V** conflict and warfare   **P** stress in word families

1 READING & VOCABULARY conflict and warfare

a Look at the stills from three movies. Have you seen any of them? If yes, are there any scenes you remember?

The scenes you'll never forget
Three movie critics choose their most memorable moments

A *Gladiator* directed by Ridley Scott, 2000

B *The Great Escape* directed by John Sturges, 1963

Gladiator, which won five Oscars, tells the story of a Roman general, Maximus Decimus Meridius, a favorite of the Emperor, Marcus Aurelius. The Emperor wants Maximus (Russell Crowe at his best) to succeed him, but Commodus, the Emperor's weak and treacherous son (wonderfully played by Joaquin Phoenix), has other plans. Commodus kills his father and becomes Emperor himself, and arranges for Maximus and his wife and child to be executed. Maximus escapes, but cannot save his family. He is captured and sold as a gladiator, and eventually makes his way to the Colosseum in Rome, where he becomes a hero by engineering a spectacular victory against overwhelming odds. In this gripping scene, Emperor Commodus descends to the arena to congratulate him—not knowing his true identity. Maximus removes his helmet and confronts the Emperor in one of the most stirring speeches in modern cinema: "My name is Maximus Decimus Meridius, commander of the armies of the north, general of the Felix Legions, loyal servant to the true Emperor, Marcus Aurelius, father to a murdered son, husband to a murdered wife, and I will have my vengeance in this life or the next." And somehow, we just know he's going to get it!

The Great Escape is set in a prisoner-of-war camp in Germany during World War II. The camp is supposedly "escape-proof," but the British and American prisoners (played by an all-star cast) are determined to get out. They dig three tunnels and forge identity documents in preparation for a large-scale escape attempt. Seventy-six prisoners manage to crawl through a tunnel and get away. Most are quickly recaptured, but in this legendary scene, Captain Virgil Hilts (played by Steve McQueen) steals a motorcycle and a German uniform and tries to get over the Swiss border. Coming to a roadblock, he breaks through and gets away, despite being shot at, but is immediately pursued by German troops. He rides across open countryside in a desperate bid to reach safety, and eventually gets to the border. But two high fences separate him from Switzerland and freedom. He jumps the first, but becomes hopelessly trapped in the second, and is forced to surrender. However many times you've seen *The Great Escape* before, you still hope he might just make it over the second fence.

b Read some movie critics' descriptions of three memorable scenes. What information does each extract give? Check (✓) the boxes as you read each one.

		A	B	C
1	prizes the movie won			
2	the book the movie is based on			
3	where and when the movie is set			
4	who the main characters are and who they are played by			

		A	B	C
5	what the movie is about			
6	one of the most memorable scenes			
7	how the director's decisions affect the scene			
8	how it makes you feel			

12 Years a Slave directed by Steve McQueen, 2013

12 Years a Slave, which won the Oscar for Best Picture in 2014, is based on the memoir by Solomon Northup in which he describes how, despite being free-born, he was kidnapped in Washington, D.C., in 1841 and sold as a slave. Northup worked on plantations in Louisiana for 12 years before his release. The book was written in 1853, eight years before the American Civil War began. It was this war that led to the abolition of slavery in the US. One of the most famous scenes is the hanging scene. It comes after Solomon (Chiwetel Ejiofor) gets pushed too far by his slave master and attacks him. He is punished by being hanged from a tree in such a way that the rope around his neck is always choking him, but his toes can touch the ground just enough to keep him from being strangled. As it goes on, and director Steve McQueen refuses to let you look away, you start to realize that all the other slaves have gone back to their normal lives. Work starts up again, children go back to playing, and you realize how common excruciating experiences like this must have been for slaves, and how thoroughly they must have been separated from their own sense of humanity.

c   Which of the three descriptions created the most vivid image of the scene in your mind?

LEXIS IN CONTEXT

d   Look at the highlighted words related to conflict and warfare. With a partner, say what you think they mean. Check their meaning and pronunciation with your teacher or a dictionary.

e   ⓥ p.165 **Vocabulary Bank** Conflict and warfare.

---

2 PRONUNCIATION stress in word families

> 🔍 **Fine-tuning your pronunciation: changing stress in word families**
> It is useful to learn words in "families," e.g., *capture* (noun) – *a captive* (person), *revolutionary* (adjective)—*to revolt* (verb), etc. However, you should check whether the stressed syllable changes within the "family."

a   Complete the chart. <u>U</u>nderline the stressed syllable in all the multisyllable words.

noun	person	adjective	verb
cap|ture	cap|tive / cap|tor	cap|tive	_____
com|mand	_____	com|mand|ing	com|mand
ex|e|cu|tion	_____		_____
_____	his|tor|i|an	his|tor|ic / _____	_____
loo|ting	loo|ter		_____
_____	_____	re|bell|ious	_____
_____	_____	re|vo|lu|tio|nar|y	re|volt
siege		be|sieged	
sur|vi|val	_____	sur|vi|ving	_____
_____	_____	vic|tor|i|ous	

b   🔊 3.11 Listen and check.

c   Practice saying the sentences.
1   The rebels were captured and executed.
2   All the captives survived the siege.
3   It was a historic victory.
4   In the end, the revolutionaries were victorious.
5   The troops rebelled against their commander.
6   Historians disagree on the causes of the rebellion.

3 SPEAKING & WRITING

> 🔍 **Describing a scene from a movie or a book**
> *In this legendary scene, Steve McQueen **steals** a motorcycle and a German uniform and **tries** to get over the Swiss border. Coming to a roadblock, he **breaks through** and **gets away**.*
> We usually use the simple present ("the dramatic present") when we describe a scene from a movie, or the plot.

a   Think of a movie or TV show you really enjoyed that was set in a historical period or based on a real event. Look at prompts 1–8 in **1b**. Think about this information for your movie or TV show.

b   Work in groups of three or four. Describe the movie or TV show and the scene to others in the group. Do those who have seen it agree with you? How does the description make you feel about the movie or TV show?

c   Now write a paragraph describing the movie or TV show and the scene, using the prompts and the three texts in **1** as models.

🔄 **Go online** to review the lesson

4 SPEAKING

a Look at the images from *Braveheart* in the movie blog below and in the movie poster on the following page. There are two historical inaccuracies. What do you think they might be?

b Answer the questions in pairs.

- Are there any movies or TV shows you've seen that you thought were historically accurate, and that you felt taught you something about the period or event?
- Are there any movies or TV shows you've seen that you were aware were historically inaccurate? Did it bother you? Why (not)?
- Have you ever checked whether a movie or a TV show was accurate either during or after seeing it?
- Do you think big studios care whether the historical movies they make are accurate or not?

c Read the extract from a movie blog and answer the questions with a partner.

1 Did the blog mention any of the movies you talked about in **b**? Do you agree about the ones that are mentioned?

2 Do you think the professor's research affected the movies' success?

3 Have you seen people "two-screening" in the movie theater? How did you feel about it?

5 LISTENING

a ◑ 3.12 You're going to listen to an interview with Adrian Hodges, who has written screenplays for several historical movies and TV shows. Listen to Part 1 of the interview and choose the best option.

1 Adrian thinks historical details don't matter as long as they're things that most people wouldn't notice.
2 Adrian thinks historical details don't matter as long as a drama is honest about whether it is history or fiction.
3 Adrian thinks historical details don't matter at all.

> **Glossary**
> **Macbeth** /mək'bɛθ/ a play by Shakespeare about a king of Scotland
> **William the Conqueror, Charles II, Victoria** English monarchs from the 11th, 17th, and 19th centuries
> **to play fast and loose with** IDM (*old-fashioned*) to treat something in a way that shows you feel no responsibility or respect for it

b Listen again and check (✓) the points Adrian makes.

1 ☐ It isn't a problem that Shakespeare's plays are not historically accurate.
2 ☐ Writers can change historical details if the drama requires it.
3 ☐ Most people never notice historical inaccuracies.
4 ☐ Nobody is certain how people spoke in ancient Rome.
5 ☐ Historical inaccuracies with costume are worse than with dialogue.
6 ☐ It's easier to be accurate when you are writing about recent history.
7 ☐ If you make it clear that something is fiction, it doesn't matter if it's not historically accurate.
8 ☐ Julius Caesar is not a good subject for drama because we know so much about him.

Did you know...?

👤 🔍 ☰

Princess Isabella of France

One of the movies that has been most criticized for historical inaccuracy is **Braveheart**. Some scenes actually had to be reshot because the extras were wearing watches and sunglasses! Other movies frequently included in the top ten most historically inaccurate movies are **JFK**, **Pearl Harbor**, **Shakespeare in Love**, and **Pocahontas**.

Historical movies that have been voted both excellent and historically accurate on numerous websites include **Downfall**, the German movie about Hitler's last days, Clint Eastwood's **Letters from Iwo Jima**, **Chariots of Fire**, and **Saving Private Ryan**.

Hollywood studios are recruiting academics as "history assassins" to help them undermine rival studios' Oscar-contending movies. A Harvard professor says he was paid a $10,000 fee by an Oscar marketing consultant to look for factual errors in the current wave of historical movies that boast that they are "based on a true story."

The concept of doing something else while watching a movie or TV show only used to stretch to eating popcorn or having a TV dinner. But since the arrival of smartphones, we have become a society of "two-screeners," that is, people who watch a movie or TV while using their smartphone. Things people do with their phones include tweeting or posting comments about what they're watching, or checking the accuracy in historical or period dramas.

c 🔊 **3.13** Now listen to Part 2. In general, is Adrian positive or negative about *Spartacus* and *Braveheart*?

d Work in pairs. Before you listen again, can you explain these phrases Adrian uses?

1 "it becomes the received version of the truth"
2 "grossly irresponsible"
3 "the notion of freedom of individual choice"
4 "a resonance in the modern era"
5 "pushing the limits of what history could stand"
6 "a matter of purely personal taste"

e Listen again and answer the questions.

1 What is the most famous scene in the movie *Spartacus*?
2 Why is it an example of a movie becoming the "received version of the truth"?
3 What does he say about the portrayal of William Wallace's life in the movie *Braveheart*?
4 What did some people think *Braveheart* was really about?

f Do you agree with Adrian's main points? Which event or period of history from your own country do you think would be most interesting as a movie or TV show?

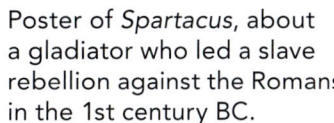
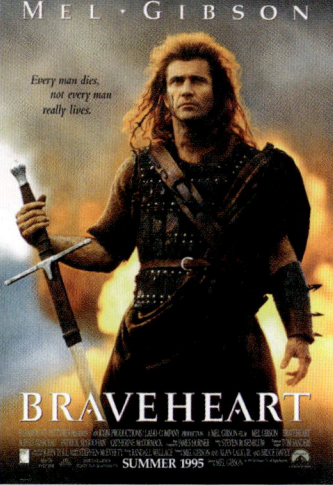

Poster of *Spartacus*, about a gladiator who led a slave rebellion against the Romans in the 1st century BC.

Poster of *Braveheart*, about William Wallace, one of the main leaders in the 13th- and 14th-century Wars of Scottish Independence.

6 GRAMMAR discourse markers (2): adverbs and adverbial expressions

a Read four extracts from the interview with Adrian Hodges. Match the **bold** discourse markers to what they are used for (A–D).

1 ▢ If you change detail to the point where history is an absurdity, then **obviously** things become more difficult.

2 ▢ So *Spartacus*…has become, I think, for nearly everybody who knows anything about Spartacus, the only version of the truth. Now **in fact,** we don't know if any of that is true, really.

3 ▢ …his whole career was invented in the film, or **at least** built on to such a degree that some people felt that perhaps it was more about the notion of Scotland as an independent country than it was about history…

4 ▢ But you know, again, these things are a matter of purely personal taste, **I mean,** I enjoyed *Braveheart* immensely.

A To introduce surprising or contrasting information
B To give more details, or make things clearer
C To introduce a fact that is very clear to see or understand
D To qualify what you have just said or to make it less definite

b 🄶 p.147 **Grammar Bank 3B** Learn more about adverbs and adverbial expressions, and practice them.

c 🄲 **Communication** Guess the sentence **A p.107 B p.111** Guess the missing phrases, and then check with a partner.

Mel Gibson portraying William Wallace in *Braveheart*

🔄 **Go online** to review the lesson

1 ▶ THE INTERVIEW Part 1

a Read the biographical information about Mary Beard. What do you think "Classics" and "classicist" refer to?

Mary Beard is Professor of Classics at the University of Cambridge and a fellow of Newnham College. She is the author of many books about ancient history, and writes a popular blog called *A Don's Life*. In 2010, she hosted the historical documentary, *Pompeii: Life and Death in a Roman Town*, which showed a snapshot of the residents' lives before the eruption of Mount Vesuvius in AD 79. In 2012, she wrote and hosted the three-part television series *Meet the Romans*, about "the world's first global metropolis." She also wrote and hosted *Caligula with Mary Beard* in 2013, where she attempts to sort the truth from the myth. Her frequent media appearances and sometimes-controversial public statements have led to her being described as "Britain's best-known classicist."

b 🔊 3.14 Watch or listen to Part 1 of the interview. What does she think is the right (and the wrong) way to get people interested in ancient history? What does she think we can learn from history?

c Now listen again. Complete sentences 1–5.

1 If a place name ends with *-chester* or *-caster*, it means that it…
2 London is the capital of Britain because…
3 In 63 BC there was a terrorist plot in Rome to…
4 When Cicero discovered the plot, he decided to…
5 Mary Beard compares this situation with…

Glossary

(63) BC Before Christ. These letters refer to the years before 1 AD (*Anno Domini*—the year of our Lord)

torch (*verb*) set fire to

Marcus Tullius Cicero /ˈsɪsərəʊ/ a Roman politician and lawyer, one of Rome's greatest orators

the Senate a political institution in ancient Rome

be exiled be sent to another country for political reasons or as a punishment

Guantanamo Bay a US military prison, where many suspected terrorists have been held

---

▶ Part 2

a 🔊 3.15 Now watch or listen to Part 2. Mark the sentences **T** (true) or **F** (false).

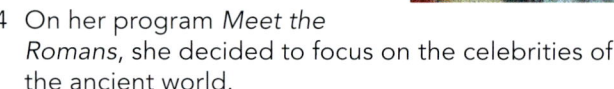

1 Mary Beard would not like to go back in time to any historical period.
2 She thinks that women have a better life now than at any time in the past.
3 She doesn't think that men would suffer from going back in time.
4 On her program *Meet the Romans*, she decided to focus on the celebrities of the ancient world.
5 She thinks that most history textbooks don't answer questions about how people dealt with practical issues in the past.
6 She thinks that questions about practical issues are just as interesting as why Julius Caesar was assassinated.
7 She doesn't think we can learn much from studying the assassination of Caesar.

b Listen again. Say why the **F** sentences are false.

Glossary

Julius Caesar /ˈdʒuːljəs ˈsiːzər/ a Roman general (100–44 BC) who played a critical role in the fall of the Roman Republic and the rise of the Roman Empire. He was assassinated by a group of senators led by his former friend Brutus

---

▶ Part 3

a 🔊 3.16 Now watch or listen to Part 3. Answer the questions.

1 How important does Mary Beard think accuracy is in historical movies?
2 What historical movie did she really enjoy and why?
3 How does she feel about the fact that there are so many historical movies nowadays?

b Listen again. What do you think the <mark>highlighted</mark> informal words and phrases mean?

1 "I think that, that, um, film and television, um, program makers can be a bit, can be a bit sort of <mark>nerdish</mark> about accuracy."
2 "…if we're going to have a dog in the film should it be an Alsatian or, you know, a Dachshund or <mark>whatever</mark>?"
3 "…look, these <mark>guys</mark> are getting the whole of Roman history…utterly wrong…"
4 "…never mind its horribly <mark>schmaltzy</mark> plot…"
5 "…there's no such good story as a true story—and that's what history's <mark>got going for it</mark>…"
6 "…nonfiction in a, in a kind of way is always a better <mark>yarn</mark> than fiction is."

> **Glossary**
> **Alsatian, Dachshund** /æl'seɪʃn, 'dɑkshɒnd/ breeds of dog

2 LOOKING AT LANGUAGE

> **🔍 Collocations**
> Many of the expressions Mary Beard uses are typical collocations, that is, where one word frequently goes with the other. Try to learn these expressions as phrases. Incorporating them into your active language will help you both to understand spoken English more easily and to sound more fluent in your own speech.

🔊 **3.17** Watch or listen to some extracts from the interview and complete the collocating words.

1 "…an _____ lot of our culture and our geography and our place names and so on are actually formed by the Romans…"
2 "…one _____ example of that is a famous incident in Roman history in 63 BC where there's a <mark>terrorist</mark> _____ in, in the city of Rome…"
3 "Now, in many ways that's the kind of <mark>problem</mark> we're still _____ …"
4 "I mean, what—how far does, how far should homeland security be more important than _____ rights…"
5 "And in part we've learned from how they debated those <mark>rights and</mark> _____ …"
6 "…if it, if it was a small antidote to modern _____ <mark>culture</mark>, I'm extremely pleased."
7 "…look, these guys are getting the whole of Roman history in, in <mark>the big</mark> _____ utterly wrong…"
8 "But I think also, I mean, it shows that you don't always have to be <mark>deadly</mark> _____ about history."

3 ▶ ON THE STREET

a 🔊 **3.18** Watch or listen to five people talking about history. Match the speakers (**D**, **He**, **Ha**, **Ad**, and **An**) with the people they admire. What reasons do they give?

Daisy	Heather	Harry	Adam	Andrew
English	*South African*	*English*	*American*	*American*

☐ Filippo Brunelleschi   ☐ Nelson Mandela
☐ Bess of Hardwick   ☐ Queen Elizabeth I
☐ Julius Caesar

b Watch or listen again. Who (**D**, **He**, **Ha**, **Ad**, or **An**)…?

☐ doesn't mention a specific time they would like to go back to
☐ would like to listen to some philosophers talking
☐ is studying the period they would like to go back to
☐ has read a lot about a specific person
☐ would like to go back to the most recent historical period

c 🔊 **3.19** Watch or listen again and complete the Colloquial English phrases. What do you think they mean?

1 "She was a real _____ _____…"
2 "I would have loved to _____ _____ in California…"
3 "…she actually stood up and was a person to _____ _____."
4 "…he was a _____ _____ person…"
5 "I think there was a lot of innovation and interesting new ideas _____ _____ in that time period…"

> **Glossary**
> **Derbyshire** a county in the middle of England
> **the Agora** the main meeting place in ancient Athens

4 SPEAKING

Answer the questions with a partner.

1 What periods and places in history did you study in school? Did you enjoy it as a subject?
2 How do you think a teacher can get students interested in history?
3 Do you think you have learned more about history from school or from books and movies?
4 Why do you think historical movies and novels are so popular?
5 Is there a person from history whom you admire or find especially fascinating?
6 Is there a period of history that you would like to go back to?

🌐 **Go online** to watch the video, review the lesson, and check your progress

Sounds interesting

I have often regretted my speech, never my silence.
Publilius Syrus,
Roman writer

| **G** speculation and deduction | **V** sounds and the human voice | **P** consonant clusters |

1 VOCABULARY & WRITING sounds and the human voice

a Try to sit for one minute in complete silence, listening carefully. Write down everything you hear. Then compare with a partner. Did you hear the same things?

b **V** p.166 Vocabulary Bank Sounds and the human voice.

c 🔊 4.4 Listen to the sounds and make a note of what they are. Then write three paragraphs based on the sounds. Begin your paragraphs as follows:

1 It was 12:30 at night and Mike had just fallen asleep…
2 Amanda was walking down Park Street…
3 It was a cold winter night…

2 PRONUNCIATION consonant clusters

> 🔍 **Fine-tuning your pronunciation: consonant clusters**
> Combinations of two or three consonant sounds, e.g., *cl*othes, *spr*ing, can be difficult to pronounce, especially if the combination of sounds is not common in your language.
>
> Three-consonant clusters at the beginning of words always begin with s, e.g., *scr*eam.
>
> Three-consonant clusters at the end of words are often either plurals (mon*ths*), third person singular verbs (wan*ts*), or regular past tenses (as*ked*).

a 🔊 4.5 Listen to the words below. Then practice saying them.

At the beginning of a word	
two sounds	**three sounds**
click	screech
slam	scream
crash	splash
slurp	
drip	
snore	
stutter	

At the end of a word	
two sounds	**three sounds**
shouts	crunched
sniffs	mumble
yelled	gasps
hummed	rattled

b 🔊 4.6 Listen and repeat the sentences.

1 She screamed when her friend splashed her in the swimming pool.
2 The brakes screeched and then there was a tremendous crash.
3 My co-worker slurps and gasps for breath when he drinks anything.

c Write three sentences of your own, using two words from **a** in each sentence. Give them to your partner to say.

3 READING

a Read the headline and the introduction to the article on p.37. With a partner, say how you think the following aspects of Vicky's life have been affected by her phobia.

- college studies
- relationships
- work
- where she lives

b Read the article and check.

c What is each paragraph about? With a partner, match paragraphs 1–7 to summaries A–H. There is one summary that you don't need.

A		how her phobia caused her to underachieve
B		the physical effects of her phobia
C		what she considers to be the most damaging effect of her phobia
D		the effect of her phobia on where she works and lives
E		her eventual diagnosis
F		how therapy has helped her
G		her ambivalent attitude to sounds
H		how her problems originated

LEXIS IN CONTEXT

d Look at the highlighted adverbs and adverbial phrases and figure out the meaning of any that you don't know. Use your dictionary.

e How sympathetic are you to Vicky's phobia? Do you know anyone with a phobia that seriously affects their life?

🏠 Previous | Next | Index

Life & style > Experience

I have a phobia of sound

For the last 30 years, I have had violent physical reactions to certain noises. Everyday sounds, like someone chewing or a pen being clicked, make me want to hide, scream, and put my fingers in my ears.

1 I feel unreasonable complaining to people about these seemingly harmless sounds, but for me they are threatening. My body reacts in the same way as it would under attack: I am flooded with adrenaline. It is as if I were in the same room as a huge, fierce dog. I am unable to focus on anything but my terror. I often have to hang up on phone calls abruptly, leave my seat, and walk around the room, trying to block out the noise.

2 My phobia began when I was 19 and started work in a busy office. The noise of a colleague next to me who chewed gum incessantly became unbearable. My ears tuned in to every sound until they filled my head, and I couldn't focus on my work. This cacophony was added to by another colleague who continually whistled, until I was forced to leave.

3 The path of my life has been dictated by the sounds around me. I have changed jobs numerous times, searching for the perfect quiet office. I have moved house, too, away from loud music or arguing neighbors. Strangely, I'd love to live near a motorway: the constant hum of traffic would be soothing to me.

4 My phobia has affected my ability to get on in life. During my final examinations at university, I was doing really well, translating Greek with ease, until the scratching of a pen against paper filtered into my consciousness, bringing me to a halt. During another exam, a nearby pub had a delivery and the sound of barrels being rolled along by whistling delivery men destroyed any chance of concentration. I discovered afterwards that I was two marks off a first.

5 My biggest regret is that it has prevented me from having a long-term relationship and children. The longest I have been with someone is two years, until the sound of their eating, breathing, just existing in proximity to me became intolerable. I would sneak off to the spare room in the night to try to get some sleep, but it would be interpreted as a rejection of them. It's hard to stay with someone who doesn't want to eat or sleep with you. I haven't ruled out love yet, though. I'm sure there is someone who could accept my limitations.

6 It took me 30 years to realize that what I have has a name: misophonia, or hatred of sound. When I recently discovered a support forum dedicated to it, I cried for two hours. I felt so relieved to know that other people—900 of them on this one site—felt like I did. I wasn't the only one.

7 It also gave me perspective. Some sufferers wish they were deaf, but I don't. I love many, many sounds: the sea, wind in the trees, music, the human voice. Time and experience have taught me that being able to hear is a beautiful thing, too important to sacrifice. I would never wish that away.

By Vicky Rhodes in The Guardian

4 LISTENING & SPEAKING

a 🔊 4.7 **Listen to five people talking about noises they don't like.**

  1 What noise does each person describe?
  2 How much do you think it affects their daily life?

b **Listen again. Who...?**

  1 ☐ feels that a sound represents a negative emotion
  2 ☐ wishes he'd / she'd complained about a noise sooner
  3 ☐ is annoyed because he's / she's powerless to stop a sound
  4 ☐ has to make a sound stop before he / she can relax
  5 ☐ describes sounds that other people clearly like

c **Talk to a partner**

- **Are there any noises that really annoy you?**

  Are you affected by them in your daily life?

  Is there anything you can do to avoid or stop them?

- **Are there any sounds that you really love or that make you feel good?**

- **Do you prefer music or silence in these situations? Why? If you prefer music, what kind?**

  - in restaurants
  - in a supermarket
  - in a gym
  - when a plane is taking off or landing
  - when you're put on hold on the phone

Glossary

two marks off a first two points away from a top score
motorway (NAmE freeway or highway) a wide road, where traffic can travel fast for long distances

🔄 **Go online** to review the lesson

5 GRAMMAR speculation and deduction

a Look at this picture and answer the questions.

1 Where **could** the photo **have been taken**?
2 Why do you think these people **might have been** in costume?
3 What do you think **might have** just **happened**?
4 How do you think the people in costume **must have been feeling** while they were walking around?

b **Ⓒ Communication** Masks for Manggao **p.108.** Find out what really happened.

c **Ⓖ p.148 Grammar Bank 4A** Learn more about speculation and deduction, and practice them.

d Look at these photos and make speculations and deductions about them.

6 LISTENING

a Have you had an interesting conversation with a stranger recently? Where? What about?

b Read about an organization called Talk to Me London. What do they aim to achieve? Does Talk to Me London sound like a good idea to you?

TALK TO ME LONDON

 What's the idea? **Why talk?** **Stories** **Get started!**

Talk to Me London is all about finding ways for people to talk to each other. We know that talking brings about many benefits, from a greater sense of well-being to friendlier communities, and increased opportunities. Think about it— just one conversation can inspire us, reassure us, or brighten up our day. Our vision is to build a friendlier city through encouraging small conversations between strangers.

> 🔍 **Note-taking**
> A good way of taking notes when you are listening to a talk, a lecture, or an interview is to try to write down the key words that you hear. These are the "content" words (usually nouns or verbs) that will help you remember the important information.

c 🔊 **4.8** Listen to an interview with Polly Akhurst, one of the founders of Talk to Me London. Make notes under these headings.

The Talk to Me London pin
How Polly has benefited from talking to strangers
Mediterranean countries and Madrid
Her reaction to negative media coverage
What she would say to people who don't want to talk

d Compare your notes with a partner and agree upon the main points under each heading. Then listen again. Can you add anything to consolidate your notes?

Talking is something most of us like to do.

We spend hours talking to our friends—at coffee shops, over dinner, or on the phone.

But we don't often talk to people we don't know.

And while this may not sound so bad, it's having a big negative impact.

Talking can help us to feel less lonely. In fact, it can make us much happier!

And this in turn, creates a greater sense of community.

e **4.9** Listen to four true stories from the Talk to Me London website. Who started a conversation, and who was approached by someone else?

James	Anneka	Philippa	Alise

f Now listen again and match the four people to the information about the conversations. Write **Al**, **An**, **Ja**, or **Ph**.

1 ☐ met someone she knew who she hadn't seen for a long time.
2 ☐ talked to someone who had recently come to London.
3 ☐ was surprised that the other person was happy to talk.
4 ☐ was unexpectedly given something.
5 ☐ talked to four different people one after another.
6 ☐ didn't expect anyone to talk to her.
7 ☐ was given a suggestion about how to make the most of traveling time.
8 ☐ ended up talking to a whole group of people.

g If you were visiting London, would you wear a Talk to Me London pin? Why (not)?

7 SPEAKING

a Read some online comments about Talk to Me London. How do you think each person feels about the project?

say hello@talktomelondon

Posts Top / All

Alex I only lived in London for three months, but I experienced my fair share of conversations with people on random benches or at train stations late at night, etc. If you want unfriendly, try Los Angeles. Honestly. I've lived here for almost a decade, but it still drives me insane. You could spend all day, every day, in the same coffee shop and you'd die, decades later, before any of the other regulars even acknowledged your presence! #talktomelondon

Mark London is no different from most cities in this respect. It's an unwritten rule, you don't talk to strangers and they don't talk to you. I can imagine few things worse than someone trying to engage me in small talk on my morning commute. You keep to your private bubble and I'll keep to mine. That's how we like it. #talktomelondon

Bella I just don't get this—London unfriendly, nobody talks to a stranger? Ridiculous. Maybe those who find London unfriendly are in fact the ones who are unfriendly, and unwilling to initiate a conversation. No problem for many of us. #talktomelondon

b **4.10** Look at some useful phrases for giving your opinion in English. Underline the words that you think have extra stress. Listen and check.

> 🔍 **Emphasizing that something is your own opinion**
> 1 I'd say that…
> 2 If you ask me,…
> 3 Personally, I think that…
> 4 Personally speaking, …
> 5 In my opinion, …
> 6 In my view,…
> 7 I feel that…
> 8 My feeling is that…
> 9 As far as I'm concerned, …

c Answer these questions in small groups. Try to use the language from the box to express your opinions.

1 Do people in your town or city tend to talk to complete strangers, or would it be considered odd?
2 Which cities or regions in your country have a reputation for being friendly or unfriendly? Do you agree?
3 Have you ever been to a city or country that struck you as particularly friendly or unfriendly?
4 "You keep to your private bubble and I'll keep to mine." Do you think this is a good approach to city life?

🔘 **Go online** to review the lesson

From cover to cover?

"Literature is the art of discovering something extraordinary about ordinary people, and saying with ordinary words something extraordinary.
Boris Pasternak, Russian author and poet

G adding emphasis (1): inversion **V** describing books and movies **P** sounds and spelling: /ɔ/

1 READING & SPEAKING

a Read the extract from the Barnes & Noble book blog and answer the questions.

- What is a "spoiler"?
- Has anyone ever spoiled a movie, a book, a sporting event, or anything else for you by telling you how it ended?

B&N BOOK BLOG

Warning: if you like to be surprised, stop reading right now. But if you're curious about these books and their endings, then read on. (Because I'm not completely cruel, I've whited out the spoilers — just highlight the empty space to see the hidden words.)

Don't say we didn't warn you…

And Then There Were None by Agatha Christie

Most Agatha Christie novels leave you speechless, but *And Then There Were None* is an absolute masterpiece of the "whodunnit?" formula. People invited to a party in a mansion keep on being murdered, but by whom? Well, if you're sure you want to know—it was

b Read the title of the article and answer the question. Then read the article and check.

c Now read the article again and answer these questions with a partner.

1 How did the reading experiment work? What was the outcome?
2 What possible reasons does the writer give for this outcome?
3 What's the writer's overall conclusion?

d Talk to a partner.

- Would you ever read the last page of a book first, or ask a friend how a movie or a sporting event ends? Why (not)?
- Do you ever re-read books or watch movies or sporting events again? Which ones? Why (not)?
- Does knowing the ending change the experience for you?

Time to rename the **spoiler**

DOES KNOWING THE ENDING AFFECT YOUR ENJOYMENT?

One of my favorite movies is *When Harry Met Sally*. I can watch it again and again and love it every single time—maybe even more than I did before. There's a scene that will be familiar to any of the movie's fans: Harry and Sally have just set off on their drive to New York City and Harry starts telling Sally about his dark side. He mentions one thing in particular: whenever he starts a new book, he reads the last page first. That way, in case he dies while reading it, he'll know how it ends.

Harry will know how it ends, true, but doesn't that also ruin the book? If you know the ending, how can you enjoy the story? As it turns out, easily. A study in this month's issue of *Psychological Science* comes to a surprising conclusion: spoilers don't actually spoil anything. In fact, they may even serve to enhance the experience of reading.

Over 800 students from the University of California in San Diego took part in a series of experiments where they read one of three types of short story: a story with an ironic twist (such as Roald Dahl), a mystery (such as Agatha Christie), and a literary story (such as Raymond Carver). For each story, there was a spoiler paragraph that revealed the outcome.

The students read the stories either with or without the spoiler. Time to reconsider, it seems, what we call a spoiler. The so-called "spoiled" stories were actually rated as more enjoyable than those that were "unspoiled," no matter what type of story was being read. Knowing the ending, even when suspense was part of the story's goal, made the process of reading more, not less, pleasurable.

Why would this be the case? Perhaps, freed from following the plot, we can pay more attention to the quality of the writing and to the subtleties of the story as a whole. Perhaps we're more likely to spot signs and clues about what might happen, and take pleasure in our ability to identify them.

Whatever the reason, it may not be as urgent as we think it is to avoid spoilers. Harry might have the right idea after all, reading the last page first. In fact, he might be getting at the very thing that lets me watch him meet Sally over and over and over again, and enjoy the process every single time.

2 VOCABULARY & PRONUNCIATION
describing books and movies; /ɔ/

a Complete some readers' comments about books and movies with an adjective from the list.

| depressing | entertaining | fast-moving | gripping | haunting |
| implausible | intriguing | moving | slow-paced | thought-provoking |

1 A wonderful movie. So _____ it brought tears to my eyes! ★ ★ ★ ★ ★
2 A _____ novel that raised many interesting questions. ★ ★ ★
3 Rather _____. I really had to make an effort to finish it. ★ ★
4 A _____ story. I was hooked from the very beginning. ★ ★ ★ ★ ★
5 A light and _____ novel. Perfect for beach reading! ★ ★ ★
6 The plot was _____. It was impossible to predict how it would end. ★ ★ ★ ★
7 The characters were totally _____. I couldn't take any of them seriously. ★
8 A _____ story that jumps from past to present and back again at breakneck speed. ★ ★ ★ ★
9 A well-written novel, but so _____ it made me feel like I'd never be happy again! ★ ★ ★
10 A _____ tale that stayed with me long after I'd finished reading it. ★ ★ ★ ★

b ◉ 4.11 Listen and check.

c Take turns with a partner to choose an adjective from the list in **a** and name a book or a movie that you could use the adjective to describe. Say why.

d ◉ 4.12 Listen and write six sentences. Then circle the /ɔ/ sounds in them. What different spellings can be pronounced /ɔ/?

e Practice saying the sentences.

3 SPEAKING
Talk to a partner about as many of the topics as you can. Tell your partner about a book that…

4 GRAMMAR adding emphasis (1): inversion

a Complete extracts 1–5 with endings A–E.

1 **No sooner** had we sat down at the kitchen table… ☐
   (Margaret Drabble, *A Day in the Life of a Smiling Woman*)
2 **Hardly** had she put the comb in her hair…
   (Grimm's Fairy Tales, *Snow White*)
3 **Only later** did I understand…
   (Mikhail Gorbachev, *On My Country and the World*)
4 **Never** have I seen so many people in an art gallery… ☐
   (review of Matisse exhibition, *The Independent*)
5 **Not only** had Silas killed the only four people who knew where the keystone was hidden, (but)… ☐
   (Dan Brown, *The Da Vinci Code*)

A looking happy.
B than the twins burst in.
C than the poison in it took effect, and the girl fell down senseless.
D he had killed a nun inside Saint-Sulpice.
E that this was not the way to proceed, that we could not live by a double standard.

b Look at the verbs after the **bold** adverbial expressions. What is unusual about the word order? What is the effect of putting the adverbial expression at the beginning of the sentence?

c Ⓖ p.149 Grammar Bank 4B Learn more about adding emphasis using inversion, and practice it.

d Complete the sentences in your own words, using inversion to make them as dramatic as possible.

1 Only after the wedding…
2 No sooner…than I realized…
3 Never in the history of sports…
4 Not until the last moment…
5 Not only…, but…

5 WRITING

Ⓦ p.118 Writing A review Write a review of a book or movie you have read or watched recently.

Go online to review the lesson

6 READING

a Would you prefer...
- to read a book written in English in the original version or translated into your language? Why?
- to watch an English-language movie subtitled or dubbed? Why?

b Read the introduction to a blog by Daniel Hahn, a translator. Why do you think he calls translation "both simple and impossible"?

c Read Part 1 and make sure you understand every word of the "rough translation." How do you picture the scene? Where are the two people, and how are they feeling?

Translation Diary

Daniel Hahn I'm translating a novel. It's written in Portuguese, and it needs to be written in English. There is a Brazilian novelist at one end, and an American publisher at the other, and there's me in the middle, tasked with giving the publisher exactly the same book the novelist has written, keeping it identical in absolutely every conceivable respect, except that I've got to change all the words. The novel is *Blue Flowers* by Carola Saavedra. Or, to be more accurate, the novel is still *Flores Azuis*, for now. *Blue Flowers* is what it's got to be when I'm done with it. So I have to immerse myself in Carola's book, in Portuguese, and write it again for the publishers in English. The process is both simple and impossible, and I'm going to be describing it on this blog.

1 In this scene, A, the main woman character, describes the moment her lover leaves her:

Eu não disse nada, não chorei, não pedi explicações, não te implorei para ficar. Eu apenas permaneci ali, imóvel, muda, deitada na cama, enquanto você se vestia, pegava a mochila e ia embora.

A rough translation might be:

I didn't say anything, I didn't cry, I didn't ask for explanations, I didn't implore you to stay. I merely stayed there, immobile, mute, lying on the bed, while you dressed, took your rucksack, and went away.

2 "Implore" isn't quite right, is it? "Beg" would be better. And "immoblie," similarly—I prefer "still" or "unmoving." In both cases my first quick version just used words that stayed close to the Portuguese ("implore" for "implorei," "immobile" for "imóvel"), but we need to move away a little further in order to arrive somewhere more like normal English. I think "merely" is a bit too formal for A's voice here, too.

I didn't say anything, I didn't cry, I didn't ask for explanations, I didn't beg you to stay. I just stayed there, unmoving, mute, lying on the bed, while you dressed, took your rucksack, and went away.

3 There are an awful lot of "I"s in that first sentence, aren't there? In Portuguese there's an "Eu" ("I") at the beginning of the first sentence and an "Eu" at the beginning of the second, so the sentences are perfectly balanced. As you can see, I've removed a pair of "I"s. And we have a "rucksack" which should probably be a "backpack," to minimize how UK-ish it sounds to US readers.

I didn't say anything, I didn't cry, I didn't ask for explanations, didn't beg you to stay. I just stayed there, unmoving, mute, lying on the bed, while you dressed, took your backpack, and went away.

4 Now, that first sentence ends on the word "stay"—which would be fine...except that "stay" appears again, three words later. Hmm, so now I've got to change that, too. One option is "I didn't beg you not to go," which helps because we imagine A saying "Please don't go!" rather than "Please stay!" which isn't quite the same.

I didn't say anything, I didn't cry, didn't ask for explanations, didn't beg you not to go.

5 I've also got to decide if the man is dressing, or getting dressed, or getting himself dressed, and my decision will be as much about the rhythm of the sentence as anything else. And I don't like the ending—"went away" is very weak. I'd rather end solidly on one word—just "left."

I just stayed there, unmoving, mute, lying on the bed, while you got dressed, took your backpack, and left.

6 Right. So—we're done now, surely? Um, not quite... I'd prefer "picked up your backpack" to just "took your backpack"—I think the latter might sound as though he's taking it from her? And I'm not sure about "mute," either. I think "silent" would do. So how about this, then?

I didn't say anything, I didn't cry, didn't ask for explanations, didn't beg you not to go. I just stayed there, unmoving, silent, lying on the bed, while you got dressed, picked up your backpack, and left.

Better?

d Now read Parts 2–6, which show the evolution of the translation. (Circle) the changes in each version and compare with a partner.

e Read Parts 2–6 again and match them to the reasons A–E Daniel gives for making the changes.

A ☐ He wants to stay close to the effects achieved in the original, and the translation needs to be accessible to American readers.

B ☐ He wants to choose the right expression to clarify exactly what is happening.

C ☐ It's better not to use the same word twice in quick succession.

D ☐ Some of the words are too close to the original and don't sound very natural in English.

E ☐ He has to decide which version of a phrase will suit the music of the sentence best.

LEXIS IN CONTEXT

🔍 **Understanding synonyms**

It is very useful to know a variety of synonyms for common words. This will help you to use a wider lexical range in your writing and not to repeat yourself. However, it is important to make sure that your synonym has exactly the meaning or register that you want.

---

f Which synonyms does the translator consider for…?

1 implore _____
2 immobile _____ _____
3 merely _____
4 rucksack _____
5 went away _____
6 mute _____

g Now find synonyms in the introduction for:

1 employed to _____
2 the same _____
3 imaginable _____
4 precise _____
5 finished with something _____

h What do you think you could learn from Daniel's blog about improving your own writing in English?

---

7 LISTENING

a You are going to listen to an interview with Beverly Johnson, a professional translator working in Spain. Before you listen, think of three questions you might ask her about her job.

b 🔊 **4.13** Listen to the whole interview. Did she answer any of your questions?

c Now listen to each part of the interview again. Choose **a**, **b**, or **c**.

🔊 **4.14** Part 1

1 One of the reasons Beverly decided to become a translator was that…
   a she thought teaching English was boring.
   b she really enjoyed the postgraduate course that she took.
   c she wanted to be self-employed.

2 Which of these does she mention as one of the drawbacks of being a freelance translator?
   a A low salary.
   b No paid holidays.
   c Time pressure.

3 Beverly's advice to would-be translators is to…
   a specialize.
   b study abroad.
   c take a translation course.

🔊 **4.15** Part 2

4 Most people who translate novels into English…
   a don't do any other kind of translation work.
   b prefer translating authors who are no longer alive.
   c often concentrate mainly on one particular writer.

5 She mentions the advertising slogan for Coca-Cola as an example of…
   a how difficult it is to convey humor in another language.
   b how you cannot always translate something word for word.
   c how different cultures may not have the same attitude to advertising.

🔊 **4.16** Part 3

6 *The Sound of Music* was translated into German as…
   a "All dreaming together."
   b "Tears and dreams."
   c "My songs, my dreams."

7 Which of these is not mentioned as a problem when translating movie scripts?
   a Having enough room on the screen.
   b Conveying the personality of the speaker.
   c Misunderstanding the actors' words.

8 The problem with translating swear words in a movie script is that…
   a they may be more shocking in other languages.
   b they may not be translatable.
   c you can't use taboo words in some countries.

d Are there any words in your language that you think are "untranslatable" into English? How would you try to express the ideas? Can you think of any English words that are "untranslatable" into your language?

🔘 **Go online** to review the lesson

3&4 Review and Check

GRAMMAR

a Complete the sentences with the right word or phrase.

1 It's 2:30 now—what time do you think we'll get _____ Miami?
2 Unfortunately, Allie got _____ cheating on her final exam.
3 The windows are filthy. Let's get someone _____ them.
4 I don't think Omar will ever get _____ doing his own laundry—his mother always did it.
5 My passport expires in two months, so I need to get it _____ .

b Right (✓) or wrong (✗)? Correct any mistakes in the highlighted phrases.

1 Basic, I think she still hasn't gotten over the breakup of her marriage.
2 We've finished the interviews and all of all we think Maria Ramirez is the most suitable candidate.
3 Dave's really late, isn't he? I think he might get lost.
4 The waiter didn't probably notice that they had left without paying.
5 I think it's unlikely that I'll be given a work permit.
6 What a wonderful smell! Somebody must bake some bread.
7 You definitely won't pass your driver's test if you drive that fast!
8 I called you yesterday. You should have gotten a message on your voicemail.
9 Not only we saw the sights, we managed to do some shopping as well.
10 Only when the main character dies does her husband realize how much he loved her.

c Complete the sentences with the right form of the verb in parentheses.

1 The traffic is really bad—she's unlikely _____ before 7:00. (arrive)
2 Monica is bound _____ the news—everybody was talking about it yesterday. (hear)
3 My neighbor can't _____ very long hours. He's always home by early afternoon. (work)
4 No sooner _____ married than Yiming lost his job. (they / get)
5 Never _____ such a wonderful view. It completely took my breath away. (I / see)

VOCABULARY

a Complete the missing words.

1 She's very shy, but you'll soon get to _____ her.
2 Let's get _____ for a coffee this weekend.
3 I've been trying to get _____ of Alan, but he's not answering his phone.
4 She's always calling me at work—it really gets on my _____ .
5 I hope I get _____ this cold by the weekend; I'm supposed to be going to a wedding.
6 His parents let him do whatever he wants, so he's used to getting his own _____ .
7 When I was a student, I had to get _____ on less than $75 a week.
8 I hope I get the _____ to talk to her before she goes home.

b Circle the right word.

1 The English archers used their bows to fire thousands of *arrows / spears* into the air.
2 After days of fighting, both sides agreed to a *retreat / ceasefire*.
3 The city finally fell after a three-month *siege / coup*.
4 During the civil war, thousands of *refugees / allies* crossed the border to safety.
5 It was a fierce battle and *civilians / casualties* were heavy on both sides.
6 The rebels *broke out / blew up* the railroad tracks.
7 Even though they were surrounded, the troops refused to *surrender / defeat*.
8 The army *shelled / looted* the capital with long-range weapons.

c Complete the sentences with verbs in the simple past.

buzz	creak	rattle	screech
sigh	slam	whisper	whistle

1 Leila _____ the door and walked off angrily.
2 "Thanks, dear," she _____ softly in his ear.
3 He _____ a happy tune as he walked down the street.
4 "I wish he was here—I really miss him," she _____ .
5 The wind was so strong that the windows _____ .
6 The car's brakes _____ as it came to a stop.
7 A bee flew in through the window and _____ around the room.
8 The door of the old library _____ open slowly, but there was nobody there!

d Write the adjectives for the definitions.

1 **th_____-pr_____** = making you think seriously about a particular subject or issue

2 **de_____** = making you feel very sad and without enthusiasm

3 **in_____** = very interesting because of being unusual or not having an obvious answer or ending

4 **gr_____** = exciting or interesting in a way that keeps your attention

5 **mo_____** = causing you to have deep feelings of sadness or sympathy

6 **im_____** = not seeming reasonable or likely to be true

CAN YOU understand this text?

a Read the article once. How do you think you would feel in "the quietest place on Earth"?

b Read the article again and complete it with phrases A–G. There is one phrase you do not need.

A Then, after a minute or two

B The kids were whining

C I booked a 45-minute session

D My experience in the anechoic chamber changed my life

E In an attempt to recapture some peace

F Despite my dislike of loud sounds

G Ironically, far from finding it peaceful

c Look at the highlighted words and phrases and work out their meaning. Check with your teacher or with a dictionary.

▶ CAN YOU understand this movie?

Watch or listen to a short movie about a comic book writer. Answer the questions.

1 Where is Midtown Comics located?

2 What kind of people does it attract?

3 How long does Chris have to finish his comic book?

4 How does Chris' father help?

5 What is the name of Chris' superhero?

6 How does Midtown Comics get people excited for new comic books?

7 How does Chris describe the superhero he created?

8 How many pages is Chris' final book?

9 Does the book get selected for the young artists' event?

10 According to Chris' father, why do people like superheroes?

Steve Orfield in the anechoic chamber

The quietest place on Earth

My quest started when I was in the New York subway with my kids. ¹_____, four trains came screaming into the station at once, and I put my hands over my ears and cowered—the noise was deafening. In cities, the ever-present, dull background roar of planes, cars, machinery, and voices is a fact of life. There is no escape from it and I was beginning to be driven mad by it.

²_____, I decided to go on a mission to find the quietest place on Earth; to discover whether absolute silence exists. The place I was most excited about visiting was the anechoic chamber at Orfield Laboratories in Minnesota. This is a small room, massively insulated with layers of concrete and steel to block out exterior sources of noise. It is the quietest place on Earth—99.9% sound-absorbent.

³_____, most people find its perfect quiet upsetting. The presence of sound around you means things are working; it's business as usual. When sound is absent, that signals malfunction. I had heard that being in an anechoic chamber for longer than 15 minutes can cause extreme symptoms, from claustrophobia and nausea to panic attacks. A violinist tried it and hammered on the door after a few seconds, demanding to be let out because he was so disturbed by the silence.

⁴_____—no one had managed to stay in for that long before. When the heavy door shut behind me, I was plunged into darkness (lights can make a noise). For the first few seconds, being in such a quiet place felt like nirvana, a balm for my jangled nerves. I strained to hear something and heard…nothing.

⁵_____, I became aware of the sound of my breathing, so I held my breath. The dull thump of my heartbeat became apparent—nothing I could do about that. As the minutes ticked by, I started to hear the blood rushing in my veins. The feeling of peace was spoiled by a tinge of disappointment—this place wasn't quiet at all. You'd have to be dead for absolute silence. Then I stopped obsessing about what bodily functions I could hear and began to enjoy it. I didn't feel afraid anymore and came out only because my time was up. Everyone was impressed that I'd beaten the record, but having spent so long searching for quiet, I was comfortable with the feeling of absolute stillness. Afterwards, I felt wonderfully rested and calm.

⁶_____. I found that making space for moments of quiet in my day is the key to happiness—they give you a chance to think about what you want in life. If you can occasionally become master of your own sound environment—from turning off the TV to moving to the country, as I did—you become a lot more accepting of the noises of everyday life.

By George Michelson Foy in The Guardian

Glossary
driven mad (NAmE driven crazy) made someone very angry

5A One thing at a time

G distancing | V expressions with time | P linking in short phrases

1 SPEAKING

a When you are working or studying, do you tend to do one task at a time and concentrate on it, or do you multitask, i.e., try to do several things at once? Give examples.

b Look at some examples of multitasking. Rate them 1–3 (1 = easy to do at the same time, 2 = possible to do at the same time, but can be distracting, 3 = very difficult or even dangerous to do at the same time).

- talking to a friend on the phone while you are cooking
- checking your email or texting while you are working or studying
- having a conversation with a friend when you are out jogging together
- checking an alternative route on your GPS when you are driving
- talking on a hands-free phone while you are driving
- listening to music while you are studying or working
- listening to music while you are exercising
- sending a message while talking to a friend

c Talk to a partner.

1 Compare your scores for **b**, and explain your ratings.
2 Which of the pairs of activities above do you do? To what extent do you think doing one thing affects how well you do the other?
3 Do you think multitasking helps you to use your time better?

2 READING

a You are going to read two extracts about time management: one from a newspaper article and one from a science website. Read the extracts once. With a partner, look at the four headings and choose the best one for each extract.

Get started, get finished

Increased efficiency, increased satisfaction

You think you can do it, but can you really?

The sport of saving time

b Read the extracts again. Mark the sentences **T** (true) or **F** (false). Correct the **F** ones.

1 It is often dangerous to talk to a friend while walking on the street.
2 It is more difficult to make a decision when you are doing two things at the same time.
3 It is difficult to maintain a conversation when you are driving if you also have to read a road sign.
4 Researchers have discovered that people trained in mindfulness are unable to multitask.
5 Mindfulness training develops people's ability to concentrate.
6 The quality of your work is not affected by how much you enjoy it.

LEXIS IN CONTEXT

🔍 **Learning verbs with dependent prepositions**
Some verbs are always followed by a particular preposition before an indirect or direct object, e.g., *depend **on**, worry **about***, etc. It is important to make a note of these prepositions when you learn new verbs.

c Look at some common verbs and verb phrases from the texts. Fill in the blanks with the preposition that usually follows them.

1 deal _____ something
2 concentrate _____ something
3 be capable _____ something
4 focus _____ something
5 become aware _____ something
6 be faced _____ something

d Talk to a partner.

1 Have you ever made a mistake or had an accident because you were multitasking? Does the first text explain in any way why it might have happened?
2 What advice do you get from the two texts about how to multitask successfully?

A

MULTITASKING is a natural everyday occurrence. We can cook dinner while watching TV and we can talk to a friend while walking down the street without bumping into anybody or getting run over. However, research suggests that there is an enormous difference between how the brain can deal with what are referred to as "highly practiced tasks," such as cooking or walking, and how it responds when, for example, you think about adding another ingredient or you decide to change the direction you are walking in. In this case, our brains require us to concentrate on the activity at hand.

Problems also arise when we try to do two or more tasks that are in some way related. Most people feel they are perfectly capable of driving and having a conversation at the same time. This is fine until they need to process language while driving, for example, read a road sign. Then the language channel of the brain gets clogged and the brain can no longer cope. A similar thing occurs if the conversation is about something visual, for example your friend describing what his new apartment looks like. In this case, as you try to imagine what he is describing, the visual channel of the brain is overloaded and you can no longer concentrate on the road.

| SPACE | TECHNOLOGY | ENVIRONMENT | HEALTH | SCIENCE IN SOCIETY |

B

MINDFULNESS refers to moment-by-moment awareness of thoughts, feelings, bodily sensations, and the surrounding environment. It focuses the brain on the present moment, instead of on the past or the future, and is gaining popularity as a practice in daily life.

A recent experiment conducted by psychologists in the US looked at the effects of mindfulness training on the multitasking behavior of workers in high-stress environments. They found that when asked to do multiple tasks in a short period of time, those who had been trained in mindfulness had a better memory for details and were able to maintain more focus on each task. They did not get distracted by worrying about the other tasks that still needed doing. This may well be because mindfulness training helps us to become more aware of where we are focusing our attention, so it makes sense that we are then better equipped to deal with a demanding work environment.

According to another study, mindfulness training can help improve people's attitudes towards work. Let's say you are faced with a large pile of invoices to process. If your mind starts to look for more interesting things to do, it is going to take you longer and you will probably make mistakes. If you can look at this task with a calm, clear, and engaged mind, you will be more efficient and you might even find some enjoyment in the process.

💬 Comment 🖨 Print

---

3 LISTENING

a You are going to listen to *The Chocolate Meditation*, a well-known exercise used to introduce people to the idea of mindfulness. Before you listen, with a partner, say what you think these verbs mean.

unwrap   inhale   pop (something) into
melt   chew   swallow

b 🔊 5.1 Close your eyes and listen. Imagine doing all the stages.

c Listen again. What does the speaker say about …?

1 the type of chocolate to choose
2 what to do before you unwrap it
3 what to notice as you unwrap it
4 what to do before you eat it
5 what to notice and do as you eat it
6 when to swallow it

d What is the main message of the meditation? Do you agree that mindfulness could "change your whole day"? Can you think of any other everyday activities you could try this approach with?

4 GRAMMAR distancing

a Read some sentences about the origins of mindfulness. Then focus on the highlighted phrases. What do they have in common? What effect would it have on the meaning if they were left out?

1 Jon Kabat-Zinn, Professor of Medicine at the University of Massachusetts, is considered to be the "father" of mindfulness.
2 He claims to help patients cope with stress, pain, and illness.
3 It appears that mindfulness is beneficial in lowering blood pressure and decreasing anxiety.

b Ⓖ p.150 **Grammar Bank 5A** Learn more about distancing, and practice it.

5 WRITING

You are a journalist. Your editor has asked you to write three breaking news stories for the website. However, you have to be careful what you say because the facts haven't been confirmed yet. Write two or three sentences for each headline, using the prompts and appropriate distancing expressions.

Politician's wife seeks divorce

Which politician? After how many years of marriage? What do people say is the reason?

Basketball player linked to cheating scandal

Which basketball player? What did he do? What is his team planning to do about it?

Sugar: the new health benefits

What are the benefits? How much sugar do you need to eat? When / In what form should you eat it?

6 SPEAKING & LISTENING

a Read an article about a survey by the watch manufacturer Timex. With a partner, complete the information with a time from the list.

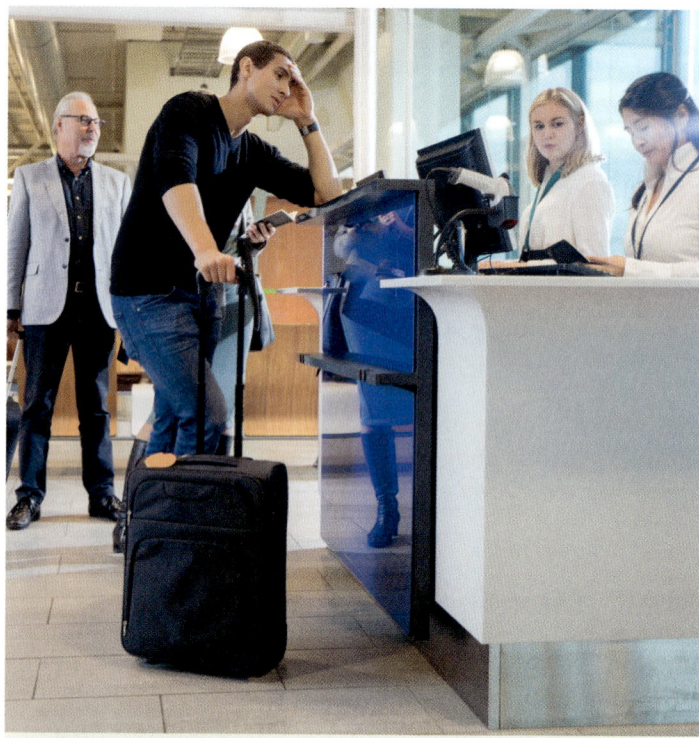

Things we hate waiting for—and how long before we freak out!

According to a US survey, there's a limit to how long people will wait for something before getting annoyed and trying to do something about it. The average wait in different situations before people lose patience is:

Survey Results

	Length of time
for a blind date to arrive	
for a bus / train	
for a car in front of you to start moving when the light turns green	
for a table in a restaurant	
for people to stop talking during a movie at the movie theater	
for the doctor	
for your partner to get ready to go out	
in a line at a coffee shop	

5 seconds	2 minutes	7 minutes	15 minutes
20 minutes	21 minutes	26 minutes	32 minutes

b **© Communication** The Timex survey **p.108** Check your answers to **a.** Then with your partner, say:
- how long you would wait.
- what you would do or say when you had gotten frustrated with waiting.

c **◆)5.2** Now listen to six people talking about waiting for things. What situations do they complain about?

d Listen again. Who…?
1 ☐ wishes other people would just be as quick and efficient as they are
2 ☐ says that the person they're waiting for always comes at the last possible minute
3 ☐ uses a strategy to try to avoid having to wait
4 ☐ doesn't mind waiting if other people follow the rules
5 ☐ says how long they're prepared to wait before getting very annoyed
6 ☐ gets frustrated by sitting watching something happen very slowly

e Do you identify with any of the speakers? In what other circumstances do you hate having to wait?

7 VOCABULARY expressions with *time*

a Can you remember the missing words in these sentences from the listening?
1 …but more often they'll say, "Could be _____ **time** 7 a.m. to 7 p.m."
2 …you actually sort of see one line loading _____ **a time**.
3 …I always turn up _____ **time**, in fact usually at least five minutes early.

b **◆)5.3** Listen to the extracts and check.

c **Ⓥ p.167 Vocabulary Bank** Expressions with time.

d Complete these sentences so that they're true for you, or reflect what you think. Then compare with a partner.
1 By the time I'm _____, I'll be _____.
2 Everyone should _____ from time to time.
3 It's only a matter of time before _____.
4 _____ is taking up a lot of my time right now.
5 I think _____ is a waste of time.
6 It's going to take me a long time to _____.
7 It's about time I _____.
8 I find _____ very time-consuming.
9 If I had more time off, I'd _____.

8 PRONUNCIATION linking in short phrases

a **5.7** Listen to sentences 1–10. Why are the words linked? Read the information box and check.

1 We need to make up for lost time.
2 He gave me a really hard time.
3 We're going to run out of time.
4 Could I have some time off next week?
5 At times I feel like giving up completely.
6 Time's up. Please stop writing.
7 Let's not waste time on that.
8 It's only a matter of time before they break up.
9 Did you have a good time last night?
10 It's about time you learned to cook!

> ### 🔍 Understanding linking
>
> When people speak quickly, many phrases are linked together so they sound like one word. This is often because:
>
> 1 a consonant sound at the end of a word is linked to a vowel sound at the beginning of the next, e.g., *I met him a long time ago.*
>
> 2 a word ending with a consonant sound is followed by a word beginning with the same consonant sound, e.g., *I need some more time.* This also applies to two very similar sounds, e.g., /d/ and /t/, e.g., *Have a good time!*, and /z/ and /s/, e.g., *Please sit down.*
>
> 3 a word ending in *-r* or *-re* (e.g., *are*) is followed by a word beginning with a vowel sound, an /r/ sound is added to link the words together, e.g., *We're early.*

b **5.8** Listen to some three-word phrases that are often heard as one word. First you will hear the phrase on its own, and then you'll hear it in context. What are the phrases?

1 _____ _____ _____
2 _____ _____ _____
3 _____ _____ _____
4 _____ _____ _____
5 _____ _____ _____

c Practice saying the sentences and phrases in **a** and **b**, trying to link the words.

9 SPEAKING

With a partner, answer the questions in *Time and you*. Give examples to illustrate your answers using language from the box.

> ### 🔍 Giving examples
>
> 1 For example, … 3 …such as… 5 …like…
> 2 For instance, … 4 …like… 6 An example of this is…

Time and you

When you take an exam or test, do you tend to **have time left** at the end or do you usually **run out of time**?

When you were younger, did your parents **give you a hard time** if you came home late? Is there anything else that they used to give you a hard time about?

On a typical weekday morning, are you usually **short on time**? Is there anything you could do to **give yourself more time**?

Do you have any apps that you think really **save you time**? How often do you use them?

What do you usually do to **kill time** while you're waiting at an airport or a train station? In what other situations do you sometimes have to kill time?

When you go shopping, do you like to buy things as quickly as possible or do you prefer to **take your time**?

Is there anything or anybody who is **taking up a lot of your time** right now? How do you feel about it?

Are you usually **on time** when you meet friends? Does it bother you when other people aren't on time?

Do you usually get to the airport or train station **with time to spare** or at the last minute? What do you think this says about your personality?

What do you most enjoy doing when you've got some **time on your hands**?

> "Too many people spend money that they haven't earned to buy things that they don't want to impress people they don't like."
> *Will Rogers, US actor*

G unreal uses of past tenses   **V** money   **P** US and UK accents

1 READING & SPEAKING

a How important do you think the following are for people who are looking for a long-term partner? Number them in order of importance for both men and women. Are there any other important criteria?

	men look for…	women look for…
a good education	☐	☐
a healthy bank balance	☐	☐
good looks	☐	☐
an attractive personality	☐	☐

b Read the first part of the article. What points in **a** does it back up? Did you find the studies mentioned surprising?

c Now read the two opposing viewpoints in the article.
Answer with **JL** (Jemima Lewis) or **JM** (JoJo Moyes).

Who…?
1 ☐ thinks that women are influenced by previous generations' lifestyles
2 ☐ admits that she understands the other viewpoint when she is under a lot of pressure
3 ☐ admits to occasional feelings of jealousy
4 ☐ says that rich husbands are hard to find
5 ☐ thinks that working mothers with children have particularly difficult challenges to deal with
6 ☐ thinks that if you marry for money you have to accept the consequences

d Now read the whole article again. With a partner, say what the writer means by:
1 By logical extension, it would appear men are keen to "marry down"… (lines 9–10)
2 We call them "trophy wives," as if to distinguish them from the real thing… (lines 27–28)
3 …calibrate your work-life balance to suit yourself, rather than your mortgage provider. (lines 41–42)
4 But marry rich and you may marry a man who views you as a commodity. (lines 51–52)
5 …the shattered dreams of traded-in middle-aged wives… (lines 56–57)
6 Earning my own money means I don't have to justify my shoe habit… (lines 61–62)
7 I wouldn't be delighted if my daughter ended up with a dropout. (lines 65–66)

Do women really want to marry for money?

1 According to a report from the London School of Economics, women are now more determined than ever to find a partner who will improve their financial prospects. "Women's aspirations to 'marry up,' if they can, to 5 a man who is better-educated and higher earning persists in most European countries," says the report's author, Catherine Hakim. "Women continue to use marriage as an alternative or supplement to their employment careers," she concludes. By logical extension, it would appear men are keen to "marry 10 down," although nobody seems to query, much less gather statistics on, their matrimonial motives. Arguably, there's nothing surprising in these findings, especially when you consider women with young children. A recent study by the National Centre for Social Research revealed that a third of all 15 mothers would prefer to give up their jobs if they could afford to and three-fifths said they would want to work fewer hours.

Glossary
keen (NAmE eager) wanting to do something or wanting something to happen very much
bloke informal BE way to refer to a man
Pilates a physical fitness systemn that focuses on posture
Waitrose an upscale UK supermarket chain

We asked journalist **Jemima Lewis** and novelist **JoJo Moyes** what they thought.

Yes, says Jemima Lewis

Women want rich husbands. Perhaps we don't often say it—perhaps we don't even like to admit it to ourselves—but women are practical creatures. A rich husband gives you options.

One of the perks of being female is that you grow up knowing there's a slim chance that you might be able to marry a millionaire and retire before you hit middle age. If he is rich enough, your husband might pay for teams of nannies to look after your children while you busy yourself with Pilates. Working mothers like me tend to regard such wives with a disapproving eye. We call them "trophy wives," as if to distinguish them from the real thing, but that is partly just to distract ourselves from the envy inside.

Whether you fill your days with Pilates or child-rearing, not having to work is...well, less like hard work. Unfortunately, rich husbands, like handsome princes, are not easy to come by. Most of us, not moving in millionaire circles, are likely to fall in love with and marry a more normal bloke. In the meantime, you might have built up a career that you are proud of, and reluctant to give up. If you then have a baby, you are doomed to an inner life of conflict and guilt as you try to find a way to bring up your child without going bankrupt or insane.

Like a winning lottery ticket, a rich husband would solve your problems at a stroke, allowing you to calibrate your work-life balance to suit yourself, rather than your mortgage provider.

No, says JoJo Moyes

Today's young women, having observed their mothers **juggling** a full-time job and all the domestic responsibility, having the odd nervous breakdown and still having to look glamorous, have now decided they'd prefer to be kept by a wealthy husband. Who can blame them? There are times—usually when sick children and deadlines **collide**—that I think the same thing.

But marry rich and you may marry a man who views you as a commodity. You may spend much of your time alone; a **high-flying** career often means an absent husband and father. You can marry for money, but it's not a marriage. It's a deal. And I suspect only the toughest of women can see that with the clarity it requires. The divorce courts are **littered with** high earners, as well as the shattered dreams of traded-in middle-aged wives who have been replaced by a younger, more glamorous model. My children have long played a game called "Who's got the **sourest** face?" in Waitrose. It's always the wives in the really expensive cars.

My husband and I have taken turns as the highest earner. Earning my own money means I don't have to justify my shoe habit, and he doesn't **shoulder** the mortgage alone. And having a career brings me more contentment than having a designer handbag.

So, I wouldn't be delighted if my daughter ended up with a dropout. But I'd feel worse if she thought the most important thing about a man was his bank balance.

By Judith Woods in The Telegraph

---

e Look at the highlighted metaphors in the "No" text. What is their literal meaning? What do they mean here?

f Who do you agree with more, Jemima Lewis or JoJo Moyes? Do you think it's acceptable for men and women to consider finance as well as romance when they choose a partner?

2 GRAMMAR unreal uses of past tenses

a Look at the highlighted verbs in these sentences and answer the questions with a partner.

- Which ones refer to things that really happened in the past?
- What do the others have in common? Which ones refer to the present or future? Which ones refer to the past?

1 When we got married, my husband and I were penniless students.
2 If he got promoted, we'd be able to afford a new car.
3 I wish we were better off.
4 It's time we thought about buying a bigger house.
5 I wasn't at all surprised when I heard that they had divorced.
6 I'd rather my husband stayed at home with the children.
7 I wish I'd accepted when he asked me to marry him!
8 If I'd married him, I would have a much better standard of living.

b **G** p.151 **Grammar Bank 5B** Learn more about unreal uses of past tenses, and practice them.

c Ask and answer the questions in small groups.

Do you ever wish...?
- you could meet a wealthy partner
- you had been born in another decade or century
- you could have a year off to travel
- you could learn a new skill
- you had chosen to study different subjects in high school or college
- you had more free time for your hobbies
- you lived in another town or city

4 VOCABULARY money

a Look at some idioms related to money. With a partner, say what you think they mean.

1 Money doesn't grow on trees.
2 He's really tight-fisted.
3 It must have cost an arm and a leg.
4 They can't make ends meet right now.
5 We're in the red. (opposite *in the black*)
6 It's highway robbery!
7 We're going to have to tighten our belts.
8 Those two are definitely living beyond their means!

b V p.168 **Vocabulary Bank** Money

c Choose the right word from each pair according to meaning, collocation, or register.

1 Mom, can you lend me some money? I'm *broke / penniless*.
2 I'm trying to get *a loan / a mortgage* from the bank to buy a car.
3 We're going to have to be a little careful this month if we don't want to end up *in the red / in the black*.
4 He took part of his pension as *a lump sum / a deposit* when he retired.
5 One of my cousins is absolutely *affluent / loaded*—she inherited a fortune from her parents.
6 When you're abroad, you get a better *currency / exchange rate* if you take money out at an ATM.
7 We like living here because we have a much better *cost / standard of living*.
8 **A** Is parking included in the price of this hotel room?
B No, sir. It's 12 *bucks / dollars* extra.

d Choose two or three of the options and tell a partner about them.

Do you know anybody who...?

is tight-fisted
lives beyond their means
was given a grant to study abroad
buys and sells shares of stock on the stock market
charges very high fees for what they do
has difficulty making ends meet
often gives donations to charity

5 LISTENING

a Read the biographical information about Sarita Gupta and Muhammad Yunus. What is the link between them?

Article | Talk | Read | Edit | View history

Sarita Gupta

From *Wikipedia, the free encyclopedia*

Sarita Gupta is an executive with more than 25 years' experience in promoting awareness and raising funds for international nonprofit organizations. She's worked for different initiatives that fight poverty around the world. From 2007 to 2010, she was the Vice President of Development and Communications at Women's World Banking. Currently, she is the President of International Nonprofit Development Consultants, which focuses on helping nonprofit organizations make a direct impact in India and South Asia.

Muhammad Yunus

Muhammad Yunus is a social entrepreneur, banker, economist, and civil society leader who was awarded the Nobel Peace Prize for founding the Grameen Bank and pioneering the concepts of microcredit and microfinance. These loans are given to entrepreneurs who are too poor to qualify for traditional bank loans. In 2008, Yunus was rated #2 in *Foreign Policy* magazine's list of the "Top 100 Global Thinkers."

b 5.13 Now listen to Sarita Gupta talking about microfinance. Complete the information with two-word phrases.

1 The idea of microfinance started in the ________ ________.
2 The Western world had been ________ ________ to developing countries for many years.
3 Yunus realized that poor people need access ________ ________.
4 Poor people can't ________ ________ relatives because their relatives are poor as well.
5 Yunus's first innovation was to make a group of people responsible for ________ ________ a loan.
6 Poor people can't repay a loan all at once with a ________ ________.
7 However, they can make small ________ ________ and repay a loan little by little.
8 Yunus's system doesn't encourage poor people to borrow a ________ ________.
9 If they pay back a small amount successfully, they can apply for a ________ ________.

Glossary

aid /eɪd/ *n* money, food, etc., that is sent to help countries in difficult situations
collateral /kəˈlætərəl/ *n* property or something valuable that you promise to give to somebody if you cannot pay back money that you borrow
peer /pɪr/ *n* a person who has the same social status as you

c 🔊5.14 🔊5.15 🔊5.16 You're going to listen to Sarita Gupta talk about three success stories. Make notes for each case study in the chart.

	The Dominican Republic	Jordan	India
The situation she was in			
The business she set up			

d Do you think there are people in your country who would benefit from microfinance?

Glossary

the DR the Dominican Republic

cantina /kænˈtinə/ *n* Spanish for a cafeteria or kitchen

recourse /ˈrikɔrs/ *n* being able to use something that can provide help in a difficult situation

embroider /ɪmˈbrɔɪdər/ *v* to decorate cloth with a pattern of stitches usually using colored thread

sari /ˈsɑri/ *n* a long piece of cloth that is worn as the main piece of clothing by women in south Asia

amass /əˈmæs/ *v* to collect something, especially in large quantities

middleman /ˈmɪdlmæn/ *n* a person or company that buys goods from the company that makes them and sells them to somebody else

---

6 PRONUNCIATION UK and US accents

🔍 **Distinguishing between UK and US accents**
Although people speaking UK English will almost always be understood in the US, and vice versa, there are several differences in pronunciation between General American and Standard English, apart from all the regional accents. Understanding these differences will help you to follow UK and US accents more easily.

a 🔊5.17 Sarita Gupta was born in India. She speaks English with a US accent, since she studied at Columbia University in the US and lives and works in New York. Listen to an extract from her interview. Focus on how she says the highlighted words.

"And the answer is obvious, they need money and all of us, in order to get started, have had access to credit. So, the poor can't get access to credit, they can't go to relatives to borrow because generally the relatives are as poor as they themselves are."

b 🔊5.18 Now listen to the same passage read by a British speaker. How does the pronunciation of the highlighted words change?

c 🔊5.19 Listen to some more examples of words spoken by US and UK speakers. Can you hear the difference?

		US	UK
1	twenty	a	b
2	internet	a	b
3	party	a	b
4	smart	a	b
5	turn	a	b
6	honest	a	b
7	coffee	a	b
8	awesome	a	b
9	new	a	b
10	route	a	b
11	vase	a	b
12	leisure	a	b
13	inquiry	a	b
14	mustache	a	b
15	address	a	b

d 🔊5.20 Now listen and circle **a** if you hear US pronunciation and **b** if you hear UK pronunciation.

e When you listen to English, e.g., in songs or on TV, which accent do you hear more often? Which do you find easier to understand?

Go online to review the lesson

stress reduction   compound nouns

1 ▶ THE INTERVIEW Part 1

a Read the biographical information about Jordan Friedman. Would you be interested in participating in one of his stress reduction programs?

Jordan Friedman, also known as "The Stress Coach," lives in New York City and is a specialist in the field of stress and stress reduction. He has been developing stress management programs and resources for individuals, companies, and colleges worldwide for over 20 years, and his client list includes Harvard University, the Massachusetts Institute of Technology, and the New York City Department of Education. He is the author of *The Stress Manager's Manual*, and his work has been featured by *The New York Times*, *The Wall Street Journal*, and *The Today Show*. Jordan is an expert on student stress, and has developed a program called Stressbusters, which helps nearly 250,000 college students and staff members.

b ◀) 5.21 Watch or listen to Part 1 of the interview. Why does he think it's important to reduce stress?

c Now listen again. Complete sentences 1–5.
1 The biggest causes of stress are…
2 Compared with 20 years ago, life today is more stressful because…
3 Nowadays we don't have time to…
4 If our immune systems are weakened by stress…
5 If we don't sleep well,…

Glossary
stressor (technical) something that causes stress
the immune system the system in your body that fights infection and disease
punching bag a heavy leather bag on a rope, used by boxers when they train
stroke a sudden serious illness when a blood vessel in the brain bursts or is blocked, which can cause death or the loss of the ability to move or to speak clearly

▶ Part 2

a ◀) 5.22 Now watch or listen to Part 2. Mark the sentences **T** (true) or **F** (false).
1 Different people should choose different ways of dealing with stress.
2 The stress management techniques Jordan Friedman mentions all take a minute or less.
3 The most important thing about stress management techniques is to make them a habit.
4 Friedman worked with a student who felt very stressed when he had to drive.
5 The student's classmates suggested that he should travel at a different time of day.
6 The solution to the student's problem was difficult for him to see for himself.

b Listen again. Say why the **F** sentences are false.

Glossary
salad bar a counter in a restaurant where customers can serve themselves from a variety of salad ingredients
walk around the block go for a quick walk near where you live or work in a town or city
subway car a section of an underground train

▶ Part 3

a ◀) 5.23 Now watch or listen to Part 3. Do students in your country suffer from similar stress?

b Listen again and answer the questions.

1 At what age do people tend to be most stressed?
2 What main reasons does Jordan Friedman give for student stress?
3 How does stress affect memory? How might this affect students?
4 What two things does the Stressbusters program give students?
5 What feedback have students given about Stressbusters?

> **Glossary**
> **back rub** a short back massage
> **campus** the buildings of a college and the land around them
> **wellness resources** facilities for helping people to stay healthy

2 LOOKING AT LANGUAGE

> 🔍 **Compound nouns**
> Jordan Friedman frequently uses compound nouns, e.g., *stress response*, *stress management*, etc. Remember that when you hear new compound nouns, the first noun usually describes the second one—this will help you to figure out the meaning.

a Try to complete the compound nouns in these extracts from the interview.

1 "...when you have emails coming in and **t**_____ **messages** left and right..."
2 "Stress is really important, and, in fact, it can be a **l**_____ saver..."
3 "Uh, stress contributes to high **bl**_____ pressure, which contributes to **h**_____ **problems** and stroke."
4 "So these are all reasons to really pay attention to our **st**_____ **levels** and to take action to reduce the stress."
5 "The great thing about stress **m**_____ is that it's like a salad bar."
6 "We can do one-minute **br**_____ **exercises**, we can, uh, exercise, we can take a ten-minute walk around the block..."
7 "Stress is a very democratic occurrence, so older people are stressed, **c**_____ **students** are stressed, babies get stressed..."
8 "...there's a greater need to get help for, uh, them while in school, but if you're not with your usual **s**_____ **network** it's even more challenging sometimes to do so."

b ◖) 5.24 Watch or listen again and check.

3 ▶ ON THE STREET

a ◖) 5.25 Watch or listen to five people talking about stress. Who do you think is the most / least stressed? Why?

Simon	Anne	Jim	Billy	Sean
English	*American*	*American*	*American*	*English*

b Watch or listen again. Match the people (**Si, A, J, B,** or **Se**) to something they do to de-stress.

▢ focuses on a certain part of their body
▢ blocks out a particular sound
▢ likes to exercise
▢ tries to accept the situation
▢ tries not to think about anything

c ◖) 5.26 Watch or listen again and complete the Colloquial English phrases. What do you think they mean?

1 "...to just _____ _____ the sound of the babies."
2 "...relaxing and being _____ _____ _____, being happy with what is."
3 "I experience very little stress, except those rare periods when I'm _____ _____ a deadline."
4 "a little stressful trying _____ _____, whereas, where I lived before I knew exactly what to do"
5 "...and every half an hour _____ _____, just if I concentrate on relaxing..."

4 SPEAKING

Answer the questions with a partner or in small groups.

* Are you currently more stressed at work or school, or at home? Why?
* How stressful do you find the following? Why?

buying clothes	driving	exams	traveling

* If you feel stressed when you get home in the evening, what's the first thing you do to unwind?
* Do you ever have back rubs or massages when you feel stressed? Do they help you?
* Where would you go for the weekend if you wanted to get away from it all? Why?
* A recent survey found that Greece was the most stressful country in the world to live in, and Estonia the least. Where do you think your country would come in? Why?

> You know how advice is. You only want it if it agrees with what you wanted to do anyway.
> *John Steinbeck, US author*

G verb + object + infinitive or gerund **V** compound adjectives **P** main and secondary stress

1 READING & SPEAKING

a Read problems 1–5.

1 your Wi-fi isn't working
2 you're having problems with your partner
3 you have some health symptoms you're worried about
4 you want to know the best way to invest a sum of money you've inherited
5 your two-year-old child wakes up a lot at night

Where would you go to get advice for each problem? Would you…?

- ask a friend, colleague, or family member
- look on the internet
- read a self-help book, newspaper, or magazine
- call a helpline or an expert

If my Wi-fi wasn't working, I'd probably…

b Work in pairs, **A** and **B**. You are going to read two different texts giving advice. Read your text carefully and try to figure out the meaning of any new words and expressions.

c Use your own words to explain to each other the tips and the reasons for them.

LEXIS IN CONTEXT

d Now read both texts. Underline idiomatic expressions or phrasal verbs that mean:

Text A
1 behave like a child
2 do the part that is your responsibility
3 save (money)
4 (in a way that is) impossible to believe

Text B
5 make you feel very stressed
6 without having eaten anything
7 panic
8 gave something to somebody in authority

e To what extent do you agree with the tips? Was there any advice that you think you might put into practice?

You're certainly old enough to keep your room neat.

How much longer can I bear this?

A

How to survive… living with your parents

Nearly a third of young adults are still living at home with mom and dad. Are you one of them? Thirty-three percent of US adults from the ages of 25 to 29 still live with their parents or grandparents. This is the highest percentage since 1939. Some researchers think this number is so high because it's difficult for young people to find jobs that pay well. Other researchers think it's because young adults are waiting until their 30s to get married. Here are some survival tips for those of you who have reluctantly moved back to your childhood bedroom in mom and dad's house.

Do your share of the cooking, cleaning, and dishes. Don't let yourself go into "child mode" just because it's the house you grew up in. Housework is just as tedious for your parents as for the rest of us. Do your share, or you lose the right to call yourself an adult.

Save, save, save. The major advantage of living at home is the price. Unless your parents are charging you full market-rate rent (in which case, surely move?) you should be able to squirrel away some money. If you're working, living at home, and not saving any money, you aren't planning for the future at all. It won't end well.

Have an exit plan. Know how, if not exactly when, you plan to leave. In the darker moments of parent–child co-habitation, when you see in your parents' behavior a worrying image of the kind of person you might end up being, the knowledge that you have an escape plan will be the only thing that keeps you sane.

Go out. A lot. Of course you and your parents love each other very much, but that doesn't mean you like each other. Frankly, if you've lived together all your life and you don't sometimes hate them, you haven't been paying attention. So go out.

Get to know these strange new housemates. This is as good a time as any to find out about your parents' past history. Learning to see them as individuals, and not just as people who are there solely to look after you both physically and emotionally, will make you a better person. It will also make it easier to forgive them when they irritate you beyond belief.

From The Guardian

I'm never going to remember all this.

How to survive...
exam stress

1 Organize
Make sure you have all the things you need for the exam the night before: stationery, your ID card, etc. Last-minute searching for things can really stress you out before an exam.

2 Diet
Never go to an exam on an empty stomach, as you can end up concentrating more on your hunger than your exam paper. Before the exam, eat foods that are energy producing, like fruit and protein, and not too heavy so that they won't make you sleepy. If possible, take a water bottle to the exam hall to rehydrate.

3 Relax
One hour before the exam, relax! Don't feed yet more information to your already over-filled brain. Whatever you have learned, be confident of it and try to picture a calm stream, or take some deep breaths. You have done your preparation and now you should prepare yourself to give your best.

4 Plan
Once you get the question paper in your hand, read all the questions and make a quick rough plan of how you are going to invest your time in order to do your best. Mark the questions which you know you can answer easily and do them first. This will make you feel more confident. Never lose your cool if a question comes up which you didn't prepare for. It is too late now and your focus should be on the present moment.

5 Cross-check
It is very, very important to check your answers again at the end. Try to allow yourself a final 15 minutes to read through your paper and make any necessary corrections.

6 Forget
Often after an exam is over, people worry about the results or waste time discussing what their friends have written. Realize that the time to do something about the results was over when you handed in the answer sheet, and knowing how your friend did isn't going to help you. Concentrate on how you will face your next exam, if you have one, or just relax and be happy that it's over!

From www.wikihow.com

Glossary
stationery materials for writing, e.g., paper and pens or pencils

2 WRITING

a With a partner, choose one of the topics below that you have some experience with. Think of some advice that you could post on wikiHow. Write headings for at least four tips and plan what information to give under the headings, e.g., reasons for the advice, examples, etc.

How to survive...
a visit from difficult relatives

How to survive...
a trip to the dentist

How to survive...
a children's birthday party

How to survive...
a family vacation

b Tell your tips to another pair. See what they think of your tips and if they have anything to add.

c Using all the ideas, write a short paragraph for each heading.

3 GRAMMAR verb + object + infinitive or gerund

a Right (✓) or wrong (✗)? With a partner, correct any mistakes in the **bold** phrases.
1 When I lived with my parents, **I was always made load** the dishwasher.
2 If your parents are fussy about mealtimes, try **not to keep them waiting**.
3 **I don't mind you not clean** your room, but at least make your bed!
4 **I hate my parents talk to me** as if I was five years old.
5 Our teacher always **recommends that we go** to bed early the night before an exam.
6 **I want that you stop** writing now.
7 **I suggest you studying** for two hours a day, no more.
8 **Could you let me have** five more minutes just to finish this question?

b **G** p.152 **Grammar Bank 6A** Learn more about verb + object + infinitive or gerund, and practice it.

c Answer the questions with a partner.
1 Is there anything you would prefer people not to do when they are invited to your house? What kinds of things do you expect them to do?
2 When you were a child, were you ever made to eat something you really disliked? Why do you think your parents tried to make you eat it?
3 Do you ever need to spend time at home waiting for something to be delivered? What happens if you are out when someone tries to deliver something?
4 Can you imagine yourself living in another country? How far and how different from your country would you prefer it to be?
5 What kind of things do you dislike people helping you to do? Why would you rather do them yourself?

Go online to review the lesson

4 LISTENING

a Read about The School of Life. Why do you think it's been successful? Would you like to do one of their courses?

Login   Sign up   Search...

The School of Life is an educational company that offers advice on life issues. It was founded in London in 2008 and now has branches around the world, including Berlin, Istanbul, São Paulo, Seoul, and Sydney. The School offers a variety of programs, courses, videos, and presentations covering finding fulfilling work, mastering relationships, achieving calm, and enjoying leisure time.

b 🔊**6.1** Listen to a School of Life presentation called *Why small pleasures are a big deal*. Number the slides the presenter mentions in order, 1–9. Which things from the slides does he say are 'small pleasures'?

c Listen again and complete the sentences with a word or short phrase.

1 We don't believe that _____ things will give us much pleasure.
2 People don't get excited about pineapples because they aren't _____ any more.
3 The famous violinist was ignored because he was wearing _____ and playing _____.
4 'Marriage, career, travel, getting a new house' are examples of _____.
5 We assume that someone who cycled to the local park didn't enjoyed themselves as much as someone who _____.
6 We think that spending time looking at a cloudy sky can't be as exciting as _____.
7 An expensive vacation can be ruined by _____.
8 If we focus on everyday pleasures, they can be very _____.

d In pairs, summarize the central message of the presentation in one sentence. Then compare with another pair. Are your summaries similar?

Glossary
the Uffizi Gallery an important art museum in Florence, Italy
Lobster Thermidor a rich French dish made with lobster, egg yolks, and brandy

lily of the valley

Why small pleasures are a big deal

A

B

C

D

E

F

G

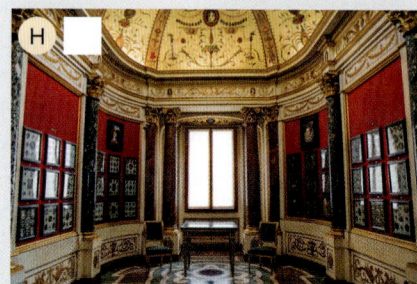

H

I

5 SPEAKING

a Look at the statements below. Choose one of them to talk about and make notes under the following headings:

- Whether you agree with the statement or not, and why
- Examples from your personal experience
- Any arguments on the other side
- Advice for your audience

Everyday life is full of small pleasures.

The best things in life are free.

Traveling abroad is more enjoyable than traveling in your own country.

A weekend at home is better than a weekend away.

b Read the tips for giving a presentation. Then, in small groups, give a short presentation about your statement. Listen to other people's presentations and ask questions.

Presentation tips

1 Organize your presentation logically, so you can remember what you're going to say.
2 Don't read your notes – use your own words.
3 Speak slowly, and pause between important points.
4 Make eye contact with the people you're talking to.
5 If the audience asks you questions, answer them clearly and concisely.

6 VOCABULARY & PRONUNCIATION
compound adjectives; main and secondary stress

> 🔎 **Compound adjectives**
>
> A **well-known** violinist once donned scruffy clothes and performed at a street corner.
>
> **Small-scale** pleasures can be anything but small.
>
> A compound adjective is an adjective made up of two parts. It can sometimes be written with a hyphen.

a Combine words from each box to make ten compound adjectives and use them to complete questions 1–10.

air	narrow		distance	made
high	second		hand	conditioned
home	self		risk	behaved
last	well		minute	minded
long	worn		out	conscious

1 Have you ever bought clothing or shoes from a _____ store? Did you have any problems with them?
2 Do you think it's possible for people to maintain a _____ relationship?
3 Do you usually do a lot of _____ studying the night before a test?
4 Do you usually feel _____ when you are having your photo taken? What do you do to try to be more natural?
5 Do you have any old clothes that you still like wearing even though they're a little _____?
6 Do you prefer _____ food to restaurant meals? Why (not)?
7 In the summer, do you spend much time in _____ buildings or cars? Do you consider it a necessity or a luxury?
8 Do you play any _____ sports? What attracts you to them?
9 Do you think as people get older they tend to get more _____ and intolerant?
10 Do you think children should be asked to leave restaurants if they are not reasonably _____?

b ◀))6.2 Listen and check.

> 🔎 **Fine-tuning your pronunciation: main stress and secondary stress**
> Some words, especially compounds or words with suffixes and prefixes, have both main stress and secondary stress. Secondary stress is shown by ˌ in a dictionary, e.g., /ˌself ˈkɑnʃəs/.

c Listen again. Which word usually has the main stress in compound adjectives? Then ask and answer questions 1–10 in **a** with a partner and give examples.

d Use these compound adjectives to complete some high-frequency collocations.

dead-end	eco-friendly	feel-good	groundbreaking
hands-free	high-heeled	high-pitched	labor-saving
life-changing	low-cost		

1 a _____ phone
2 a _____ job
3 a _____ movie
4 _____ research
5 a _____ voice
6 a _____ device
7 _____ shoes
8 a _____ airline
9 _____ detergent
10 a _____ experience

e ◀))6.3 Listen and check. Now use three compound adjectives from **a** or **d** to write questions to ask your partner.

Go online to review the lesson

6B Can't give it up

> My cell phone is my best friend.
> *Carrie Underwood,*
> *US singer and actress*

G conditional sentences   **V** phones and technology; adjectives + prepositions   **P** /æ/ and /ʌ/

1 VOCABULARY phones and technology

a Talk to a partner.
- What kind of phone do you have? How often do you upgrade? Would you like to upgrade right now?
- What apps do you have that you use a lot?
- What do you use your phone for apart from making calls?
- Do you use the internet most on your phone, a tablet, or a computer?

b **V** p.169 **Vocabulary Bank** Phones and technology.

2 PRONUNCIATION /æ/ and /ʌ/

> 🔍 **Fine-tuning your pronunciation: /æ/ and /ʌ/**
> The sounds /æ/ and /ʌ/ are very similar and it can be difficult to hear and produce the difference. The /æ/ sound is always spelled with the letter *a*, and the /ʌ/ sound is usually spelled with the letter *u*, though it can also be *o*, e.g., *come*, or *ou*, e.g., *touch*.

a 🔊 6.6 Listen to the difference between the two vowel sounds.

	a	b
1	a rang	b rung
2	a app	b up
3	a hang up	b hung up
4	a cat	b cut
5	a ran out	b run out
6	a match	b much
7	a track	b truck

b 🔊 6.7 Listen. Which word or phrase did you hear?

c Practice saying the sentences.
1 What is the number one app in your country?
2 Jack was cut off so he hung up.
3 My cell phone ran out of memory so I had to upgrade to a new one.

3 READING & SPEAKING

a Approximately how many hours do you think you spend a day using your phone? Are you happy with the amount of time you spend, or would you like to cut down?

b Read the article and fill in the blanks in the Rules and Challenges text with suitable verbs.

A beginner's guide to divorcing your phone

What's the first thing you do when you wake up? Read the news? Check your emails? Scroll through social media? Now, imagine your phone's not in the room. If that makes you feel uncomfortable, it may be time for a digital detox.

Tanya Goodin, a digital detox specialist, has devised a seven-day detox. She recommends first downloading a tracking app that measures how much time you spend looking at your screen and how many times a day you pick up your phone, so then you can compare your normal phone use with the end results.

Rules for a digital detox

▶ ¹D _____ all social media apps from your phone; check these only from a desktop computer.

▶ ²T _____ off all banner-style / pop-up / sound notifications from all other apps.

▶ ³L _____ your phone in your pocket or somewhere where you can't see it for meetings / get-togethers / conversations / meals involving other people.

▶ ⁴K _____ your phone out of sight during your commute.

▶ ⁵Don't t _____ your phone with you into the bathroom.

Challenges

Day 1	Day 2	Day 3
Leave your phone outside your bedroom overnight; get an alarm clock or ⁶t_____ up the volume on your phone, so you can hear its alarm easily from your bed through the door. Continue this all week.	Put your phone in a central place when you return home and go to the location of the phone (rather than carrying it around with you) if you need to ⁷ch_____ it.	⁸T_____ your work email account off your phone (notify everyone in advance that you're doing this.)

Day 4	Day 5	Day 6 and 7
Go out to dinner, lunch, or to an evening event / gym session and ⁹l_____ your phone behind.	¹⁰K_____ your phone on airplane mode as default all day; take it off this mode only when you need to use it.	Your complete digital detox: ¹¹t_____ off your phone and put it away from 7:00 p.m. Friday to 8:00 a.m. Monday.

c Read about Anisah Osman Britton. <u>Underline</u> all the positive effects and (circle) all the negative ones.

Anisah Osman Britton, 24, is the founder of 23 Code Street, a coding school for women. She has lived on a boat for the last five years, with her dog.
Before detox
Daily phone screen time: 3 hours 50 minutes
Number of pick-ups a day: 88

I rely on my phone for everything; I leave my laptop at work because there is no wi-fi on the boat. My top four apps are WhatsApp, Telegram, Instagram, and Twitter, and when it comes to deleting them, I think, "I can do this!" I substitute Instagram with reading books and finish two by the
5 end of the week, which makes me cringe at how much time I must waste on my phone.

I struggle with insomnia and often wake up at 4:00 a.m. and scroll through my phone. I'm amazed that, without it at hand, I simply go back to sleep. I set the alarm on my old-fashioned Casio watch now, and stay asleep a
10 lot longer.

By day three, I'm feeling left out of my family's WhatsApp group, but I welcome taking work emails off my phone. Things take a turn for the worse on day four, when I'm sick and have to stay home. I decide there is no way I'm doing it without my phone – I need it in bed with me – and I go back to
15 checking work emails, WhatsApp-ing my family, and watching dog videos on YouTube.

I'm not worried about switching my phone off on the weekend. I tell my family, and my business partner, Tom, that I'll speak to them on Monday. By Saturday lunchtime, I have a meltdown. It's so dead and quiet; I can't
20 even listen to music because my only source is my phone. I don't see a single person until my neighbor knocks on my door on Sunday morning with some chocolate. I almost cry. Later, I walk to the supermarket, just so I can speak to someone. This is the worst weekend of my life.

After the detox...
I couldn't cope with... not being able to take photos. I missed that so much.
I can now do without... flicking through social media in bed before getting up. I've given myself an extra hour in the morning.

After detox
Daily phone screen time: 3 hours
Number of pick-ups a day: 70

LEXIS IN CONTEXT

d With a partner, say what you think the writer means by the following words and phrases:

1 makes me cringe (line 5)
2 at hand (line 8)
3 take a turn for the worse (line 12)
4 have a meltdown (line 19)
5 cope with
6 flicking through social media

e Answer the questions with a partner.

1 How would you score for "daily phone screen time" and "number of pick-ups a day"? How dependent is your work or social life on having a phone?
2 Have you ever spent a long time without your phone, either as a detox, or because of circumstances? How did you feel?
3 Which of the rules and challenges would you find the most difficult?

4 GRAMMAR conditional sentences

a Match the halves of the conditional sentences.

1 If I'd had my phone with me,
2 If my laptop wasn't so new,
3 If they bring out a new iPhone,
4 If I didn't have fast broadband,
5 If my phone numbers weren't all in my phone,
6 If I hadn't sent you a message,

A you wouldn't have known where I was.
B I wouldn't be able to work from home.
C I'd have texted you to say where I was.
D I might be able to remember some of them.
E I'm definitely going to get one.
F I wouldn't have bothered to get it repaired.

b Which sentences refer to present or future situations and which ones refer to the past? What is different about sentence 2?

c **G** p.153 **Grammar Bank 6B** Learn more about conditional sentences, and practice them.

d Complete the sentences so that they are true for you. Then compare with a partner.

1 I could manage for a week without the internet provided that...
2 I would only lend someone money on the condition that...
3 Even if I had all the time in the world, I would never...
4 Had I not decided to learn English, I...
5 I'd be prepared to move abroad as long as...

Go online to review the lesson

5 VOCABULARY adjectives + prepositions

> 🔍 **Adjectives + prepositions**
> I'm not **worried about** switching my phone off on the weekend...
>
> Some adjectives need a certain preposition when they are followed by a noun or gerund. It is essential to learn these prepositions with the adjectives.

a Complete the prepositions column.

		Prepositions
1	Our country depends on young people to **come up** ____ new ideas.	*with*
2	Many 30-year-olds are still **dependent** ____ their parents.	_____
3	People are totally **fed up** ____ the number of reality shows on TV.	_____
4	Older people aren't as **open** ____ new ideas as younger people are.	_____
5	People are **sick** ____ being bombarded with depressing news.	_____
6	A lot of people are **hooked** ____ superhero movies.	_____
7	As a nation, we are very **proud** ____ our sporting achievements.	_____
8	A lot of young people are **addicted** ____ social networking.	_____
9	A lot of people are **obsessed** ____ celebrities and their lifestyles.	_____
10	People are usually very kind and **helpful** ____ foreign tourists.	_____

b 🔊 **6.8** Listen and check.

c Cover the **Prepositions** column and say the sentence with the correct preposition.

d With a partner, say to what extent sentences 1–10 are true for your country, giving examples.

6 LISTENING

a Read the website information and look at the photos of people who are addicted to certain types of behavior. With a partner, for each picture, discuss:
1 what kind of behavior the person is addicted to.
2 what effect this addiction might have on their daily life.

Home	Health A–Z	Medicines and treatments	Women's health	Men's health	Children's health

Hooked

When most people hear the word "addiction," they think of dependence on a substance such as drugs or alcohol. But if you just substitute the word "behavior" for "substance," you open up the definition of addiction to all kinds of dependencies, some of which may surprise you. Whether it's food, the internet, or bungee-jumping, the desire to experience that "high" becomes so strong that the addict loses control and seeks the activity despite all negative consequences.

b You're going to listen to a doctor talking about addiction. First look at some words and phrases that he uses related to addictions. Do you know what any of them mean? How are they pronounced?

1 dopamine
2 to quit a substance or a behavior
3 depression
4 brain chemistry
5 cravings
6 to go cold turkey
7 nicotine patches
8 to have counseling
9 to have a relapse

c ◀)) **6.9** Listen and check.

d Look at statements 1–8. Do you think they are true or false?

1 You get "a flood of dopamine" when you take or do something you are addicted to.
2 The more dopamine there is in your brain, the less effect it has and the more you need of what you are addicted to.
3 When people give up an addiction their first reaction is pleasure at their achievement.
4 People's addictions not only make them feel good, they stop them from feeling bad.
5 The best way of quitting all addictions is to go cold turkey.
6 It is helpful to use aids such as nicotine patches when trying to stop some addictive behavior.
7 All addicts need to be treated with a combination of medication and counseling.
8 Family support is important to stop addicts from having a relapse.

e ◀)) **6.10** Now listen to the doctor and mark the statements **T** (true) or **F** (false). Say why the **F** statements are false.

f Do you know anybody who is addicted to any of the things in the photos? How does it affect their lives? Are they doing anything about it?

7 SPEAKING

a What is the difference between being *addicted to* or *hooked on* something, and being *obsessed with* something (or someone)?

b Look at some tweets about obsessions. What do you think the highlighted phrases mean?

> 🐦 **#imobsessed**
>
> **Tweets** Top / All
>
> 1 My best friend's completely obsessed with her new boyfriend. She goes on and on about him the whole time. #imobsessed
>
> 2 I have to admit I've got a little bit of an obsession with bikes. I'm always looking at websites and checking out new models. #imobsessed
>
> 3 My sister always has her phone either in her hand or on the table next to her and she keeps checking it the whole time. #imobsessed
>
> 4 I always look at my reflection whenever I walk past a store window. I don't think I'm vain, but I just can't help it. #imobsessed
>
> 5 A friend of my brother's is an absolutely rabid New England Patriots fan. He goes to all their games. #imobsessed
>
> 6 My sister-in-law has a thing about not eating any processed food. She doesn't let her kids eat anything that's not homemade. #imobsessed

c Talk in small groups. Use some of the phrases from **b**.

Are you / Do you know anyone who is (a little bit) obsessed with…?

- their appearance
- a celebrity
- a sportsperson or team
- a particular object, e.g., their car, their phone, etc.
- staying in shape
- healthy eating
- organizing or cleaning
- a hobby or free-time activity
- anything else

8 WRITING

Ⓦ p.120 **Writing** A discursive essay (1): A balanced argument Analyze a model essay and write a discursive essay about online shopping or ready-made meals.

Go online to review the lesson

GRAMMAR

a Circle **a, b, or c.**

1 It _____ that the senator is to retire at the end of her term.
   a has announced   **b** announced it
   c has been announced

2 Excuse me. _____ to be a problem with this seat—I can't change its position.
   a It seems   **b** There seems   **c** It appears

3 _____ to a recent article, eating a lot of salt may not cause long-term health problems.
   a According   **b** Apparently   **c** Considering

4 _____ that the murderer is being concealed by friends.
   a There is thought   **b** It is thought   **c** It thought

5 My house is a mess—if only I _____ so messy!
   a 'm not   **b** weren't   **c** was

6 I'd _____ you didn't come in with your muddy shoes.
   a rather   **b** prefer it   **c** wish

7 I really wish we _____ that white sofa—it gets dirty much too easily.
   a haven't bought   **b** hadn't bought   **c** don't buy

8 I'd like _____ it in the morning, if that's possible.
   a that they deliver   **b** them delivering
   c them to deliver

9 If we hadn't had to work late, _____ the game now.
   a I'd be watching   **b** I'd have watched   **c** I'll watch

10 I'll pay for the classes _____ you agree not to miss any.
   a supposing   **b** unless   **c** providing

b Complete the sentences with the right form of the verb in parentheses.

1 The president is believed _____ his vacation in the Caribbean currently. (spend)

2 It's time you _____ to think about what subjects you want to study next year. (start)

3 My parents always encouraged me _____ foreign languages. (learn)

4 My new job involves me _____ to South America two or three times a year. (travel)

5 They're incredibly generous people and they wouldn't let me _____ for anything. (pay)

6 Daniel can stay the night as long as he _____ sleeping on the sofa. (not mind)

7 Supposing the Yankees lost their last two games, _____ they still _____ the division? (win)

8 Marcus might have hurt his head badly if he _____ a helmet when he fell off his bike. (not wear)

9 _____ you _____ me earlier that you were coming, I would have taken the day off. (tell)

10 If my wife hadn't inherited a lot of money, we definitely _____ in a house like this now. (not live)

VOCABULARY

a Complete the sentences with a preposition.

1 We arrived _____ time to spare.

2 Don't tell me you're still listening to Nickleback! You're really _____ the times.

3 Let's set off early. There's so much to see, and I don't want to run _____ of time.

4 We've decided to stay here _____ the time being.

5 We missed the bus, so _____ the time we got to the theater the play had started.

6 The reservation is for 8:30, so please make an effort to be _____ time.

7 He met Lara in Moscow, where he was working _____ the time.

8 It's _____ time you started studying.

b Circle **the right word or phrase.**

1 The *standard / cost* of living is higher in the city than it is in the suburbs. Rents are almost double.

2 Liz spent a fortune on her new bag! She must be *loaded / affluent*.

3 *Fares / Fines* on the New York City subway have gone up a lot recently. The cost of a SingleRide ticket is now $3.

4 **A** This hat cost $20.
   B Twenty *bucks / spots*? You're kidding!

5 They wanted to buy a house, but the bank wouldn't give them *an installment / a mortgage*.

6 The highest rate of *income / inflation* tax in the US is currently 37%.

7 Our vacation *budget / grant* is only $1,500, so we won't be able to go abroad.

8 Would you like to make a *donation / deposit*? It's for UNICEF.

c Complete the compound adjectives.

1 My father is very intolerant and **narrow-_____**.

2 Don't say anything about her new hairstyle. She's feeling very _____**-conscious**.

3 Jane gets her vintage clothes from **second** _____ stores.

4 You shouldn't have gone to the interview in those _____**-out** jeans.

5 Their kids are really **badly-_____**. They never do what they're told.

6 Our trip to Uganda was a _____**-changing** experience.

7 The local bakery sells good _____**made** cakes.

d Complete the sentences with a verb or adjective.

1 I was on the phone when we suddenly got _____ off and the line went dead.
2 I tried to call Bill at the office, but I couldn't _____ through. The line was busy.
3 You'll have to _____ up a little. My grandmother is very deaf.
4 I'm so _____ of you. That was a wonderful performance.
5 My sister is totally _____ on that new reality show on TV.
6 I'm completely _____ to potato chips. I buy a package almost every day.
7 I hope Franz and Amy _____ up with some great ideas for the April meeting.

CAN YOU understand this text?

a Read the article once. What two strategies do the people have in common?

b Read the article again and choose a, b, or c.

1 **a** But **b** And **c** So
2 **a** easily **b** hardly **c** never
3 **a** less valuable than **b** as valuable as **c** more valuable than
4 **a** rather than **b** in addition to **c** despite
5 **a** after **b** without **c** instead of
6 **a** neck **b** behalf **c** shoulders
7 **a** in spite of **b** as well as **c** because of
8 **a** in my control **b** out of my control **c** under control
9 **a** Nor will I ask **b** I will also ask **c** I love asking
10 **a** at home **b** at the front door **c** in the kitchen

c Look at the highlighted words and phrases and figure out their meaning. Check with your teacher or with a dictionary.

▶ CAN YOU understand this movie?

Watch or listen to a short movie on giving presentations. Complete the sentences with two or three words.

1 The one thing Louise hates about her job is _____ _____.
2 Nowadays in most jobs you need to be able to deliver a message _____ and _____.
3 RADA opened in the Haymarket in _____ in the year _____.
4 Actors and public speakers use a lot of the _____ _____ to engage an audience.
5 The RADA approach can be summarized as "_____, _____, _____."
6 After Louise's first presentation, the instructor gives her some _____ _____.
7 If you can get your _____ _____ right it will help your breathing.
8 In public speaking it's important to _____ an _____ from the beginning.
9 It's equally important to end on a _____ _____.
10 The RADA technique gives you the skills to _____ in _____.

THINK
BREATHE
SPEAK
PERFORMANCE IS DISCOVERED. HERE.
www.radaenterprises.org

How I stay calm

The school principal
Education transformed my life. I wasn't academic, I was a plodder. ¹_____ I had the most fantastic teachers. In a way, that's where the stress and worry of this job comes from, the knowledge that a school can make a huge difference to the lives of young people. Children are here for only a fixed period; any time that is lost, they'll ²_____ get back.

There are 1,100 people in the building whose jobs are all essential to the running of the school, and I need to make sure that every single one of them is doing what they need to be doing. Our cleaners are ³_____ our teaching staff. Nothing can prepare you for being responsible for it all. However, most stressful situations that arise, be it with antisocial behavior or angry parents turning up, we have systems to deal with them. When I arrived in 2012, I introduced a policy for both teachers and students of always remaining calm and non-confrontational. The minute you shout, people don't listen to you; they just focus on the noise you're creating ⁴_____ what you're saying. The other thing that helps me remain calm is being highly visible, so that everyone—parents and those in school—can talk to me as soon as something is niggling them. It's when things fester that they create the most stress. So I'm at the school gate at the start and end of every day.

I'm an organized person; I won't leave my office ⁵_____ getting everything ready for the next morning. One rule I try to stick to is that I do my work at work; I'll stay late to get it finished, but I won't take it home. And I run. If there's something I need to deal with, I can usually find a solution on my run, and by the time I get home I'm relaxed.

The high school wrestling coach
When I'm watching one of my guys wrestle a match, my heart is usually racing pretty fast. I can get pretty worked up if I think the referee made a bad call, but most of the time I can stay calm and in control. I'm no use to my guys if I'm constantly yelling at the referee.

As a junior varsity wrestling coach, I have a lot of responsibility resting on my ⁶_____. I'm teaching my guys how to wrestle, ⁷_____ how to balance practice with schoolwork. I also have to deal with the kids' schedules—who can't make a practice because their mom scheduled a dentist appointment, who can't come to an important match on a Saturday because he's going to a family wedding. Most of these things are ⁸_____, and there's really nothing I can do about them, so I just try to just go with the flow.

The best way for me to stay calm while surrounded by 23 energetic boys is to remind myself that they wouldn't be on the team if they weren't interested in the sport. When the kids are showing effort and staying focused in practices, I won't discourage them by yelling or being mean. ⁹_____ them to do moves they're not ready for yet.

When I was a wrestler in college, there was a period when I was injured and I felt I was letting my coaches down. Then one of them told me the best thing I could do was to give my injury time to heal. He told me to go home, rest up, and leave all my stress ¹⁰_____. And I did. So, I guess the point is whether I'm dealing with 23 high school kids or a season-ending injury, as long as I'm calm and I have a good attitude, I can handle anything!

7A Quite interesting

| G permission, obligation, and necessity | V word formation: prefixes | P intonation and linking in exclamations |

1 LISTENING & SPEAKING

a Which of these subjects did you enjoy most in school? What made the classes interesting? Were there any you really didn't enjoy?

geography   history   science   sports

b Work in pairs, and try to agree on answers to questions 1–12, which come from a book based on a popular TV quiz show.

c **C** Communication QI quiz A **pp.108–109** B **p.112**. Find the answers to the quiz questions and explain them to each other.

d **7.1** Listen to a journalist explaining the quiz. Answer the questions.

1 Why was the show called *QI*?
2 What is the basic principle behind the show and its books?
3 What two examples are given from *The QI Book of General Ignorance*?
4 What does the popularity of the books prove?
5 What are the two reasons Lloyd and Mitchinson give for why children often do badly in school?

e **7.2** Now listen to the journalist explaining Lloyd and Mitchinson's ideas about education. Complete the five suggestions they make.

1 Education should be more _____ than _____.
2 The best people to control what children learn are the _____ _____.
3 Children should also be in control of _____ and _____ they learn.
4 There should never be _____ without _____.
5 There's no reason why school has to _____ _____ at 17 or 18.

f Listen again and make notes about the reasons.

g What do you think of Lloyd and Mitchinson's suggestions? Can you make any other suggestions that would improve learning in schools?

everything you think you know is probably *wrong...*

The natural world

1 How many legs does an octopus have?
2 What is Australia's most dangerous animal?

Science

3 At what temperature does seawater freeze?
4 What's the best color to wear to keep cool in the shade?

Statistics

5 If you toss a coin, what is the probability of it landing on "heads"?
6 How tall was Napoleon?

History

7 What did the Russian Vyacheslav Molotov invent?
8 What was the most commonly spoken language in ancient Rome?

Geography

9 Which country is most of the Nile River in?
10 When people say "The Iron Lady," what are they referring to?

Sports

11 Where was soccer first played?
12 What is the last name of the famous Portuguese soccer player whose first name is Cristiano?

2 PRONUNCIATION intonation and linking in exclamations

a ◔ 7.3 Listen to two dialogues, and complete the exclamations.

> 1 A Did you know that America was named after a British merchant named Richard Ameryk?
>   B _____! I'd always wondered where the name came from.

> 2 A Lloyd and Mitchinson think that school shouldn't be mandatory.
>   B _____! If it wasn't mandatory, no one would ever go.

b Listen again and answer the questions with a partner.

1 Which word has extra stress in each exclamation? What happens to the intonation?
2 Why do you think a /w/ sound is added between *How* and the adjective?

c Practice saying some more common exclamations with *How* and *What*.

> What a great idea!   What an amazing coincidence!
> What a terrible experience!   How annoying!
> How embarrassing!   How weird!

d ⓒ **Communication** What a ridiculous idea! **A p.109 B p.112.** Respond to what your partner says with an exclamation.

3 VOCABULARY word formation: prefixes

a Look at ten more QI facts at the bottom of the page. Which do you find the most surprising?

b Look at the prefixes in the highlighted words. Answer the questions with a partner.

1 Which four are negative prefixes and simply mean "not"?
2 What do the other prefixes mean?

c Ⓥ p.170 **Vocabulary Bank** Prefixes.

d Add a prefix to the **bold** words and make any other necessary changes to complete the sentences.

1 I completely _____ Alan. I thought he was self-centered, but I see I was wrong. **judge**
2 This paragraph in your essay is unclear. I advise you to _____ it. **write**
3 I can't read my doctor's handwriting. It's completely _____. **legible**
4 Having to take care of my sister's dogs while she's on vacation is very _____. **convenient**
5 My husband is _____. He never wants to come with me to parties or dinners. **social**
6 The expedition failed because they were _____. **equip**
7 It's going to be an _____ struggle to motivate the team after last week's defeat. **hill**
8 Could you work some overtime this week? We're _____. **staff**
9 We're not going back to that restaurant—they _____ us last time we went. **charge**
10 The hotel has an _____ swimming pool that's only open from June to September. **door**

..and everything is **interesting**

1 10% of US electricity is made from dismantled Soviet atomic bombs.

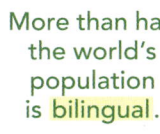
2 More than half the world's population is bilingual.

3 Most antibiotics are made from bacteria.

4 In Switzerland, it's illegal to keep a guinea pig on its own.

5 N X 12 ⊕ Over 100 billion neutrinos pass unnoticed through your head every second.

6 Paper can only be recycled six times. After that the fibers are too weak to hold together.

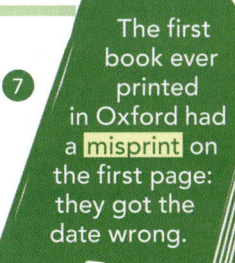
7 The first book ever printed in Oxford had a misprint on the first page: they got the date wrong.

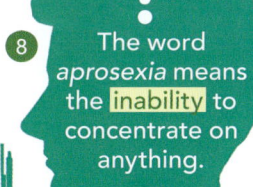
8 The word *aprosexia* means the inability to concentrate on anything.

9 You could listen to a radio on the moon, but it's virtually impossible on a submarine. Radio waves travel much more easily through space than through water.

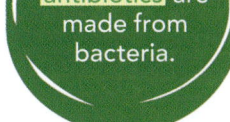

10 A typical microwave oven uses more electricity keeping its digital clock on standby than it does heating food.

4 READING

a You are going to read a review of a book called *In the Interests of Safety*. First look at some current rules in the US. With a partner, say what you think the missing words are.

1 You can't walk through airport security with anything made of _____.
2 You can't take any kind of _____ on board a plane in carry-on bags.
3 You can't take liquids of more than _____ through airport security.
4 You can take anything bought in airport _____ stores on planes.
5 You can't take _____ in some public places.
6 You can't use _____ below 3,048 meters (10,000 feet) on an airplane.
7 You can drive in all US states when you are _____ years old.

b Read the article once and check.

c Now read the article again. Answer the questions with a partner.

1 Do the authors think that the rules in **a** are…?
  • applied too strictly
  • unnecessary
  • dangerous
2 What do they say about the relative danger or safety of…?
  • butter knives
  • jogging in an area where there are hippos
  • taking children to the beach
  • large trucks in cities
  • unpasteurized cheese
  • traffic near schools

It's health and safety gone mad!

Steven Poole reviews Tracey Brown and Michael Hanlon's book *In the Interests of Safety* about "the absurd rules that blight our lives."

1 On my way to Poland the other week, I was going through security at Heathrow behind an elderly man who walked with an aluminium crutch. He went through the metal detector leaning on his wife, having left the crutch next to the conveyor belt. The detector beeped, so the man was given his crutch and forced to go back through to remove his shoes, a procedure that obviously caused him some annoyance and discomfort. Now in socks, he was ordered to pass through the metal detector again. But he wasn't allowed to take his crutch with him and his wife wasn't allowed to go back through the detector. Eventually, the security guard himself reached a hand through the detector to help him, and the man, grimacing, limped through, while his crutch passed through the baggage scanner.

2 We've all seen such examples of the meaningless "security theater" at airports. One pilot had his butter knife confiscated, just before taking the controls of an enormous metal machine packed with flammable fuel. Liquids over 100 milliliters (3.4 ounces) were banned in carry-on baggage even though the initial incident which led to prohibition of liquids—a plot to mix chemicals in the plane's toilet to produce explosives—almost certainly wouldn't have worked. And yet, as Tracey Brown and Michael Hanlon point out in this book, passengers are not only allowed, but encouraged to buy and take on board large duty-free bottles of alcoholic spirits, which could easily be turned into Molotov cocktails.

3 This book about absurd rules considers such "security" restrictions as well as more general "health and safety" rules. While "security" promises to protect us from external threat, "safety" protects us from accident or ourselves. Actually, the phrase "health and safety" has become so familiar that we don't quite notice that the two concepts are not necessarily mutually reinforcing. What is healthy might be unsafe (going jogging along a river populated by irritable hippos) and what is safe might be unhealthy (staying indoors binge-watching Netflix series 24 hours a day).

4 Although many stories of absurd official regulations turn out to be simply rules imposed by unimaginative bosses or supervisors, some do seem to be true. In Kent recently, schoolteachers had to fill out a 30-page questionnaire before taking pupils to the beach—the safety-assessment form for workers on an oil rig is only one page! In general, whenever officials cite "terrorism laws" to stop you taking photographs in public places, or a call center worker cites "data protection" as a reason not to tell you something, the authors recommend being polite, but firm. "Really? Which rule are you thinking of? And how does it apply here?"

5 "The core philosophy of the book," the authors say, "is *ask for evidence.*" It turns out that there is no evidence that, say, using your phone at a petrol station is dangerous. Nor has there ever been any evidence that using your phone, or any other electronic equipment, will interfere with the systems on commercial aircraft. So that rule is, finally, being relaxed.

6 If we were really interested in "evidence-based safety," the authors argue, we would ban large trucks from city centers (they kill a lot of cyclists), as well as raising the driving age from 17 to 21. But some options, unfortunately, are simply political impossibilities. "In America, this is why people can't buy unpasteurized cheese. In Britain, it is why people worry about dangerous dogs, but do little to reduce or calm the traffic around schools and playgrounds."

Glossary
Kent a county in southeastern Britain
pupil (NAmE student)
oil rig a large structure with equipment for getting oil from under the ocean or under the ground
petrol (NAmE gas)

LEXIS IN CONTEXT

🔍 **Learning new verbs**
When you learn a new verb, always make sure you check whether it is regular or irregular in the past tense. Remember that, in fact, 97% of verbs are regular.

d Find regular verbs in the text that mean:

Paragraph 1
1 make a short high electronic sound
2 make an expression with your face to show pain
3 walk with difficulty, e.g., because one leg is injured

Paragraph 2
4 officially take something away from somebody
5 say officially that something is not allowed

Paragraph 3
6 make an idea stronger

Paragraph 4
7 make somebody accept something, e.g., a rule or regulation
8 mention something as a reason

Paragraph 5
9 prevent something from working

Paragraph 6
10 make safer by slowing down

e Are there any laws or regulations where you live that you think are unnecessary or contradictory?

5 GRAMMAR permission, obligation, and necessity

a Look at the pairs of sentences. With a partner, say if they are the same or different in meaning. In which pair of sentences is there a difference in register?

1 **It is not permitted to** use your phone here.
  You're not allowed to use your phone here.

2 **You'd better** finish your water before we go through security.
  You ought to finish your water before we go through security.

3 **We're not supposed to** walk along the river bank.
  We must not walk along the river bank.

4 **You don't have to** fill out the form now. You can do it later.
  You needn't fill out the form now. You can do it later.

5 **We should have** left home early.
  We had to leave home early.

b **G** **p.154 Grammar Bank 7A** Learn more about permission, obligation, and necessity, and practice them.

6 SPEAKING

a Talk in small groups. Imagine the following rules or laws have been proposed for your country. Would you be in favor of them or not? Say why. Try to use expressions from the box.

🔍 **Talking about rules**

I think	people should be allowed to…
I don't think	we ought to be encouraged to…
	parents should be made to…
	it should be against the law to…
	it should be illegal to…
	it should be mandatory to…
	…ought to be banned.

On the road
▶ People over 85 should not be allowed to drive.
▶ It should be against the law for pedestrians to cross the street while wearing headphones.
▶ Bicyclists ought to be made to pass a test to get a bicycle license before they are allowed on the road.

At home
▶ It should be mandatory to turn off all electrical appliances at night in order to save energy.
▶ It ought to be illegal to leave children under 12 alone in the house.
▶ It should be against the law for parents to give fast food to obese children.

Public health
▶ Smoking on the street should be banned.
▶ Restaurants should not be allowed to serve more than one large soda per person.
▶ People who abuse their health should be made to pay higher health insurance premiums.

Society
▶ It should be against the law not to vote in elections.
▶ All advertising aimed at children under the age of 12 ought to be banned.
▶ Couples should be required to attend three months of marriage counseling before they are allowed to get divorced.

b In your groups, agree on a new law or regulation that you would like to see introduced for two of the categories. Then try to convince other groups to vote in favor of passing your law.

7 WRITING

W p.122 Writing A report Analyze a model report and write a report about a language school.

Go online to review the lesson

G verbs of the senses **V** art; color idioms **P** -ure

1 LISTENING & SPEAKING

a Look at the photos. Four of them show famous works of art. With a partner, decide which ones they are.

b 🔊 7.6 Read the definition of "installation art." Then listen to Ghislaine Kenyon, who has worked in education at the National Gallery in London, talking about the four works of art. Match four of the photos to descriptions A–D.

c Listen again and complete the descriptions. What is the idea behind each piece?

d 🔊 7.7 Now listen to Ghislaine talking about understanding modern sculpture and installations. Does she think that, compared to normal painting or sculpture, these types of art are a) easier, b) more difficult, or c) about as easy to understand?

e Listen again and answer the questions.
1 Where in a gallery might you find information about installations or modern sculptures?
2 What does Ghislaine recommend that you do to get the most out of a modern art exhibition?
3 What does she say that your job as a viewer is?
4 How does she think people might find Mona Hatoum's cot beautiful?

f Would you like to go and see these modern sculptures and installations? Who would you choose to go with?

Glossary
installation art an artistic genre that is designed to transform people's perception of a space, often incorporating everyday or natural materials and media such as video or sound
cot (NAmE crib)

A ☐ **Title: Kobe** _____
by _____ artist **Florentijn Hofman**
It's ten meters (32.9 feet) high and was made for the roof of a _____ in Kobe in _____.

B ☐ **Title: Blaenau Ffestiniog** _____
(Blaenau Ffestiniog is a place in _____.)
by British artist _____ _____
It was part of an exhibition of art created from different landscapes, called "_____ and _____."

C ☐ **Title:** _____
by Mona Hatoum
It's a sculpture by a _____ artist born in _____, but who was stranded in _____ after civil war broke out in Lebanon.

D ☐ **Title:** _____
by British artist **Damien Hirst**
It's like a real room with some unusual things, such as four _____ with _____ of _____ on them and a machine for _____ _____ suspended from the ceiling.

2 GRAMMAR verbs of the senses

a ▶7.8 Complete these sentences from the listening script with the correct form of one of the following verbs or verb phrases. Listen and check.

look (x2)   look as if   look at   look like   see

1 "It doesn't _____ a modern cot"
2 "it _____ it might be a hospital cot from, say, 50 years ago"
3 "But when you _____ it a bit more closely you notice…"
4 "but if you start _____, you'll start _____ things which _____ strange"

b Answer the questions with a partner.

1 What's the difference between *look as if* and *look like* and between *look at* and *see*?
2 Apart from *sight*, what are the other four senses?
3 What verbs do you associate with the other senses?

c **ⓖ p.155 Grammar Bank 7B** Learn more about verbs of the senses, and practice them.

d Ask and answer the questions with a partner.

- Are there any paintings or images that you like or dislike looking at because of how they make you feel?
- If you could look like a celebrity, which celebrity would you choose, and why?
- What makes a voice sound attractive or unattractive to you?
- Are there any sounds or kinds of music that you don't like hearing because they make you feel uncomfortable?
- Are there any foods you dislike because of their smell or their texture rather than their taste?
- What kinds of perfume or cologne do you really like or dislike on yourself or on other people? Why?
- Would you be prepared to touch these creatures in a zoo? Why (not)?

a lion   a lizard   a parrot   a rat   a snake
a tarantula

- Are there certain materials you love to wear, or never wear, because of the way they feel?

3 PRONUNCIATION -ure

a Put the words in the correct column according to the pronunciation of *-ure*.

picture   sculpture   allure   architecture   capture   culture
endure   feature   furniture   future   immature   impure   leisure
measure   nature   obscure   pleasure   secure   signature
structure   sure   temperature   texture   treasure

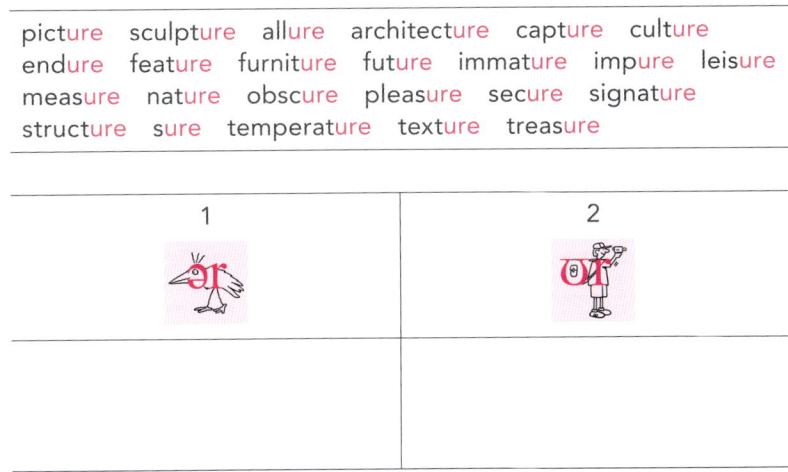

1	2

b ▶7.9 Listen and check.

c Look at the words in the two columns. Answer the questions.

1 In column 1, where is the stress in all the words?
2 What sounds do the *t* and the *s* make before *-ure*?
3 In column 2, which syllable is stressed?

d Practice saying the sentences below.

1 In this picture, the artist captures the allure of nature.
2 This sculpture is representative of today's immature culture.
3 He has a treasured collection of old furniture.
4 Are you sure the new structure is secure?
5 The architecture has some unusual features.

4 VOCABULARY & SPEAKING art

a Look at the words for six different kinds of art. With a partner, say what each one is.

a portrait /ˈpɔrtrət/
a landscape /ˈlændskeɪp/
a still life /stɪl ˈlaɪf/
a self-portrait /self ˈpɔrtrət/
an abstract painting /ˈæbstrækt ˈpeɪntɪŋ/
a sculpture /ˈskʌlptʃər/

b Talk in small groups.

- Can you think of a famous example for any of the six kinds of art in **a**?
- Do you have a favorite work in any of these categories, or a favorite artist?
- Do you go to museums or art galleries? Do you have a favorite one? Are there any in your town?
- What do you have as decoration…?
  - on the walls of your bedroom or living room
  - for the screensaver on your computer, phone, or tablet

Go online to review the lesson

5 READING & LISTENING

a Look at the portrait of Max Ernst. Approximately when do you think it might have been taken? What do you think he's famous for?

b 🔊 **7.10** Read and listen to the first part of an article called *The Secret of The Forest*. Then, with a partner, say who the people in the list are, and what their connection is to Max Ernst.

Werner Spies   Helene Beltracchi   Werner Jägers   Alfred Flechtheim
Wolfgang Beltracchi

c Now read the article again. Answer the questions with a partner.

1 What controversy was there about *La Forêt*?
2 How had the painting ended up in Helene Beltracchi's house?
3 What was Spies's conclusion about *La Forêt*? What evidence was it based on?
4 What happened to the painting next?

d 🔊 **7.11** What do you think the "little problem" was? Listen once to find out. Where are the Beltracchis now?

The Secret of *The Forest*

About ten days before Christmas in 2003, Werner Spies, one of the world's pre-eminent experts on 20th-century art, took the train from Paris to the picturesque port of Sète on the
5 Mediterranean coast. Spies, a specialist in the works of the painter Max Ernst, was coming to look at and hopefully authenticate an Ernst painting that had been unknown to him—and thus unknown to the art world—until earlier that year. The painting was *La Forêt* (*The Forest*) and, although
10 it was undated, Spies thought it had been painted in 1927. Ernst produced a number of "forest" paintings around that time; they are considered among his most important works.

Spies had previously authenticated another Ernst work, *Oiseau en Hiver*, which was then sold for €500,000. But the
15 scientific analysis suggested that there was some doubt about *La Forêt*. It apparently included traces of two pigments which had generally only been used by artists after 1945. Spies, however, preferred to trust his own judgement and because *La Forêt* was not dated, he believed Ernst might
20 have used the pigments at an early experimental stage. But he wanted to look at the painting to make sure.

The following morning, Helene Beltracchi picked up Spies and drove him to the beautiful Beltracchi estate. Helene was 45 and a striking woman—intelligent, cultured,
25 animated, with thick, blond hair almost to her waist. Spies had already met her in Paris and knew something of her background. She was German, from near Cologne, and she had inherited an extensive collection of modern art from her grandfather, the industrialist Werner Jägers.
30 As Helene liked to tell the story, in the 20s and early 30s, her grandfather had been a close friend of Alfred Flechtheim, the most important modern art dealer in Germany, and had bought many paintings from him. After Hitler came

Werner Spies

to power in 1933, Flechtheim, who was Jewish, fled to
35 London. His galleries were seized and his art collection was sold by the Nazis, because the paintings were considered disreputable. But Werner Jägers managed to hide the paintings he had bought from Flechtheim, including a number of works by Max Ernst, which Helene later
40 inherited. She liked to show potential buyers an old black and white photograph of her grandmother, Josefine Jägers, sitting in the family dining room in an austere black dress, strings of pearls around her neck, with some of the art collection on the wall behind her. Helene was now gradually
45 selling these paintings, to which faded *Sammlung Flechtheim* (Flechtheim Collection) labels were attached on the back.

The Ernst painting, *La Forêt*, hung upstairs in the master bedroom. Taking it into the light, Spies was thrilled with what he saw: the intensity of the color, the power of the
50 imagery. Despite the scientific analysis, Spies had no doubt

e Listen again. What did you find out about...?

1 Wolfgang's teenage years
2 what he did during the 1980s
3 what happened in 1992 and the last name Beltracchi
4 how Wolfgang created his pictures
5 the photo of Helene's grandmother
6 the labels on the back of the paintings
7 the Campendonk painting *Red Picture with Horses*
8 what they feel now and Wolfgang's plans

LEXIS IN CONTEXT

f ◉ 7.12 Listen to five extracts from the listening script and complete the time expressions.

1 ..._____ a _____ of _____.
2 _____ days...
3 ..._____ a year _____...
4 ...in _____ a _____ minutes...
5 ..._____ the _____.

g What do you think about the Beltracchis? Do you think you would feel differently about a painting if it turned out to be a fake?

Helene and Wolfgang Beltracchi in their studio

he was holding a genuine, previously unknown Max Ernst in his hands. Following this authentication, a Swiss gallery owner paid Helene and her husband Wolfgang Beltracchi €1.7 million for the painting in November 2004.
55 He quickly resold *La Forêt* for a small profit and in 2006 it was exhibited at the Max Ernst Museum in Brühl, Germany, adding to its value. *La Forêt* was finally sold later that year for $7 million.

From the early 90s onwards, many more paintings
60 made a similar journey from the Beltracchi's lovely home to the walls of the world's top collectors and museums. There was just one little problem...

By Christopher Goodwin in The Times

6 SPEAKING

a In small groups, answer questions 1 and 2 about the things in the list.

bags books clothes and shoes movies music
sports equipment sunglasses watches

1 Are many fakes or pirate editions sold (or downloaded) in your country? Where can people get them?
2 Are the fakes as good as the originals? If they are worse, in what way?

b Now answer questions 3 and 4.

3 Do you think it should be illegal to sell fakes?
4 Have you ever bought or been given something that was a fake? Did you know it was a fake when you got it? How do you feel about it? Do you think you would like it more if it was the real thing?

7 VOCABULARY color idioms

a Complete the eight idioms with a color.

black (x2) blue gray red (x2) white (x3)

1 John Singer Sargent's lost great flamenco picture, *El Jaleo*, turned up **out of the** _____ , and amazingly, it was absolutely genuine.
2 It's very difficult for thieves to sell famous paintings, even on **the** _____ **market**.
3 We tried to organize an exhibition tour, but there was so much _____ **tape** to deal with that we had to cancel.
4 When you said how nice her dress was, were you telling **a** _____ **lie**? I thought it was awful.
5 My uncle is very narrow-minded. He **sees everything in** _____ **and** _____ , and he's always convinced that he's right.
6 That huge clock my sister-in-law gave me is **a** _____ **elephant**. It doesn't fit anywhere, and it's taking up space in the spare room.
7 There are lots of rules about copyright for printed text, but online copyright is still **a** _____ **area**. Nobody's quite sure who owns what.
8 The anonymous letter was **a** _____ **herring**—it had nothing to do with the murder at all.

b With a partner, say what you think the idioms mean.

Glossary
muralist a person who paints murals, i.e., pictures directly on walls
Campendonk a Dutch painter (1889–1957)
Titanium White a pigment used in white paint

🔄 **Go online** to review the lesson

1  THE INTERVIEW Part 1

a Read the biographical information about Quentin Blake. Have you ever read any books illustrated by him? What else has he done apart from book illustrations?

Quentin Blake is probably one the best-known illustrators of children's books. Apart from his illustrations of stories by other authors, for example, his famous drawings for the Roald Dahl books, he has also both written and illustrated many stories of his own. In recent years his work has increasingly appeared in public places such as galleries and museums, and he has produced work for the walls of several hospitals and mental health centers. He has also illustrated adult books such as Cervantes' *Don Quixote*. He is a trustee of the House of Illustration, a center for exhibitions and other activities, and was the subject of the first exhibition held there in 2014.

b 🔊 7.13 Watch or listen to Part 1 of the interview. What does he think is the most important thing for someone who wants to become an illustrator?

c Now listen again. Complete sentences 1–5.
1 Quentin Blake describes himself as…
2 When he was in his early 20s, he…
3 In 1960, he and John Yeoman…
4 He finds it touching when…
5 A lot of young people say they want to become illustrators because…

Glossary
ceramic *adj* (objects, e.g., pots) made of clay that has been permanently made hard by heat
John Yeoman author of *A Drink of Water*, the first children's book illustrated by Quentin Blake

 Part 2

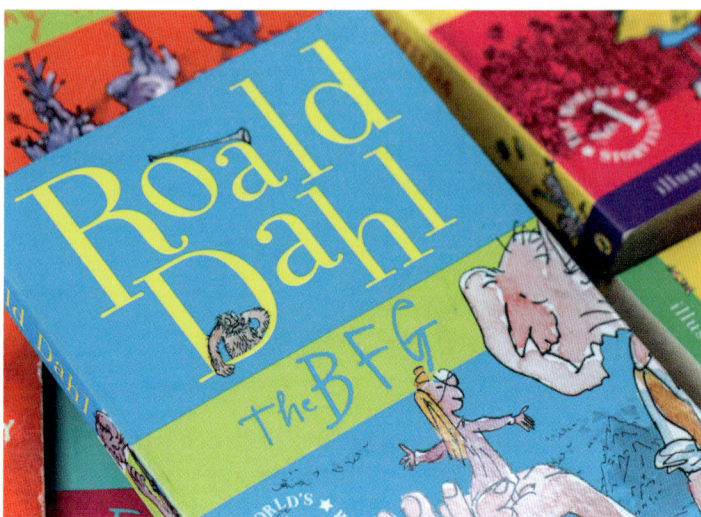

a 🔊 7.14 Now watch or listen to Part 2. Mark the sentences **T** (true) or **F** (false).
1 Quentin Blake says that authors and illustrators usually need to have a lot of conversations.
2 The most important thing is the relationship between the illustrator and the words in the book.
3 Quentin Blake never drew any of Roald Dahl's characters without first talking to him about them.
4 He thinks conversations with Dahl helped him to get into the mood of the books.
5 Roald Dahl sometimes changed his text if an illustration wasn't working.
6 The BFG was originally described as wearing a leather apron.
7 It was decided that the apron made the BFG look too old.
8 The shoes the BFG wears were based on a pair of Quentin Blake's own shoes.

b Listen again. Say why the **F** sentences are false.

Glossary
The BFG a book by Roald Dahl published in 1982; BFG stands for Big Friendly Giant

▶ Part 3

a 🔊 **7.15** Now watch or listen to Part 3. What does Quentin Blake say about…?

1 his relationship with the characters he creates in an illustration
2 his attitude toward children
3 drawing from life
4 digital drawing
5 the advantage of quills, nibs, and reed pens
6 Ronald Searle and André François
7 his exhibition in Paris

b Listen again. Can you add any more details?

> **Glossary**
> **reed pen** a pen made from a tall plant that grows in or near water
> **Ronald Searle** British artist and satirical cartoonist
> **André François** Hungarian-born French cartoonist

quill   nib

2 LOOKING AT LANGUAGE

> 🔍 **get**
> *get* is one of the most common verbs in English; it is frequently used by Quentin Blake in this interview. Learning expressions with *get*, and thoroughly assimilating the variety of meanings of this important verb, will help you to understand native speakers better.

a 🔊 **7.16** Watch or listen to some extracts from the interview and complete the missing words.

1 "…but we got _____. And I thought, 'Well, I'll, I'll try—keep—I'll try and keep on with this until I'm 30…'"
2 "Um, and I got _____, but I passed 30 and I didn't notice!"
3 "But um, uh, we talked quite a lot, again, some of it was about the, about the technicalities of the book, getting it _____ _____ better…"
4 "…but I think, to get, to get _____ the _____ of the book, which is a terribly important thing…"
5 "So he—after a bit he said, 'This apron's getting _____ the _____, isn't it?'"
6 "…if you have a quill, or a nib, or a reed pen, you get a _____ _____ of scratch"
7 "When I was a young man I got _____ _____ and went to see him."

b With a partner, say what the phrases mean, using a synonym for *get* where possible.

3 ▶ ON THE STREET

a 🔊 **7.17** Watch or listen to five people talking about illustrations and art. Match the people (**La**, **Mar**, **Lo**, **Mau**, or **A**) with the books they mention.

Laura	Marcus	Louise	Maura	Ally
Danish	*Australian*	*American*	*Irish*	*American*

☐ *The Little Prince*, Antoine de Saint-Exupéry
☐ *Garfield*, Jim Davis
☐ *A Little Princess*, Frances Hodgson Burnett
☐ *The Lord of the Rings*, J.R.R. Tolkien
☐ *The Happy Prince and Other Stories*, Oscar Wilde

b Watch or listen again. Match the people (**La**, **Mar**, **Lo**, **Mau**, or **A**) to the artwork they have at home.

☐ it's a collage of photos
☐ it's from a place its owner visited as a child
☐ it has two predominant colors
☐ it shows an activity that its owner also does
☐ it wasn't originally owned by them

c 🔊 **7.18** Watch or listen again and complete the Colloquial English phrases. What do you think they mean?

1 "I have a painting I bought in, uh, Buenos Aires once, with two tango dancers, which I'm _____ _____ _____…"
2 "It's very vibrant and at _____ _____ _____ simple."
3 "…and he's got watercolor illustrations and they're just, they're so _____ and _____."
4 "…I think I read that as a child, so it must have really _____ _____ _____…"
5 "It's a _____ _____ this, um, Roman, um, mural…"

4 SPEAKING

Answer the questions with a partner or in small groups.

- Can you remember a book you read when you were a child where you liked the illustrations? What did you like about them?
- Can you remember any children's books where you really disliked or were scared of the illustrations?
- Do you like comics? Do you think the illustrations in comics are more important than the story?
- Do you think any adult books would benefit from being illustrated? Which ones? Why?
- Look at the illustrations in this book on pages 10, 11, 68, 110, and 169. Which do you like the most / least? Why?

8A Doctor's orders

> The only way to keep your health is to eat what you don't want, drink what you don't like, and do what you'd rather not.
> *Mark Twain, US author*

G gerunds and infinitives **V** health and medicine; similes **P** /ə/

1 VOCABULARY & SPEAKING
health and medicine

How much medical vocabulary do you know? Take the quiz in small groups.

How good a doctor are you?

1 When might you get...?
a a bruise
b a blister
c a rash
d side effects

2 Why might you be given...?
a a bandage
b a cast
c antibiotics
d stitches
e an X-ray
f an ultrasound
g an anesthetic

3 When might you need to see...?
a your primary care physician
b a specialist
c a surgeon

4 What are the symptoms of...?
a a cold
b the flu
c food poisoning
d a heart attack
e asthma
f a stroke

5 What might happen to you if you...?
a had to stand for a long time in a hot, crowded room
b were stung on your hand by a bee
c turned on a light with wet hands

2 READING

a With a partner, look at the list below. Which things do you think most doctors might not want to do themselves?

follow a low-carb diet
go to the doctor with a long list of symptoms
have a full health check
have cosmetic surgery
see a life coach
eat fried, fatty foods
sunbathe
take anti-malaria pills when visiting a country where it is endemic
take sleeping pills
take vitamin supplements
use alternative medicine
vaccinate their children against childhood illnesses like measles

b Read the article on page 77 once and complete the headings A–G with a treatment or habit from **a**.

c Read the article again. Why wouldn't the doctors do these things? Match reasons 1–7 with paragraphs A–G.

1 ☐ Because it might be difficult later to stop doing this.
2 ☐ Because the doctor may take you less seriously.
3 ☐ Because the short-term benefit may be outweighed by long-term problems.
4 ☐ Because you may develop another illness as a result of unnecessary treatment.
5 ☐ Because you may end up getting treatment you didn't really need.
6 ☐ Because you may not necessarily be treated by a professional.
7 ☐ Because you are doing something that is deliberately damaging.

LEXIS IN CONTEXT

d Look at the highlighted phrases. With a partner, figure out what they mean and try to paraphrase them.

e Work in small groups.
- Do any of the doctors' opinions surprise you?
- Might their opinions affect the way you behave? Why (not)?
- Is there anything connected with medicine or health that you would never do?

What doctors won't do...

Doctors reveal the treatments or habits they would avoid

I would never...

From The Guardian

A

I would never take up the regularly advertised offers by private medical companies. Why? Well, if you have symptoms, you go to your GP and they listen to your history, examine you, request investigations, and reach a decision. This process is known as "diagnosis." A full check when you feel totally well is not diagnosis, it is "screening." There are few screening tests where the advantages outweigh the disadvantages and they could lead you to have potentially harmful investigations, or indeed treatment, that you may not have needed.

Mike Smith, GP

B

Patients often think this helps, but it makes the doctor's heart sink. They're not going to be able to deal with everything in one go and, most importantly of all, it makes them think you haven't got one particular problem, you've got a multiplicity of problems, which is a sure sign of a hypochondriac.

Carol Cooper, GP

C

People underestimate the risk. They think, "My skin looks all right; how can it be damaged?" Even if your skin doesn't look aged, you can end up with skin damage that sets you up for potential cancers in the future. Tanning in your teens and early 20s is a strong risk factor. We are now seeing cancers in the under 40s that we used to see only on the faces of old, weather-beaten guys who had spent a lifetime outdoors. I would go out in the sun, but I would never lie in it just to get a tan.

Carol Cooper, GP

D

I have come across many patients who have been taking them for decades. They are addictive and it can be very difficult for people to wean themselves off them; the side-effects can include falls, confusion, sleepiness in the daytime, and the feeling that increasingly high doses are needed to achieve the same effects. I can't imagine any situation in which I would start using them.

Helen Drew, GP

E

Why? Because although you will probably lose weight, it may kill you. Don't take my word for it—read about the 43,396 Swedish women followed for an average of 15 years. Those who stuck to low carbs and high protein had a rising risk of dying from heart attacks and strokes. There was a staggering 62% higher risk among the women eating the strictest diet over those who ate normally. Eating is for enjoyment; these diets turn food into medicine and it's the wrong medicine.

Tom Smith, GP

F

The reason for my reluctance? Nothing to do with anesthetics (safe these days), but entirely to do with surgery, which should never be undertaken for what you might call "soft" reasons. It's not that surgery is so dangerous that I would worry about death. Mainly it's the worry of an infection, which can be very unpleasant.

Mark Patrick, consultant anesthetist

G

I would never see a "counselor" if I was having mental health problems. Absolutely anyone can claim to be a counselor—it's an entirely unregulated area. So, there's a huge variation in quality and I have seen too many patients who have been further psychologically damaged by poorly qualified counselors.

Max Pemberton, psychiatrist

Glossary

GP (general practitioner) a doctor who is trained in general medicine and who treats patients in a local community rather than at a hospital

screening the testing or examining of people to see if they have a disease when they have no symptoms

counselor (NAmE therapist) a person who has been trained to advise people with problems, especially personal problems

3 LISTENING & SPEAKING

a Look at these types of alternative medicine. Do you know what any of them involve?

acupuncture	aromatherapy	chiropractic
homeopathy	hypnotherapy	osteopathy

b ◔ **8.1** Listen to four people talking about alternative medicine. Answer these questions for each speaker.

Did they have any treatment?
Yes What treatment did they have?
What for?
Was it successful?
No Why not?

c Listen again. Which speaker...?

1 ▢ doesn't believe in alternative medicine of any kind
2 ▢ was told by a doctor to use alternative medicine
3 ▢ had been trying traditional medicine, but it hadn't worked
4 ▢ doesn't really believe in alternative medicine, but was willing to try it
5 ▢ thinks alternative medicine only works because of the placebo effect
6 ▢ felt better with fewer than the recommended number of treatments
7 ▢ might consider repeating the treatment as a last resort
8 ▢ was having one alternative treatment when he / she was given another type of alternative medicine

d Which forms of alternative medicine are popular in your country? Have you ever tried any forms of alternative medicine, or do you know anyone who has? Was your / their experience positive or negative?

Go online to review the lesson

4 GRAMMAR gerunds and infinitives

a Write the verbs or phrases in the correct column.

> afford   agree   avoid   can't help
> can't stand   deny   had better   happen
> imagine   involve   be worth
> look forward to   manage   miss   practice
> pretend   refuse   regret   risk   suggest
> tend   threaten   would rather

+ infinitive	+ gerund	+ base form

b ◖)) 8.2 Listen and check.

c Cross out the wrong form. Check (✓) if both are possible.

1 I regret *not going / not having gone* to the doctor earlier.
2 I hate *telling / being told* that I've gained weight.
3 I'd like *to have stopped / to stop* smoking sooner, but at least I've finally done it.
4 I was unwise *not to take / not to have taken* all the antibiotics.
5 Is it easier *to park / park* at the hospital now?
6 I exercise enough *to stay / for staying* in reasonably good shape.
7 It's no use *worrying / to worry* about being out of shape if you don't change your diet.
8 She was the first woman *to become / becoming* a professor of cardiac surgery.

d Ⓖ p.156 **Grammar Bank 8A** Learn more about gerunds and infinitives, and practice them.

e Ⓒ **Communication** Guess the sentence A p.109 B p.113. Imagine the missing phrases. Then check with a partner.

5 LISTENING & SPEAKING

a Look at these infographics. What medical advice do you think each image represents?

A

B

C

D

E   F

b ◀)) **8.3** Listen to the radio program and check your ideas.

c Listen again and make notes for each piece of advice about what we should <u>really</u> be doing.

d ◀)) **8.4** Look at some sentences from the listening script. Try to complete them with the correct form of *make* or *do*. Then listen and check.

1 You're constantly _____ **decisions** based on what you want versus what you think is good for you.
2 Does it really _____ **a difference**?
3 So, although five will _____ **you good**, more might be better.
4 So, eight hours a night is probably about right, though a little more or a little less shouldn't _____ **you any harm**.
5 _____ **the recommended amount** of moderate activity, but try to do more if you can, especially if you spend a lot of the day sitting down.
6 …but a large-scale UK study of 11,000 children showed no relationship between screen time and emotional or social problems, or an inability to concentrate or _____ **friends**.
7 Instead we should _____ **up our own minds** about what's best for our children—and for ourselves.

e Talk to a partner.

1 Which piece of advice in **a** was the most accurate? Which was the least accurate? Were you surprised?
2 Have you heard similar advice in your country? Do you know where it comes from? Do people follow it? How seriously do you take it?
3 Do you think advice like this is helpful, or should people be left to make their own decisions?
4 Is there a piece of health advice you strongly believe in and try to put into practice?

6 VOCABULARY similes

Some people can eat like a horse and not put on weight.

a Look at the example from the listening script and read the information about similes. Then complete sentences 1–10 with a word from the list.

🔍 **Similes for comparisons**
A simile is a fixed informal / colloquial expression of comparison using *as* or *like*. Similes add emphasis to an adjective, adverb, or verb, e.g., *I think Jane's underweight for her age—she's **as light as a feather**.* (= extremely light).

angel   bat   dream   flash   gold   log   mule   post   rail   sheet

1 My husband's **as stubborn as a** _____—he refuses to go to the doctor about his bad back.
2 She's **as white as a** _____. I think she's going to faint.
3 He **sings like a** _____. He really should be on a singing competition show.
4 He's **as deaf as a** _____. You'll have to speak up a little.
5 She **sleeps like a** _____. I don't think she's ever had problems with insomnia.
6 Your mother's **as blind as a** _____. She should get her eyes tested.
7 She's been **as good as** _____. She took all her medicine without making any fuss.
8 He's lost a lot of weight since his illness. He's **as thin as a** _____.
9 When I pressed the button, the nurse came **as quick as a** _____ and changed my IV drip.
10 My new medication **works like a** _____. I feel 100 times better.

b ◀)) **8.5** Listen and check.

7 PRONUNCIATION /ə/

🔍 **Fine-tuning your pronunciation: the most common sound in English**
/ə/ is the most common sound in English. If you use it, it will help your word stress and sentence stress sound more natural and fluent.

/ə/ is the vowel sound in many common unstressed words in a sentence, e.g., *a / an, the, to, as, than*, etc.

My **husband's** as **stubborn** as a **mule**—he **refuses** to **go** to the **doctor** about his **bad back**.

a Look at the sentence from the vocabulary exercise. Circle the unstressed words with the /ə/ sound. Which one of the stressed words also has the /ə/ sound?

b ◀)) **8.6** Listen and check. Practice saying the sentence. Then practice saying sentences 2–10 in **6a**.

c Try to think of three people or things you could describe with the similes. Compare with a partner.

🔄 **Go online** to review the lesson

> "Tourists don't know where they've been; travelers don't know where they're going."
> *Paul Theroux, US travel writer*

G expressing future plans and arrangements   **V** travel and tourism   **P** homophones

What kind of traveler are you?

What do your vacation habits say about you? Do you love soaking up the sun or immersing yourself in the culture? Find out what kind of globetrotter you are…

Start here!

Flip flops *or* Comfy shoes?

A good book *or* A guidebook?

Going rambling *or* Happy meandering?

Guidebook *or* Survival guide?

The open sea *or* Seaweed face mask?

City life *or* The quiet life?

Pampered princess

Sleeping under the stars *or* Who needs sleep?

Day trips *or* Spiritual journey?

Action addict

Hippie at heart

All about me *or* All at sea?

Peace and quiet, A piece of history, A piece of the action, *or* Peace, man?

Culture vulture

Sand between your toes *or* Go where the wind blows?

The great ocean waves *or* The great outdoors?

Museum hopping *or* A spot of shopping?

Lazy cruiser

Beach bum

Happy camper

City slicker

1 VOCABULARY & SPEAKING
travel and tourism

a What kind of traveler are you? Take the quiz and find out.

b **C Communication** What kind of traveler are you? p110 Read about your traveler type.

c **V** p.171 **Vocabulary Bank** Travel and tourism.

2 READING

a What's the difference between people who…?

- go to Las Vegas or Cancún
  go to Outer Mongolia
- enjoy meeting local people
  enjoy meeting people from their own country
- buy lots of souvenirs
  think souvenirs are tacky

b Read the article. Which of these sentences best summarizes its message?

1 Travelers think they're superior to tourists, but in fact it's the other way around.
2 There's no real difference between travelers and tourists.
3 Tourists' bad reputation is partly deserved.

Why I'm absolutely sick of the traveler vs. tourist debate
Courtney Jones

Travelers really experience places. Tourists rush around too much to check things off a list. Travelers are cultured. Tourists only care about getting good Instagram photos...and on and on and onnnnn.

Am I a tourist because I take selfies? Or am I a traveler because I have a GoPro and capture some pretty intense moments? Seriously, I'm beyond sick of this debate. First of all, who cares? Not me. Secondly, just because someone travels differently than you, it doesn't mean their traveling style is wrong.

I've heard this argument surface in a million ways. When I was backpacking Australia in an old van, my peers would make comments about how people staying in hostels "weren't really seeing the country." The people staying in hostels would comment that people staying in luxury hotels weren't experiencing Australia properly. Now that my travel style is more aligned to luxury, I hear comments about how backpackers are just out to party and totally miss out on culture. There are countless articles out there about how annoying "tourists" are; that they're selfie-stick obsessed and don't respect cultural behaviors. Sure, there are people out there like that, but why do we have to label that person a tourist?

Being rude doesn't make someone a tourist, it makes them a rude person.

The traveler vs. tourist debate is not a new one. It's been around for ages, and I feel like every "serious" traveler is trying to prove they're not a tourist. They're trying to prove that they really get the world. You know, that unlike most people, they immerse themselves in culture. Whatever.

I really hate narrow stereotypes. I'm not a tourist because I have a shirt that says "Texas," just like I'm not a traveler because I spent six months living in a van in rural Australia. I'm someone who enjoys exploring. End of conversation.

I don't care how other people travel. My travel style has changed significantly over the past few years. It changes as my lifestyle, situation, and preferences change, and I'm OK with that. Just because I enjoy luxury travel now doesn't mean I've sold out. It means I'm in a different place in life and it's what works for me now. Do I judge backpackers? Well, yeah, sometimes, when they annoy me. But I also judge super pretentious luxury travelers. I don't judge people because they're a "traveler" or because they're a "tourist"; I judge people when they're inappropriate. It doesn't matter how someone travels, annoying people will always annoy me.

Why do we have to be either a traveler or a tourist? Why can't we just be a person who likes the world?

Take advantage of the opportunities that arise for you. Sometimes places are overdone, so leave the beaten path if you feel it's right; however, keep in mind that sometimes places are popular for a reason. You know, because they're awesome! Try not to rule a place out just because you know someone who took a selfie there, but also don't avoid a place just because you haven't seen it on Instagram. There is no right way to travel. One basic rule: respect the culture of the place you're in and don't be so obnoxious that people hate you. Aside from that, it's your life and your own experience. Do what you want and have an amazing time doing it!

What do you think? Should people be labeled one or the other? Does it matter? Leave a comment with your thoughts!

---

c Read the article again. According to the writer, are the following sentences **T** (true) or **F** (false)? Underline the parts of the text that show her opinion.

1 Tourists don't take the time to really experience a destination.
2 There is only one way to travel correctly.
3 The author's travel style has remained the same since she traveled through Australia in a van.
4 The traveler vs. tourist debate is a relatively new argument because of the rise of Instagram.
5 The writer judges people based on their behavior.
6 Be wary of travel that takes you to remote places.
7 It's best to avoid places you've seen posted about on social media.
8 Both travelers and tourists should honor the customs and beliefs of the places they visit.

LEXIS IN CONTEXT

d Look at the highlighted phrasal verbs and try to figure out their meaning. Then match them to 1–7.

1 give up one's beliefs _____
2 move with great speed _____
3 not take part in _____
4 decide something is not suitable _____
5 hate someone or something very much _____
6 worth worrying about _____
7 put a mark beside an item on a list to show that it has been dealt with _____

e Work in groups and answer the questions.

1 Do you agree with the writer's opinion of the traveler vs. tourist debate?
2 Do you consider yourself to be more of a tourist than a traveler, or vice versa?
3 Has tourism had a significant effect where you live? Has it been positive or negative?

3 WRITING

Ⓦ p.124 Writing A discursive essay (2): Taking sides Analyze a model essay and write a discursive essay about road charging or healthy lifestyles.

4 GRAMMAR expressing future plans and arrangements

a Look at the messages and (circle) the correct form of the verbs in *italics*. Check (✓) if you think both are possible.

> ¹*I'm leaving* / *I'll be leaving* for the airport soon, so I should be there in plenty of time. ²*I'll let* / *I'm going to let* you know if there's any delay.

> Fingers crossed! Can't wait to see you!

> Delayed! ³*It now leaves* / *It's now leaving* at 6:30. Hope they're telling the truth... 😞

> Typical! Oh, well. ⁴*I'll be waiting* / *I'm waiting* for you in Arrivals.

> We're due ⁵*to start* / *starting* boarding at 6:00, so it looks as if it really is leaving at 6:30! 🙂

> 🙂 🙂 🙂

> We're about ⁶*board* / *to board* at last! See you soon.

b **ⓖ p.157 Grammar Bank 8B** Learn more about expressing future plans and arrangements, and practice it.

c Are you planning any trips or journeys right now? Have you made any of the arrangements? If so, tell a partner.

5 LISTENING

a You're going to listen to Clive Oxenden, who lives in Spain, describing a disastrous journey. Look at the headline. Where do you think he was trying to travel to and why? What kind of problems might he have had?

Christmas getaway crippled by storms

b Listen to Clive's story. After each part, answer the questions with a partner.

🔊 8.9
1 Where was Clive traveling to / from? Who with? When?
2 What happened before take-off and why did it worry him?
What do you think might have happened next?

🔊 8.10
3 When did things start going wrong?
4 What did the pilot tell them?
5 How do you think Clive felt and why?
What do you think might have happened next?

🔊 8.11
6 What did the pilot decide to do?
7 How did the people on the plane react?
8 How did the pilot explain what had happened?
What do you think might have happened next?

🔊 8.12
9 Where did they end up going?
10 Why did the pilot think they would be able to land there?
11 How did the passengers feel when they landed and what did they do?
What do you think might have happened next?

🔊 8.13
12 What were the passengers then told to do? Why?
13 What alternative were they given?
What do you think might have happened next?

🔊 8.14
14 What did the people with children all decide to do?
15 What did Clive and his family do?
16 When did Clive and his family eventually get home?

LEXIS IN CONTEXT

c Look at the highlighted words and expressions from the listening exercise. Explain what they mean in your own words.

1 he said in the message that there was a very bad storm in London with gale-force winds...
2 as we were approaching Gatwick...
3 we're going to circle for a while...
4 then we started getting the worst turbulence I've ever experienced...
5 the plane suddenly shot back up in the air...
6 The plane started gaining height...
7 we're off to Holland now.
8 it was a good landing, little bit bumpy...
9 everyone was very relieved to get down on the ground...
10 So then, everyone had a little bit of a dilemma...

d How would you have felt in Clive's position? Do you think you would have made the same decisions?

6 SPEAKING

a Think about a bad trip you've had (it could be when you were on vacation, or just something that happened on your way to work or school). Look at the plan below and decide what you are going to say.

1 Set the scene
One of the worst trips I've ever had…
It happened (a few months) ago…
I was traveling…

2 Give the details
Everything was fine until…
What happened was that…
Suddenly…
So anyway…
Finally…

3 End with a comment about how you felt
It was certainly the most…
I've never been so…
I'll never forget it.

b Work in groups of three or four and tell each other about your experience. Use the plan to help you tell your story.

7 PRONUNCIATION homophones

> **Homophones**
> *You're not **allowed** to use this gym unless you have a membership.*
> *I read **aloud** to my children before they go to bed every night.*
> *allowed* and *aloud* are homophones. They are words that are spelled differently and have different meanings, but are pronounced exactly the same.

a With a partner, complete each pair of sentences with homophones.

1 /pɪr/
  a We walked along the <u>pier</u>, watching the fishing boats on the water.
  b Searching for elephants, the safari guide continued to <u>peer</u> into the distance.

2 /weɪt/
  a We've got a three-hour _____ before the flight leaves.
  b What's the maximum _____ for carry-on bags on this flight?

3 /bɔrd/
  a We're _____! We don't want to visit anymore museums!
  b The passengers are waiting to _____ the plane.

4 /breɪk/
  a We spent spring _____ in Mexico.
  b The airport bus had to _____ suddenly when a truck pulled out.

5 /fɛr/
  a My ticket cost twice as much as yours. It's not _____!
  b How much is the air _____ to Australia?

6 /pis/
  a Where's the _____ of paper with our flight details?
  b We're going off the beaten track for some _____ and quiet.

7 /kɔt/
  a I slept in a tent on an old army _____.
  b We just barely _____ the train—it left seconds after we got on it.

8 /saɪt/
  a We visited an archaeological _____ on the banks of the Nile.
  b My first _____ of the Grand Canyon completely took my breath away.

9 /θru/
  a After we arrived it took us a long time to get _____ immigration.
  b The screener at Security _____ away my perfume because it was more than 3.4 ounces.

10 /swit/
  a We've booked the hotel's bridal _____ for our honeymoon.
  b I don't really like to eat desserts. They're usually too _____ for me.

11 /ˈsɪriəl/
  a You'll need the _____ number of your laptop to make an insurance claim.
  b There wasn't much for breakfast, just toast and _____.

12 /ˈwɛðər/
  a We can't decide _____ to go to Miami or Malibu for our next trip.
  b Our flight was delayed for three hours because of bad _____.

b Test a partner. **A** say one of the homophones, **B** say what the two spellings and meanings are. Then switch roles.

Go online to review the lesson

GRAMMAR

a Complete the sentences with the right form of the verb in brackets.

1 Do you think I should _____ to Mario yesterday? (apologize)
2 You'd better _____ to the doctor about that cough. (go)
3 You're not supposed _____ your cell phone at work, but everyone does. (use)
4 Alex seems _____ a lot recently. Do you think he's studying enough? (go out)
5 Isn't there anywhere _____ here? (sit down)
6 Rick hates _____ that he doesn't dance very well. (admit)
7 I would love _____ the exhibition, but it finished the day before we arrived. (see)
8 There's no point _____ him. He always has his phone turned off while he's driving. (call)
9 It's important for celebrities _____ at all the right parties. (see)
10 Let's go and have a coffee. The meeting isn't due _____ until 10:30. (start)

b Circle the right phrase. Check (✓) if both are possible.

1 It is *not allowed / not permitted* to wear jewelry at school.
2 *You should have listened / You should listen* to my advice, but it's too late now.
3 I'll *have a white suit on / be wearing a white suit*, so you'll easily recognize me at the airport.
4 *You look / You seem* down today. Is everything OK?
5 It smells *as if / as though* someone has burned the toast.
6 Is that your father upstairs? *I can hear / I'm hearing* his voice.
7 This coffee *tastes like / tastes of* tea. It's undrinkable!
8 *I'll be working / I'm working* at home this afternoon, so you can call me there.
9 You'd better get on the train now. It *is to / is about to* leave.
10 The mayor *is to / is due to* open the new hospital early next month.

VOCABULARY

a Complete the sentences with a form of the **bold** word and a prefix.

1 Sorry, but you _____ my name. It's K-A-T-Y, not K-A-T-I-E. **spell**
2 I get very _____ when I feel that I'm not making any progress. **motivate**
3 Nowadays in Hong Kong, local residents are completely _____ by tourists. **number**
4 The movie isn't as good as everyone says it is. I think it's very _____. **rate**
5 Look, I think they've _____ us. The check should be $80, not $60. **charge**
6 I'm afraid this style of jeans has been _____—we won't be receiving any more. **continue**
7 The staff meeting has been postponed and will be _____ for a later date. **schedule**
8 Trying to improve people's lives by imposing all kinds of new laws on them is _____. **logical**

b Write the expressions or idioms for the definitions.

1 a _____ _____ *noun* a painting or drawing of arrangements of objects such as flowers, fruit, etc.
2 a _____-_____ *noun* a painting or drawing that an artist does of him / herself
3 a _____ _____ IDM an unimportant fact or idea that takes people's attention away from the important things
4 a _____ _____ IDM a thing that is useless even though it may have cost a lot of money
5 the _____ _____ IDM an illegal form of trade in which goods that are difficult to obtain are bought and sold
6 _____ _____ IDM bureaucracy

c Circle the right word.

1 I wore my new shoes to work today and now I have a *blister / cast* on my toe.
2 That's a very deep cut. It may need *bandages / stitches*.
3 Do you know which *surgeon / GP* will be operating on you?
4 I have a strange *ultrasound / rash* on my hands. I think it might be an allergy to laundry detergent.
5 My husband is as stubborn as a *horse / mule*.
6 Grandad never hears the doorbell. He's as deaf as a *bat / post*.
7 I was so tired I slept like a *fish / log* last night.
8 Now that my laptop's been fixed it works like a *dream / flash*.

d Complete the missing words.

1 It's a quiet place, completely off the **b**_____ track.
2 We **s**_____ off at 7:00 and we were there by 11:00.
3 As soon as we get there, let's **h**_____ the stores!
4 It used to be an unspoiled village, but now it's really **t**_____—there are ten hotels!
5 Sadly, my father-in-law died suddenly, so we had to **c**_____ our vacation.
6 It's been such a stressful couple of months. I need a break to **r**_____ my batteries.
7 Our room had a **br**_____ view of the mountains.
8 On the first day we decided to go to the market and **s**_____ the local street food.

CAN YOU understand this text?

a Read the article once. What does the writer recommend getting insurance for?

b Read the article again and mark the sentences **T** (true) or **F** (false).

1 When traveling in the US, most Americans don't take a long time making their travel arrangements.
2 Having flight insurance won't help you if your flight is canceled .
3 Booking flights for international travel in advance will usually result in cheaper airfares.
4 It's often easy to find medical help while traveling in remote locations.
5 Those traveling on cruises tend to encounter more problems than other kinds of travelers.

c Look at the highlighted words and phrases and figure out their meaning. Check with your teacher or with a dictionary.

▶ CAN YOU understand this movie?

Watch or listen to a short movie on the history of penicillin and mark the sentences **T** (true) or **F** (false).

1 Alexander Fleming was the first person to find a way to prevent infection.
2 After discovering penicillin, his problem was that he couldn't produce enough of it.
3 Florey and Chain weren't interested in Fleming's results.
4 By early 1940, they had discovered a way to produce penicillin in large quantities.
5 The drug was urgently needed because of World War II.
6 In 1945, Fleming, Florey, and Chain won the Nobel Prize for Chemistry.
7 Doctors are not to blame for the reduction in effectiveness of antibiotics.
8 Antibiotics can be bought without a doctor's prescription in some countries.
9 If we do not control the use of antibiotics, it will be impossible to carry out operations.
10 We need national legislation to restrict the use of antibiotics.

Three times you can skip travel insurance—and three times you should buy it

Travel insurance can offer peace of mind while you're on a trip—but at a price. Here's some advice for US travelers planning their next vacations.

Skip It: For US travel

Road-tripping around the American Southwest? You can probably skip any extra insurance. Travel within the US is typically a less expensive investment — and most people tend to plan only a few weeks in advance. The average domestic trip spans about four days and costs $576 per person.

Plus, if you have medical insurance, you're typically covered for any emergencies that occur. As always, double check the fine print, but experts generally recommend opting out of trip insurance for short trips within the US.

Skip It: For flights

If your flight is canceled, you're generally entitled to have the next available seat on the next available flight going to your destination. Having insurance is not going to make much difference in getting you re-booked faster.

Skip It: Just for flexibility

Trip insurance should not be used just so you can keep your options open. Instead of purchasing a whole comprehensive policy, opt for a hotel reservation with free cancelation right up until your stay.

Buy It: For international trips

International trips last about 12 days on average and cost $3,242 per person. Travelers also tend to book trips outside the US much further in advance — and for good reason. To get a good deal on an international flight, you'll need to book almost five months beforehand on average.

Because of the advanced planning and the cost, you should definitely consider buying insurance that will cover you in a wide range of situations.

Buy It: For medical reasons

If something goes wrong in a faraway place, medical help may be difficult to come by, and it could be expensive, too. That's when a comprehensive travel insurance policy can come in handy: It can help you avoid out-of-pocket expenses.

Buy It: For cruises

Cruises involve a big, upfront payment, international travel and higher risk of problems. We'd recommend investing in a comprehensive policy which covers all types of situations, including hurricanes. It's a good way of protecting your investment so you're not on the hook for exorbitant fees.

⟲ **Go online** to download the video, review the lesson, and check your progress

> **G** ellipsis   **V** animal matters   **P** auxiliary verbs and *to*

> "A rattlesnake loose in the living room tends to end all discussion of animal rights.
> *Lance Morrow, US writer*

1 READING

a Would you say that people in your country are animal lovers? Have you ever had a pet? How attached to it were you?

b Look at the title of the article. Does it imply that the writer likes animals or dislikes them?

c Now read the article. In which paragraph does the writer talk about…?

- [ ] his attitude toward dogs
- [ ] his current feelings about kittens
- [ ] future plans about pets in his household
- [ ] people's preference for animals over children
- [ ] his general attitude toward cats
- [ ] his children's attitude toward animals
- [ ] his childhood experience with pets

d Read the article again. Choose **a**, **b**, or **c**.

1 The writer _____ kittens are cute.
  a agrees that
  b disagrees that
  c isn't sure whether

2 He thinks that in general cats are _____ .
  a more loveable than annoying
  b equally loveable and annoying
  c more annoying than loveable

3 He _____ .
  a prefers cats to dogs
  b prefers dogs to cats
  c doesn't have a preference

4 He thinks that some animal lovers would consider his attitude toward animals _____ .
  a oversensitive
  b unnatural
  c normal

5 He _____ people who prefer animals to children.
  a sometimes understands
  b half-agrees with
  c strongly disapproves of

6 His children have _____ attitude toward animals.
  a an inconsistent
  b a rigid
  c an unhealthy

In defense of NOT liking animals

1 Our household at the moment is infested—sorry, blessed—with cats. Six of them. Having gotten rid of one, Dylan, last year—may he rest in peace—leaving only his infirm and senile brother, Floss, behind, my wife accepted a kitten. This kitten has just given birth to four of her own fluffy balls. I have to admit that the expression "cute as a kitten" does not seem to be an arbitrary one. They are extraordinarily loveable. They meow and play and generally make the world a fluffier place. I like them.

2 But I doubt that it will last. I am a lifelong pet skeptic. Confronted with the kittens, it briefly slipped my mind why I was skeptical. I am now beginning to remember. The house is starting to smell. Cats come on to the bed in the morning at 6 a.m., sit on your head, and wake you up. They drink the water in your bedside glass. If you close the door, they wait outside complaining until you open it so they can sit on your head, etc. Their lovability is more than offset by their extraordinary flair in the art of being annoying.

3 My prejudice is not confined to cats. To dogs I am positively averse. They are needy, time-consuming, easy to trip over, and frequently smell bad. Also, they have been known to bite people—certainly a lot of dogs in my neighborhood appear to have evolved specifically for this purpose.

4 There are people—"animal lovers" is the term—who find people like me, people who care very little about other species, barely human. If I were feeling apologetic, I would only say that I grew up in a house without pets, and so have never quite become acclimatized to them. My only pet was a stickleback I caught in the canal, which died after six hours in my mother's household bucket. And a tortoise, whose shell I found mysteriously empty one day.

5 But I'm not feeling apologetic. Should I feel sorry because I can stare at my children awestruck by love, but not feel the same way about another species? I cannot accept that people who don't much care for animals are emotionally defective. If anything, the reverse is true. Anybody who leaves their inheritance to a donkey sanctuary rather than research for, say, children's cancer strikes me as profoundly cynical about the human race.

6 Human beings are difficult to love—they are complex, contrary, and they often let you down. Animals are simple and easy to love. But it's a soft option. My children appear to adore animals, but in a highly partial way. They ooh and aah when they see lambs frolicking in the fields, but then sit down and eat their Sunday lunch with mint sauce without a second thought. This is sentimentality rather than genuine love.

7 But for the moment, cynic or not, I am content to have the gorgeous balls of fluff around the house. Three are being given away, we're keeping one, and Floss can't be for this earthly realm much longer. That will leave us with two. I can live with that, just about, as long as no one asks me, ever, to clean out the litter tray.

By Tim Lott in The Guardian

> **Glossary**
> **stickleback** a small, freshwater fish with sharp points on its back
> **mint sauce** a sauce traditionally eaten with roasted lamb
> **litter tray** (NAmE litter box) a shallow box full of a dry substance used by cats as an indoor toilet

e Look at the <mark>highlighted</mark> verbs and expressions related to feelings and try to figure out their meaning. Then match them to 1–6.

1 _____ be happy and satisfied with
2 _____ really dislike something
3 _____ not feel strongly about
4 _____ really love
5 _____ have doubts about something
6 _____ PHR V accept something that isn't perfect

f Talk to a partner.

1 Do you think the writer's attitude toward animals is…?
   a realistic b sentimental c hard-hearted
2 What is your attitude toward animals: **a**, **b**, or **c**? Explain why.

2 VOCABULARY & SPEAKING
animal matters

a Look at the definition of "stickleback" in the glossary. Then make dictionary-style definitions for these words from the article:

donkey kitten lamb pet tortoise human being

b V p.172 **Vocabulary Bank** Animal matters.

c Choose five circles. Tell your partner something about a person you know who…

goes hunting or fishing regularly

has an unusual pet

doesn't eat meat or fish because of their principles

is afraid of certain animals or insects

is allergic to bee or wasp stings

doesn't look after an animal properly

has a really annoying pet

doesn't believe in wearing fur / leather

is passionate about animal rights

is a member of an organization that protects the environment

has had an infestation of insects or animals recently in their house / garden

can't eat shellfish

has been attacked by a wild animal

d Read the idioms and their definitions. Choose the correct word to complete the expressions.

1 **twitter grunt neigh**
   I **did all the** _____ **work** on this project, so I hope I'm going to get the credit for it.
   = did the hard, boring part

2 **duck goldfish penguin**
   I told him what I thought of him, but **it's like water off a** _____**'s back**.
   = criticism doesn't affect him

3 **duck fish frog**
   He **was like a** _____ **out of water** when he left his small hometown and moved to Los Angeles.
   = felt uncomfortable or awkward in unfamiliar surroundings

4 **calves chickens lambs**
   You think you passed the exam, but **don't count your** _____ **before they hatch**.
   = don't be too confident that you will be successful

5 **cat dog horse**
   I didn't think Omar could compete in the race, but he turned out to be **a dark** _____, and he came in first!
   = a person taking part in a race, etc., who surprises everyone by winning

6 **lion leopard tiger**
   When they divorced, Nick's wife got **the** _____**'s share** of everything they owned.
   = the main part

7 **mouse pig rat**
   The company says they're not going to downsize anyone in the restructuring, but I **smell a** _____.
   = think that something is wrong or that somebody is trying to deceive you

8 **birds cats fish**
   If the meeting's in Chicago, I can go and visit my mother at the same time—**it'll kill two** _____ **with one stone**.
   = achieve two things by doing one action

9 **bark meow roar**
   My boss can seem very aggressive, but in fact, **her** _____ **is worse than her bite**.
   = her words are worse than her actions

10 **beak paws tail**
   After playing so badly, he walked off the field **with his** _____ **between his legs**.
   = feeling ashamed, embarrassed, or unhappy because you have been defeated or punished

e Do you have the same or similar idioms in your language?

3 GRAMMAR ellipsis

a 🔊9.6 Read a conversation about pet owning and fill in the blanks with one word. Listen and check. What is the function of these words in the sentences?

> **W** Have you ever had a pet?
> **M** Sadly not. I've always wanted ¹_to_ , but I've never been able ²_____ because I'm allergic to cats and dogs.
> **W** Are you? I'm not, but my sister ³_____ , which is why we never had them either. But my kids really want a puppy and so ⁴_____ my husband.
> **M** I think you probably ⁵_____ then. What's stopping you? You should go to a shelter for abandoned dogs.
> **W** I already ⁶_____ .
> **M** So, you really are going to get one then?
> **W** I think ⁷_____ . I'm not 100% convinced, but the children ⁸_____ .

b 🇬 **p.158 Grammar Bank 9A** Learn more about ellipsis, and practice it.

4 PRONUNCIATION auxiliary verbs and *to*

a 🔊9.7 Read the conversations and <u>underline</u> the auxiliaries or *to* when you think they are stressed. Listen and check. Then practice the conversations.

1 **A** Do you like dogs?
  B No, I don't, but my husband does.
  A So does mine. We have three rescue dogs.
2 **A** I went to Alaska last summer.
  B Lucky you. I'd love to go there. Did you see any whales?
  A No. I wanted to, but I got seasick and I mostly stayed in my cabin.
3 **A** Allie doesn't have any pets, does she?
  B She does have a pet. She has a hamster.
  A Ugh. I don't like hamsters.
  B Neither do I. They're too much like mice.

b 🇬 **Communication** Match the sentences **A p.111 B p.113.** Read sentences and choose responses.

5 LISTENING

a Answer the questions in small groups.

1 Do you know anyone who…?
  • eats fish, but not meat
  • doesn't eat meat or fish, but does eat eggs and dairy products
  • doesn't eat any animal products at all
  • says they're vegetarian, but sometimes eats meat
2 Are there many vegetarians or vegans in your country? How easy is it for them to eat out?
3 What is your attitude toward vegetarians and vegans?

b You are going to listen to a radio program where two people are debating the pros and cons of being vegetarian. Before you listen, try to predict two arguments that the pro-vegetarian might make and two that the anti-vegetarian might make.

c 🔊9.8 Listen to the pro-vegetarian making her points. Did she make any of the arguments you predicted?

d Listen again and make notes in the chart. Write her main arguments next to **1**, **2**, and **3**, and write the details underneath.

We should stop eating meat		
1 _____	2 _____	3 _____

e 🔊9.9 Now listen to the anti-vegetarian opposing these arguments. Did he make any of the points you had predicted?

f Listen again and make notes in the chart. What is his final argument when he sums up?

We should not stop eating meat		
1 _____	2 _____	3 _____

g Who did you find more convincing? Are there any other arguments you would add?

6 SPEAKING

a 🔊 9.10 Listen to some short extracts of people discussing the pros and cons of zoos and complete the expressions in the box with an adverb.

> 🔍 **Common adverb collocations**
> 1 *It's something I feel _____ _____ about.*
> 2 *Well, I don't feel _____ _____ about it either way.*
> 3 *I have to say I am _____ against zoos nowadays.*
> 4 *I don't _____ agree with you.*
> 5 *Well, I'm _____ convinced that the animal does not want to be there.*
> 6 *I'm _____ sure that kids could get the same amount of pleasure from seeing animals in the wild.*

b Work in groups of three or four. You are going to discuss some of the issues below. Each person in the group should choose a different issue, for which they will start the discussion. Decide whether you agree or disagree with the statement and make notes with reasons and examples.

c Hold your discussions. Try to use language from **a**.

d On which topic, in your group, do you most strongly a) agree, b) disagree?

Animals raised for food should be kept in humane conditions. #animalissues

Zoos nowadays serve no useful purpose and should be banned. #animalissues

Animal rights activists are wrong to object to animals being used in experiments. #animalissues

It is hypocritical for people who call themselves animal lovers to eat meat and fish. #animalissues

Fishing is a traditional sport that has existed for centuries and should not be banned. #animalissues

In today's society, there is no place for entertainment that exploits animals. #animalissues

People should not be allowed to keep very aggressive breeds of dog such as pit bulls as pets. #animalissues

People who live in apartments should not be allowed to have pets that need exercise. #animalissues

Go online to review the lesson

9B How to eat out...and in

"A first-rate soup is more creative than a second-rate painting."
Abraham Maslow, US psychologist

G nouns: compound and possessive forms | **V** preparing food; food adjectives with -y | **P** words with silent syllabl

1 VOCABULARY preparing food

a Imagine you are in a restaurant and are given the menu below. Study it for a couple of minutes and choose what to have. Compare with a partner.

BEN'S BRASSERIE

APPETIZERS

cobb salad $9.95
grilled chicken, avocado, blue cheese, and arugula with raspberry vinaigrette

steamed mussels $13.95
with coconut and chili peppers

grilled sardines $11.95
with parsley, lemon, and garlic

MAIN COURSES

Thai chicken curry $22.95
stir-fried chicken, Thai spices, peppers, onions, cashew nuts, and coconut milk with jasmine rice or egg noodles

spicy sausages $21.95
with garlic mashed potatoes and onion purée

herb-crusted lamb chops $22.95
with potatoes, steamed green beans, and balsamic sauce

hot-smoked salmon $20.95
with mashed potatoes, poached egg, and hollandaise sauce

baked eggplant $18.95
stuffed with basmati rice, pecorino cheese, and pistachios

DESSERTS

plum and almond tart $7.95
with amaretto whipped cream

apple and blackberry pie $8.95
with vanilla ice cream

A service charge of 15% will be added to your bill.

b Complete the chart with words from the menu. Find three for each category.

Ways of preparing food	
Vegetables	
Fruit and nuts	
Sauces and dressings	
Fish and seafood	

c What fruits, vegetables, and meat, fish or seafood are really popular in your region or country? Do you know how to say them in English?

d **V** p.173 **Vocabulary Bank** Preparing food.

2 PRONUNCIATION words with silent syllables

a ◀)) 9.13 You are going to hear eight sentences. For each one, write down the last word you hear.

> 🔍 **Fine-tuning your pronunciation: silent syllables**
> Some common multi-syllable words in English have vowels that are often not pronounced, e.g., the middle *e* in *average* and the *o* in *favorite*. When this happens, the word loses an unstressed syllable. If you pronounce these vowels, you will still be understood, but leaving them out will make your speech sound more natural, and being aware of them will help you to understand these words in rapid speech.

b Cross out the vowels that are not pronounced in the words you wrote down in **a**.

c ◀)) 9.14 Listen and check. Practice saying the words.

3 LISTENING & SPEAKING

a You are going to listen to extracts from a book called *How to Eat Out* by restaurant critic Giles Coren, giving advice about how to get the best out of restaurant meals. Before you listen, with a partner, decide what you think the missing words are in his tips.

1 Always order the _____ .
2 Never eat the _____ .
3 Have the vegetarian option—but not in a _____ restaurant.
4 Never sit at a table _____ .
5 Insist on _____ water.
6 How to _____—and get a result.
7 Be nice to the _____ .

b 🔊 9.15 Listen once and complete the tips. Did you guess any of them right?

c Listen again. Why does he mention the following?

- ordering steak in a restaurant
- an ex-girlfriend of his
- meat-eating chefs
- smokers
- bottled water
- free main courses
- waitresses and foreign staff

LEXIS IN CONTEXT

d 🔊 9.16 Listen to some extracts from the book and try to complete the missing words. How do you think they are spelled and what do you think they mean?

1 It's often _____ to prepare and very smelly to cook.
2 So, whenever we meet for dinner, she is utterly starving and _____ up the entire bread basket and three pats of butter without pausing for breath.
3 But in an expensive place with a TV chef and a whole range of exciting things to _____ on for the next couple of hours…
4 …personally I would much rather restaurants focused on doing one or two things brilliantly than offered a whole load of _____ that was just about OK.
5 "I'm awfully sorry to make a _____ ," you might say, "but this fish really isn't as fresh as I'd hoped."

e In groups, discuss the questions.

1 Do you agree with Giles Coren's tips? Are there any other tips that you could give visitors to your country that would help them to get the most out of local food and restaurants?
2 Where would you recommend eating out…?
   - for a weekday lunch
   - to celebrate a friend's birthday
   - with a wealthy relative
3 Think of a good meal out you've had. Where was it? Who were you with? Can you remember what you had to eat and drink?
4 Have you ever had a disastrous meal out? Why was it so awful?
5 In general, do you think that eating out is good value in your country? Why (not)?

4 WRITING

W p.126 **Writing** A complaint Analyze a model email and write an email of complaint to a hotel.

5 GRAMMAR

nouns: compound and possessive forms

a (Circle) the correct phrase in each pair. If you think both are possible, explain the difference between them, if any.

1 a recipe book / a recipe's book
2 a tuna salad / a salad of tuna
3 children's servings / children servings
4 a coffee cup / a cup of coffee
5 a chef hat / a chef's hat
6 a can opener / a cans opener
7 James' kitchen / James's kitchen
8 a John's friend / a friend of John's

b **G** **p.159 Grammar Bank 9B** Learn more about compound nouns and possessive forms, and practice them.

6 READING

a Read the introduction to an article. What exactly is "comfort food"? Do you have an equivalent expression in your language?

b Now read about five people describing their comfort food and fill in the blanks for 1–5 with sentences A–F below. There is one sentence you don't need.

A Who am I kidding, it's still great.
B The kitchen is where the love comes from.
C It's when this connection between a dish and a certain context comes together that food makes most sense and is comforting to me.
D Nobody has ever made it quite like my mother used to.
E It's one of those dishes that seems so simple, but takes years of practice to perfect.
F It was light, but incredibly comforting.

> **Glossary**
> **Ladbroke Grove** a road and an area in west London
> **Dalston** an area in northeast London

Well-known faces reveal their ultimate comfort food

Comfort food takes us somewhere safe and cozy and simple. Many of the things we eat have a unique ability to transport us – a fresh tomato salad with basil and peppery olive oil can help us re-experience, for a moment, a long-gone summer in Tuscany. Comfort food can also take us back to our childhood and remind us of exactly who we are. A photograph is good at doing that, but the way something tastes is the greatest, most comforting time machine of all.

Goldie, musician

Growing up in a children's home, I got used to the kind of meals that work for feeding 25 to 30 kids—things like sausage and mash, bacon and eggs—but I first associated comfort with food when I'd go home at the weekends and visit the Jamaican side of the family. The smell of Jamaican cooking, be it in a home kitchen, a patty shop in Ladbroke Grove or Junior's Caribbean takeaway in Dalston is, to me, home. And home means comfort. [1]_____. The smells, the pots and pans, all the dried and fresh ingredients, the heat from the Scotch bonnet chilis catching your throat, it's all so beautiful.

Beth Ditto, singer

If we're talking homemade dishes, it has to be biscuits and gravy, southern-style. My mom makes the most incredible biscuits, but I can't make gravy as good as hers. There's even a chocolate gravy which very few people have heard of—it's a dish that only true southerners know. I make mine simple, with no herbs, just bacon scratch [the sticky bits left on the pan], milk, flour, salt and pepper. [2]_____. Biscuits and gravy is a long process and when my mom, a nurse who worked a lot and was gone on weekends and holidays, took the time to make that for us seven kids, it made us feel taken care of.

Cornelia Parker, artist

Something like fish soup rates high on the comfort-food list for me. A *bouillabaisse*, or a fish stew—anything wet with fish in it, really. If I see something soupy and fishy like that on a menu, I have to have it. I went to Portugal at the beginning of the summer and we went to the same restaurant every night of the week, as you do, and I had monkfish stew four nights out of six. ³_____.

Yotam Ottolenghi, chef

Comfort food is about eating the right food in the right place at the right time. ⁴_____. In this way, any food can be comforting depending on the time and place, whether that's a can of smoked oysters for breakfast or pasta at the end of the day. But my true comfort dish, I think, would be brown rice with miso vegetables.

Azealia Banks, singer

If we're talking guilty, comforting pleasures, mine has to be candy. Particularly Haribo gummy bears. As well as candy, I love steak. It's a guilty pleasure because red meat is so bad for you! When I was a kid, I used to really love McDonald's. ⁵_____.

LEXIS IN CONTEXT

c Read the article again. Write the food words for photos 1–5.

1 _____
2 _____
3 _____
4 _____
5 _____

d Underline all the other types of food mentioned in the article. With a partner, say what you think they mean. Check with your teacher or with a dictionary.

e Work in groups and answer the questions?

- Is there any food that the people mentioned that you also find comforting? Why?
- What are your comfort foods?
- What do they remind you of?
- How do they make you feel?
- How often do you eat them?
- Where do you eat them, and who with?

7 VOCABULARY food adjectives with -y

> 🔍 **Making food words into adjectives**
> *A fresh tomato salad with basil and* ***peppery*** *olive oil.*
>
> A lot of food words can be made into adjectives by adding -y. Common examples include *buttery, cheesy, chocolatey, creamy, fishy, fruity, herby, lemony, meaty, minty, peppery, salty, spicy, sugary,* and *watery.*

a Which of the adjectives in the box might you use to describe…?

| a cake | coffee | Indian food | pizza |
| a sauce | soup | a stew | toothpaste |

b Tell your partner about five things you really like or dislike eating or drinking using adjectives from the box.

(*I love really fruity drinks.*

8&9 Colloquial English Insects and animals

entomology phobias

a plant hopper /plænt 'hɑpər/

1 THE INTERVIEW Part 1

an ant /ænt/

a Read the biographical information about George McGavin and look at the photos of insects on these pages. How many of them have you seen?

George McGavin is a well-known entomologist, academic, author, explorer, and TV host. He is Honorary Research Associate at the Department of Zoology of Oxford University. He studied zoology at the University of Edinburgh before completing a Ph.D. at the Natural History Museum and Imperial College London. He is a Fellow of the Linnean Society and the Royal Geographical Society, and has several insect species named in his honor. He has hosted several TV shows for the BBC, including *Expedition Borneo, The Dark: Nature's Nighttime World*, and *Monkey Planet*, as well as for the Discovery Channel. He enjoys eating insects, which he describes as "flying shrimp."

b 9.17 Watch or listen to Part 1 of the interview. What is an arthropod, and why does he think they are so important?

c Now listen again. Answer the questions.

1. What examples does George McGavin give of animals with a spine, and why does he think they are less important than arthropods?
2. When did he first decide to focus on arthropods? What insect caught his attention?
3. What usually influences how new species are named? How many does he have named after him?
4. What currently makes him sad about arthropods?

Glossary

crustacea /krʌ'steɪʃʌ/ creatures with a soft body and a hard outer shell, usually aquatic, e.g., crabs, shrimp
mammal /'mæml/ an animal that gives birth to live babies (not eggs) and feeds its young on milk, e.g., a cow
amphibian /æm'fɪbiən/ an animal that can live on land and in water, e.g., a frog
badger /'bædʒər/ a nocturnal animal with gray fur and wide black and white lines on its head
Borneo /'bɔrnioʊ/ a large tropical island in southeast Asia

Part 2

a 9.18 Now watch or listen to Part 2. How sympathetic is George McGavin to people who have phobias of insects? Has he ever been afraid of a living creature?

b Listen again. Mark the sentences **T** (true) or **F** (false). Correct the false sentences.

a shield bug /ʃild bʌg/

1. People say they have a phobia of insects because of the way insects look and move.
2. George McGavin thinks children develop phobias as a result of adults' fears.
3. He thinks a fear of spiders is never justifiable.
4. In the UK there are spiders whose bite can make you seriously sick.
5. He thinks curing people of phobias always takes a long time.
6. His first reaction when he saw the snake in the Amazon was excitement.
7. The snake didn't like the clothes McGavin was wearing.
8. When he realized how dangerous the snake was, he dropped it and ran away.

Glossary

tarantula a large hairy spider
fer-de-lance a poisonous snake native to South America and the Caribbean
head torch (NAmE head lamp) an electric lamp that uses batteries that you wear on your head

a moth /mɔθ/

Part 3

a 9.19 Now watch or listen to Part 3. What does George McGavin say about...?

1. killing insects at work
2. killing insects at home
3. "optimal foraging theory"
4. harvesting insects in cold and hot countries
5. a mealworm in a snack
6. cooking crickets for children in Oxford
7. one boy's mother

a flea /fli/

a bee /bi/

a cockroach /'kɑkroʊtʃ/

b Compare with a partner. Then listen again. Can you add any more details?

a wasp /wɒsp/

Glossary
a flash in the pan IDM a sudden success that lasts only a short time and is not likely to be repeated
ecology the relation of plants and living creatures to each other and to their environment
swarm *verb* (of insects) move around together in a large group, looking for a place to live
harvest *verb* cut and gather a crop; catch a number of animals or fish to eat
snail a small soft creature with a hard round shell on its back, that moves very slowly and often eats garden plants
prawn (NAmE shrimp) a shellfish with ten legs and a long tail, that can be eaten

2 LOOKING AT LANGUAGE

> 🔍 **Informal and vague language**
> George McGavin uses a lot of informal expressions, as well as vague language, which is common in colloquial English when we don't want to be too specific or precise. Vague language makes us sound more informal and chatty.

a ▶9.20 Watch or listen to some extracts from the interview and complete the missing words.

1 "And the sad truth is that although we are _____ sure there are eight million species of arthropods _____ there unknown…"
2 "And I think adults sometimes pass their fears on by, by _____, 'Oh, what's that? Oh, it's a spider.'"
3 "…but, but still there are _____ like seven million people in the United Kingdom who are terrified of spiders, and, and moths."
4 "…however, if you have a cat and you don't control the fleas, are a _____ of a pest…"
5 "No, it, it isn't a flash in the pan, um, we will have to, to address this quite seriously in the next, you know, hundred or _____ years."
6 "…lots of people say it's because insects are dirty or they look funny or _____."
7 "…and the kids went wild! They, they ate the _____ lot."
8 "I _____, 'Yeah, and your point is?' She was _____, 'At home he doesn't even eat broccoli.'"

b With a partner, say how you could express the phrases in more formal or neutral language.

a mealworm /ˈmiːlwɜːm/

a cricket /ˈkrɪkət/

3 ▶ ON THE STREET

a ◀9.21 Watch or listen to five people talking about animals. Who (Je, A, S, Ja, or K) saw an animal or a group of animals…?

Jenny	Alex	Sarah	James	Karen
American	*English*	*American*	*English*	*English*

☐ that really impressed them by the elegant way it moved
☐ that were much larger than expected
☐ that were recovering from injuries
☐ completely unexpectedly, while they were traveling across the country
☐ despite having been warned that they probably wouldn't see any

b Watch or listen again. Who mentions an animal that they would like to see in the wild rather than a place they would like to visit? What places do the other four people mention?

c ◀9.22 Watch or listen again and complete the Colloquial English phrases. What do you think they mean?

1 "…they actually allowed them to just _____ _____ _____, uh, so it was really impressive."
2 "But, we'd been told the _____ of seeing them in the wild were _____ _____…"
3 "…you see them on TV, but never in _____ _____."
4 "I mean, it's _____ _____ _____ I suppose, but I did see it in the wild."
5 "…so, um, it's very rare that you can, actually, um, _____ _____…"

sanctuary an area where wild birds or animals are protected
David Attenborough an English broadcaster and naturalist

4 SPEAKING

Answer the questions with a partner or in small groups.

- How do you feel about insects in general? Are there any you particularly like or dislike?
- Would you be prepared to eat insects?
- Do you ever watch wildlife shows on TV? Why do you think they are so popular?
- What's the most interesting animal that you've ever seen in the wild? Where was it?
- Is there anywhere you would particularly like to go to see animals or the natural world?

🔵 **Go online** to watch the video, review the lesson, and check your progress

10A Where do I belong?

G adding emphasis (2): cleft sentences | **V** words that are often confused | **P** intonation in cleft sentences

1 LISTENING & SPEAKING

a Can you think of some reasons why people decide to go and live in another country, or in another city in their country?

b 🔊 **10.1** You are going to listen to an interview with David and Emma Illsley, who went to live in Mairena, a small village in southern Spain, in 1997. Number pictures a–g in the order they mention them (1–7).

c 🔊 **10.2** Listen again to the first half of the interview. Answer the questions with **D** (David), **E** (Emma), or **B** (both).

Who…?
1 ☐ first got a job in Spain
2 ☐ studied at Warwick University
3 ☐ taught English
4 ☐ fell in love with Mairena
5 ☐ taught in Granada for a year
6 ☐ worked in local government
7 ☐ thinks having children helped them to integrate
8 ☐ employs local people

d 🔊 **10.3** Now listen again to the second half of the interview. Make notes under the following headings:

What they like most about living in Mairena
What they don't like about living in Mairena
What they miss about the UK
Whether or not they will go back to the UK

David and Emma Illsley

LEXIS IN CONTEXT

e ◀))10.4 **Listen to some extracts from the interview and complete the idioms and phrasal verbs. With a partner, say what you think they mean.**

1 …he'd agreed to, to let us rent this house for, for _____ to _____ …
2 …we wandered around and cycled around and finally _____ _____ this little village of Mairena where we live now…
3 …we were _____ a _____ and enjoying it too much really to, to want to go back…
4 …as long as I can remember I always _____ a _____ , I really wanted to live in a very small community…
5 …on the one hand, it's great being away from shops, it's like a kind of a, real kind of _____ _____ …
6 …so we, we've never really _____ it _____ , it would be tricky I think to come back, largely for economic or financial reasons…
7 …to take them back to the UK, I think now, that would be perhaps a, a _____ _____ .
8 …I think once you've spent 15 years building up a business then also that's something you don't want to, to easily _____ your _____ on.

f **Talk to a partner.**

Do you (or friends of yours) have any experience with going to live in another country?

Yes

Where did you (they) move from or to?
Why did you move?
What are / were the pros and cons?
How integrated do / did you feel?
What do / did you miss?
Did / Will you go back home?

No

What do you think are the pros and cons of…?
• living in a country that is not your own
• living in a city in your country that is not your own
Would you like to move to another country or city yourself?

2 GRAMMAR adding emphasis (2): cleft sentences

a **Sentences 1–4 below convey ideas that the speakers expressed, but they phrased them in a slightly different way. Can you remember what they actually said?**

1 David convinced me it was a good idea.
"It was _____."
2 When we had children it really made a difference.
"The thing _____."
3 I really like the sense of cultural diversity in the UK.
"What I _____."
4 I can't see us going back because of Dan and Tom…
"The main reason _____."

b ◀))10.5 **Listen and check. Now look at the pairs of sentences. What's the difference between them?**

c Ⓖ p.160 **Grammar Bank 10A** Learn more about adding emphasis using cleft sentences, and practice them.

3 PRONUNCIATION intonation in cleft sentences

> 🔍 **Fine-tuning your pronunciation: intonation in cleft sentences**
> Cleft sentences beginning with *What…* or *The person / place / thing*, etc., typically have a fall-rising tone at the end of the *What…* clause.
> *What I hate about my job is having to get up early.*
> *The reason why I went to Japan was that I wanted to learn the language.*
> Cleft sentences beginning with *It…* typically have a falling tone in the clause beginning with *It…*.
> *It was her mother who really broke up our marriage.*
> *It's the commuting that I find so tiring.*

a ◀))10.6 **Read about intonation in cleft sentences. Then listen to each example sentence twice.**

b ◀))10.7 **Listen and repeat the sentences, copying the intonation.**

1 What I don't understand is why she didn't call me.
2 The thing that impresses me most about Jack is his enthusiasm.
3 The reason why I left early was that I had an important meeting.
4 The place where I would most like to live is Thailand.
5 It was the neighbors who made our lives so difficult.
6 It was then that I realized I'd left my keys behind.

4 SPEAKING

Complete the sentences in your own words. Then use them to start conversations with your partner.

• What I would find most difficult about living abroad is…
• What I love about living here is…
• What I least like about living here is…
• The person I get along with best in my family is…
• The place where I can relax the most is…
• The reason I decided to continue learning English was…

🔄 **Go online** to review the lesson

a Look at these requirements for becoming an American citizen. Do they seem fair to you?

> You must have had a Permanent Resident (Green) Card for at least five years, or for at least three years if you're filing as the spouse of a US citizen, before you can apply to be a citizen.
>
> You must be at least 18 years of age at the time of filing, be able to read, write, and speak basic English, and be a person of good moral character.
>
> You must take and pass a civics test and an English test.

b Read an article by Angela Masajo. Number the emotions 1–5 in the order they appear in the text.

- ☐ She felt relieved.
- ☐ She felt confident.
- ☐ She felt nervous again.
- ☐ She felt worthy of respect.
- ☐ She felt nervous.

Angela Masajo is a graduate of Marquette University in Milwaukee, Wisconsin. She recently became an American citizen after living in the US for 14 years.

Glossary

The Star-Spangled Banner the national anthem of the US

The Pledge of Allegiance a formal promise to be loyal the US, which citizens make standing in front of the flag with their right hand on their heart

Bayanihan from the Filipino word "bayan," meaning nation, town, or community

Why I became a US citizen

1 **"I hereby declare, on oath…"**

After a year of waiting, I found myself reciting the words I had been practicing and preparing to speak. I took time away from school and work to travel down to Chicago. And now here I was, in this large auditorium with 98 other people, speaking in unison: *"I will
5 support and defend the Constitution and laws of the United States of America against all enemies, foreign and domestic; that I will bear true faith and allegiance to the same…"*

The room felt small as families filed in to support their loved ones. I didn't know why I was still so anxious. This was the easiest part of the whole process. *Why am I so nervous??* At the ceremony, we watched videos about America and patriotism, took the Oath of
10 Allegiance, sang *The Star-Spangled Banner*, and said the Pledge of Allegiance while being led by the children in the audience. In the end, we received our naturalization certificate. And just like that, I could finally call myself a US citizen.

Starting my path

I'm like any other college student, active in both my studies and extracurriculars. As
15 an undergrad at Marquette University, I majored in Speech Pathology and Audiology and Public Relations. Now I'm getting my master's degree in Speech-Language Pathology. I took an active role in Bayanihan Student Organization. I love to work on art as a creative outlet. What most people around me didn't know was that—despite moving to the United States almost 14 years ago—I wasn't a US citizen. I've been a permanent
20 resident since I was a child.

Now that I'm 23 years old, I'm starting to think more about the future. I've lived in the United States since I was nine years old, and I am pretty certain that I'm not planning to move out of the country any time soon. There was no reason for me not to become a citizen. My family was supportive of me. We'd had the conversation years
25 prior about where I wanted to be, and I chose to stay. So this next step was to finally make things "official." Even knowing what I wanted, this wasn't going to be a simple process. After I sent in my paperwork, I was scheduled to come in for biometrics testing— fingerprinting—a month after they received my application. I had to wait another five months until I received the notice for my interview. Then the waiting really began.

30 **The nerves set in**

I couldn't sleep all week leading up to the interview. It was definitely the most nerve-wracking part of this process. I drove from Milwaukee to Chicago in the middle of the week so I had to notify my work that I'd be taking a couple days to take care of "personal matters." I didn't tell them what I was actually doing. I didn't want to jinx it before it
35 was official.

Once I was in the building, I was so anxious. It was like getting sent to the principal's office knowing that I did nothing wrong—but I was questioning my innocence anyway. They went through my whole application to make sure my answers were consistent. I was asked to read and write in English and I took the civics test. I memorized the 100
40 questions and answers in the prep packet they gave me. It's safe to say I passed with flying colors.

Taking the oath

I received the notice for my oath ceremony quickly. When I told my mom the good news it was pretty apparent that she'd been nervous too when I heard her yell through
45 the phone:

"Ay nako! Bakit hindi mo agad sinabi ipinagdadasal pa kita araw araw!!"

Translation: *Why didn't you tell me right away! I was praying for you every day!!*

Now I've given myself a little bit of time to reflect on what's happened so far. In some ways, it's like earning your degree. Nothing and everything changes at the same time.
50 My friends accepted me before I was an American citizen, and that hasn't changed. I had the same hopes and dreams before I had that certificate as I do now. I'm worthy of being treated with respect yesterday and today. Today, the anxiety about the whole process is gone, but overall, nothing much about me has changed. Now, I'm a US citizen. I'm a college graduate. And I'm still me.

c Read the article again. Then answer the questions with a partner.

1 Why did Angela know the process of becoming an American citizen wasn't going to be simple?
2 How did Angela feel immediately after the ceremony to become a US citizen?
3 Why didn't Angela want to tell the people at her work about the interview?
4 What did Angela mean when she said, "Nothing and everything changes at the same time."
5 How did Angela know that her mother had been nervous too?
6 What was Angela's biggest realization about becoming a US citizen?

LEXIS IN CONTEXT

d Look at the highlighted words and phrases that are all quite formal and try to figure out their meaning. Then match them with the informal or neutral equivalents 1-10.

1 _____ activity or hobby
2 _____ before
3 _____ bring bad luck
4 _____ easy to understand
5 _____ make a promise
6 _____ officially tell someone something
7 _____ saying something you've learned
8 _____ the same
9 _____ think about
10 _____ walk into

e Could you imagine ever becoming a citizen of another country?

6 VOCABULARY
words that are often confused

a The words *foreigner*, *outsider*, and *stranger* are often confused. What is the difference in meaning?

b Look at some more words that are often confused. For each pair, complete the sentences with the correct word.

1 **suit** /sut/ / **suite** /swit/
   a The hotel upgraded us and gave us a _____ instead of a double room.
   b You should definitely wear a _____ to the interview—you'll make a better impression.

2 **beside / besides**
   a Let's not go out tonight. I'm tired and _____, I want to read.
   b They live in that new apartment building _____ the school.

3 **lay** /leɪ/ / **lie** /laɪ/
   a Please _____ down and relax. This will only take a minute.
   b If you _____ the baby on the sofa gently, I'm sure she won't wake up.

4 **actually / currently**
   a The rate of inflation has gone up since last month; it's _____ 2%.
   b I thought I wouldn't enjoy the movie, but _____ it was very funny.

5 **announce / advertise**
   a It is rumored that the president will _____ the latest recipient of the Medal of Honor this week.
   b The company is planning to _____ the new product both on TV and online.

6 **affect** /əˈfɛkt/ / **effect** /ɪˈfɛkt/
   a How does the crisis _____ you?
   b What is the main _____ of the crisis?

7 **ashamed / embarrassed**
   a As soon as the plumber arrived, the leak stopped! I was so _____ .
   b When the teacher told my father I had cheated on the test, I felt so _____ .

8 **deny / refuse**
   a The accused does not _____ being in the house, but he insists that he did not touch anything.
   b I love parties. I never _____ an invitation.

9 **compromise / commitment**
   a I know we will never agree about what to do, but we should try to reach a _____ .
   b The company's _____ to providing quality at a reasonable price has been crucial to its success.

10 **economic / economical**
   a I think we should buy the Toyota. It's nicer looking, and it's much more _____ .
   b I don't agree with this government's _____ policy.

c Complete the sentences with words from **b**. Then, with a partner, say if you think they are more true of men or women, or equally true of both.

1 They let personal problems _____ them at work.
2 They feel _____ when they have to talk about feelings.
3 They are afraid of making a long-term _____ to a relationship.
4 They tend to buy things because they are _____ on TV.
5 They often say they can do something well when _____ they can't.
6 They _____ to admit they are wrong in an argument.

Go online to review the lesson

> Runners run because they like running, joggers jog because they like cake.
> *Stuart Heritage, British journalist*

G relative clauses   **V** word building: adjectives, nouns, and verbs   **P** homographs

BATTLE OF THE WORKOUTS

TENNIS OR SQUASH? YOGA OR PILATES? Making the decision to get fit is the easy part—choosing how to go about it is more difficult. We answer four key questions to help you decide for yourself.

1 How quickly will it make a difference?
2 How many calories does it burn?
3 Will it keep me motivated?
4 What are the benefits?

TENNIS VS. SQUASH

1 After six weeks of twice-weekly matches.
2 476 per hour in a singles match, 340 in doubles.
3 Tennis is competitive and there is nothing better than playing outdoors. However, your motivation may diminish if you keep having to cancel due to the weather!
4 The strength for a great serve is provided by your thigh muscles. Sharp turns and twists put the abdominals and upper body through a vigorous workout.

1 Two to three weeks if playing three times a week.
2 748 per hour.
3 Squash is sociable and if you join a club, there will be a league structure.
4 Rated the number one healthy sport by *Forbes* magazine, squash is easier to learn than tennis and you can play all year round. It helps to strengthen your legs, arms, and core region.

WINNER [ ]

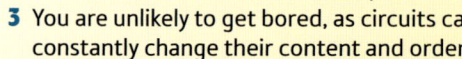
WEIGHTS VS. CIRCUITS

1 After the first session, your muscles will feel more toned, but significant changes will take three to four weeks.
2 136–340 per hour depending on weight lifted and the recovery time between repetitions.
3 If improved body tone is your goal, then yes.
4 Great for toning your muscles and improving overall bone density. Weight training speeds up the rate at which calories are burned, resulting in quicker weight loss.

1 After two weeks of twice-weekly circuits.
2 476 per hour.
3 You are unlikely to get bored, as circuits can constantly change their content and order.
4 Circuits address every element of fitness—aerobic, strength, balance, and flexibility. A good instructor should introduce new tools like skipping ropes and weights to make sure you are always developing new skills.

WINNER [ ]

YOGA VS. PILATES

1 After eight weeks of thrice-weekly sessions.
2 102 per hour for a stretch-based class. Power yoga burns 245 per hour.
3 Yoga is about attaining a sense of unity between body and mind rather than achieving personal targets. However, you will feel a sense of accomplishment as you master the poses and there are lots of different types to try.
4 The American Council on Exercise found that women who did yoga for eight weeks experienced a 13% improvement in flexibility. They were also able to perform six more push-ups and 14 more sit-ups at the end of the study.

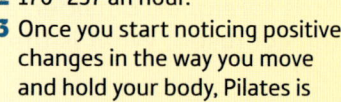
1 After five to six weeks of thrice-weekly sessions.
2 170–237 an hour.
3 Once you start noticing positive changes in the way you move and hold your body, Pilates is hard to give up.
4 Widely used by dancers and top athletes, Pilates improves your posture and strength. It develops the abdominal muscles which support the trunk.

WINNER [ ]

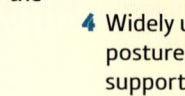 
SPINNING VS. STEP

1 After two to three weeks of twice-weekly sessions.
2 408–646 an hour.
3 Although it's a group session, you can increase the workload as you get fitter. Avoid boredom by looking out for classes with video screens that take you on a virtual ride through pleasant scenery.
4 Pedaling works most of the muscles in the legs and buttocks, so you will get an unbelievably toned lower body. But your heart and lungs are the biggest beneficiaries.

1 After four weeks of twice-weekly classes.
2 510–612 per hour (depending on height of step).
3 You will notice changes in your body shape fairly quickly, but there are only so many times you can step on to a platform before utter boredom takes hold.
4 A study carried out in California showed that women who did step for six months experienced a 3.3% increase in the bone density of their spines, and hip and leg bones. It has good aerobic benefits as well as toning muscles in the bottom and legs.

From The Guardian

WINNER [ ]

1 READING & SPEAKING

a Look at the activities in the article. Do you know what they all are? Do you do any of the activities, or have you ever done them? Is / Was your experience positive or negative?

b Read the article. For which activity are these statements true?

1 Once you start you won't want to stop.
2 It's probably the most boring of all the activities.
3 It takes the longest time to show any benefits.
4 Having the right instructor will make it more varied.
5 It will make some difference immediately.
6 The amount of calories you burn depends on the number of people you do it with.
7 Some gyms have equipment that can make it less dull.
8 You will burn the most calories in an hour.

c Read the article again. For each pair of workouts, which do you think, according to the article, was the winner? Why? Compare with a partner.

LEXIS IN CONTEXT

d In pairs, think of words related to exercise and the body that match the definitions below. Then find them in the article.

1 **th**_____ *noun* the top part of the leg between the knee and the hip
2 **v**_____ *adj* very active and energetic
3 **tr**_____ *noun* the process of improving your fitness by exercising
4 **fl**_____ *noun* the ability to bend
5 **str**_____ *noun* the act of making your muscles longer
6 **p**_____-_____ *noun* an exercise in which you lie on your stomach and raise your body off the ground with your hands until your arms are straight
7 **s**_____-_____ *noun* an exercise for making your stomach muscles strong, in which you lie on the floor on your back and raise the top part of your body
8 **tr**_____ *noun* the main part of the body apart from the head, arms, and legs
9 **l**_____ *noun* the organs in the chest that you use for breathing
10 **sp**_____ *noun* the bones down the middle of the back

e Think of a sport or physical activity that you have done, or know something about. In small groups, say as much as you can about it, answering some of the questions in the article.

2 VOCABULARY word building: adjectives, nouns, and verbs

a Without looking back at the text, complete sentences 1 and 2 with a word made from the adjective *strong*.

1 It helps to _____ your legs, arms, and core region.
2 Widely used by dancers and top athletes, it improves your posture and _____ .

b Complete the chart.

adjective	noun	verb
strong		
long		
deep		
short		
wide		
high		*heighten**
weak		
thick		
flat		

* Note that *heighten* (verb) doesn't mean *make higher*; it means *intensify*.

c Complete the sentences with words from **b** in the correct form.

1 I often have to _____ new pants because they're usually too long for me.
2 Can you measure the _____ and _____ of the living room? I want to order a new rug.
3 I'm more or less the same _____ as my sister, but my brother's much taller than us.
4 People's muscles tend to _____ as they get older.
5 **A** What's the _____ of the water here?
   B About 15 feet, I think.
6 If you want to _____ the sauce, add flour.
7 The building was completely _____ in the explosion.
8 He's almost unbeatable. He doesn't have any real _____ .
9 This road needs to be _____ . It's too narrow.
10 My grandfather suffered from _____ of breath when he had the flu.

Go online to review the lesson

3 PRONUNCIATION homographs

> **Homographs**
> Homographs are words that are spelled the same but pronounced differently, and which have different meanings, e.g.,
> **bow** /baʊ/ = move your head or the top half of your body forwards and downwards, as a sign of respect
> **bow** /boʊ/ = 1 a weapon used for shooting arrows; 2 a hair decoration made of ribbon
> There are not very many words like this, but the common ones are sometimes mispronounced, and learning the correct pronunciation will avoid misunderstandings.

a Read the information box. Then look at the sentences that contain homographs. Match them with pronunciation **a** or **b**.

close   a /kloʊz/   b /kloʊs/
1 ☐ It was a really close race and they had to study the replay to see who won.
2 ☐ What time does the ticket office close? We need to get our tickets for the game on Saturday.

upset   a /ˈʌpsɛt/   b /ʌpˈsɛt/
3 ☐ The lowest-ranked baseball team in our division pulled off an amazing upset when they played the top team and defeated them five to four.
4 ☐ He was really upset because he missed an easy shot that would have won the basketball game for the team.

minute   a /ˈmɪnət/   b /maɪˈnut/
5 ☐ He was disqualified because they found a minute quantity of a banned substance in his blood sample.
6 ☐ He scored a goal just one minute before the referee blew the final whistle.

tear   a /tɛr/   b /tir/
7 ☐ If you tear a muscle or a ligament, you may not be able to train for six months.
8 ☐ As she listened to the national anthem, a tear rolled down her cheek.

content   a /ˈkɑntɛnt/   b /kənˈtɛnt/
9 ☐ Professional athletes never seem content with their contracts. They're always trying to negotiate better terms.
10 ☐ The content of the program wasn't very interesting—just a long analysis of the game.

wound   a /wund/   b /waʊnd/
11 ☐ He wound the tape tightly around his ankle to prevent a sprain.
12 ☐ You could see his head wound bleeding as he was taken off the field.

use   a /yuz/   b /yus/
13 ☐ If you use a high-tech swimsuit, you'll be able to swim much faster.
14 ☐ It's no use complaining—the umpire's decision is final.

b ◾)10.8 Listen and check. Practice saying the sentences.

4 GRAMMAR relative clauses

a Look at the blanks in the sentences below. Complete them with a relative pronoun (*who*, *which*, etc.) where necessary.

1 He ran the marathon in 2 hours 22 minutes, _____ was a new course record.
2 I feel really sorry for the players _____ lost.
3 The coach, _____ daughters also play on the team, has had a really successful season.
4 She got along well with the players _____ she trained.
5 John McEnroe, _____ won Wimbledon in the 1980s, now works as a sports commentator.
6 New sneakers! Thanks, that's just _____ I wanted.
7 Those are the gloves _____ Muhammed Ali wore when he beat Joe Frazier.

b **G** p.161 Grammar Bank 10B Learn more about relative clauses, and practice them.

> **Defining relative clauses in spoken English**
> In informal spoken English, we tend to use *that* rather than *who* or *which* and almost always leave out the relative pronoun when the subject of the clause changes, e.g., *There's the restaurant (that) John told us about.*

c Choose five new words from this lesson and define them for your partner to identify. Use *that* instead of *who / which* and leave out the relative pronoun where appropriate.

5 SPEAKING & LISTENING

a Read the information on page 103 about a book called *Foul Play*, and six of the points the author makes. Decide what you think about each point and write **A** (agree), **HA** (half-agree), or **D** (disagree).

b In groups of three or four, discuss each point, explaining what you think and giving examples where possible.

c  ◗ **10.9** Now listen to Ron Kantowski, a sports journalist in Las Vegas, talking about the topics in **a**. Mark the statements **A**, **HA**, and **D**. Do any of his opinions coincide with what you said in your groups?

Glossary
Super Bowl the annual championship game of the National Football League (NFL), the highest level of professional football in the United States

d Listen again and write a summary of the reasons he gives in answer to each of the interviewer's questions.

1 Sports teach you to…
   People who do individual sports…
2 Sports can enhance your life because…
   On the other hand…
3 The World Cup is an example of…
   Sports should be entertainment, not…
4 It's hard to see a difference between…
   Drugs have improved performance less than many things, including…
5 Athletes are only human, and…
   They're under a lot of pressure from…
6 There's too much media coverage of…
   But the media are just…

e Do you agree or disagree with his arguments? Do you think these aspects of sport will ever change?

Foul Play

What's wrong with sports?

In *Foul Play*, sports journalist Joe Humphreys challenges the idea that sports are a positive influence on athletes, spectators, and the world as a whole.

According to Humphreys:

1 Sport brings out the worst in people, both fans and athletes. It does not improve character or help to develop virtues such as fair play and respect for opponents. You ☐ Ron ☐

2 Sports don't make you happy. Spectators as well as athletes have higher than normal levels of stress, anxiety, and hopelessness, especially in relation to professional sports. You ☐ Ron ☐

3 Sports are like a religion in its ability to "move the masses." You ☐ Ron ☐

4 Doping is no worse than any other kind of cheating and really no different from using technology to gain an advantage, e.g., high-tech running shoes. You ☐ Ron ☐

5 It's ridiculous to expect professional athletes to be role models. You ☐ Ron ☐

6 Sports have too high a profile in the media, often making the headlines in the papers and on TV. You ☐ Ron ☐

9&10 Review and Check

GRAMMAR

a Right (✓) or wrong (✗)? Correct any mistakes in the highlighted phrases.

1 She's never been to Canada, but her son has.
2 They bought the house immediately after see it.
3 A Do you think it's cold outside?
  B I hope no.
4 Do you have a cans opener?
5 A I'd love a coffee cup.
  B Sure. Regular or decaf?
6 Jim hasn't called back, that is a little strange.
7 This is the café I used to work in.

b Circle the right word or phrase. Check (✓) if both are possible.

1 A Can I come with you?
  B I suppose so / yes, but hurry up.
2 A You have to read her latest book.
  B I already am / have.
3 Look, I found an old photo album / album of photos in the attic!
4 Come over about 9:00. We'll be at Alex's / at Alex's house.
5 I can't find my car's keys / car keys. Have you seen them?
6 She has two sisters, both of whom are very pretty / who are both very pretty.
7 I got exactly that / what I wanted for my birthday—a Kindle.
8 Her aunt, who / that never usually said a word, suddenly burst out laughing.

c Rewrite the sentences using the **bold** word.

1 I didn't bring sunscreen because the weather forecast said rain. **reason**
  The _____ because the weather forecast said rain.
2 I spoke to the head of customer service. **person**
  The _____ the head of customer service.
3 I don't like the way he blames other people for his mistakes. **what**
  _____ the way he blames other people for his mistakes.
4 I only said that I thought she was making a big mistake marrying him. **all**
  _____ I thought that she was making a big mistake marrying him.
5 A boy from my school was chosen to carry the Olympic torch. **it**
  _____ was chosen to carry the Olympic torch.

VOCABULARY

a Write the words for the definitions.

1 _____ noun a young cow
2 _____ noun a small shelter for a dog to sleep in
3 _____ verb (of a horse) to make a long, high sound
4 _____ noun pl the sharp curved nails on the end of an animal or a bird's foot
5 _____ noun a group into which animals, plants, etc., are divided
6 _____ verb to chase wild animals or birds in order to catch or kill them for food or sport
7 _____ noun the hard pointed outer part of a bird's mouth
8 _____ _____ noun a thing you use to cut vegetables on
9 _____ verb to cook something slowly in liquid
10 _____ verb to rub food against a sharp surface in order to cut it into small pieces
11 _____ verb to fill with another type of food
12 _____ verb to make something become liquid as a result of heating
13 _____ verb to beat very quickly until it becomes stiff, e.g., cream
14 _____ verb to place food over boiling water so that it cooks in the steam, e.g., vegetables

b Circle the right word.

1 I definitely don't want to go to the party, and beside / besides I'm going to have to work late that night.
2 Could you lay / lie the baby in his crib for a nap?
3 The movie theater will be closed until June because it is actually / currently being refurbished.
4 You don't deny / refuse that you were responsible, do you?
5 Gas is so expensive—a smaller car would be much more economic / economical.
6 I looked like such a mess after painting my living room that I was ashamed / embarrassed of myself.
7 What affect / effect do you think climate change is having on the weather in your country?
8 The names of the six finalists will be announced / advertised next week.

c Complete the sentence with the right form of the **bold** word.

1 The real _____ of the movie is its witty dialogue. **strong**
2 I need to get someone to _____ my new jeans. **short**
3 The pole-vaulter Sergei Bubka was the first man to clear the _____ of six meters. **high**

4 The custard will _____ as it cools. **thick**

5 I can't express the _____ of my feelings for you. **deep**

6 The team has been _____ by the injury to its top player. **weak**

7 Can you measure the _____ of the window? **wide**

8 The school has decided to _____ winter break by three days. **long**

CAN YOU understand this text?

a Read the article once. What technological advances described in the article have affected sports? Do you know of any others?

b Read the article again and complete it with phrases A–F. There is one phrase you do not need.

A Even more remarkable is a state-of-the-art clothing line that allows athletes to coach themselves.

B The "Hawk-Eye" system is an example of successful technology that has been used in professional tennis for several years now.

C Where will technology take us next?

D Many people think that new technology is creating even more inequality in sports than doping.

E Because athletes are always looking for an edge against the competition, many are taking advantage of the latest trends in technology.

F Years ago, the instant replay was considered a giant technological leap because, for the first time, it allowed judges and fans to watch the video of an event almost immediately after it happened.

c Look at the highlighted words and phrases and figure out their meaning. Check with your teacher or with a dictionary.

▶ CAN YOU understand this movie?

Watch or listen to a short movie on Ellis Island and answer the questions.

1 Which three countries does the host say she has ancestors from?

2 Who was Annie Moore?

3 How many people passed through Ellis Island between 1892 and 1954?

4 Why was 1907 a significant year?

5 Which passengers were allowed to disembark in Manhattan?

6 What was the Great Hall used for until 1924?

7 What did the doctors check immigrants for?

8 What kind of people got sent back?

9 Roughly how many people left New York for other parts of America?

10 Who are the three well-known immigrants mentioned, and what did they become famous for?

How is technology affecting sports?

Technology plays a major role in sports: it has changed the way athletes perform, the way professional sports are officiated, and the way fans watch the game.

1 _____. For example, some competitive ice skaters are taking their experience on the ice to the design table. They have developed a new way to make skates using a process called rapid prototyping, using CAD (computer-assisted design). This process allows athletes to get a custom-made pair of boots in record time and be on the ice with them faster than ever before.

2 _____. Unlike a video or instructional pamphlet, the "Haptic Sports Garment" senses your every move and lets you know which areas you need to improve. The garment uses vibrations to help improve posture, target key muscle groups, and even help maintain optimal speeds.

3 _____. But there is no longer a need for instant replay with the new RFID tags (Radio Frequency Identification technology), which European rugby teams are experimenting with. This amazing micro-location technology can transmit the exact coordinates of the ball and players an astounding 2,000 times per second. It can also be used to calculate movement, speed, accuracy, and even force of impact. It essentially eliminates the guesswork from officiating.

4 _____. High-speed cameras mounted around the stadium, combined with a 3D (three-dimensional) model of the tennis court, can track the position of the tennis ball in space. This not only affects the game itself, but also the ability of players to self-analyze at a new level of detail.

5 _____. Will there one day be tiny live cameras and microphones inserted into basketballs and footballs that allow fans to get an even closer view of the action? In the future, will we all be playing video games with holographic players on a life-size field? It may all sound far-fetched, but the technology is there, and it may be on the market sooner than you think.

From www.sportsnetworker.com

Communication

1A WHAT'S YOUR PERSONALITY?
Students A + B

a Use your four types to find out which personality you have and read the description.

b Now find out what your partner's personality is and read the description.

PLANNER + FACTS + HEAD + INTROVERT = REALIST
How you see yourself mature, stable, conscientious
What you are like loyal, straightforward, good at meeting deadlines, respect facts and rules, can be obsessed with schedules, critical of others, may not have faith in other people's abilities

PLANNER + FACTS + HEAD + EXTROVERT = SUPERVISOR
How you see yourself stable, practical, sociable
What you are like natural organizer and administrator, irritated when people don't follow procedures, other people find you bossy

PLANNER + FACTS + HEART + INTROVERT = NURTURER
How you see yourself gentle, conscientious, mature
What you are like caring, may have trouble making decisions that could hurt others, tend to avoid conflict, others may take advantage of you

PLANNER + FACTS + HEART + EXTROVERT = PROVIDER
How you see yourself sympathetic, easygoing, steady
What you are like warm, caring, traditional, tend to avoid conflict, not afraid to express your beliefs

PLANNER + IDEAS + HEAD + INTROVERT = MASTERMIND
How you see yourself logical, thorough, bright
What you are like efficient, independent, rarely change your mind, critical of those who don't understand you

PLANNER + IDEAS + HEAD + EXTROVERT = LEADER
How you see yourself bright, independent, logical
What you are like organized, good at solving large-scale problems, can be critical and aggressive

PLANNER + IDEAS + HEART + INTROVERT = COUNSELOR
How you see yourself gentle, peaceful, cautious
What you are like relaxed and creative, deeply private, can be difficult to get to know

PLANNER + IDEAS + HEART + EXTROVERT = MENTOR
How you see yourself intelligent, outgoing, sensitive
What you are like articulate, warm, lively, extremely sensitive to people's needs, may become overbearing

SPONTANEOUS + FACTS + HEAD + INTROVERT = RESOLVER
How you see yourself understanding, stable, easygoing
What you are like independent, rational, good at finding solutions, natural risk taker, enjoy an adrenaline rush, often focus on short-term results, sometimes lose sight of the bigger picture

SPONTANEOUS + FACTS + HEAD + EXTROVERT = GO-GETTER
How you see yourself inventive, enthusiastic, determined, alert
What you are like resourceful, tough-minded, may become frustrated by routines and constraints

SPONTANEOUS + FACTS + HEART + INTROVERT = PEACEMAKER
How you see yourself steady, gentle, sympathetic
What you are like sensitive to the feelings of others and the world around you, can be self-critical, often difficult to get to know

SPONTANEOUS + FACTS + HEART + EXTROVERT = PERFORMER
How you see yourself enthusiastic, sociable, sensitive
What you are like fun-loving, outgoing, often a good motivator, can be unreliable

SPONTANEOUS + IDEAS + HEAD + INTROVERT = STRATEGIST
How you see yourself bright, logical, individualistic
What you are like quiet, easygoing, intellectually curious, logical, may be critical or sarcastic, can be insensitive to the emotional needs of others

SPONTANEOUS + IDEAS + HEAD + EXTROVERT = BIG THINKER
How you see yourself talkative, curious, logical, self-sufficient
What you are like ingenious, bored by routine, can be rude, rebellious, critical of others

SPONTANEOUS + IDEAS + HEART + INTROVERT = IDEALIST
How you see yourself bright, forgiving, curious
What you are like generally easygoing, flexible, can be stubborn, may refuse to compromise

SPONTANEOUS + IDEAS + HEART + EXTROVERT = INNOVATOR
How you see yourself imaginative, sociable, sympathetic
What you are like energetic, sensitive, creative, sometimes illogical, rebellious, unfocused

p.9

3A BLIND DATE Student A

a Read what Stef says about her blind date with Graham.

Life & style ⟩ Blind date

🏠 Previous | Next | Index

....

Stef on Graham

....

First impressions? Friendly, funny, attractive, and forgiving: I was late.

What did you talk about? Music, comedy, food, bad dancing.

Any awkward moments? Only when we were playing pool – neither of us are fabulous players.

Good table manners? Impeccable, even though it was burgers. He faced the ultimate date challenge well.

Best thing about him? Really genuine and friendly.

Did you go on somewhere? No, but then we didn't leave till 2 a.m.

Marks out of 10? 9 (being a teacher, I can never give full marks).

Would you meet again? I'd really like to, yeah.

b Using your own words, tell **B** about Stef's opinion of the date.

> When Stef met Graham at the restaurant her first impressions were positive. She thought he was…

c Now listen to **B** describing Graham's opinion of the date. How do you think their relationship might develop?

d Turn to p.113 and see if you were right!

3B GUESS THE SENTENCE Student A

a Look at sentences 1–5 and guess what the missing phrase could be. Remember: ⊞ = positive verb and ⊟ = negative verb.

> 1 A lot of people say the book is better than the movie, but actually I _____ . ⊞
> 2 It wasn't a particularly nice day for the barbecue, but at least it _____ . ⊟
> 3 The sea was blue, the sun was shining, and the picnic was marvelous. All in all, it was _____ . ⊞
> 4 On the one hand, dogs are much better company than any other pets, but on the other hand, you have to _____ at least twice a day. ⊞
> 5 Make sure your suitcase weighs less than 40 pounds, otherwise you may _____ . ⊞

b **B** has the complete sentences 1–5. Read your sentences to **B**. Keep trying different possibilities until you get each sentence exactly right.

c Listen to your partner's sentences. Tell them to keep guessing until they get it exactly the same as yours.

> 6 I'm not sure you would enjoy the play, and in any case it will be very difficult **to get tickets**.
> 7 Some of the teachers aren't very inspiring, but on the whole I think it's **a good school**.
> 8 Laura's husband only thinks of himself and he always gets his own way. In other words, **he's totally selfish**.
> 9 I don't feel like going to Miranda's birthday party and besides, I **don't have anything to wear**.
> 10 It's no big surprise that Leo didn't do very well on his exam. After all, he **didn't study at all**.

↪ p.33

Masks for Manggao

People of the Miao culture from the Guangxi Zhuang Autonomous Region in South China were walking around wearing wooden masks and grass costumes at last years' Manggao Festival. They had just finished dancing in the middle of the village and entertaining the crowd.

Like every year, the local villagers were dancing along, playing music, smearing black ash on their faces, and putting on the masks to celebrate Manggao the "masked god". They do this believing that the legendary creature will bring them good luck.

These customs have been passed on from generation to generation, so the dancers were feeling proud and happy to be celebrating for another year.

⬅ p.38

5A   THE TIMEX SURVEY   Students A + B

Survey Results

	Length of time
for a blind date to arrive	26 minutes
for a bus / train	20 minutes
for a car in front of you to start moving when the light turns green	5 seconds
for a table in a restaurant	15 minutes
for people to stop talking during a movie at the movie theater	2 minutes
for the doctor	32 minutes
for your partner to get ready to go out	21 minutes
in a line at a coffee shop	7 minutes

⬅ p.48

7A   QI QUIZ   Student A

a   Read the answers to questions 1–6 of the quiz and remember the information.

b   Explain the answers to 1–6 to **B** in your own words. **B** will tell you the answers to 7–12.

1   Octopuses have eight limbs (= arms or legs), but recent research about how they use them has redefined what they should be called. In fact, they use only their two back limbs to move and the other six to feed themselves, so biologists now refer to them as having **two legs** and **six arms**.

2   Although Australia is home to many of the world's most dangerous spiders, snakes, jellyfish, crocodiles, and sharks, the creature that causes most animal-related deaths per year is the **horse**. The second is the **cow**, followed by the **dog**.

everything you think you know

Qi

is probably **wrong**...

3 Not at 0 degrees, which is the temperature at which pure water freezes. Seawater freezes at about -2° C. Scientists have also "supercooled" pure water to below -40° C without it freezing.

4 It's true that white reflects sunlight and black absorbs it, so in direct sunlight you will be cooler wearing white. However, in the shade dark colors are more effective, because they radiate heat better, and **loose black clothes** will carry heat away from your body faster than they absorb it.

5 It isn't 50/50. If the coin is heads up to begin with, it is slightly more likely that it will land on heads. Students at Stanford University in the US recorded thousands of coin tosses with high-speed cameras and discovered that the chances are approximately **51/49**.

6 Napoleon was not short. The universal belief that he was tiny comes from a mistranslation of a French term of measurement, and propaganda. It is now accepted that he was **1.69 meters**, which is 5 centimeters taller than the height of the average Frenchman at the time.

← p.66

7A WHAT A RIDICULOUS IDEA! Student A

a Read your sentences to **B**. He / She will respond with an exclamation.

- Did you know that you're not supposed to call a female actor an actress because it's considered sexist?
- I got a ticket from a police officer yesterday for talking on my cell phone while I was parked.
- My sister got married on Saturday and it rained all day.
- I thought we could go to the movies and then have dinner at the new Italian place near the mall.
- My daughter's goldfish died this morning.
- Did you know my parents were both born on exactly the same day?
- You won't believe it, but my sister just won $250,000 in the lottery!

b Respond to **B**'s sentences with an exclamation beginning with either *How…!* or *What (a / an)…!* Make sure you use expressive intonation and link the words where appropriate.

← p.67

8A GUESS THE SENTENCE Student A

a Look at sentences 1–7 and imagine what the missing phrase could be. Remember: ⊞ = positive verb and ⊟ = negative verb.

> 1 I would love _____ the boss's face when you told him you were quitting. ⊞
> 2 There's no point _____. He never goes to parties. ⊞
> 3 It's no good _____ pay you back. She's completely broke. ⊞
> 4 We would rather _____ vacation in July, but in the end we had to go in August. ⊞
> 5 I absolutely hate _____ to do. I prefer to make my own mistakes. ⊞
> 6 You'd better _____. There are speed cameras on this road. ⊟
> 7 Jack completely denied _____ his ex-girlfriend again, but I don't believe him. ⊞

b **B** has the complete sentences 1–7. Read your sentences to **B**. Keep trying different possibilities until you get each sentence exactly right.

c Now listen to your partner's sentences. Tell them to keep guessing until they get it exactly the same as yours.

> 8 It's a very rewarding job that involves **working as a** team.
> 9 Lucy seems **to be seeing** Danny a lot recently. Do you think they're going out together?
> 10 We hope **to have found** a new apartment by the end of the year.
> 11 Our plan is **to drive to** the National Parks in Utah for two weeks in September.
> 12 There's absolutely **nothing to do** in this town. There isn't even a movie theater.
> 13 My father was the first person in my family **to go to** college.
> 14 I really regret **not having known** my grandfather. He died before I was born.

← p.78

WHAT KIND OF TRAVELER ARE YOU? Students A + B

Read about your traveler type. Then compare with a partner. Are the descriptions accurate for you? Would you be good vacation companions?

What kind of traveler are you?

Pampered princess

You're at your happiest when you're relaxing in the spa, indulging in beauty treatments, or simply curled up in a fluffy bathrobe sipping a fruit tea. You've worked hard all year, so it's time to put those freshly pedicured feet up and let everyone else take care of you. After all, you deserve it.

Action addict

You're not the average vacationer and following the typical tourist trail is never enough for you. You can't sit still for a minute – even on vacation. Whether it's extreme sports or going off the beaten track, you see every trip as an adventure.

Hippie at heart

You're a free spirit and love discovering far-flung places. Whether traveling alone or with an equally laid-back companion, it's all about going where the mood takes you. You have your guidebook and your roll-up mattress and the rest can take care of itself.

Culture vulture

You don't just want to visit a country – you want to immerse yourself in it. You'll see all the sights, learn the language, and find out about the history of a place. If you find the time to sit down, it's because you're sampling the local cuisine – no English menu for you, thank you very much!

Lazy cruiser

You like to take things at a slower pace on vacation – doing as much or as little as you please. You love being out on the ocean waves and you enjoy exploring new places, but you're equally happy sitting on deck taking in a beautiful sunset.

Beach bum

You're in your swimwear almost as soon as the plane touches down – and once you're on that sun-lounger, you won't be moving far. Reaching for your ice-cold drink is about as energetic as you get, and why not? That's what vacations are for, aren't they?

Happy camper

You like to get away from it all and you'll happily switch your creature comforts for a sleeping bag if it means waking up to birdsong every morning. Whatever you fill your days with, you'll do it at your leisure. And if it happens to rain buckets, it's all part of the fun.

City slicker

You love the buzz of the city and you'd rather hit the stores than the beach any day. You're happy to take in the famous sights and check all the touristy boxes – but you have to bring back a few souvenirs, right? It's the best way to explore a new city...

← p.80

9A MATCH THE SENTENCES Student A

a Read your sentences 1–6 to **B**. Make sure you stress auxiliaries where appropriate. **B** will choose a response.

> 1 Have you seen the latest Avengers movie?
> 2 I absolutely hate getting up early.
> 3 Is Lina coming swimming this afternoon?
> 4 Your brother lives in San Diego, doesn't he?
> 5 Your aunt doesn't drive, does she?
> 6 You do like cabbage, don't you?

b Now **B** will read you his / her sentences. Choose a response from below. Stress auxiliaries and *to* where appropriate.

> ☐ He is! He made the varsity team this year.
> ☐ I don't, but my partner does. I'm too lazy!
> ☐ No, and neither does her brother. Maybe they were adopted.
> ☐ No, there weren't. Where were you, by the way?
> ☐ She said she wanted to, but she wasn't sure if she'd be able to.
> ☐ We'd like to, but we're not sure if we can afford to.

c Practice the dialogues again, focusing on the stress.

⬅ p.88

3A BLIND DATE Student B

a Read what Graham says about his blind date with Stef. Then listen to **A** describing Stef's opinion of the date.

b Now, using your own words, tell **A** about Graham's opinion of the date. How do you think their relationship might develop?

> *(When Graham met Stef he thought she was beautiful. Unfortunately...*

Life & style ▶ Blind date

🏠 Previous | Next | Index

Graham on Stef

First impressions? Effortlessly beautiful and unforgivably late. But she had called.

What did you talk about? Music, cooking, and why Abba is the greatest pop band ever.

Any awkward moments? Not really.

Good table manners? I've never seen a burger crammed into a face with such grace and finesse.

Best thing about her? Anyone who knows the full routine to *Saturday Night Fever* and is prepared to strut their stuff scores highly with me.

Did you go on somewhere? Cash machine, bus stop.

Marks out of 10? 9. Would have been higher, but I lost a game of pool.

Would you meet again? Yes, it'd be great to do it again.

c Turn to p.113 and see if you were right!

⬅ p.28

3B GUESS THE SENTENCE Student B

a Look at sentences 6–10 and guess what the missing phrase could be. Remember: ⊞ = positive verb and ⊟ = negative verb.

> 6 I'm not sure you would enjoy the play, and in any case it will be very difficult _____ . ⊞
> 7 Some of the teachers aren't very inspiring, but on the whole I think it's _____ . ⊞
> 8 Laura's husband only thinks of himself and he always gets his own way. In other words, _____ . ⊞
> 9 I don't feel like going to Miranda's birthday party and besides, I _____ . ⊟
> 10 It's no big surprise that Leo didn't do very well on his exam. After all, he _____ . ⊟

b Listen to your partner's sentences. Tell them to keep guessing until they get it exactly the same as yours.

> 1 A lot of people say the book is better than the movie, but actually I **preferred the movie**.
> 2 It wasn't a particularly nice day for the barbecue, but at least it **didn't rain**.
> 3 The sea was blue, the sun was shining, and the picnic was marvelous. All in all, it was **a great day**.
> 4 On the one hand, dogs are much better company than any other pets, but on the other hand, you have to **take them for a walk** at least twice a day.
> 5 Make sure your suitcase weighs less than 40 pounds, otherwise you may **have to pay extra**.

c **A** has the complete sentences 6–10. Now read your sentences to **A**. Keep trying different possibilities until you get each sentence exactly right.

⬅ p.33

7A   QI QUIZ Student B

a   Read the answers to questions 7–12 of the quiz and remember the information.

b   **A** will tell you the answers to 1–6. Then explain the answers to 7–12 to **A** in your own words.

everything you think you know is probably wrong…

Qi

7   **Molotov didn't invent anything.** Molotov cocktails, handmade incendiary devices made from bottles filled with flammable liquid, were named after him as an insult by the Finns, who used them against the Russians during World War II. Molotov, who was the Soviet foreign minister, had authorized the invasion of Finland. The Finns had themselves copied the devices from weapons invented by Franco's forces during the Spanish Civil War.

8   The language most commonly spoken in ancient Rome was not Latin, but **Greek**. Rome was the capital city of a rapidly expanding empire and many of its inhabitants were not native-born Romans. **Koine**, or "common Greek," was the **lingua franca** used by all tradespeople and Greek was also the language of choice for Rome's elite, as it was considered more educated.

9   Although the Nile is usually associated with Egypt, in fact, most of it is in **Sudan**. The main river (the White Nile) rises in Rwanda and flows through six countries on its journey to the sea.

7A   WHAT A RIDICULOUS IDEA!
Student B

a   Respond to **A**'s sentences with an exclamation beginning with either *How…!* or *What (a / an)…!* Make sure you use expressive intonation and link the words where appropriate.

b   Read your sentences to **A**. He / She will respond with an exclamation.

   • I was at home all morning waiting for the electrician to come and they never showed up.
   • We're going to New York on Friday for a long weekend.
   • Jack's going to take Sue to the theater for their anniversary and then they're having a candlelit dinner at the new Italian restaurant.
   • My parents were robbed last night. They took all my mom's jewelry.
   • I failed the class even though I got a 70 on the final exam.
   • I really messed up at the party last night. I called Tom's wife "Anna," but that's his ex-wife's name!
   • Maria's husband collects old rock and roll albums. He has hundreds of them.

← p.67

10   Apart from **Margaret Thatcher**, Prime Minister of Great Britain from 1979–1990, who was given this nickname, it could also be **the Eiffel Tower** in Paris. It was called "The Iron Lady" because of the material used to make it.

11   A game that involved kicking a leather ball stuffed with fur or feathers and trying to score a goal without using hands was played in **China** over 2,000 years ago. The game was called **cuju**, and it was first recorded in the 5th century BC.

12   His full name is Cristiano Ronaldo **dos Santos Aveiro**, so his last name is dos Santos Aveiro. He was called Ronaldo after the US president Ronald Reagan, who his parents admired.

← p.66

8A GUESS THE SENTENCE Student B

a Look at sentences 8–14 and imagine what the missing phrase could be. Remember: ⊞ = positive verb and ⊟ = negative verb.

> 8 It's a very rewarding job that involves _____ team. ⊞
>
> 9 Lucy seems _____ Danny a lot recently. Do you think they're going out together? ⊞
>
> 10 We hope _____ a new apartment by the end of the year. ⊞
>
> 11 Our plan is _____ the National Parks in Utah for two weeks in September. ⊞
>
> 12 There's absolutely _____ in this town. There isn't even a movie theater. ⊟
>
> 13 My father was the first person in my family _____ college. ⊞
>
> 14 I really regret _____ my grandfather. He died before I was born. ⊟

b Listen to your partner's sentences. Tell them to keep guessing until they get it exactly the same as yours.

> 1 I would love **to have seen** the boss's face when you told him you were quitting.
>
> 2 There's no point **inviting him**. He never goes to parties.
>
> 3 It's no good **expecting her to** pay you back. She's completely broke.
>
> 4 We would rather **have gone on** vacation in July, but in the end we had to go in August.
>
> 5 I absolutely hate **being told what** to do. I prefer to make my own mistakes.
>
> 6 You'd better **not drive so fast**. There are speed cameras on this road.
>
> 7 Jack completely denied **having seen** his ex-girlfriend again, but I don't believe him.

c **A** has the complete sentences 8–14. Now read your sentences to **A**. Keep trying different possibilities until you get each sentence exactly right.

← p.78

9A MATCH THE SENTENCES Student B

a **A** will read you his / her sentences. Choose a response from below. Make sure you stress auxiliaries and *to* where appropriate.

> ☐ I love it. It's cauliflower I can't stand.
> ☐ No, she doesn't, but she owns three cars.
> ☐ No, but I'd love to.
> ☐ She isn't, but her children are. She didn't want to.
> ☐ So do I. Luckily I don't often have to.
> ☐ Yes, and so does my sister.

b Now read your sentences 7–12 to **A**. Make sure you stress auxiliaries where appropriate. **A** will choose a response.

> 7 Are you going to go skiing during winter break?
> 8 Katie doesn't look like her parents, does she?
> 9 Were there many people in class yesterday?
> 10 Do you do a lot of gardening?
> 11 Erica did say she was coming, didn't she?
> 12 Adam isn't particularly good at tennis, is he?

c Practice all 12 mini-dialogues again, making sure you get the stress right.

← p.88

3A BLIND DATE Students A + B

Life & style Blind date

🏠 Previous | Next | Index

Stef and Graham on their wedding day

← p.28

Writing

A JOB APPLICATION

ANALYZING A MODEL TEXT

a You see the following advertisement on the Skyscanner website. Would you be interested in applying for the job? Why (not)?

Skyscanner

Receptionist

Location: Miami

The receptionist is the first point of contact for staff and visitors. The role involves a variety of tasks including answering and directing calls, welcoming visitors, scheduling meetings, and general administration support.

Core hours are 8 a.m.–6 p.m. and you will need to be available to work earlier shifts some days and later shifts other days.

About you:

The ideal candidate will have a customer-focused personality with a strong can-do attitude. We're looking for someone with proven communication skills for liaising with individuals at all levels in a very fast-moving environment.

Interested? The closing date for applications is Wednesday, June 18—click "Apply" before this opportunity flies away!

b Read the first draft of an email written in response to the advertisement. What information does Azra give in the three main paragraphs?

To:	irena.foster@skyscanner.net
From:	Azra Osman
Subject:	Application

Dear ~~Miss~~ *Ms.* Foster,

~~My name is Azra Osman.~~ I am writing to apply for the position of receptionist advertised in your website.

1 I have recently graduated from Ankara University, where I completed a degree in business studies. I have a high level of spoken english (C1 on the CEFR), as I lived in the United States during six months as part of an ekchange programm between my school and a high school in Utah. I made many American friends during this period, but we lost touch when I came home.

2 As you will see from my résumé, I have some relevant experience because I am currently an intern at a leading Turkish travel company. I have worked in various roles, including marketing asistant and administrator and my tasks have included organizing and running meetings and dealing with clients by phone and email. The director of company would be happy to provide a reference. He is, in fact, my uncle.

3 I am very enthusiastic on travel and would welcome the chance to be part of such a high-profile and successful company. I believe I would be suitable for the job advertised as, apart of my work experience, I am an outgoing person and get along well with people. Friends describe me as calm and consciensious and I would enjoy the variety and excitement the job would offer. I would definitely not panic when things got busy!

I attach a full résumé and if you require a further information, I would be very happy to provide it.
I look forward to hearing from you.

Yours sincerely,
Azra Osman

🔍 **Improving your first draft**
Check your writing for correct paragraphing, mistakes, irrelevant information, and language that is in an inappropriate register.

c Read the draft email again and try to improve it.

1 Cross out three sentences (not including the example) that are irrelevant or inappropriate.
2 Correct ten more mistakes in the highlighted phrases, including spelling, capital letters, grammar, and vocabulary.

d Do you think Skyscanner would have given her an interview if she had sent her first draft?

e Look at 1–9 below. How did Azra express these ideas in a more formal way? Use the **bold** word(s) to help you remember. Then look at the text again to check your answers.

1 This letter is to ask you to give me the job of receptionist. **apply**
   I am writing to apply for the position of receptionist.

2 I've just finished college, where I did business studies.
   graduate / degree
   _____

3 I can speak English very well. **high**
   _____

4 I've done this kind of job before. **relevant**
   _____

5 My tasks have included talking to people on the phone.
   dealing / clients
   _____

6 I'd love to work for such a famous company.
   welcome / high-profile
   _____

7 I'm sending a full résumé with this email. **attach**
   _____

8 If you need to know anything else, I'll tell you. **require / provide**
   _____

9 Hope to hear from you soon! **forward**
   _____

PLANNING WHAT TO WRITE

a Read the job advertisement below and underline the information you will need to respond to. Then make notes about:

- any qualifications you have.
- any relevant experience you could include.
- what aspects of your personality you think would make you suitable for the job and how you could illustrate them.
- any other information you think you need to include.

Festival staff members needed to work at Global Stage, a world music event in California from July 12th to 14th

Responsibilities
- To ensure the safety and comfort of the public and to assist in the running of a successful festival.
- To reduce any crowd-related problems, including maintaining a state of calm to minimize any injury.
- To prevent unauthorized access to the site by members of the public.

Requirements
- You must be 18 or older on the date of the festival and be eligible to work in the US.
- You must be physically fit and healthy and able to work under pressure in a demanding atmosphere.
- You should speak English well and have some experience dealing with the public.

How to apply
Send an email and full résumé to Emma Richards: e.richards@worldmusic.org

---

b Compare notes with a partner and discuss how relevant you think each other's information is, what you think you should leave out, and what else you might want to include.

TIPS for writing a cover email / letter to apply for a job, grant, etc.

- Use appropriate sentences to open the email / letter.
- Organize the main body of the email / letter into clear paragraphs.
- Use a suitable style:
  Don't use contractions or very informal expressions.
  Use formal vocabulary where appropriate, e.g., _require_ instead of _need_, _as_ instead of _because_.
  The use of a conditional can often sound more polite, e.g., _I would welcome the chance to…_
- When you say why you think you are suitable for the job, be factual and positive, but not overconfident. Be careful not to sound arrogant.
- Use appropriate phrases to close the email / letter.

WRITING

You have decided to apply for the festival job advertised to the left. Write a cover email of between 200 and 250 words.

DRAFT your email.
- Write an introductory sentence to explain why you are writing.
- Paragraph 1: Give personal information including skills and qualifications.
- Paragraph 2: Talk about any relevant experience you have.
- Paragraph 3: Explain why you think you would be suitable for the job.
- Write a closing sentence.

EDIT the email, checking paragraphing, cutting any irrelevant information, and making sure it is the right length.

CHECK the email for mistakes in grammar, spelling, punctuation, and register.
◀ p.11

WRITING AN ARTICLE

ANALYZING A MODEL TEXT

a You are going to read an article about childhood covering the areas below. What information would you include if you were writing about your country?

   • What are the main differences between children's lives 50 years ago and children's lives now?
   • Why have these changes occurred?
   • Do you think the changes are positive or negative?

b Now read the article. Did the writer include any of your ideas? With a partner, choose what you think is the best title from the options below and say why you prefer it to the others.

   How childhood has changed
   Children of the past
   My childhood

c Answer the questions with a partner.

   1 What is the effect of the direct question in the introduction? Where is it answered?
   2 What does paragraph 1 focus on? What examples are given?
   3 What are the changes that the writer focuses on in paragraph 2 and what reasons are given for the changes? Do you agree?
   4 Underline the discourse markers that are used to link the points in paragraphs 2 and 3, e.g., *First…*

Children's lives have changed enormously over the last 50 years. But do they have happier childhoods?

1 It's difficult to look back on one's own childhood without some element of nostalgia. I have four brothers and sisters and my memories are all about being with them, playing board games on the living room floor, or spending days outside with the other neighborhood children, racing around on our bikes, or exploring the nearby woods. My parents hardly ever appear in these memories, except as providers either of meals or of severe reprimands after some particularly hazardous adventure.

2 These days, in the US at least, the nature of childhood has changed dramatically since the 1960s. First, families are smaller and there are far more only children. It is common for both parents to work outside the home and far fewer people have the time to bring up a large family. As a result, today's boys and girls spend much of their time alone. Another major change is that youngsters today tend to spend a huge proportion of their free time at home, inside. This is due more than anything to the fact that parents worry much more than they used to about real or imagined dangers, so they wouldn't dream of letting their children play outside by themselves.

3 Finally, the kinds of toys children have and the way they play is totally different. Computer and video games have replaced the board games and more active pastimes of my childhood. The fact that they can play electronic games on their own further increases the sense of isolation felt by many young people today. The irony is that so many of these devices are called "interactive."

4 Do these changes mean that children today have a less idyllic childhood than I had? I personally believe that they do, but perhaps every generation feels exactly the same.

USEFUL LANGUAGE

> 🔍 **Using synonyms**
> Try not to repeat the same words and phrases too often in your writing. Instead, where possible, use a synonym or similar expression if you can think of one. This will both make the text more varied for the reader and help to link the article together. A good monolingual dictionary or thesaurus can help you.

d Find synonyms in the article for…
1 at the present time _____ , _____
2 children _____ , _____ , _____
3 alone, without adults _____ , _____

> 🔍 **Using richer vocabulary**
> You can make your writing more colorful and interesting to read by trying to use a richer range of vocabulary instead of the most obvious words.

e Can you remember how the words in *italics* were expressed in the article, to make the style more interesting?
1 Children's lives have changed *in a big way*… _____
2 …spending days outside with the other *children who lived near us*… _____
3 …*going* around *fast* on our bikes… _____
4 My parents *don't* appear *very often* in these memories… _____
5 …after some particularly *dangerous* adventure. _____
6 …*usually both parents* work outside the home _____
7 …that children today have a less *happy* childhood than I had? _____

PLANNING WHAT TO WRITE

a Look at the test question below.

> Many aspects of life have changed over the last 30 years. These include:
>
> **marriage   dating   the role of women and / or men**
>
> Write an article for an online magazine about how <u>one</u> of these areas has changed in your country and say whether you think these changes are positive or negative.

With a partner, brainstorm for each topic…
1 what the situation used to be like.
2 whether the situation has changed a lot in your country.
3 whether you think the changes are positive or negative and why.

Now decide which topic you are going to write about and which ideas you want to include.

b Think of a possible title for your article.

TIPS for writing an article:
- Remember that this is not an essay. In an essay, you would focus on the most important points, but for an article, you should choose the points that you could say something interesting about, or where you can think of any interesting personal examples.
- There is no fixed structure for an article, but it is important to have clear paragraphs. Use discourse markers to link your points or arguments.
- Use a suitable style, neither very formal nor very informal.
- Make the introduction reasonably short. You could use a question or questions that you then answer in the article.
- Try to engage the reader, e.g., by referring to your personal experience.
- Vary your vocabulary using synonyms where possible.

WRITING

Write an article of between 200 and 250 words.

DRAFT your article.
- Write a brief introduction that refers to the changes and asks a question.
- Write two or three main paragraphs saying what the situation used to be like and how it has changed.
- Write a conclusion that refers back to the question in the introduction and that says whether you think the changes are positive or negative.

EDIT the article, checking paragraphing, cutting any irrelevant information, and making sure it is the right length.

CHECK the article for mistakes in grammar, spelling, punctuation, and register.

⬅ p.21

WRITING A REVIEW

ANALYZING A MODEL TEXT

a Which of the following would normally influence you to read a book?

- a friend of yours recommended it
- it's a bestseller—everybody is reading it
- you saw and enjoyed a movie based on it
- you were told to read it at school
- you read a good review of it

b Read the book review. In which paragraph 1–4 do you find the following information? Write **DS** if the review doesn't say. Does the review make you want to read the book?

- [ ] the strong points of the book
- [ ] the basic outline of the plot
- [ ] what happens in the end
- [ ] where and when the story is set
- [ ] the weakness(es) of the book
- [ ] whether the reviewer recommends the book or not
- [ ] who the author is
- [ ] who the main characters are
- [ ] how much the book costs
- [ ] who the book will appeal to

c Look at these extracts from a first draft. Which words did the reviewer leave out or change to make it more concise? Then read the information box about **Participle clauses** to check.

1 A thriller, **which is set in the present day** in a small town in Missouri in the US, it immediately became an international bestseller.

2 …a couple, Nick and Amy Dunne, **who are now living in Nick's hometown** of Carthage,…

3 Nick now owns a bar, **which was opened with his wife's money**, which he runs with his sister Margo.

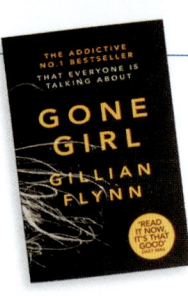

1 *Gone Girl* is the third novel by American writer Gillian Flynn. A thriller, set in the present day in a small town in Missouri in the US, it immediately became an international bestseller.

2 The main characters in the novel are a couple, Nick and Amy Dunne, now living in Nick's hometown of Carthage, after Nick lost his job as a journalist in New York City. Nick now owns a bar, opened with his wife's money, which he runs with his sister Margo. On the day of his fifth wedding anniversary, Nick discovers that his wife, Amy, is missing. For various reasons, he becomes a prime suspect in her disappearance. The first half of the book is told in the first person, alternately by Nick, and then by Amy through extracts from her journal. The two stories are totally different: Nick describes Amy as stubborn and antisocial whereas she makes him out to be aggressive and difficult. As a result, the reader is left guessing whether Nick is guilty or not. In the second half, however, the reader realizes that neither Nick nor Amy have been telling the truth in their account of the marriage. The resulting situation has unexpected consequences for Nick, Amy, and the reader.

3 The great strength of this book is how the characters of Nick and Amy unfold. Despite having the typical devices common to thrillers, for example, several possible suspects and plenty of red herrings, the novel is also a psychological analysis of the effect on personalities of failure and disappointed dreams. My only criticism would be that the first half goes on too long and perhaps could have been slightly cut down.

4 Not only is this a complex and absolutely gripping novel, but it also tackles real problems in society, such as the unhappiness that is caused by problems with the economy and the effect of the media on a crime investigation. For all lovers of psychological thrillers, *Gone Girl* is a must.

> **Glossary**
> **red herring** an unimportant fact, event, idea, etc., that takes people's attention from the important one

---

🔎 **Participle clauses**

The writer uses participles (*set, living, opened*) instead of a subject + verb. Past participles replace verbs in the passive, and present participles (*-ing* forms) replace verbs in the active. The subject of the clause is usually the same as the subject of the main clause.

Participle clauses can be used:

- instead of a conjunction (*after, as, when, because, although*, etc.) + subject + verb, e.g., *Having run out of money…* instead of *Because she has run out of money…*
- instead of a relative clause, e.g., *set in the present day / opened with his wife's money* instead of *which is set… / which was opened…*

When you use a participle clause, you do not need to link the next clause with *and*, e.g., *It is set in 1903 and it tells the story of a young girl…* ➜ *Set in 1903, it tells the story…*

d Rewrite the sentences, making the highlighted phrases more concise by using participle clauses.

1 As she believes him to be the murderer, Anya is absolutely terrified.

_____

2 Armelle, who was forced to marry a man she did not love, decided to throw herself into her work.

_____

3 Simon, who realizes that the police are after him, tries to escape.

_____

4 It was first published in 1903 and it has been reprinted many times.

_____

5 When he hears the shot, Mark rushes into the house.

_____

6 It is based on his wartime journals and it tells the story of a young soldier.

_____

USEFUL LANGUAGE

The two stories are totally different…

…and perhaps could have been slightly cut down.

e Underline the adverbs of degree in these phrases from the review. What effect do they have on the adjectives?

f Cross out any adverbs that don't fit in these sentences. Check (✓) if all are possible.

1 My only criticism is that the plot is **somewhat / slightly / a little** implausible.
2 The last chapter is **really / very / absolutely** fascinating.
3 The end of the novel is **rather / pretty / quite** disappointing.
4 The denouement is **absolutely / incredibly / extremely** thrilling.

PLANNING WHAT TO WRITE

a Think of a book or movie that you have read or seen recently. Make a list of the main things about the characters and plot that you should cover in a review. Don't include a spoiler. Use the present tense and try to include at least one participle clause.

b Exchange your list with other students to see if they can identify the book or movie.

TIPS for writing a book / movie review:
- Choose a book or movie that you know well.
- Organize the review into clear paragraphs.
- Use a suitable style, neither very formal nor very informal.
- Give your reader a brief idea of the plot, but do not give away the whole story. This is only part of your review, so choose only the main events and be as concise as possible.
- Use the present tense when you describe the plot. Using participle clauses will help to keep it concise.
- Use a range of adjectives that describe as precisely as possible how the book or movie made you feel, e.g., _gripping, moving_, etc. (see p.41). Use adverbs of degree to modify them, e.g., _absolutely gripping_.
- Remember that an effective review will include both praise and criticism.

WRITING

A student magazine has asked for reviews of recent books and movies. Write a review of between 200 and 250 words.

DRAFT your review.
- Paragraph 1: Include the title of the book or movie, the genre, the author or director, and where / when it is set.
- Paragraph 2: Describe the plot, including information about the main characters.
- Paragraph 3: Talk about what you liked and any criticisms you may have.
- Paragraph 4: Give a summary of your opinion and a recommendation.

EDIT the review, making sure you've covered all the main points, checking paragraphing, cutting any irrelevant information, and making sure it is the right length.

CHECK the review for mistakes in grammar, spelling, punctuation, and register.

⬅ p.41

WRITING A DISCURSIVE ESSAY (1): A BALANCED ARGUMENT

KEY SUCCESS FACTORS

- constructing an argument on both sides
- writing an effective introduction and conclusion
- using appropriate discourse markers to contrast and balance points

ANALYZING A MODEL TEXT

a   You have been asked to write the following essay:

Do smartphones really improve our lives?

With a partner, discuss three reasons why you think smartphones make our lives better and three reasons why they do not. Order them 1–3 according to their importance.

b   Read the model essay and check if the writer has mentioned some or all of your arguments. Where does the writer put the main argument in each paragraph?

🔍 **Introductions and conclusions**

- In an essay, it is important that the introduction engages the reader's attention. A good introductory paragraph describes the present situation and gives supporting evidence. It should introduce the topic, but should not include the specific points that you are going to mention in the body of the text. It should refer to the statement or question you have been asked to discuss. This can often be done in the form of a question to the reader, which the subsequent paragraphs should answer.

- The conclusion should briefly sum up the arguments you have made and can include your personal opinion. The opinion you express should follow logically from the arguments you have presented. It is important that this is not just a repetition of your arguments. It is a summary of what you believe your arguments have proved.

Do smartphones really improve our lives?

Introduction

Arguments in favor

Perhaps the greatest benefit of smartphones is that they give us an incredible amount of information. They are not just phones—we can also use them as maps, encyclopedias, novels, entertainment systems, and much more. We live in an age of information and smartphones help us to make the most of it all. In addition, they allow us to live our lives spontaneously. Whether you need a taxi, have to make reservations at a restaurant, or want to identify stars in the night sky, you can do it immediately. Finally, they keep us in touch with our friends and family and the social role they play in a fast-moving society is hugely important.

Arguments against

However, there are strong arguments to suggest that the advantages of smartphones can also be disadvantages. One drawback is the cost—monthly contracts are far from cheap and smartphones tend to become obsolete quickly, so people feel they need to buy the newest model. What is more, they are a constant distraction and they encourage people to spend hours checking social networking sites when they could be doing something more useful. But perhaps the most significant downside is for professionals. On the one hand, smartphones offer great convenience, but they also mean that employees can be contacted by their boss all the time, even on vacation.

Conclusion

c   Read the information box. Then look at the three introductory paragraphs below and choose which one you think is best for the essay. Compare with a partner. Discuss why you think it is the best and why the other two are less suitable. Then do the same with the concluding paragraphs.

Introductions

1   Smartphones dominate the field of personal communications and it sometimes seems that nearly everyone owns one. The technology is universal, but do smartphones really make our lives better?

2   Smartphones clearly have important advantages and disadvantages. In this essay, I am first going to analyze the advantages of this technology and then I will outline some important disadvantages, before finally drawing my conclusions.

3   Can you imagine life without your smartphone? Probably not, as this fantastic technology has become such a crucial tool for our work and social lives. So how did we manage before smartphones were invented?

Conclusions

1 To sum up, smartphones have both advantages and disadvantages, but all things considered, I believe that their influence is entirely beneficial—after all, we could not live without them.

2 In conclusion, smartphones have improved our lives considerably in my view, especially if you want to use the internet. They are very useful, for example, if you are in a store and you decide to buy something online instead.

3 On the whole, smartphones are a wonderful tool, but they have both pros and cons and they have to be used appropriately. It is very important that we control them and not the other way around.

USEFUL LANGUAGE

d Complete the missing words. Some (but not all) are in the model essay.

Expressing the main points in an argument

+
1 The greatest **b**_____ is that…
2 **First and most im**_____, smartphones give us an incredible amount of information.

−
3 One **d**_____ of smartphones is that…
4 Another **dr**_____ to smartphones is that monthly contracts can be expensive.

Adding supporting information to a main argument, or introducing other related arguments

5 In **a**_____
6 **What is m**_____
7 **Not o**_____ **that**, but…
8 **Another point in f**_____ of this technology is that smartphones allow us to live our lives spontaneously.

Weighing up arguments

9 **On the wh**_____,
10 **On b**_____,
11 **A**_____ **in a**_____,
12 **All things c**_____, smartphones have both pros and cons.

PLANNING WHAT TO WRITE

a Look at the essay titles below and, with a partner, choose one of them. Brainstorm the pros and cons. Then decide on three main arguments on each side that are relevant to the title.

The growth of online shopping has greatly improved life for the consumer.

Ready-made meals have revolutionized eating at home—but at what price?

b Write an introduction for the essay. Follow this pattern:

1 Write an introductory sentence about how important online shopping or ready-made meals have become.
2 Write a second sentence supporting the first one.
3 Ask the main question that you intend to answer in the essay.

c Compare your introduction with a partner. Together, make a final version.

TIPS for writing a discursive essay giving both sides of an argument:

• Brainstorm points for and against and decide which two or three you think are the most important.
• Use a neutral or formal style.
• Write a clear introduction that engages the reader. You could end the introduction with a question you are going to answer.
• An essay is not just a list of ideas and opinions. Link your ideas in a logical sequence. Use phrases to order, contrast, and weigh up the points in your argument.
• Make sure your conclusion is a summary of what you have previously said and refers back to what you were asked to write about.

WRITING

Write an essay of between 200 and 250 words.

DRAFT your essay.
• Paragraph 1: Write an introduction.
• Paragraph 2: Give arguments in favor of online shopping or ready-made meals.
• Paragraph 3: Give arguments against online shopping or ready-made meals.
• Paragraph 4: Write your conclusion, saying whether you think the advantages outweigh the disadvantages or vice versa.

EDIT the essay, making sure you've covered the main points, cutting any irrelevant information, and making sure it is the right length.

CHECK the essay for mistakes in grammar, spelling, punctuation, and register.

◀ p.63

Go online for more Writing practice

WRITING A REPORT

ANALYZING A MODEL TEXT

a The owners of a language school are doing some research into student satisfaction and have asked several students to interview all the students at the school and write a report. Read their report and then, from memory, tell a partner what the school's main strengths and weaknesses are in each area.

b Can you remember how some of the highlighted phrases below were expressed in a more formal way? Then look at the text again to check your answers.

1 What this report is for is…
The _____ is…

2 … is to find out how happy students are with the classes and facilities.
… is to _____ with the classes and facilities.

3 In general, students thought the teachers were very good.
In general, students _____.

4 About class sizes, most students think there should be no more than 12 students in a class.
_____, most students think there should be no more than 12 students in a class.

5 As for how long the classes last, they officially last an hour…
_____, they officially last an hour…

6 We suggest buying more computers…
We suggest _____ more computers…

7 Most students are extremely positive…
_____ are extremely positive…

8 …that if you make the changes we suggest, it will be an even better place to study.
…that _____, it will be an even better place to study.

English Time Language School

A report

Introduction
The aim of this report is to assess student satisfaction with the classes and facilities at the English Time Language School and to make suggestions for improvements.

Testing and registration of new students
Most students were satisfied with the testing process for new students. However, they complained about the long lines at registration. We believe it would be preferable either to have more staff members available to deal with registration, or to give students a specific day and time to register.

The classes
In general, students rated the teachers very highly. Their main criticisms were of class sizes and the length of classes. With regard to class sizes, most students think there should be no more than 12 students in a class. In terms of the duration of classes, they officially last an hour, but in practice they are usually only 45 minutes because of latecomers. We propose that all students who arrive more than five minutes late should have to wait until the break for admittance.

The self-study center
It is generally thought that the self-study center, while useful, has two major drawbacks. There are not enough computers and at peak times they are always occupied. Also, the center closes at 7 p.m., so students who come to the later classes cannot use the center at all. We suggest purchasing more computers and extending the center's hours to 9 p.m.

The cafeteria
The cafeteria was recently replaced by vending machines for drinks and snacks. Although it is true that people often had to wait to be served, most students greatly preferred the cafeteria and would like it to be reopened.

Conclusion
Overall, the majority of students are extremely positive about the school and feel that if the suggested changes are implemented, it will be an even better place to study.

c Complete the missing words. Some (but not all) are in the model report.

Some common expressions for generalizing

1 **In g_____** , people think…
2 **Generally sp_____** , people think…
3 **It is generally co_____** / thought…
4 **The general v_____** is that certain improvements need to be made.
5 **Ov_____** , the majority of students think…

d Rewrite the following sentences.

Making suggestions

1 Please buy new computers.
   We suggest _____
   _____ .

2 The registration process ought to be improved.
   It would be advisable _____
   _____ .

3 Why don't you make the classes smaller?
   We propose _____
   _____ .

4 You really should extend the center's hours.
   I strongly recommend _____
   _____ .

5 It would be much better if classes lasted an hour.
   It would be far preferable for classes
   _____
   _____ .

 p.69

PLANNING WHAT TO WRITE

a Read the following task and study the relevant information. Then, with a partner, decide:

1 how many headings you will need and what they should be.
2 how to express the relevant information in your own words.
3 what suggestions for improvements could be made under each heading.

> Your language school has just started four-week study trips to the US. You have been asked by the principal of the school to get feedback from all the students who participated in the first trip and write a report detailing what students were positive about, what problems they had, and making suggestions for improving future study trips.
>
> You have made the following notes about the views of the majority of participants:
>
> – *People with families much happier than ones who stayed in the dormatories, because they were able to practice their English with the families.*
> – *School OK and classes good, but almost everyone complained about the lunch (just a sandwich). Some thought six hours a day too much.*
> – *People not very interested in some weekend cultural programs. Trips to New York City and Philadelphia great, to Gettysburg and Valley Forge boring. On all trips too much sightseeing and not enough time for shopping!*

b Together, suggest improvements to the study trips, beginning with a different expression each time.

TIPS for writing a report:

- Look carefully at who the report is for and what they need to know. This will help you choose what information you have to include.
- Decide what the sections of the report are going to be and think of headings for them.
- Use an appropriate professional style, avoiding very informal expressions.
- In the introduction, state what the aim of the report is.
- For each paragraph, state the situation (strengths and weaknesses) and then make a recommendation.
- If on a test you are given information on which to base your report, try not to use exactly the same words.
- Use a variety of expressions for generalizing and making suggestions.

WRITING

Write a report of between 200 and 250 words.

DRAFT your report, using the headings and suggestions you worked on in the planning stage.

EDIT the report, making sure you've covered all the main points, checking paragraphing, cutting any irrelevant information, and making sure it is the right length.

CHECK the report for mistakes in grammar, spelling, punctuation, and register.

WRITING A DISCURSIVE ESSAY (2): TAKING SIDES

KEY SUCCESS FACTORS

- constructing an argument
- sustaining your case with examples
- showing that you have considered the opposing viewpoint

ANALYZING A MODEL TEXT

a   You have been asked to write the following essay:

Tourism always does a place more harm than good.

Discuss the question with a partner. Do you think that the effect of tourism on a country, city, or region is in general more positive or more negative? Why?

> 🔍 **Topic sentences**
> In a well-written essay, the first sentence of a paragraph usually establishes what the paragraph is going to be about. This is sometimes called the "topic sentence."

b   In pairs, read each topic sentence below and imagine how the paragraph will continue. Do you think the essay will be in favor of or against tourism?

A   The infrastructure of an area is also often improved as a result of tourism.

B   It is often claimed that popular tourist destinations are spoiled as a result of over-development.

C   Tourism is one of the world's great growth industries.

D   Another point in favor of tourism is that governments are becoming aware of the need to protect tourist areas in order to attract visitors.

E   The main positive effect of tourism is on local economies and employment.

c   Now read the model essay and match topic sentences A–E to paragraphs 1–5.

Tourism always does a place more harm than good

1   _____ People today are traveling further and further, not only in the summer, but throughout the year. Although some people argue that mass tourism has a negative effect on destinations, in my view its influences are generally positive.

2   _____ Tourists need places to stay and things to do and this creates a wide range of jobs for local people. Vacationers also spend a great deal of money, which stimulates the economy of the region as well as benefiting the country as a whole.

3   _____ For example, when tourists start visiting an area, roads and public transportation tend to improve, or an airport may be built, all of which benefit local people as well as tourists.

4   _____ This is leading to better conservation not only of areas of natural beauty and endangered habitats in rural areas, but also of historic buildings and monuments in towns and cities.

5   _____ For instance, many people argue that tourist development results in ugly hotels and apartment buildings. This may have been true in the past, but nowadays developers recognize that new buildings should blend in with old ones and should not change the character of a place.

6   To sum up, I believe that, on the whole, tourism has a positive influence provided its development is properly planned and controlled. Tourist destinations have a lot to gain from visitors and the business they bring. In my opinion, it is possible for both tourists and local people to benefit and for popular tourist destinations to have a sustainable future.

d Read each paragraph again, with its topic sentence. Answer the questions with a partner.

1 Where does the writer state his overall opinion about tourism?
2 How many arguments are given to support his view?
3 What is the purpose of paragraph 5?

🔍 **Using synonyms and richer vocabulary**
When you are writing an essay, remember to vary and enrich your vocabulary by using synonyms where appropriate.

---

e Find synonyms in the essay for the following words and expressions:

1 tourists   _____ , _____
2 effects   _____
3 for example _____
4 in general   _____ , _____

USEFUL LANGUAGE

f Complete the missing words. Some (but not all) are in the model essay.

Giving personal opinions
1 I **b**_____ that…
2 I **f**_____ that…
3 **In my v**_____, the influences of tourism are generally positive.
4 **In my o**_____, …
5 **P**_____, I think that…

Introducing opposite arguments
6 Some / Many people **ar**_____…
7 It is often **cl**_____ **that** popular destinations are spoiled by tourism.
8 There are **th**_____ who say…

Refuting them
9 This **m**_____ **h**_____ been true in the past, but **n**_____…
10 There are a number of **fl**_____ in this argument.
11 That is simply not the **c**_____ .

PLANNING WHAT TO WRITE

a Read the essay titles below. For each one, decide which side of the argument you are going to take, and think of three or four reasons with examples.

Drivers should be charged for using roads linking major towns and cities.

Our lifestyles are less healthy than our grandparents'.

b Compare with a partner. Decide which you think are the three most important reasons. Decide on typical opposing arguments that you could refute.

c Choose which of the essays you are going to write. Decide on the main paragraphs and write topic sentences for each one. Show your topic sentences to a partner and see if you can improve each other's sentences.

TIPS for writing a discursive essay where you take one side of an argument:

• Organize your essay into paragraphs, with a clear introduction and conclusion (see *p.120*).
• Begin each paragraph with a clear topic sentence and then develop the idea.
• Use synonyms to avoid repeating yourself.
• Use a variety of phrases for giving your opinion and introducing an opposing argument and refuting it.

WRITING

Write an essay of between 200 and 250 words on one of the topics above.

DRAFT your essay.
• Introduction: Introduce the topic and state your opinion.
• Main argument: Write two or three paragraphs giving your reasons.
• Opposing arguments: Write a paragraph stating one or more common opposing arguments and refuting each one.
• Conclusion: Sum up, stating what your arguments have shown.

EDIT the essay, making sure you've covered the main points, cutting any irrelevant information, and making sure it is the right length.

CHECK the essay for mistakes in grammar, spelling, punctuation, and register.
 p.81

WRITING A COMPLAINT

KEY SUCCESS FACTORS
- summarizing the issue clearly
- maintaining an assertive but respectful tone
- being clear and reasonable about what you expect to be done

ANALYZING A MODEL TEXT

a Have you ever had a very bad experience at a restaurant or a hotel? What happened? Did you make a complaint either in person or in writing? What response did you get?

b Read the model formal email. What exactly is the complaint about?

To: manager@fiorellis-nyc.net
From: a.knight10798@gmail.com
Subject: Complaint

Dear Sir or Madam,

1   I am writing to complain about the meal that my husband and I had on Thursday, March 16th, at Fiorelli's on Riverside Street. ¹_____ that the dinner ²_____ .

2   First of all, according to our online reservation, the table was booked for 7:00 and we ³_____ leave the table by 9:00, which we ⁴_____ . However, the service was extremely slow and at 8:45, we had only just been brought our dessert. At this point, the waiter not only brought us the check, but also asked us to hurry because he would need the table back very soon. This left us feeling extremely ⁵_____ .

3   Second, when we were ordering our meal, the waiter recommended several dishes that were not on the menu and we both chose *tagliatelli al tartufo.* We assumed that the price of this item would be in line with those on the menu, ⁶_____ , between $10 and $15. However, when the waiter brought the check, we discovered that ⁷_____ a total of $50, making them more than twice as expensive. When we complained to the waiter, he said that we should have asked the price when we ordered; however, in my opinion the waiter himself should have pointed out that this dish was considerably more expensive than the other choices.

4   I feel strongly that if customers are given a table that has a time limit, the service should be efficient enough to ensure that ⁸_____ within that time. I also think that, while it is understandable that some of the daily "specials" may be more expensive because of the ingredients used, this should always be made clear from the start.

5   Under the circumstances, we believe that ⁹_____ and that we should receive ¹⁰_____ . I look forward to hearing your views on this matter.

Respectfully,
Andrew Knight

---

c With a partner, discuss which phrase, **a** or **b**, is better for each blank and why.

1   a   I'm sorry to say
     b   I am afraid to say
2   a   did not live up to our expectations
     b   was a complete disaster
3   a   were requested to
     b   were told we had to
4   a   thought was OK
     b   considered reasonable
5   a   fed up
     b   dissatisfied
6   a   that is to say
     b   I mean
7   a   we had been charged
     b   you had charged us
8   a   they can eat their food
     b   their meal can easily be completed
9   a   we are owed an apology
     b   you ought to say sorry
10 a   some form of compensation
     b   a lot of money back

d Can you remember how the writer expressed the following in a more formal way? Then look at the text again to check your answers.

1 In this letter I want to complain…

2 It said on our online booking…

3 The waiter gave us the check <u>and</u> asked us to hurry.

4 I really think that if customers are given a table…

5 I'd like to know what you think about this.

PLANNING WHAT TO WRITE

a Read part of a website post by Hannah. What problems did she have at the Westfield Hotel?

Hannah Jones
2 hours ago

Just got back from Florida. That's the last time we stay at the Westfield Hotel! We stayed there a couple of years ago and had a good time, so I booked again for a week in April. The website described it just as I remembered it and said you could order food from the hotel kitchen in the evening—you know what a pain it is to have to go out with the kids, much easier to get room service—so I just went ahead and booked. Anyway, when we got there we were totally speechless! The kitchen and restaurant were under construction and they said that in fact they didn't do any food except for breakfast because of the construction. It was too late to find anywhere else, so we decided to stay, but it was a nightmare. The constructions workers started making noise at 7:30 in the morning, the breakfast was horrible—just cold food because the kitchen wasn't up and running—and we had to buy drinks and sandwiches from a nearby fast-food restaurant and take them back to our room in the evening for dinner. I tried to complain, but somehow the manager was never there, only the reception staff who weren't really responsible and obviously felt sorry for us. So I'm going to email the manager and if I don't hear anything, I'm definitely going to put something on Twitter…

Like • Comment • Share

b You are going to write Hannah's email to the Westfield Hotel. With a partner:
- underline the relevant information in the website post.
- summarize exactly what you are dissatisfied with.
- discuss what it would be reasonable for the hotel to do to compensate you for the inconvenience.
- invent any other details you think might be important to include in the email, for example, the exact dates of your stay, the room number, etc.

TIPS for writing an email or letter of complaint:
- Make a note of all the relevant details you want to include before you start drafting your email.
- Decide what action you want the person you are writing to take.
- Use appropriate expressions for opening and closing the email.
- Use a formal style and be clear and assertive, but not aggressive.
- Use the passive, e.g., *we were told*, *we are owed an apology*, etc., to make it more impersonal, or to make it clear that you are not accusing individuals.
- Use a variety of expressions for generalizing and making suggestions.

WRITING

Write an email of complaint of between 200 and 250 words.

DRAFT your email.
- Introduction: Explain why you are writing.
- Main paragraphs: Say what the complaint relates to and give the details.
- Summary paragraph: Restate your complaints briefly.
- Closing sentences: Ask for some action from the hotel.

EDIT the email, checking paragraphing, cutting any irrelevant information, and making sure it is the right length.

CHECK the email for mistakes in grammar, spelling, punctuation, and register.

← p.91

Go online for more Writing practice

Listening

🔊 **1.2**

Frida Kahlo is Latin America's best-known twentieth-century painter, and a key figure in Mexican art. She has also become a kind of cultural legend. She was born in Mexico in 1907, the third of four daughters, and when she was six, she caught polio—a disease which left her with one leg shorter than the other. Her second tragedy came when she was 18: she was riding in a bus when it collided with a tram. She suffered serious injuries, which affected her ability to have children. Although she recovered, she was in pain for much of her life and had three miscarriages. But it was this accident and the long periods of recuperation that changed Frida's career plans: she had wanted to study medicine, but instead she started to paint. This work is an unfinished one—you can see patches of bare canvas behind the row of women at the bottom of the picture and some of the faces have been painted over, suggesting she may have wanted to repaint them. Frida started it in 1949, five years before the end of her short life—she died in 1954 at the age of 47. She actually carried on trying to finish it on her deathbed, which suggests that it had a strong meaning for her.

As with many of her other works, the image contains at least one self-portrait: she is the third woman from the left in the bottom row, but the unborn child next to her may also be a representation of her—it is placed below her father, to whom she was very close. The painting is a kind of visual family tree: at the top are both sets of grandparents. On the left are her father's parents, whose ancestors were German-Hungarian. On the right are her maternal grandparents: her grandfather Antonio had American Indian origins, while her grandmother Isabel was the great-granddaughter of a Spanish general. Her parents Matilde and Guillermo, who were dead by the time this picture was painted, are in the middle of the picture. Their portraits are based on photographs and it is interesting that they are shown turning away from each other—their marriage was an unhappy one. They appear with their dead parents in a kind of cloud above their four daughters. From left to right the daughters are Matilde, the eldest, then Adriana, followed by Frida herself (with her niece Isolda) and then, with a blanked-out face, her sister, Cristina. Frida was very close to Cristina, but also jealous of her, especially because she had an affair with Frida's husband, the painter Diego Rivera. The next figure is Cristina's son Antonio, but it is not clear who the last unfinished face in the very bottom right-hand corner might be.

🔊 **1.13**

Interviewer Well, today I'm very pleased to be visiting the Edinburgh offices of Skyscanner, a company which did extremely well in this year's *Sunday Times Best Companies to Work For* awards, coming sixth overall and winning outright in the categories for most exciting future and best personal growth. So today we're speaking to a PR Manager at Skyscanner, could you start by telling us a bit about what you do?

PR Manager So I am the PR Manager for the Danish, Swedish, and Turkish markets. I look after the, our PR agencies there, and what that really means is that I work with them to get Skyscanner messages and stories into the media, so that could be anything from a big report on trends, on the future of travel, to smaller stories about where the Turkish people are going on summer holidays.

I And how long have you worked at Skyscanner?

PR I have just celebrated my year anniversary.

I Oh, well, congratulations!

PR Lots has changed in a year, but all good changes.

I And what was it that attracted you to apply for a job here?

PR I had always want, wanted to work somewhere that was kind of travel-focused. My previous job was in a very dry environment, so much so that I decided I would go traveling and then the day before I flew to South America for a few months, I had an interview here and found out when I was in the Bolivian Salt Flats that I got the job, so really nice, yeah.

I Skyscanner did very well in this year's *Sunday Times* survey of Best Companies to Work For. Do you agree that it's a good place to work?

PR Yeah, absolutely it's, it's a very funny thing, actually, because it very quickly becomes the norm for someone who works here, all these amazing benefits we have, so when you talk to someone else, you know, in another company, you suddenly think, "Wow, we're so lucky," so, you know, anything from flexible working to the small things like free fruit, to people being able to work from their home country, they are all massive benefits that you quite quickly get used to, but I think everyone really does appreciate it.

I So I guess it would be difficult to go anywhere else after this?

PR Yes, very much—maybe that's the plan, maybe that's the ploy that they've gone with!

I Is, is there one thing that you'd identify for you as a particularly significant benefit?

PR I have to admit what I really love is, the flexible working policy, it's a quite casual thing, there is no formal procedure, but it, it very much places the trust with the, the employees, so, you know, if I want to leave early on a Friday, there is kind of this, relaxed understanding, "Do you know what? You'll make up the time when you can, you're in charge, you're the, you're the one who knows your workload and your own role," which is really nice, it's quite refreshing

because it's quite unusual, especially within quite a large corporate–, you know, organization and so I particularly like that.

I Is there anything that you might change about, about the company or about its, the way it treats its employees?

PR I think, so we're growing at quite a, kind of rapid pace and I think because we have six different offices—you know, Beijing, Miami—I think as we grow it will probably be something that we need to tackle in terms of how we all work together across different time zones, so I think at some point that will be something that becomes more of an issue—it's not at the moment, but I'm pretty confident that Skyscanner will be able to tackle that, and tackle that in good time.

I Wonderful. OK, well, thank you very much indeed. Thanks for your time.

PR Thank you.

🔊 **1.18 Part 1**

Interviewer Eliza Carthy, could you tell us a bit about your family background, your parents and grandparents?

Eliza Um, I come from a musical family; my parents are folk singers, my father is a guitarist who is known for playing for playing the guitar, um, and inventing a particular style of English folk guitar. Um, he started playing when he was 17, back in the fifties, and, um, really was, was quite instrumental in his youth in sort of building the the, the sixties folk club scene in London. He was a friend of Bob Dylan and Paul Simon many, many years ago, and, um, is known for reconstructing old traditional ballads, traditional English ballads. My mother comes from a folk-singing family called The Watersons, and they were from the north of England, they're from Hull, which is in the north of England, and they were also instrumental in the beginning of the sixties folk revival, the formation of the folk clubs, and the, the beginning of, basically, the professional music scene that I work on now.

I And were your parents both from musical families?

E Um, really, both sides of my family are musical: my, my mother's side of the family were all travelers and gypsies, my– uh, her grandmother, she was brought up by her grandmother, both of her parents died when she was very young. She had an uncle that played the trumpet, you know, her father played the banjo, he used to listen to American radio in–during the Second World War and he used to learn the songs off the radio like that. Her grandmother was very into the sort of old romantic ballads like *The Spinning Wheel* and things like that, and she used to– she used to sing when they were little; the whole family sang, the whole family danced. And I was brought up in that kind of a family: my mother and her, her brother and her sister were in a singing group, my dad joined that singing group, and then, when I was old enough, I joined the family as well.

I So you had a very musical upbringing?

E My upbringing was– I suppose some people might think it was quite a hippy upbringing. I was brought up on a farm, um, that had three houses in a row, with me and my mum and dad in the end house, my uncle—my mum's brother—and his wife and their four children in the middle house, and then my mum's sister and her husband and their two children on the other end house. And we grew up basically self-sufficient, we had animals and we had chickens and goats and pigs and horses and things like that, and we, we grew up singing together and living together in that environment in North Yorkshire in the 1970s. Um, we had– Because our parents were professional musicians and touring musicians, we had a lot of touring musician friends who would come and stay at the farm and they would sing and play all the time and there was music all around when I was a child, and that really, that really formed the basis of of, of how I live now.

🔊 **1.19 Part 2**

Interviewer Do you think it was inevitable that you'd become a professional musician?

Eliza Well, if you if you were ever to ask any of us, were it– we would definitely have all said no. I wanted to be, I wanted to be a writer; my mum certainly didn't want me to go on the road. My mum retired in 1966..65..66 from professional touring to raise me. I mean, the road is a difficult place, whether you're traveling with your family or with a band or on your own, and she certainly didn't want that for me. My dad also probably never thought that I would do it, but I ended up following– exactly following his footsteps and quitting school when I was 17 and going on the road, and I've been on the road ever since.

I Can you tell us about your first public performance?

E My dad says that my first public performance was at the Fylde Folk Music Festival in Fleetwood in Lancashire when I was six, and we were at the Marine Hall and they were singing, The Watersons, the family– the family group were, were singing, and I asked if I could– I asked if I could go on stage with them, and I was six. And Dad said, "Well, you know, you probably don't know everything so just stand next to me on stage and we'll start singing and if you, if you know the song just pull on my leg and I'll lift you up to the microphone and you can, you can join in." God, I must have been awful! But yes, apparently I just– the first song they started up singing, tugged on his leg, and he picked me up and held me to the microphone and I sang that, and he was like, "Did you enjoy that?" "Yes, I did!" Put me down again and they started singing the next one, tugged on his leg, same thing! And he just ended up doing the whole concert with me sitting on his hip! Which uh– now I have a six-year-old and I know how heavy she is–it must have been quite difficult, God bless him!

I Has having children yourself changed your approach to your career?

E Uh, yes, in a way. Yes, in a way it has. I've just reordered my working year because my eldest daughter has just started school, so I, you know– I'm, I'm not free to, to take the children with me on the road anymore and, and I'm now bound by the school terms. So I try to work only on the weekends and in school holidays now and I try to, to be Mummy from Monday to Friday, taking them to school, bringing them back again. I'm not getting a great deal of sleep, but then I don't know many mothers of– many mothers of six- and four-year-olds that are getting a great deal of sleep!

1.20 Part 3

Interviewer You do a lot of collaborations with other musicians. What is it that appeals to you about working like that?

Eliza I like working with other–I don't like working alone. I don't know if that's because I don't trust myself or I just don't like being alone; I like being surrounded by a big crowd of people. I suppose that's, that's partly to do with my upbringing, there were always so many people around, that, um, I, I'm at my best, I'm at my best in a, in a large event where loads of people are running around doing things and we're all sort of collaborating with each other and there's lots of ideas and everyone's having, you know, a creative time, and that's how I feel– yeah, that's how I feel I, I work best, and that's why at the moment I have a 13-piece band and it's just heaven for me being with so many people and just feeling like a part of a big machine, I love that.

I Is there a difference between playing with your family and playing with other people?

E Um, yes, very much so. I'm not sure if I could tell you how different or why it's different. My dad is very eloquent on how and why it's different and he, he knows that uniquely because he joined The Watersons, and The Watersons was, was a brother and two sisters, and he joined that, and of course he was married to my mum, but he wasn't related to her. And there is this thing within family groups, this blood harmony thing, this intuition, you have similar sounding voices, you know where a relative is going to go, and that may be because you know each other so well, but it also may be whatever it is that binds a family together anyway.

I Would you like your children to follow in your footsteps?

E I get very, very excited when the children, um, when the children love music, I get very excited. My daughter Florence is very, very sharp, she listens and she can already– she plays *Twinkle, Twinkle* on the violin, plucking like that, and on the guitar as well, and she's– yeah, she has a very, very good sense of rhythm. And she loves foreign languages as well, there's a real, um, there's a real sort of correlation there between, between language and singing, she has great pitch, she is able to learn songs and things very, very quickly, and I love that. And Isabella, my youngest as well, she's really, she's really showing interest in it and I love it when they do that. As to whether or not I'd want them to be touring musicians, I think I'm probably of the same opinion as my mother, which is, "No, not really!" But, you know, I, I think the– I think the world is changing anyway, I don't know how many touring musicians there are going to be in the world in 20 years when they're ready, I don't know.

1.22

Interviewer How much do you know about your family tree?

Sarah Uh, I actually know quite a bit about my family tree on my dad's side. I don't know very much about my mom's side.

I Have you ever researched it?

S Yeah, um, my dad actually has done a lot of research, uh, and he can trace us all the way back to The Mayflower.

I Is there anyone in your family that you'd like to know more about?

S I would like to know more about my mom's side. Her father was adopted, so we don't, there's a lot we don't know.

Interviewer How much do you know about your family tree?

Kent I know a fair about– amount about my family tree. Um, I know we come back from ancestors in Sweden and, uh, England, and I know we've traced it back I think to, to the 1500s for some of the lines.

I Have you ever researched it?

K Um, you know, I haven't personally done a lot of research about my ancestors. I know we have the books and we have the stories and the journals and it's all there, so I guess I, I, I'd be interested to know a little bit about, uh, what my my ancestors did, uh, before they came to America. Um, 'cause I think they were farmers, I'm not entirely sure.

Interviewer How much do you know about your family tree?

Alison Um, I know a little bit because, um, my dad's done some research into his side of the family. Um, we know that my father's side stretches back to the 1700s in Cornwall. Um, my great-great-grandfather went down on the *Titanic*. Interesting piece of family history. Um, and we've got some family artifacts for that.

I Is there anyone in your family that you'd like to know more about?

A Um, probably the wife of the man who went down with the *Titanic*. I think she had quite an interesting and quite difficult life. Um, she had a baby, uh, brought it up by herself, so sounds like a, an amazing woman.

Interviewer How much do you know about your family tree?

Marylin Um, I know quite a lot because a relative of my father's, um, did some research on our family tree, oh about 20 years ago. So, well, I know that my father's family, um, is from Luxembourg and, in fact, when I worked there, I tried to get in touch with some distant relatives, but they weren't interested.

I Is there anyone in your family that you'd like to know more about?

M Um, well, guess what, it's precisely those relatives who are still living in Luxembourg. But what can I do, if they didn't want to meet me, oh well, I guess it's just destiny.

Interviewer How much do you know about your family tree?

Hannah You know, I, I know a little bit about my family tree because I was lucky enough to grow up with having great-grandparents in my life until about, like, ninth grade, so I know a lot from them and they told me a lot of stories about their parents and grandparents, but it doesn't go much further than that and that's only on my dad's side. I know about, um, immigration from Russia but that's all I know and then my mom's side I really don't know a lot about, but it's something that I'm interested in looking into.

I Have you ever researched it?

H I've tried to research it a little bit, uh, like doing the ancestry dot com thing, but, um, I haven't really gotten much further than that.

I Is there anyone in your family that you'd like to know more about?

H I'd love to know more about my great-grandmother's grandmother so I guess that would be my great, great, great-grandmother.

2.6

1 I'm from a small village on the southeast coast of Scotland, it's a very small place, not very many people live there. I liked growing up there, but I think it's a better place to visit than it is to actually live because there isn't very much for young people to do there. The people are quite nice and friendly, but most people have spent their whole lives there and their families have been there for several generations, so sometimes it can seem a bit insular.

2 I'm from Vancouver, which is on the western coast of Canada, in the province of British Columbia. It's a great place to raise a family, uh, it has a good mix of city things and outdoor activities to do. Vancouver has a population of around 632,000, so it's quite a big city, but it's not so big that you feel overwhelmed. I'd say the people there are friendly and quite welcoming.

3 I'm from Oxford in the southeast of England, I, I was born here and I've, I've lived here my whole life. It's difficult to say what the people are like because it's, in a way it's a city of two halves, famous for its university, but also, which obviously has people from all over the world, but also, it's a city in its own right, it has a very large BMW factory where they make Minis, so, but it's a nice place, I like it, I've lived here my whole life pretty much, so, so there we are.

4 So I'm from Melbourne which is on the southeast coast of Australia, just in, in the state of Victoria, this is a really cultural city, very European, you've got everything from beaches to art galleries, lots of shopping, and bars and restaurants, so it's a fantastic city to be in. The people are really laid back and and quite friendly there. We've got a very big mixture of cultures there, so a very multicultural city. So it's quite diverse and a really interesting place to be.

5 I'm from New Jersey and it's a nice mix between rural and city life because it, it has a lot of nature and nice kind of mountain landscapes where you can go hiking or walking, but it also has nice access to the city and lots of nice little shops and restaurants as well.

6 OK, I was born in Johannesburg in the late, in the late 50s. I moved to Cape Town when I went to university and of course it's a very beautiful old colonial center, with lovely buildings, and the aspect of Table Bay with the beautiful backdrop of Table Mountain, wonderful vegetation and a wonderful friendly community of people. It's very vibrant and exciting, people like bright colors in the strong sunlight, it's a very creative environment.

2.7

Interviewer Do you find it easier to understand native or non-native speakers of English?

Cristina Well, I've been in the United States for seven years now, and I've been exposed to a lot of different accents, not only people from the United States, but from different parts of the world, so I'm used to it. In terms of regional accents in the US, I still sometimes have trouble with Southern accents… they're a little more challenging for me, because I don't live in the South. The most stressful thing, I think, is talking on the phone, because you don't have the face-to-face interaction, so it can be tricky.

Interviewer How do you feel about having your English corrected?

Cristina Well, it hasn't happened much lately, but I don't mind, because that's how we learn, you know, we learn from our own mistakes. Sometimes when I'm tired, I might make a mistake with the third-person form, you know, but usually people are quite tolerant. And sometimes I catch my own mistakes, so I'm able to correct myself.

2.8

Interviewer Do you have any funny or embarrassing stories related to misunderstanding someone?

Cristina Yes, this happened a few years ago. I was trying to organize an evening out with some friends, and one of my friends picked a place for all of us to meet, and he said, "Let's all meet at Hideout." He meant H-I-D-E-O-U-T, you know, like a hiding place, which was the name of a bar. But I completely misunderstood him and thought he said "high doubt," two words, like H-I-G-H D-O-U-B-T. So, this caused a lot of confusion because I passed on the information to a bunch of other people and everybody got extremely confused and we couldn't find the place. We had to call him to find out where it was, and then we all figured out that I had misunderstood and gotten the name of the place wrong. Yeah, it took us a while, but in the end we all got together and had a good laugh. So, it all worked out.

Interviewer Is there anything you still find difficult about English?

Cristina I find that certain idioms related to sports don't come easily to me because I don't know anything about baseball or basketball or American football, and there's quite a few idioms in American English that come from those sports, like "hit it out of the park" or "slam dunk." So even though I do understand them in context, I don't use them, because I don't always see the

Go online to listen to the audio and see all the Listening scripts connection...Oh, and spelling. Romanian is a phonetic language, so spelling isn't necessarily as important as it is in English. Sometimes I have to write words out in English, maybe because I'm a visual learner. I have to visualize the letters in my head before I can spell the word.

2.15

1 My, my earliest memory, I must have been about three, I guess, maybe two, was, when we'd been to, to a county fair and I would have gone with my brother, who's a little older than me, and my parents, and I'd been bought, a, a helium balloon, and for some reason the balloon had a snowman inside it, it was only September; I don't know why there was a snowman, but, but there was, and I took it out into the back yard and because it was full of helium, obviously, it was pulling on the string, it wanted to, to fly away, and I let go, I didn't let go by accident, I remember letting go on purpose, to see what would happen, and of course what happened was the balloon flew up into the sky over the neighbors' trees and disappeared, and I was absolutely devastated, heartbroken by the loss of the balloon, and stood there crying and crying, and my dad had to go back to the county fair and get me another identical balloon, which did nothing to console me, I kept crying and crying and crying and that's my, my earliest memory, not a very happy one!

2 My earliest memory is probably from when I was about three or four years old and it was Christmas and I was at my nana's house with, all my family and my uncle was reading to me, he was reading *The Little Mermaid*, except that he was making it up, he wasn't actually reading the words in the book, he was just saying things like "Ariel went to buy some peanut butter and jelly" and things like that, and that made me really mad because I was at an age where I couldn't really read myself, but I knew that he was reading it wrong. So I got really annoyed with him and told him to read it the right way, but yeah, that's my earliest memory.

3 My earliest memory is from when, I must have been about three, and we were moving to a new house, we moved to an apartment building and I remember arriving and it was, it was dark and we'd had very a long trip, and we arrived and we went in the door and we turned the lights on and nothing happened, and the whole apartment was completely black and dark, no power, no electricity, no lights, and I thought this was terrific, and we had a flashlight and I was just running around, running around the, the hall and the rooms, finding all these new rooms all with a flashlight, and I imagined that it was always going to be like that, that we'd, we'd arrived in an apartment that wasn't going to have lights, so I was always going to have to use a flashlight. And I thought that was going to be amazing. My mother was in tears, obviously she, she was stressed out from the trip and arriving somewhere and having no power. But I, I was really, really excited by it, and the next day when the power came on I was really disappointed.

2.16

Host Are our first memories reliable, or are they always based on something people have told us? What age do most people's first memories come from? John Fisher has been reading a fascinating new book about memory by Professor Draaisma called *How Memory Shapes Our Past,* and he's going to answer these questions for us and more. Hello, John.

John Fisher Hello.

H Let's start at the beginning, then. At what age do first memories generally occur?

J Well, according to both past and present research, 80% of our first memories are of things that happened to us between the ages of two and four. It's very unusual to remember anything that happened before that age.

H Why is that?

J There seem to be two main reasons, according to Professor Draaisma. The first reason is that before the age of two, children don't have a clear sense of themselves as individuals—they can't usually identify themselves in a photo. And you know how a very small child enjoys seeing himself in a mirror, but he doesn't actually realize that the person he can see is him. Children of this age also have problems with the pronouns *I* and *you*. And a memory without *I* is impossible. That's to say, we can't begin to have memories until we have an awareness of self.

H And the second reason?

J The second reason is related to language. According to the research, first memories coincide with the development of linguistic skills, with a child learning to talk. And as far as autobiographical memory is concerned, it's essential for a child to be able to use the past tense, so that he or she can talk about something that happened in the past, and then remember it.

H I see. What are first memories usually about? I mean, is it possible to generalize at all?

J Early memories seem to be related to strong emotions, such as happiness, unhappiness, pain, and surprise. Recent research suggests that three quarters of first memories are related to fear, to frightening experiences like being left alone, or a large dog, or having an accident—things like falling off a swing in a park. And of course this makes sense, and bears out the evolutionary theory that the human memory is linked to self-preservation. You remember these things in order to be prepared if they happen again, so that you can protect yourself.

H Are first memories only related to emotions or are there any specific events that tend to become first memories?

J The events that are most often remembered, and these are always related to one of the emotions I mentioned before, are the birth of a baby brother or sister, a death, or a family visit. Festive celebrations with bright lights were also mentioned quite frequently, much more frequently than events we might have expected to be significant, like a child's first day at school. Another interesting aspect is that first memories tend to be very visual. They're almost invariably described as pictures, not smells or sounds.

H First memories are often considered unreliable, in that perhaps sometimes they're not real memories, just things other people have told us about ourselves or that we have seen in photos. Is that true, according to Professor Draaisma?

J Absolutely! He cites the famous case of the Swiss psychologist Jean Piaget...

2.17

Host First memories are often considered unreliable, in that perhaps sometimes they're not real memories, just things other people have told us about ourselves or that we have seen in photos. Is that true, according to Professor Draaisma?

John Fisher Absolutely! He cites the famous case of the Swiss psychologist Jean Piaget. Piaget had always thought that his first memory was of sitting in his stroller as a one-year-old baby when a man tried to kidnap him. He remembered his nanny fighting the kidnapper to save him. The nanny was then given a watch as a reward by Jean's parents. But many years later, I think when Jean was 15, the parents received a letter from the nanny in which she returned the watch to them. The nanny, who was by now an old woman, confessed in the letter that she'd made up the whole story, and that was why she was returning the watch. Of course, Jean had heard the story told so many times that he was convinced that he'd remembered the whole incident.

3.6

Host A first date is loaded with expectation. Will I like them, and will they like me? Is this person going to be "the one" or will I want to run for the door before the appetizer? Will we have anything to talk about and, if not, how will we get through the evening? Here's relationship expert Jenny with some suggestions on how to make sure that your first date is the best it can be—even if it turns out to be your only date.

Jenny Hello there. My first tip is "Choose the venue carefully," that is, the place where you're going to meet. Try to avoid very noisy places where you can't hear each other, or places where you can't talk, like movie theaters. So a good place to meet might be a quiet coffee shop for some locally roasted coffee, for example, or lunch in a little local place you know. The advantage of keeping the first date short and sweet, meeting for coffee or for lunch rather than dinner, is that if you don't like each other, you don't have to make it through a seven-course meal together. And of course if you do like each other, you can either extend the date, or plan a longer one for next time.

Tip number two is "Make an effort with your appearance." Obviously you don't want to make so much of an effort that your date wouldn't recognize you if they saw you on the street the next day. But getting your hair done, say, or wearing something you know you look good in, those kinds of things show that you care—and that you want to make a good impression. I mean, if you turn up with unwashed hair, wearing yesterday's clothes, you aren't likely to win anyone over.

The third tip, and it's an important one, is "Be kind," even if you think the date is going nowhere. It doesn't cost anything, and it'll make a big difference to how much the other person enjoys themselves. Of course, being kind also means not lying or giving your date false hope. Don't tell someone that you'll call and that you can't wait to see them again if you have absolutely no intention of following through!

Tip number four, which is sort of related to number three, is "Don't forget your manners." Make sure you turn up on time, and if you're going to be late for whatever reason, let your date know. Try not to yawn even if you're getting a little tired. Turn off your phone, and if the other person is footing the bill, remember to say "thank you." And one last thing while we're on the subject of manners—you can tell a lot about a person by how they treat waiters and waitresses. So don't just be polite to your date, be polite to the other people, too.

Number five is "Don't pretend to be anything you're not." It can be very tempting to exaggerate, or to dress up the truth, or just to plain lie to try to get your date interested. Of course, you may get away with it if you don't see the person again after the first date, but if the relationship does last any longer, you may find yourself in a tricky situation further down the line. So, for example, if you're separated, don't say that you're divorced. If you hate baseball, don't say that you can't think of a better way to spend a Saturday afternoon than cheering for the Chicago Cubs. And if you work part-time in a call center, don't say you're something big in communications.

Finally, and this is my last tip, "Don't make an instant judgement." Many of us make up our minds about whether we like someone in the first few seconds or minutes of meeting them. But you know, first impressions can be misleading, so try not to rule someone out right away. It's much better to spend a little time getting to know them, and if you're not sure about someone, it may take two or three dates before you can really decide. If you make a snap decision, you may risk missing out on the love of your life.

P Jenny, thank you very much for the advice. And now we turn to the next...

3.12 Part 1

Interviewer How important is historical accuracy in a historical movie?

Adrian The notion of accuracy in history is a really difficult one in drama because you know, it's like saying, well, "Was *Macbeth* accurate? Was– is Shakespearean drama accurate?" The iro- the thing is, it's not about historical accuracy, it's about whether you can make a drama work from history that means something to an audience now. So I tend to take the view that, in a way, accuracy isn't the issue when it comes to the drama, if you're writing a drama you, you have the right as a writer to create the drama that works for you, so you can certainly change details. The truth is nobody really knows how people spoke in Rome or how people spoke in the courts of Charles II or William the Conqueror or Victoria, or whoever, you have an idea from writing, from books, plays, and so on. We know when certain things happened, what sort of dates happened. I think it's really a question of judgement, if you make history ridiculous, if you change detail to the point where history is an absurdity, then obviously things become more difficult. The truth is, the, the more recent history is, the more difficult it is not to be authentic to it. In a way, it's much easier to play fast and loose with the details of what happened in

Rome than it is to play fast and loose with the details of what happened in the Iraq War, say, you know. So it, it, it's all a matter of perspective in some ways. It, it, it's something that you have to be aware of and which you try to be faithful to, but you can't ultimately say a drama has to be bound by the rules of history, because that's not what drama is.

I Do you think that the writer has a responsibility to represent any kind of historical truth?

A Not unless that's his intention. If it's your intention to be truthful to history and you, and you put a piece out saying "This is the true story of, say, the murder of Julius Caesar exactly as the historical record has it," then of course, you do have an obligation, because if you then deliberately tell lies about it, you are, you know, you're deceiving your audience. If, however, you say you're writing a drama about the assassination of Julius Caesar purely from your own perspective and entirely in a fictional context, then you have the right to tell the story however you like. I don't think you have any obligation except to the, to the story that you are telling. What you can't be is deliberately dishonest, you can't say, "This is true," when you know full well it isn't.

3.13 Part 2

Interviewer Can you think of any examples where you feel the facts have been twisted too far?

Adrian Well, I think the notion of whether a film, a historical film has gone too far in presenting a dramatized fictional version of the truth is really a matter of personal taste. The danger is with any historical film that if that becomes the only thing that the audience sees on that subject, if it becomes the received version of the truth, as it were, because people don't always make the distinction between movies and reality and history, then obviously if that film is grossly irresponsible or grossly fantastic in its, in its presentation of the truth, that could, I suppose, become controversial. I mean, if you—you know, the only thing anybody is ever likely to know about *Spartacus*, for example, the movie, is Kirk Douglas and all his friends standing up and saying, "I am Spartacus, I am Spartacus," which is a wonderful moment and it stands for the notion of freedom of individual choice and so on. So *Spartacus*, the film made in 1962, I think, if memory serves, bec– has become, I think, for nearly everybody who knows anything about Spartacus, the only version of the truth. Now in fact, we don't know if any of that is true, really. There are some accounts of the historical Spartacus, but very, very few, and what, virtually the only thing that's known about is that there was a man called Spartacus and there was a rebellion and many people were, you know, were crucified at the end of it, as in, as in the film. Whether that's irresponsible I don't know, I, I can't say that I think it is, I think in a way it's, it's, it's *Spartacus* is a film that had a resonance in the modern era.

There are other examples, you know, a lot of people felt that the version of William Wallace that was presented in *Braveheart* was really pushing the limits of what history could stand—the whole, in effect, his whole career was invented in the film, or at least, yeah, built on to such a degree that some people felt that perhaps it was more about the notion of Scotland as an independent country than it was about history as an authentic spectacle. But you know, again, these things are a matter of purely personal taste, I mean, I enjoyed *Braveheart* immensely.

3.14 Part 1

Interviewer Professor Beard, what's the secret to getting people interested in the Romans, in ancient history?

Mary Well, you have to go about it in the right way, really. Um, you know, I think perhaps starting from rather arcane and difficult bits of literature isn't the right way. But, you know, one thing that you see in Britain, you know, one thing that we know is that an awful lot of our culture and our geography and our place names and so on are actually formed by the Romans, you know. You ask somebody, um, "Why do you think so many English place names end in *-chester* or *-caster*, you know, Manchester, Doncaster?" And they'll often say, "I don't know." And then you say, "That's because that bit—*-caster*—is from the Latin for 'military camp,' and every place that ends *-caster* or *-chester* once had a Roman fort on it." And I've got a pretty 99% success record with getting people interested after that, because suddenly it is a question, not of these, um, uh, remote people who wrote some literature that you probably suspect would be boring; it's the people who formed the geography of our country and much of Europe. Why is London the capital of, of Britain? It's because the Romans made it so.

I What do you think we can learn from Roman history?

M In political terms many of the issues and questions and dilemmas that we face now, uh, were faced by the Romans. And in many ways, we're still thinking about and using their answers. I mean, one classic example of that is a famous incident in Roman history in 63 BC where there's a terrorist plot in, in the City of Rome to, to assassinate the political leaders, to torch the city, um, and to take over—revolution. Um, and that plot is discovered by, uh, one of the most famous Romans of all, Marcus Tullius Cicero, the great orator and wit of Roman culture. And he discovers the plot. He lays it before the Senate. He then decides to execute the leading conspirators without trial, summary execution. Um, and a couple of years later he's exiled. Now, in many ways that's the kind of problem we're still facing, uh, with modern responses to terrorism. I mean, what…how far does, how far should homeland security be more important than civil rights, you know? Uh, you know, what about those people in Guantanamo Bay without trial? Um, you know, where, where does the boundary come between the safety of the state and the liberty of the citizen? Now, the Romans were debating that in the 60s BC. And in many ways we're debating it, uh, along the same terms. And in part we've learned from how they debated those rights and wrongs.

3.15 Part 2

Interviewer If you could go back in time, is there one particular historical period that you'd like to go back to?

Mary I think it would be a terrible kind of, uh, punishment to be made to go back in history, you know, particularly if you're a woman, you know. There's, you know, there is not a single historical period in world history where women had halfway as decent a time as they do now. So, deciding to go back there, uh, you know, that would, that would be a self-inflicted punishment. I think I'd rather go in the future. Um, and there's also, I mean, even for men there's considerable disadvantages about the past, you know, like, you know, no antibiotics and no aspirin.

I Today we live in a celebrity culture, but in *Meet the Romans*, you focus on the lives of the ordinary people in Rome. Was that a conscious decision, to try to get people away from celebrity culture?

M I was rather pleased that people did actually find, you know, the non-celebrity, um, version of the Romans interesting. Um, and in some ways if it, if it was a small antidote to modern celebrity culture, I'm extremely pleased. Um, I think that, that wasn't quite what was driving me, though, because, uh, I think the celebrities of the ancient world are so remote from us in some ways. Um, and one of the things that puts people off ancient history is that, you know, you know, the big narrative books, the kind of the history of "the big men," you know, never seem to answer all those questions that we know we all want to know about the ancient world, you know, or any period in the past, you know: where did they go to the loo, you know. Um, and actually I think people are often short-changed, uh, about, um, the…in, in terms of providing an answer to questions which are really good ones, you know. Um, you know, in the end most of us, most women—don't know about men—most women, you know, do really want to know what having a baby was like, um, uh, before the advent of modern obstetrics, you know. That's a big question. It's not a– it's not, simply because it's, uh, intimate and female doesn't mean it's a less important question than why Julius Caesar was assassinated. And actually world history contains a lot more people like me and my family and women and slaves and people who, you know, want to do many of the things that we want to do, you know. But they can't clean their teeth 'cause there's no such thing as an ancient toothbrush, you know. Now, how does that feel? And I'm not saying in that I guess that those big blokeish issues aren't important, you know. The assassination of Julius Caesar, you know, is an event in world history that has formed how we look at every other assassination since, you know. When Kennedy's assassinated we see that partially in relation to that, that formative defining bit of political assassination in Rome. But it's not the only way that Rome is important.

3.16 Part 3

Interviewer As a historian, how important do you think it is that historical movies should be accurate?

Mary I'm not sure quite how keen I am on accuracy above everything else. The most important thing, if I was going to make a historical movie, I'd really want to get people interested. And I think that, that, um, film and television, um, program makers can be a bit, can be a bit sort of nerdish about accuracy. I remember a friend of mine once told me that, uh, he'd acted as advisor for some Roman film and the, the crew were always ringing up when they were on location, um, saying things like, "Now, what kind of dog should we have?" You know, "Should it, you know, if we're going to have a dog in the film, should it be an Alsatian or, you know, a Dachshund or whatever?" And to start with, he said he'd go to the library and he'd kind of look up and he'd find a breed. And eventually after question after question he'd think, look, these guys are getting the whole of Roman history in, in the big picture utterly wrong, and yet there they are worrying about the damned dogs, you know.

I Can you think of any historical movies that you've really enjoyed?

M I absolutely loved *Gladiator*. Um, you know, never mind its horribly schmaltzy plot, you know; I thought in all kinds of ways it was just a wonderful, uh, brilliant, and I don't know if it was accurate, but a justifiable re-creation of ancient Rome. Um, the, the beginning scenes of *Gladiator* which show, you know, Roman combat, um, just in a sense punctured the kind of slightly sanitized version of, you know, legionaries standing, you know, with all their shields, you know, face to–, you know, facing the enemy, um, you know, all looking ever so kind of neat and tidy. I mean, it was messy and it was bloody and it was horrible. And it was such a different kind of image of, uh, Roman combat that I remember we set it in Cambridge as an exam question, you know, um, you know: how, how would, how would students judge that kind of representation of Roman warfare.

I It's very interesting that there seem to be more and more historical movies recently, and many have won Oscars. Is that because history has all the best stories?

M Yes, there's no such good story as a true story—and that's what history's got going for it, you know, actually. Um, you know, nonfiction in a, in a kind of way is always a better yarn than fiction is. Um, and I think it's, you know…I feel very pleased because, uh, I think, you know, for one thing it gets, it gets some of the best stories from history into the popular, into popular attention, popular consciousness. But I think also, I mean, it shows that you don't always have to be deadly serious about history. I mean, you know, history, like classics, you know, is often treated as something which is good for you; but isn't actually going to be much fun, you know. You'll be improved by knowing about it, but it probably will be a bit tedious in the process. And I think that, you know, showing that history can be larky, it can be funny, it can be surprising, um, it can be something that you can sit down and have a good two and a half hours at the cinema enjoying, is really all to the good.

3.18

Interviewer Is there a period of history that you would like to go back to?
Daisy I'd really like to go back to Tudor England, sixteenth-century England.
I Why that period?
D Well I'm doing a PhD in the music of that period and I just think it's such a fascinating time because there was so much change happening and the way people lived their lives, their religion, the way the politics of the country was working. It must have been a really exciting time to live.
I Is there a person from history that you admire or find especially fascinating?
D There was a lady called Bess of Hardwick, um, who owned a lot of property in Derbyshire. She was a real social climber, and she lived through Henry VIII, Edward VI, Mary I, and Elizabeth I and into a bit of James I as well. Um, so she had a really long life, a really exciting life and she started from absolutely nothing and worked her way right to the top. I think she must have been a really amazing lady to know.
Interviewer Is there a period of history that you would like to go back to?
Heather I think I would have loved to be around in California in the sixties. I think, it, it sounds like it was a really exciting time. I think, uh, there was a lot of frightening things happening, in Vietnam, and, but it– but people were excited and, um, excited about the potential, I think of, of something new and really exploring their freedom, I guess.
I Is there a person from history that you admire or find especially fascinating?
H I think I most admire Nelson Mandela. I'm South African. So, uh, he's the first person that comes to mind. I think he was, um, an incredible person and an amazing leader. So, um, yeah, I would have loved to have met him.
Interviewer Is there a period of history that you would like to go back to?
Harry Um, ooh, that's a really, that's a weird one. I don't know. Um, history was pretty brutal, life was really quite hard. Um, I mean, there are some parts, some aspects of it that I'd like, where time was slower, life was defined by the seasons and daylight, um, and you didn't have the same sort of pressures as you do now. So, I'd like aspects of it, but I'm not sure I'd really like to go back to the actual way of life.
I Is there a person from history that you admire or find especially fascinating?
H Um, probably, uh, probably Queen Elizabeth I, because she, she managed to be the queen in a society where women weren't expected to have or hold or command any power and respect and that they were meant to do the bidding of men and their families and she actually stood up and was a person to be counted.
Interviewer Is there a period of history that you would like to go back to?
Adam Yes, there's a period I'd like to go back to, absolutely! I love ancient Greece. I love, uh, ancient Athens. I think it would be so amazing to spend time there and see what it was like being in the Agora with, you know, uh, Plato and Aristotle and talking. And, uh, that entire world be very, very interesting to me.
I Is there a person from history that you admire or find especially fascinating?
Ad Hmm. A person from history that I find, uh, that I admire. There are a lot of people, I study a lot of ancient history, so I would love to meet Julius Caesar or someone like that who really transformed the entire world with his actions and you know he has a very unique personality, he was a very cocky person and it'd be fun to, uh, just see what he was like in person and see how he was able to kind of take over the entire Roman Empire by himself.
Interviewer Is there a period of history that you would like to go back to?
Andrew I think I'd like to go back to, um, the Renaissance, like, the fourteenth and fifteenth century. Maybe in Italy.
I Why that period?
An I think there was a lot of innovation and interesting new ideas coming up in that time period.
I Is there a person from history that you admire or find especially fascinating?
An I've read a lot about, uh, Filippo Brunelleschi who was in Florence, in Italy, during the Renaissance and helped build the Duomo, the dome in Italy.

4.7

1 Sounds or noises that particularly annoy me, I would say dogs barking, very irritating, they just don't stop, especially the small yappy dogs, they just go on and on and on and just keep yapping at you and I just find that extremely irritating because there isn't any real way to quiet them down like a child, or something—you can tell them to be quiet, but a dog, no, they'll just keep going.
2 Any noises that annoy me? I suppose I'm annoyed by excessively creative cell phone ringers, that can be of overly popular songs or themes from television shows that people obviously think are really cute, but I probably don't think they are as cute.
3 The one sound I really hate is car horns, which you hear an awful lot of in cities. And the reason I hate them is because in my mind, at least, a car horn is meant to be a warning, but of course nobody uses them for warnings anymore, they use them because they're angry and impatient, and it, it seems to me that it's like shouting at somebody, and I don't like hearing that expression of anger all around me from dozens of cars.
4 For me, the most annoying sound is the buzzing noise of a mosquito. When you're just falling asleep in your bedroom at night and you hear that sound, and it's just terrible, I actually can't sleep until I've stopped the sound by killing the mosquito. So what I tend to do is, I tend to leave the light off actually, and just follow the sound, and just search the room for the sound for as long as I can until I can track it down and kill it, because otherwise I, I can't sleep knowing that I will wake up in the morning covered in mosquito bites.
5 I work in an office, and the person who sits next to me, Julie, she crunches on rice cakes every lunchtime, and it's really annoying, and I don't know what to say to her, or how to put it, and if I do tell her now, she'll know I've been annoyed for

the last four years, but I think she's leaving soon, so maybe I'll just have to deal with it for the next few weeks, or months.

4.8

Interviewer London, as well as other big cities, has often been accused of being an unfriendly place, but is it really, and if it is, does it matter and what could or should we do about it? Today I'm talking to Polly Akhurst, one of the co-founders of Talk to Me London, an organization whose goal is to get people talking to each other. Hello, Polly.
Polly Hello.
I Could you start by telling us about Talk to Me London?
P Sure. Talk to Me London is all about finding ways for people to talk to other people they don't know. And we do this through fun activities including a badge or pin, which says *Talk to Me London* on it and shows that you're open to conversation, as well as through regular events that, that get people talking, and we are also organizing, a "Talk to Me London" day at the end of August.
I And how did you get the idea for it, I mean, do you personally find London unfriendly?
P Well, I personally talk to a lot of people I don't know, and I think that's where the idea came from, I found that the conversations that I have with people just kind of randomly, have been hugely, kind of, beneficial, really, so I've made, I might have made new friends, new business connections, sometimes they just kind of just cheer up my day. So Talk to Me London comes from this idea of, you know, what happens if we do start talking to each other more and you kind of, you know, are able to see more opportunities and possibilities there.
I Have you ever been anywhere either in the UK, the US, or maybe abroad, a, a large city, which you thought really was a friendly place, which made you think you wish London was like that?
P There are definitely places that I've found friendlier than London, but I think that we all kind of change a bit when we travel and when we're out of our normal circumstances, we feel like, you know, more free to, to do things and perhaps talking to people is one of them. There is a tendency for, people say that Mediterranean countries are friendlier, however, or Latino countries even, but there was a similar initiative to this which was set up in Madrid a couple of years ago which I think indicates that, that they're facing the same problem as us, and perhaps, you know, points to the fact that this is a phenomenon in all large cities.
I So you wouldn't say it was a uniquely London problem?
P No, I wouldn't, no.
I You've had some very high profile support of Talk to Me London, on your website I think there's a quote from Boris Johnson (the former mayor of London) saying what a wonderful idea it sounds like. But on the other hand, there's, there's been some negative media coverage that must have been discouraging for you?
P I mean, I don't think so, I think that this idea is quite controversial in some ways because we're trying to encourage people to think about the way that they act and to reflect on that and to possibly change that, so, it hasn't really been surprising for us that we've had the negative coverage.
I And what would you say to people, and there are plenty of them I think, people who would say, "I'm sitting on the bus, I'm sitting on the train, I really don't want to talk to anybody, I really don't want anyone to talk to me, I just want to read my book or listen to my music, or whatever...." What would you say to those people?
P I would say that it's not about everyone talking to everyone else, it's about enabling those people who want to talk to do so, basically, so that's why all the things that we do are opt in, so the pin, for example, you wear it if you want to talk, if you don't want to talk you don't have to wear it, so you know, this, this isn't something for everyone, but we want to give people the choice between talking or not talking and currently there doesn't really seem to be that choice.
I Well, I wish you all the best with the project, I hope it's extremely successful and thank you very much for talking to us.
P Thanks a lot.

4.9

James's story
I was heading home at rush hour a few weeks ago. I was tired and bored, and there was this guy standing beside me reading a book. So I started reading it over his shoulder—it was all about the history of popular social movements. I couldn't see the title, so I asked him what it was called. Surprisingly, he reacted positively and told me the name. He told me that he commuted for two hours each day and that he always tried to read something enlightening because it made him feel better about his life and being productive by the time he got home! It was such a nice unexpected conversation—and it got me thinking about my own reading habits!

Anneka's story
I was getting the last train back home one evening, and I had to wait a long time on the platform, so I started talking to the girl sitting next to me. She was Czech and had just come to the UK with her boyfriend for work. She was a science graduate in the Czech Republic, but was working at a sandwich shop. I suppose in many ways it was a pretty typical story, but she was so upbeat and positive about London and living in the UK. At the end of the journey she emphasized how good it was to talk, and pulled out a sandwich from her bag and gave it to me. I was both shocked and grateful! Maybe my stomach had been rumbling too loudly...

Philippa's story
I was on the train home today and this young man asked me how my day had been. We talked about the area and iPads and TV and that kind of thing. Then I mentioned the concept of "Talk to Me London" and encouraged him not to stop talking to people. An older lady in the meantime had sat down by us and thought

the fact that we were talking was nice! And then I bumped into an old neighbor from about ten years ago, and we caught up. When he got off the train, the guy opposite me mentioned how nice it was to see us catching up, and then we got talking too. It was exciting. It was contagious. I had a smile on my face for the rest of the day.

Alise's story

I was standing on a bus, and I would have thought I'd looked unapproachable, but instead a man sitting close by saw I was carrying a guitar. He gave me a big smile and asked if I'd play him a song! Before long we were talking about traveling and living in different countries and cities around the world, and about music. He was leaving the next day for a few months of travel around South America. Because the man was a small distance away from where I was standing, quite a few people nearby were able to hear us talk, and many of them also joined in. It felt a little surreal, stepping off the bus later, smiling and saying goodbye to a bunch of strangers as though they were long-time friends.

4.13

Interviewer What made you want to be a translator?

Beverly It was something that I'd done when I was in college and when I moved to Spain it was difficult to get a job that wasn't teaching English, so I went back home and I took a postgraduate course in translation. After taking the course I swore that I would never be a translator, I thought it would be too boring, but I kept doing the odd translation, and eventually I, I came around to the idea because I liked the idea of working for myself, and it didn't require too much investment to get started. And, and actually, I enjoy working with words, and it's, it's very satisfying when you feel that you've produced a reasonable translation of the original text.

I What are the pros and cons of being a translator?

B Well, um, it's a lonely job, I guess, you know, you're on your own most of the time, it's hard work, you're sitting there and, you know, you're working long hours, and you can't schedule things because you don't know when more work is going to come in, and people always have tight deadlines. You know, it's really rare that somebody'll call you up and say, "I want this translation in three months." You know, that, that just doesn't really happen.

I And the pros?

B Well, the pros are that it, it gives you freedom, because you can do it anywhere if you have an internet connection and electricity, and I guess you can organize your time, because you're freelance, you know, you're your own boss, which is good. I, I like that.

I What advice would you give someone who's thinking of going into translation?

B I'd say that– I'd say, in addition to the language, get a speciality. Take another course in anything that interests you, like, economics, law, history, art, because you really need to know about the subjects that you're translating into.

I What do you think is the most difficult kind of text to translate?

B Literary texts, like novels, poetry, or drama because you have to give a lot of consideration to the author, and to the way it's been written in the original language.

I In order to translate a novel well, do you think you need to be a novelist yourself?

B I think that's true ideally, yes.

I And is that the case? I mean are most of the well-known translators of novels, generally speaking, novelists in their own right?

B Yes, I think in English anyway, people who translate into English tend to be published authors, and they tend to specialize in a particular author in the other language. And of course if it's a living author, then it's so much easier because you can actually communicate with the author and say, you know, like, what did you really mean here?

I Another thing I've heard that is very hard to translate is advertising, for example, slogans.

B Yeah, well, with advertising, the problem is that it has to be something punchy, and, and it's very difficult to translate that. For example, one of the Coca-Cola ads, the slogan in English was "the real thing," but you just couldn't translate that literally into Spanish—it, it just wouldn't have had the same power. In fact it became *Sensación de vivir*, which is "sensation of living," which sounds, sounds really good in Spanish, but it, it would sound weird in English.

I What about movie titles?

B Ah, they're horrific, too. People always complain that they haven't been translated accurately, but of course it's impossible because sometimes a literal translation just doesn't work.

I For example?

B OK, well, think of, you know, the Julie Andrews movie, *The Sound of Music*. Well, that works in English because it's a phrase that you know, you know like "I can hear the sound of music." But it doesn't work at all in other languages, and in Spanish it was called *Sonrisas y Lágrimas* which means "Smiles and tears." Now let me– in German it was called *Meine Lieder, meine Träume* which means "My songs, my dreams," and in Italian it was *Tutti insieme appassionatamente* which means I think, "All together passionately"or, I don't know, something like that. In fact, I think it was translated differently all over the world.

I Do you think there are special problems translating movie scripts, for the subtitles?

B Yes, a lot. There are special constraints, for example the translation has to fit on the screen as the actor is speaking, and so sometimes the translation is a paraphrase rather than a direct translation, and of course, well, going back to untranslatable things, really the big problems are cultural, and humor, because they're, they're just not the same. You can get across the idea, but you might need pages to explain it, and, you know, by that time the movie has moved on. I also sometimes think that the translators are given the movie on DVD, I mean, you know, rather than a written script, and that sometimes they've simply misheard or they didn't understand what the people said. And that's the only explanation I can come up with for some of the mistranslations that I've seen. Although sometimes it might be that some things like, like humor and jokes, especially ones that depend on wordplay are just, you know, they're, they're simply untranslatable. And often it's very difficult to get the right register, for example with, with slang and swear words, because if you literally translate taboo words or swear words, even if they exist in the other language they may well be far more offensive.

5.1

Again and again people tell us that mindfulness greatly enhances the joys of daily life. In practice, even the smallest of things can suddenly become captivating again. For this reason one of our favorite practices is the chocolate meditation. In this, you ask yourself to bring all your attention to some chocolate as you're eating it. So if you want to do this right now, choosing some chocolate, not unwrapping it yet, choosing a type that you've never tried before, or one that you've not eaten recently. It might be dark and flavorful, organic, or fair-trade, or whatever you choose. Perhaps choosing a type you wouldn't usually eat, or that you consume only rarely.

Before you unwrap the chocolate, look at the whole bar or package—its color, its shape, what it feels like in your hand—as if you were seeing it for the very first time. Now very slowly unwrapping the chocolate, noticing how the wrapping feels as you unfold it, seeing the chocolate itself. What colors do you notice? What shapes? Inhaling the aroma of the chocolate, letting it sweep over you. And now taking or breaking off a piece and looking at it as it rests in your hand, really letting your eyes drink in what it looks like, examining every nook and cranny. At a certain point, bringing it up to your mouth, noticing how the hand knows where to position it, and popping it in the mouth, noticing what the tongue does to receive it. See if it's possible to hold it on your tongue and let it melt, noticing any tendency to chew it, seeing if you can sense some of the different flavors, really noticing these.

If you notice your mind wandering while you do this, simply noticing where it went, then gently escorting it back to the present moment.

And then when the chocolate has completely melted, swallowing it very slowly and deliberately, letting it trickle down your throat.

What did you notice? If the chocolate tasted better than if you'd just eaten it at a normal pace, what do you make of that? Often, we taste the first piece and perhaps the last, but the rest goes down unnoticed. We're so often on autopilot, we can miss much of our day-to-day lives. Mindfulness is about bringing awareness to the usual routine things in life, things that we usually take for granted. Maybe you could try this with any routine activity, seeing what you notice? It could change your whole day.

5.2

1 One thing I really hate waiting for is waiting at home for a delivery to arrive, because sometimes you get, like, a two-hour delivery window, and that's fine, but more often they'll say, "Could be any time 7 a.m. to 7 p.m." and you're stuck in the house—you don't even dare go and buy a gallon of milk—and of course it always ends up arriving at five to seven in the evening, and you've spent the whole day waiting.

2 It annoys me if I have to wait for web pages to load, if there's a really bad internet connection and the pages are really slow to load and you actually sort of see one line loading at a time, pixel by pixel it seems, but, you know, invariably, if you need the information you sit and wait as long as it takes.

3 Is there anything I really hate having to wait for? Not really, I'm, I'm pretty patient. If I'm in a line I'm pretty patient, but I will get annoyed if people start to disregard the laws of lines, and try to cut in or try and get to the front in some other way. As long as there's a system to follow, that usually keeps me calm.

4 I really hate waiting for anything where I've been given an appointment time for a specific hour, you know, a specific time, and then having to wait forever before I have it, so, well, you know, for example a hair stylist or, or a dentist or a doctor. I think particularly things like hair stylists and dentists, because I think they must know how long the previous person's going to take, you know, they don't have to deal with emergencies or anything like that, so why can't they give me a correct time? I mean, I'm very punctual so I always turn up on time, in fact usually at least five minutes early, and it really, really annoys me if I have to wait for a long time. Anything more than fifteen minutes past the appointment time drives me completely insane.

5 Waiting for Jerry, my husband, is a complete nightmare, because he's never ready on time and I always tell him to be ready fifteen minutes before we need to be ready, and even so he's so late, it drives me completely bananas. I don't know why it drives me completely bananas because, in fact, often we don't need to be there on time, or it doesn't need to be that kind of precise, but it does. I hate it. He's preening himself, you know, getting his jacket on and looking at himself in the mirror, I mean, he takes much more time than I do.

6 I can't abide waiting in check-in lines at airports, because I'm standing in the line watching people take for-ev-er to check in, and I know when I get to the front of the line I'll do my check-in in twenty seconds. I don't know why these other people can't do the same.

5.13

Interviewer Where did the idea of microfinance come from?

Sarita The idea behind microfinance again goes back to the mid-70s. There had been, by that time, several decades of what we call the Western World giving massive amounts of aid to the developing world and a realization that a lot of it was not working, there were still many people who were left poor. So, you know, Muhammad Yunus is credited as being the father of microfinance, he's an economist living in Bangladesh, a very poor country, and he looked around and he said—what, what is it that the poor lack, what is that they need? And the answer is obvious, they need money and all of us, in order to get started have had access to credit. So, the poor can't get access to credit, they can't go to relatives to borrow because generally the relatives are as poor as they themselves are and they certainly cannot go into a bank and borrow because they have no collateral.

I How did Dr. Yunus solve these problems?

S There are really three innovations that he came up with that are brilliant in, in hindsight. One was, OK, the poor have no collateral, but let's figure out a way to create collateral which means, collateral is basically if you're not going to pay back the loan, that somebody's held responsible. So he came up with a lending methodology where there was a group of peers that were given the loan and they would be lending to each other and the group held each member accountable for paying back. The second innovation that he came up with is that it is very difficult for the poor to gather a lump sum to pay back a loan, but if you can break up that payment into very small regular payments that are coming out of your daily income, then it's feasible to pay back the loan. So what micro-credit did was, to break up the, the loan payment into these very sort of regular small payments. And the third was really an incentive system, that the poor were not encouraged to borrow a large amount, they only borrowed what they could use in their business and then pay back, and if they paid back successfully then they were eligible for a larger loan.

🔊 **5.14**

Interviewer Do you have any examples of individual success stories?

Sarita Oh, I love talking about, individual success stories, because this is what, sort of gets us up in the morning and, you know, gets us to come to work and stay late, and, and do this, this work, since I've been at Women's World Banking I have been to the Dominican Republic, Jordan, and India, so I am happy to give you a story from each, each, each of the three countries.

The DR is a more established economy, if you will, and so the, the woman I met had already had successive loans that she had taken from our partner in the DR and what she did was to start out, she was basically selling food from her, kitchen, making excess food and selling it to the factory workers, took out a loan, sort of increased that business and then set up a little cantina out of her living room. So that along with food she was selling cigarettes, beer, candy, etc. That business did well, took out another loan and built a room on top of her house and started to rent it out and so over seven years what she's been able to do is to completely build a new home for herself and rent out the old one, and this is going to ensure income in her old age, because at some point she's going to be too old to, to work in the kitchen, and to be, you know, standing on her feet behind the cantina counter and she's looking at the, the, these rental rooms that she has been able to put on as her, her old age security.

🔊 **5.15**

In Jordan, I'll, I'll tell you about a young women that, that we met, you know, sort of the, the, cultural, norm in Jordan is that, a fairly old husband can marry again and marry a, a fairly young woman, so the one that we met, her husband was now too old and sick so while, while, he took care of the…having a roof over her head, she had absolutely no means of earning more money for herself or her kids, and at her socio-economic level it's not considered proper for a woman to go out and work. So the only thing that she was able to do, was she had taken a loan to buy cosmetics, and was selling them from her living room to her neighbors and this was considered to be an OK business for her because primarily she was dealing with other women, but it gave her that sort of extra money, to use for herself.

🔊 **5.16**

And then in India where I was recently in the city of Hyderabad, and Hyderabad is this up-and-coming city, you know, it's gleaming, it's, Indians themselves are thinking of it as the next cyber city. But across town they have slums, where even now, both men and women have not gone to school, they're not educated and their only recourse is to work in the informal economy, so the family that we met, the husband, was a vegetable cart– a vegetable seller, so he took his cart and went out into the more affluent neighborhoods, the son had dropped out of school to join his father, to push a similar car…cart, and the mother had taken a loan to embroider saris, and, she did this at home, sort of in her spare time and what she really wanted to do was to, amass enough income so that she would cut out the middleman, because she basically got half of what the sari was worth, because she was handing it over to a, a middleman, so that if she could buy the materials herself, embroider it herself, and sell it herself to the store she could in effect double her income without doubling her labor.

🔊 **5.21 Part 1**

Interviewer In your experience, what are the main causes of stress?

Jordan My clients and audiences tell me that their big stressors are, uh, too much to do, too little time, uh, money stressors, commuting is a big stressor. I think that the opportunities to be stressed are everywhere.

I Do you think life is more stressful now than it was, say, 20 years ago?

J I think that today there are many more opportunities to be stressed, there are many more distractions, especially ones that are technology-driven. And I'm a big fan of technology, we can use technology to help us reduce stress, but when you have emails coming in and text messages left and right, and Twitter feeds and Facebook messages, and, uh TV, and the kids and a job, and maybe school, it really divides our attention and it produces a stress response that is often ongoing, continuous within us. And all of that stuff can take away the time to just relax, uh, take a walk, not think about who's trying to communicate with us, and not needing to be on all of the time. So, uh, so I think there are just more chances to be stressed today, uh, and therefore we need to really pay more attention to reducing stress.

I Can you tell us something about the effects of stress on the body and mind?

J Stress impacts the body because it produces wear and tear, and when we are constantly stressed, our organs, our immune system, become the punching bags of our stress response. Stress is really important, and, in fact, it can be a lifesaver, but when it kicks into action all the time, it, uh, has a corrosive effect on us. So, for example, our immune systems are weakened when we are under a lot of stress,

and especially for a long period of time. When our immune systems are weaker, it opens us up to be more susceptible to illnesses in the environment. Uh, stress contributes to high blood pressure, which contributes to heart problems and stroke. Stress impacts our sleep, so when we get stressed during the day it often makes it more difficult for us to fall asleep at night or to stay asleep or to have a quality night's sleep, and if we don't get a good night's sleep, then we are tired the next day, which makes us more stressed in many cases, so it becomes a stress–poor-sleep cycle that is stressful and tiring. So these are all reasons to really pay attention to our stress levels and to take action to reduce the stress.

🔊 **5.22 Part 2**

Interviewer How can you help people deal with stress and how long does it take to find a solution?

Jordan The great thing about stress management is that it's like a salad bar. There are 30 different choices on a salad bar and some of us like most of the things that are offered, but some of us don't like everything, but we get to choose what works for us and what we enjoy. Same thing with stress management—there are more than 30 different ways you can manage stress, there are probably, uh, 30 million and counting, and we should pick the techniques, many of them easy and simple and fun, that we like, and therefore we'll be more likely to use them on an ongoing basis. So stress management can take as little as ten seconds. You can look at a beautiful picture that you took on your last vacation, you can put it on your computer screen, you can put it next to your bed, you can put it on your desk, and just focusing on that photo of the ocean or a mountain or a beach can alleviate stressed feelings immediately. We can do one-minute breathing exercises, we can exercise, we can take a ten-minute walk around the block, we can meditate each day. So there are many different ways to prevent and reduce the stress that we're experiencing. The key is to do it on a regular basis.

I Are the solutions to stress physical, mental, or both?

J Stress management involves both the mind and the body, they make great partners when we're trying to feel better and to cut down on the stress that we're experiencing. I once worked in a school where a student identified his stressor as riding on the subway. He felt very stressed going to school every day and very stressed when it was time to go home, because the subway made him feel very closed in and like he wanted to escape, he couldn't stand the, the crowds. And then we opened up to the rest of the group and we asked them for different ways that this student might think about this stressor and different ways that he might act to try and reduce it. And the group came up with all sorts of great possibilities, including that he ride in a different car, in the first car or the last car, because it's often less crowded compared to the center car, which is where he always used to ride. And he liked that idea, and I heard from the principal of the school a few weeks later that he in fact had started riding in the first car, and for the first time in his subway-taking life, he didn't feel stressed, he didn't feel anxious, because the car was less crowded and he felt so much better. And you might think, "Well, that's such an easy answer, why didn't he think of that himself?" The truth is, and I think we all identify with this, we get into very fixed ways, habits almost, of thinking and acting, because we, we deal with our stressors and have dealt with them in similar ways for a long, long time, so we lose the perspective, we don't take as much time to think about how we could deal with our stressors in different ways. So this is an example of how the mind and body and actions and thoughts can work together to really make a big difference in the way we feel.

🔊 **5.23 Part 3**

Interviewer Are some age groups more susceptible to stress than others?

Jordan Stress is a very democratic occurrence, so older people are stressed, college students are stressed, babies get stressed, 30-somethings get stressed, men are stressed, women are stressed, so, uh, it's hard to say if one group is more stressed than another.

I What makes students stressed? How does stress affect their lives or their studies, and what are the most stressful times in a typical student's life?

J College, and being a student can be really fun and exciting and rewarding. There are also a lot of stressors associated with it: there's the studying, there's the pressure to do well on exams so that you can get a better job and perhaps make more money. You are in a different environment that doesn't have the same support that you used to have, especially if you were back home. Uh, there is the social stress of needing to meet new people, and also for a lot of young people, especially those in their teens and twenties, we see a lot of mental, uh, health issues arise and there's a greater need to get help for, uh, them while in school, but if you're not with your usual support network it's even more challenging sometimes to do so. Stress makes it difficult to study, to focus, to concentrate. When you're sitting down to take an exam and you studied really hard for the exam, and then all of a sudden, you're having trouble remembering what you studied, stress can play a big role in making it more difficult for us to recall information. If you're doing a presentation, public speaking, that can be very stressful for a lot of students as well as professionals. In fact, still, public speaking is feared more than death by most people. Then there's the financial stress of being in school, not only, uh, not having a lot of money to spend on things that you want to do, fun activities, but what awaits you when you graduate, which for many, uh, students is a lot of financial, uh, stress and loans to repay. So being a student—great fun, and also can provide a lot of– great stress.

I You set up Stressbusters as an anti-stress program for students. Can you tell us something about it and how it works?

J We train teams of students to provide five-minute free back rubs at events all over campus, all year long, and people on campus come to the events, and not only do they get an amazing stress-relieving back rub, but they also learn about other stress reduction and wellness resources on campus that we train our students to provide. And we have seen incredible reductions in feelings of stress, tension, anxiety, lowering of feelings of being overwhelmed, from before someone has the Stressbusters experience to after. We also find students telling us that they're better able to cope with their stressors and they're better able to complete the tasks that they have at hand after they have one of our Stressbusters experiences.

5.25

Interviewer Are you currently more stressed at work or at home?

Simon Am I more stressed– uh, I'm more stressed at home at the moment because my wife, um, has just had, or, I say my wife has had, we have just had twin little girls. Eight months old or eight and half months old now, so it is far more stressful being at home than being at work. I found work easy compared to being at home at the moment.

I When things are stressful, what do you do to try to de-stress?

S I put my earphones on and listen to music, to drown out the sound of the babies.

Interviewer Are you currently more stressed at work or at home?

Anne I'm stressed at both work and home. Um, my mom is really sick right now, work is busy, and, um, we're going through all sorts of changes with the project. Um, and I just got married! So there's been a lot going on.

I When things are stressful, what do you do to try to de-stress?

A This is my problem. I try to plan ahead, and, so that I won't be stressed at some point. But, after a while, there's nothing you can do so then you just have to practice letting go and relaxing and being in the moment, being happy with what is.

Interviewer Are you currently more stressed at work or at home?

Jim Uh, well, I work at home, uh, I'm a self-employed writer and, uh, I experience very little stress, except those rare periods when I'm up against a deadline. So, uh, I have no commute, I– my commute is walking from one room to the other, and I have a cozy little office and I'm very happy, uh, and unstressed with work, which I think is very unlike most New Yorkers and I'm very fortunate.

I When things are stressful, what do you do to try to de-stress?

J Ah, I de-stress by, uh, sitting uh down and breathing calmly and thinking about nothing, or sometimes thinking about the cosmos and thinking about, uh, the illusory nature of time. And, um, that usually works, uh, but as I say, I experience very low levels of stress, uh, because I actually spend a lot of time thinking about cosmological matters and that has a very calming effect, I think, and, uh, I commend it to my fellow New Yorkers.

Interviewer Are you currently more stressed at work or at home?

Billy More at home. I just recently moved from one place to another and, um, getting used to the new neighborhood, um, you know, where to shop, where to eat, um, how to get to work, um, a little stressful trying to navigate whereas, where I lived before I knew exactly what to do.

I When things are stressful, what do you do to try to de-stress?

B Work out. Um, I work out, I read, um, I listen to music, I meditate. Um, yeah.

Interviewer Are you currently more stressed at work or at home?

Sean I would say definitely more stressed at work. Um, I think stress is quite contagious. I think I spend a lot of my time around stressed people, um, either in a room with them, or on the phone to them, or, or just having emails from them, so I think that that builds a lot of stress, um, just from the environment, really.

I When things are stressful, what do you do to try to de-stress?

S I've realized quite recently that when I am stressed, I build a lot of tension in my shoulders, um, and I think it's not just a metaphor when we say we have things, we carry the weight of things on our shoulders. So I think it really helps just to be conscious of that and every half an hour or so, just if I concentrate on relaxing my shoulders, everything seems to be a little bit more bearable.

6.1

Nowadays we're surrounded by some powerful ideas about the sort of things that will make us happy. The first of these is that we tend to think that really to deliver satisfaction, the pleasures we should aim for need to be rare. We've become suspicious of the ordinary, which we assume is mediocre, dull, and uninspiring, and likewise we assume that things that are unique, hard to find, exotic, or unfamiliar are naturally going to give us more pleasure.

Then, we want things to be expensive. If something is expensive, we value it more, whereas if something is cheap or free, it's a little harder to appreciate. The pineapple, for instance, dropped off a lot of people's wish list of fruit when its price fell from exorbitant (they used to cost the equivalent of hundreds of dollars) to unremarkable. Caviar continues to sound somehow more interesting than eggs.

Then, we want things to be famous. In a fascinating experiment, a well-known violinist once donned scruffy clothes and performed at a street corner and was largely ignored, though people would flock to the world's greatest concert halls to hear just the same man play just the same pieces.

Lastly, we want things to be large scale. We're mostly focused on **big** schemes that we hope will deliver **big** kinds of enjoyment: marriage, career, travel, getting a new house.

These approaches aren't entirely wrong, but they unintentionally create an unhelpful bias against the cheap, the easily available, the ordinary, the familiar, and the small-scale. As a result, if someone says they've been on a trip to a Caribbean island by private jet, we automatically assume they had a better time than someone who went to the local park by bike. We imagine that visiting the Uffizi Gallery in Florence is always going to be nicer than reading a paperback novel in the backyard. A restaurant dinner at which Lobster Thermidor is served sounds a good deal more impressive than a supper of a cheese sandwich at home. The highlight of a weekend seems more likely to be a hang-gliding lesson, rather than a few minutes spent looking at the cloudy sky. It feels odd to suggest that a modest vase of lily of the valley (the cheapest flower at many florists) might give us more satisfaction than a Van Gogh original.

And yet the paradoxical and cheering aspect of pleasure is how unpredictable it can prove to be. Fancy vacations are not always 100% pleasurable. Our enjoyment of them is remarkably vulnerable to emotional trouble and casual bad moods. A fight that began with a small disagreement can end up destroying every benefit of a five-star resort. Real pleasures often seem insignificant—eating a fig, taking a bath, whispering in bed in the dark, talking to a grandparent, or scanning through old photos of when you were a child—and yet these small-scale pleasures can be anything but small. If we actually take the opportunity to enjoy them fully, these sort of activities may be among the most moving and satisfying we can have.

Fundamentally, this isn't really about how much small pleasures have to offer us. It's about how many good things there are in life that we unfairly neglect. We can't wait for everything that's lovely and charming to be approved by others before we allow ourselves to be delighted. We need to follow our own instincts about what is really important to us.

6.9

Interviewer Can you begin by explaining exactly what an addiction is?

Doctor Stork I think we often think of addiction as being something like an illegal drug, but the truth is you can be addicted to a lot of things—caffeinated drinks, fatty, sugary foods, it could be drugs, but it could be a whole host of other things. What's happening in your brain's pleasure centers, is that whenever you do this thing, it rewards you, you get a flood of dopamine in your brain's pleasure centers. And over time you start having more and more dopamine. Well, the brain responds to that in an interesting way. All this dopamine in your brain, just like with the radio when it's turned up too loud, your brain turns down the volume. So if you've been drinking too much caffeine, eating too much sugar, your brain actually turns down the volume, so you have to drink even more or eat even more just to get back to your normal state.

I So what does that mean for someone who's addicted to something and wants to give it up?

Dr. S Well, have you ever noticed how people, when they quit a substance, or a behaviour, they're angry, they're depressed, they're unhappy. The reason is because their brains rely on the "drug" to make them not only feel good, but to stop them from feeling bad. So this is all a matter of reward centers in the brain, and when you become addicted to a behavior you are just trying to get that pleasurable feeling, to not feel so bad any more. And that's why it's so difficult to give up, because once you're addicted it's so hard to stop.

I If someone wants to give up an addiction, would you recommend that they went cold turkey?

Dr. S Well, it depends on what they're addicted to, and it also depends on the person. If you're truly addicted to video games, to the point where you're not eating or sleeping properly, or you have migraine headaches from intense concentration, or maybe you have a video game addiction coupled with depression; we will give people medicine to change their brain chemistry—to help them decrease their cravings to play video games. They couldn't go cold turkey without some kind of serious risk. But food addiction, you know, if you're addicted to fatty and sugary foods, you can't stop eating food, but you can quit that kind of food cold turkey. There's not going to be any problem in your body from doing that. And for some people, stopping smoking cold turkey is the best way to do it, but other people may be dependent on nicotine patches or gum for a while, or some other substitute.

I I see. What other kind of treatment do addicts need?

Dr. S The best treatment options are multi-pronged, so you may need counseling, and sometimes you may need medication, and it's also vital if you can get support from your family, because these addictive personalities, they tend to push the limits, and they need all the help they can get not to have a relapse, fall back into their bad habits.

I Dr. Stork, thank you very much.

7.1

Why is it that so many children don't seem to learn anything in school? A TV producer-turned-writer has come up with some very revolutionary ideas.

A few years ago, TV producer John Lloyd thought up a formula for a new quiz show. The show is called *QI*, which stands for "Quite Interesting," and which is also IQ backwards. It's a comedy quiz show hosted by actor Stephen Fry, where panelists have to answer unusual general knowledge questions, and it is perhaps surprising that it's particularly popular among 15 to 25 year olds. Along with co-author John Mitchinson, Lloyd has since written a number of QI books, for example, *The Book of General Ignorance*, and these have also been incredibly successful. Lloyd's basic principle is very simple: everything you think you know is probably wrong, and everything is interesting. *The QI Book of General Ignorance*, for example, poses 240 questions, all of which reveal surprising answers. So we learn, for example, that you are more likely to be killed by an asteroid than by lightning, or that Julius Caesar was not, in fact, born by Caesarian section.

The popularity of these books proves Lloyd's other thesis: that human beings, and children in particular, are naturally curious and have a desire to learn. And this, he believes, has several implications for education. According to Lloyd and Mitchinson, there are two reasons why children, in spite of being curious, tend to do badly at school. First, even the best schools can take a fascinating subject, such as electricity or classical civilization, and make it boring, by turning it into facts that have to be learned by heart and then regurgitated for exams. Second, QI's popularity seems to prove that learning takes place most effectively when it's done voluntarily. The same teenagers who will happily choose to read a QI book will often sit at the back of a geography class and go to sleep, or worse still, disrupt the rest of the class.

7.2

So how could we change our schools so that children would enjoy learning? What would a "QI school" be like? These are Lloyd and Mitchinson's basic suggestions.

The first principle is that education should be more play than work. The more learning involves things like storytelling and making things, the more interested children will become.

Second, they believe that the best people to control what children learn are the children themselves. Children should be encouraged to follow their curiosity. They will end up learning to read, for example, because they want to, in order to read about something they are interested in.

Third, they argue that children should also be in control of when and how they learn. The QI school would not be mandatory, so students wouldn't have to go if they didn't want to, and there would be no exams. There would only be projects, or goals that children set for themselves with the teacher helping them. So a project could be something like making a movie or building a chair.

Fourth, there should never be theory without practice. You can't learn about vegetables and what kind of plants they are from books and pictures; you need to go and plant them and watch them grow.

The fifth, and last point Lloyd and Mitchinson make, is that there's no reason why school has to stop dead at 17 or 18. The QI school would be a place where you would be able to continue learning all your life, a mini-university where the young and old could continue to find out about all the things they are naturally curious about.

7.6

Interviewer So, could you tell us a little about the four pieces of art, and explain the ideas that they are somehow communicating?

Ghislaine OK, let– let's start with the frog. It's called *Kobe Frog* and it's by the Dutch artist Florentijn Hofman, and it's an enormous inflatable 10-meter-high object, and it was made in 2011 for a particular place—the roof of the Museum of Art in Kobe, in Japan. And Kobe was the site of a very severe earthquake in 1995. And the frog is wearing a party hat and it sits very close to the edge of the roof. The artist says that it's about enjoying life and having a flexible attitude in times of disaster. I'm not sure whether the people of Kobe would agree with that.

Next, we come to the stones. This is a work called *Blaenau Ffestiniog Circle*—Blaenau Ffestiniog is the name of a town in Wales and this work is by the artist Richard Long, and it was in an exhibition of his called "Heaven and Earth." And what Richard Long does is that he spends months of the year walking through different landscapes and he creates art out of the things he finds there. His main theme is the relationship between art and landscape, and here he has created a beautiful harmonious arrangement of different local stones that he's chosen, and what he wants to do is to make people stop and look and realize how beautiful the countryside and in this case the stones also can be.

Then we come to the cot, and this is a modern sculpture by Mona Hatoum, and it's called *Incomunicado,* and at first sight you might think it was a baby's cot. It doesn't look like a modern cot, but it looks as if it might be a hospital cot from, say, 50 years ago. But when you look at it a bit more closely you notice that there's something strange about the bottom of the cot, where the support for the mattress should be, and in fact it's a series of very sharp wires. Mona Hatoum is a Palestinian artist who was born in Beirut, but she was stranded in London after civil war broke out in Lebanon, and I think if we ask ourselves what her idea might be, well, it's a cot and a cot is normally a protective bed for a baby, where a baby will be safe, but this cot is the opposite of that, so if you got into this cot instead of being safe, you'd be seriously damaged, or seriously injured. I think this cot is a kind of metaphor for the idea of the state, the country that should look after you, your mother country or your fatherland, but in an extreme political situation, instead of being safe, or being at home, you feel threatened because of political oppression, and I think probably that's the metaphor that she's making here.

Finally, there's *Pharmacy.* This is an installation by Damien Hirst, and it occupies a whole room. If you were in an art gallery and you suddenly walked into this room, you might almost think you'd walked into a real pharmacy by accident, but if you start looking, you'll start seeing things which look strange, for example, there are four little stools that– the kind of stools you use to reach up to higher shelves and on top of each one is a bowl with honey in it, and if you look up, suspended from the ceiling there is a kind of machine for killing insects. And there are four old-fashioned apothecary bottles, which originally were in pharmacies because they were meant to represent the elements of earth, air, fire, and water, but which you wouldn't often see in a pharmacy today. So what could the idea be about here? Well, most of Hirst's works, like the work of many artists of the past, are about life and death. The honey attracts flies to come in, or other insects, but they end up zapped in the insectocutor, the, the killing machine. Drugs, medicines, to us represent healing, so people might come into a pharmacy to get better, but even if you spend thousands of pounds on drugs, in the end you, like the flies, will die. But we also have the four bottles, which are the four primary colors, the, the tools, the materials of the artist, and I think he's also saying that art, like drugs, can cure, can heal, if not the body, then the spirit.

7.7

Interviewer Well, this is all very fascinating, but my problem is that I don't think I could ever have gotten there by myself. I needed you, an expert, to explain these works of art to me, whereas if I went to a gallery to see normal paintings or sculptures I could probably enjoy them without needing to have them explained to me. What, what do you think…?

Ghislaine Well, I disagree there. I don't think you do need an expert to explain them to you, actually. In any case with modern sculpture and installations, there's normally some interpretation on the walls so you can read about it if you want to. But I think if you're going to go to a gallery to see modern sculpture and installations, and perhaps a lot of modern, modern art in general, the best way is to go with someone else, or with a group of people, and to talk about the work, to ask each other questions about the things you see, and very often you find that by asking questions, and coming up with the answers you can get much more out of it. You know, even though it may not look like the kind of art that you're used to, you have to believe that the person who made it is an artist, or was an artist, and that they have things to say, and it's your job to find out what they might be.

I Don't you think then that they're making you work much harder to enjoy their works than artists did in the past?

G Actually, no I don't, because plenty of other works are just as elusive, you know, abstract art or sculpture, many Old Master paintings where you don't actually understand the symbolism, there's always more to understand.

I OK, so then, in that case do you think artists today want to make you think, they don't just want to create something of beauty?

G I think they always have done. They have ideas and feelings, and they want to give form to them. And actually, I think many people would find Richard Long's stones beautiful. And other people might think that Mona Hatoum's cot is beautiful, maybe not exactly a beautiful object, but a beautiful and rich idea. Beauty can be a beautiful landscape, or a portrait of a beautiful person, but I think it can also be a beautiful idea.

I Thank you so much, Ghislaine, for coming in and talking to us today, I'm sure our audience will be…

7.11

There was just one little problem. Every single painting that left the Beltracchi's house, including *La Forêt*, was a forgery. In what is believed to be the most lucrative art forgery scam in history, all these paintings were the work of Wolfgang, Helene Beltracchi's husband.

Wolfgang was quite young when he realized he had a unique gift. His father was a church muralist and sometimes produced copies of seventeenth-century Old Masters to sell for small amounts of money. To his father's amazement, the teenage Wolfgang painted a "Picasso" in a couple of hours. He later went to art school; three of his paintings sold for reasonable amounts in a show in Munich in 1978.

But Wolfgang was more interested in his free and easy lifestyle than in the struggle of building a career as an artist. He forged a number of paintings in the 1980s, mainly selling them through dealers in Berlin, but his criminal career really took off after he met Helene Beltracchi in 1992. They fell in love immediately. Within days he told her that he was an art forger. He says he knew she wouldn't go to the police. "The first minute, I saw my future life with her," he says. Helene became his perfect accomplice. They married about a year later, and he took her last name.

Although Wolfgang was a forger, he did not copy paintings. He created totally new works of art, but in the style of the original painters. His greatest gift was the ability to look at a painting and, in just a few minutes, figure out exactly how the painter did it: where he started, when he added the blue, the white, the clouds, the water. He could even tell the time it took to complete the painting. Before tackling a forgery, Wolfgang would sometimes go to where the painter lived to get a feeling for the light there. He wanted to make sure of the colors, but also to pick up something more mystical, a sense of the painter's soul.

It was Wolfgang who came up with the idea of creating "old" photographs of Helene's grandmother sitting in front of some of the family's art collection. Wolfgang used a pre-war box camera and paper. The photos actually show Helene Beltracchi herself. The "paintings" on the wall are black and white photocopies. Wolfgang also devised the *Sammlung Flechtheim* labels which he fixed to the backs of paintings. To age them he stained them with tea and coffee.

The painting that brought about their downfall was a fake Campendonk, called *Red Picture with Horses*. In 2006, they sent it to an auction house in Cologne, with the usual fake label on the back. But in 2008, the company that bought it commissioned a scientific analysis from a British expert, which showed that the painting contained traces of the pigment Titanium White, which was not in general use until the forties. Another expert then realized that the *Sammlung Flechtheim* label on the back of the painting was fake. That led to the discovery of numerous other paintings bearing the false labels, including the Max Ernst *La Forêt*.

Wolfgang and Helene Beltracchi were arrested in Germany on August 27, 2010. Helene was released from prison in February 2013 while Wolfgang was in prison until January 2015. He agreed to paint only in his own name and to move from Germany to France. The Beltracchis say they have no regrets. Wolfgang insists he has no plans to return to forgery, although he admits it's hard. As he says, "If you imagine that after breakfast you can paint a little painting that can earn you €1 million or €2 million, then it's not so easy <u>not</u> to do it."

7.13 Part 1

Interviewer Would you describe yourself as an illustrator or as an artist?

Quentin I think those are two overlapping categories. I'm an artist and an illustrator, in the way that one might be an artist and a ceramic artist, or an artist and a sculptor, or something like that, so it's a department of being an artist.

I When did you decide to become an illustrator?

Q I don't think I ever quite decided to become an illustrator, I knew I wanted to draw, and I think I knew I wanted to draw situations. Um, I think it was– First of all, I knew that I could do pictures in magazines, and it was I suppose when I was about 20-something, 23, 24, when I was finding my own way of drawing, I also wanted to get a book to myself, so that I could have the– not only do the drawings, but tell the whole story and design the book in the way that I wanted to.

I And when did you realize that it was going to work out for you as a career?

Q Um, when I was 20-something, a bit older than that, when I'd when I'd left university and art school, I thought– I managed to get a book published in 1960, and written by John Yeoman, who's a friend, and he didn't know how to write a book and I didn't know how to illustrate it, but we got it published. And I thought, "Well, I'll, I'll try, keep– I'll try and keep on with this until I'm 30, and if it's not working out then I'll go back to teaching." Um, and I got to 30, but I passed 30 and I didn't notice!

I If a young person who was interested in becoming an illustrator, age 18, say, asked you for any advice you could give them, what would you say?

Q They, they do ask me, actually, it's very, it's very, it's very touching they still come and say– Some of them say, "I'm doing it because of you," and but also they, they ask that question. Um, and it's, it's– I mean, I really don't know the answer, but it must be something about drawing and doing a lot of drawing and a lot of different kinds of drawing, because then you become completely familiar with the activity, and in a sense, that's the most important thing.

7.14 Part 2

Interviewer How important is the relationship between author and illustrator?

Quentin Well, in some respects it has to be terribly important, I think! But it's, it's– the thing about it is initially it's, um, collaboration very often isn't what people think it is. You don't spend a lot of time talking much, "Shall we do this? Shall we do that?" and I, I never want to do that. Essentially, the collaboration, the relationship, is with the text to begin with, with the book to begin with, and you have to read that first and you have to keep collaborating with– those, those are the messages from the writer, that is the thing that you're dealing with. You may want to talk to the writer as well, but if, if the– if you can establish the, the relationship with, with the words, that's the important thing.

I Are there any authors to whom you did talk a lot?

Q With Roald Dahl, I think our view of things, in many respects, is very, very different, and I think we, we did talk a lot and we needed to talk. Um, but it was on the basis of what he'd written, initially, so that I would– the way of going about it, which we established after a while, was that I would draw some pictures of what I thought the characters looked like, and the moments that I thought would be useful to draw and interesting to draw, then I would go and talk to him about it, and he would say, "Could you do this and could you do this? We need to see more tortoises," you know, or something like that! But um, uh we talked quite a lot, again, some of it was about the about the technicalities of the book, getting it to work better, I think. Um, but I think to get to get into the mood of the book, which is a terribly important thing, it's something you have to do on your own, really, I think. The author can't tell you that.

I I can imagine that an author might ask an illustrator to redraw something. Does it ever work the other way around, that the illustrator asks the author to change things?

Q Uh, it can do, yes. Actually, Roald volunteered to alter things, I didn't ask him to, I mean, in the case of *The BFG*, which we spent a lot of time working on, um, the BFG had a different costume to begin with. Uh, he had a long leather apron and long boots and that sort of thing. Of course, if you say an apron, when the character is introduced you say he was wearing an apron and you don't talk about it after that probably. But I had to draw it in every wretched drawing– picture, that there is in the book! So he– after a bit he said, "This apron's getting in the way, isn't it?" because the chap has– you know, the giant has to run and it has to leap in the air, and so on and so on. So we went back and talked about what he would wear, uh, that would keep his character the same, but, um, and, and that– also what came out of that, we couldn't decide what to put on his feet. And I went home, and a day or two later, arrived this strange brown paper parcel, which is– was one of Roald's own Norwegian sandals, and of course, that's– it solved the problem as far as what he wears is concerned, but in a funny way it also told you how near he was to his creation.

7.15 Part 3

Interviewer Do you like all the characters you create in an illustration, or are some more interesting to you than others?

Quentin You have a sympathetic feeling for all of them, I think, but of course some are more interesting than others, I think! Um, that's not a question I've ever thought about, I don't think. Um, yes, I think some are more interesting, but I think the, the essence of that question, though I'm not sure I've got this right, is that you have to be able to, whether they're nice or not, or interesting or not, you have to be able to identify with them, so that you imagine, in some sense, as you're drawing, that you are them, and that's much more important than whether you're interested in them or like them.

I So you're not thinking of the children who are going to be reading the books?

Q What I'm interested in about children is children and about children in books, but I, I'm not illustrating children's books because I love children or because I have children, which I don't, or because– anything of that kind. What you have to do while you're illustrating that book is to identify with them for that moment, in the same way that that's how I know what they're doing, because I just become them for a moment, you know. In the same way that you become the elderly grandparent or you become the dog, or, or whatever the characters are!

I Do you draw from life?

Q I never draw from life, no, I make it all up. Um, and, um, I think I'm fortunate in that respect, I, I can imagine people. I do a rough drawing first to see how, you know, where the gestures are or what the, what the activity is, how the figures relate to each other, what the expressions on their faces are, so I get a rough drawing and then I, I work from that. But, um, I've mostly just invented.

I Do you ever draw digitally?

Q Digitally, curiously enough, I was probably one of the first people who did it, did it, because I did, um, like 40 years ago, start– did drawing on a television screen, I mean, in a television studio, so that you could draw on the screen, but I haven't gone on with it. Um, I mean, I wouldn't mind doing it, the disadvantage to it from my point of view is that I like the feeling of the implement on the paper, so that it's– you get– you know, if you have a quill or a nib or a reed pen, you get a different kind of scratch, but if you're inventing what is happening, the reed pen is actually doing it. It's, it's not copying something, it's actually creating it as you're going along, so it's the fact that you can feel it on the paper is enormously helpful.

I Is there an artist or an illustrator that inspired you?

Q I mean I was very influenced by a lot of, of, uh, people who were drawing when I started drawing in the 50s, um, I mean, Ronald Searle, for instance, who was, was– who you couldn't avoid being influenced by to a considerable extent, but the person that I think most had an effect on me was a French artist, a contemporary and friend of Searle, André Francois. When I was a young man I got his address and went to see him. And, um, I suppose—he died a few years ago, he was nearly 90, but, um, just two or three years before that, I had an exhibition in Paris and it was rather wonderful because he turned up. I mean, I didn't invite him, the gallery owner invited him, um, so it was nice that he hadn't forgotten who I was, exactly.

7.17

Interviewer Is there a book that you particularly like because of the illustrations?

Laura *Garfield*, I love *Garfield*. They have wonderful illustrations. With the– this stupid human, and the stupid dog, and the clever cat. I love it. That would be it.

I Do you have a favorite painting or poster in your house?

L I have a painting I bought in, uh, Buenos Aires once with two tango dancers which I'm very fond of, I dance tango myself and it it has a meaning to me.

I Can you describe it?

L Mmm, not very strong colors. It's sort of black and white and she's wearing a, uh, a red dress, which is also very classical tango-like and he's in black clothes and they're like, like from above, uh, you see her leaning back. It's nice.

Interviewer Is there a book that you particularly liked or like because of the illustrations?

Marcus Um, uh, it's difficult, but, uh, I guess a book that I would enjoy the most because of the illustrations would be, uh, actually, uh, Tolkien's, uh, *Hobbit* and *The Lord of the Rings*. He did a lot of original illustrations himself and they're, they're quite whimsical in their, in their design. I really enjoy that sort of originality.

I Do you have a favorite painting or poster in your house?

M Uh, I have a really nice picture from Canada, by a, uh, a, a local artist and it's, um, it's, it's inspired by the traditional Canadian styles. So, it's, it's a black and red painting, very, very, uh, striking, and, um, sort of a tribal style and I really, I really like that one. It's very vibrant and at the same time simple.

Interviewer Can you remember a book you read when you were a child where you liked the illustrations?

Louise Um, probably *The Little Prince*, because the author illustrated the book himself and he's got water-color illustrations and they're just, they're so unique and timeless.

I Do you have a favorite painting or poster in your house?

L Um I have a calendar that my friend made. So it's got pictures of all of us, which is really nice.

Interviewer Is there a book that you particularly liked because of the illustrations?

Maura There's probably two books that I can think of that I liked because of the illustrations. One is *Alice in Wonderland*, um, by Lewis Carroll, which had all the very famous line drawings, uh, in the book of Alice going down, uh, into Wonderland, following the White Rabbit, and I guess I really liked those because they kind of show you the characters and they help you to kind of fix the images of, uh, the people within the book, so I really liked that one. And another one that I liked, and I don't know if they were the original illustrations that come with the book, were Oscar Wilde's *Short Stories*, and I always remember there was a picture of the Selfish Giant crying in the garden and I think I read that as a child so it must have really stuck with me that I can still see this image and again I think it was just a black and white line drawing.

I Do you have a favorite painting or poster in your house? Can you describe it?

M OK, I do have a fav– a favorite painting in my house at the moment. I actually got it for Christmas. And it was actually in my friend's bedroom and I saw it and I said, oh, that's really nice and she said, "Oh, OK, well, you can have it for your Christmas present." And I have it hanging up in my house at the moment. And it's two birds, uh, in a garden about to, uh, eat a plant. And, uh, it's very, it's very cute, it's not realistic, um, and I just really like it, it's kind of a tree and underneath it it says something like "We found love," which is probably sentimental, but anyway, it was quite sweet and I really liked it and it's in my house at the moment.

Interviewer Is there a book that you particularly liked because of the illustrations?

Ally When I was younger I had this copy of *A Little Princess* which had really beautiful illustrations and I really loved it.

I Do you have a favorite painting or poster in your house? Can you describe it?

A At my parents' house, in my room, I have this poster that I got when we went to Pompeii when I was in fifth grade. It's a recreation of this, um, Roman, um, mural and so it's this lady with flowers and it's beautiful.

8.1

1 I'm not sure if I've ever had experience with what you would call alternative medicine, I've used chiropractic, but not everyone considers chiropractic to be alternative. I had been doing some sort of extreme exercises in the gym and I got a slipped disc and the pain was excruciating, and although my boyfriend at the time was an orthopedic surgeon, he told me to see a chiropractor, ha, and I must say it worked really well. The only problem was that although I felt fine after, I think, three or four visits, the chiropractor wanted me to keep coming back, and so I ended up having to make an excuse for not going back, I said that I was leaving the country basically, but it worked!

2 I'm very skeptical, you know, about alternative medicine, all, all sorts of alternative medicine, in fact I don't believe in them, except I guess osteopathy, if you can call that "alternative"—but the only time I've had something that you would really call alternative medicine was when I went to an osteopath because I had a bad back, and at the same time as having a bad back, I had this really awful cold, terrible pain in my sinuses, and I could hardly breathe and the osteopath said, "I can give you a sort of acupuncture, but it's with very small needles that they put in your ear," and I was lying face down having the osteopath deal with my back, and I could hardly breathe, so I said, "OK," so he put these tiny needles in my ear, and I have to admit that the next day I was almost completely better—I felt so good, and it convinced me really that– in the sense that it definitely wasn't a placebo effect because I didn't believe in it, but I really felt much, much better.

3 I don't use alternative medicine, because I think it's a waste of time and it doesn't work. If alternative medicine worked, it wouldn't be alternative, it would be actual conventional medicine. The reason that it's alternative is because we don't have any solid proof that it works. You only ever hear anecdotal evidence that it's worked for individual people, that's not real evidence, and I would say to anyone who's heard stories like that, look up "the placebo effect." There's no evidence that alternative medicine works beyond the placebo effect, and so as far as I'm concerned, it's a waste of time and money, and at its worst it could even be dangerous or harmful if people are using it in place of real medicine that might cure their very real illness.

4 So, having had endless pain as a result of this inflamed tendon in my foot, and after tons of antibiotics that seemed to take a very long time to have any effect, I decided to try acupuncture. It just so happened that the doctor who was doing it was somebody that I'd known from the doctors' group where I used to go to, so I went to him, and it was an extremely pleasant experience, but unfortunately it didn't do any good at all, however if I was very sick or something and had tried like all sorts of normal cures I think I'd give it a try again.

8.3

Think about your average day as a series of choices. You get up, you choose what to eat, you decide whether to go for a run, whether or not to have a second helping of dessert. You're constantly making decisions based on what you want versus what you think is good for you. But how do you know what's good for you? Nowadays we are bombarded with research and statistics telling us what we should or shouldn't do—but are the numbers really right?

First of all, the classic advice to eat five servings of fruit and vegetables a day. Does it really make a difference? Well, it's a lot more useful than just saying "eat a varied diet," because how do we know what that really means? But five servings may not be enough. A World Health Organization study found that in the countries with the lowest levels of heart disease, the average person was eating around ten servings a day of fruit and veggies. So although five will do you good, more might be better. In the US, by the way, only one in ten adults eat enough fruit and vegetables each day.

From food to water. The claim that we should drink eight glasses of water a day is widely attributed to a report by the American National Academy of Sciences, which estimated that we needed 2.5 liters of fluid a day, which is approximately eight glasses. But, and this is the key thing, the fluid doesn't need to be water. For example, we already take in three quarters of a liter of fluid from the food we eat each day. The eight glasses of water idea might seem fairly harmless, but it has created a belief that we don't drink enough water. In fact, the best advice is, if you're thirsty, have a drink—water, tea, juice, whatever you feel like. If not, you're probably fine.

Now the tricky question of how much we should *eat*—or, more specifically, how many calories a day we should consume. The standard guidelines are 2,000 calories a day for women and 2,500 for men. But this is a simplification. The actual amount you need depends on your weight and height, the amount of activity you do, and your metabolism—some people can eat like a horse and not put on weight. Every individual is different and needs to balance their own food intake against their own calorie needs.

What about sleep? Well, for everyone who tells you they can get by on four hours a night, studies show that most people need between seven and nine hours of sleep to function well. If you regularly average less than seven hours, then you have an increased risk of depression, diabetes, and heart problems. But sleeping for more than nine hours a night has also been associated with an increase in health issues. So eight hours a night is probably about right, though a little more or a little less shouldn't do you any harm.

On to exercise. You've probably heard that the recommended amount of exercise is a minimum of half an hour's moderate activity five times a week. But even if you're doing the recommended amount, it may not be enough if you then drive to work and sit at a computer all day. A review by the *American Journal of Clinical Nutrition* said that an average of 30 minutes daily may not prevent unhealthy weight gain in many people. The message? Do the recommended amount of moderate activity, but try to do more if you can, especially if you spend a lot of the day sitting down.

And finally, we all know how addicted our kids are to anything with a screen. But given the amount of panic there is about children watching TV, playing computer games or going online, there is surprisingly little research into the long-term effects of screen time. So, should we limit screen time to protect our children's physical or emotional health? It's a difficult question to answer. Obviously sitting down for too long is as bad for children as it is for adults, but a large-scale UK study of 11,000 children showed no relationship between screen time and emotional or social problems, or an inability to concentrate or make friends. So, while the internet may be changing how our brains work, the idea of limiting screen time to two hours a day isn't supported by research. Instead we should make up our own minds about what's best for our children—and for ourselves.

8.9

I was, I was traveling back from Spain to the UK, I was with my family, with my wife and two young children, it was two days before Christmas, and we were traveling back to London to visit my family there. It was an evening flight, I think the flight left around 10 o'clock, and it was leaving from Valencia. The weather there was really good, but just before we were going to take off, I was just reading my, you know, the messages at the last minute and I saw there was a message from my brother, so I read it, and he was asking me whether the flight had been canceled, because he said in the message that there was a very, very bad storm in London with gale force winds. I sent a message back to him saying, well, no, actually we're just taking off, but obviously it made me wonder what the weather was going to be like when we got there.

8.10

It was a two-hour flight, everything was normal, until we got to Gatwick. As we were approaching Gatwick the pilot came on and he said, "I'm sorry, we can't land yet because there's really bad weather here, so we're going to circle for a while." So the plane started circling, and then we started getting the worst turbulence I've ever, ever experienced. The plane just seemed to be going up in the air, then dropping, then rising up again and then dropping. And this went on for about 20 minutes. Then the pilot obviously decided he was going to have a go at landing, but as he got nearer and nearer to the ground, the wind just got stronger and stronger, and the plane was being knocked around, and I really thought, "This is it, we're going to crash."

8.11

Just at the very last moment, the pilot obviously realized that it was impossible to land and he changed his mind and the plane suddenly shot back up in the air and this was a really scary moment and a lot of people on the plane they sort of gasped in alarm. The plane started gaining height, the pilot didn't say anything, and when we finally got up, well, really high again then he came on and he said, "I'm very sorry, but I just couldn't land, it was too windy, and I'm afraid we can't land at Gatwick now because the airport's been closed. In fact, I have to tell you that we can't land anywhere in the UK because all the airports are closed." Everyone on the plane was sort of looking at each other and I think we were all thinking, "So where are we going to land? Have we got enough petrol to land somewhere else?"

8.12

Well, then the pilot said, "Fortunately, Amsterdam airport has said we can land there, so we're off to Holland now. Then we had a two-hour journey to Holland, that was OK, fairly calm, fairly normal, and then as we came in to land at Amsterdam, the pilot warned us, he said, "It's going to be windy here too, but not as bad as at Gatwick," and it was quite a good landing, little bit bumpy, and everyone was very, very relieved to get down on the ground, in fact, all the passengers applauded. And we all started getting up, to be honest we couldn't wait, you know, to get off, to get our feet on firm ground again.

8.13

But then, just as we were getting all our things from the overhead locker, one of the crew got on the loudspeaker and he said, "Well no, no, don't get off because what's happening now, is we're going to refuel, and then we're going to fly back to Gatwick. We're going to have another try, because we think that in a couple of hours, the weather should be better at Gatwick. And he said, if you want to get off, you can get off, but there won't be a hotel for you, because this plane's going back to Gatwick."

8.14

So then everyone had a bit of a dilemma, and in fact what happened was that pretty well everyone who had children, all the parents, there were a lot of children on the plane, because it was Christmas, pretty well everyone who had children got off the plane and the others stayed on. We were really happy to get off that plane and we spent the night in Amsterdam airport, and then in the morning we got a train from Amsterdam to Belgium. In Brussels, we picked up the Eurostar, and that took us through France, under the Channel, and back to London. So, after traveling all day, we finally got home around seven o'clock in the evening, just in time for the children to hang up their stockings for Christmas. Definitely the most frightening experience I've ever had.

9.8

John Good afternoon, and welcome to *The Food Program*, where each week we debate issues related to food. In this week's debate, and some people may think this is long overdue, the subject is "Being vegetarian." Should we or shouldn't we be giving up meat? With me today in the studio are Abby Fisher, from an online newspaper about vegetarian issues, and Dr. Mark Carol, a nutritionist. Before we start the debate, let me just clarify that we are just debating about not eating meat, not giving up fish and dairy, too, or going vegan. Abby, you have the floor, to propose that we should all give up meat.

Abby Thank you, John. People are drawn to vegetarianism by all sorts of motives. Some of us want to live longer, healthier lives, or do our part to reduce pollution. Others of us have made the switch because we want to preserve the Earth's natural resources, or because we've always loved animals and are ethically opposed to eating them. I'm going to focus on three clear reasons for giving up meat.

First, for your health. I think it's pretty generally accepted that vegetarian diets are healthier than the average US diet. It's estimated that 70 percent of all diseases, including one third of all cancers, are related to diet. A vegetarian diet reduces the risk for diseases such as obesity, coronary artery disease, high blood pressure, diabetes, and certain types of cancer. Being a vegetarian also means being slimmer, which as we all know, means being healthier. In a recent study where overweight people followed a low-fat, vegetarian diet they lost an average of 26 pounds in the first year and, by sticking to a vegetarian diet, had kept off that weight five years later. You'll also live longer—according to other studies, vegetarians live on average 13 years longer than meat eaters.

Now, let's move on to pollution. Many people have become vegetarians after they realized the devastation that the meat industry is having on the environment. According to the US Environmental Protection Agency, chemical and animal waste from factory farms—that is, farms that keep large numbers of animals, and usually in terrible conditions— this waste is responsible for more than 173,000 miles of polluted rivers and streams and it's one of the greatest threats to water quality today. So, by stopping eating meat, you'll help to reduce pollution, especially water pollution.

My third main argument is cost. If you give up meat, you'll save money. The average American spends about $585 a year on meat. If you have four people in your family, that's over $2,000 a year! If you start eating vegetables, grains, and fruits instead of the 222 pounds of meat, chicken, and pork each non-vegetarian eats per year, you'll cut individual food bills right down.

So, to sum up, stopping eating meat will improve your health, will reduce pollution, and will save you money. So rather than asking yourself, "Why go vegetarian?" the real question is, "Why haven't you gone vegetarian already?"

9.9

John Thank you very much, Abby. And now it's Dr. Mark Carol's turn to oppose these arguments. Mark, over to you.

Mark Well, let me deal with those arguments one by one. I'll start with the area that is obviously my speciality, and that's health. While there is some evidence that eating too much meat can negatively affect your health, the vast majority of research suggests that a well-balanced omnivorous diet, that is, a diet that includes all the main food groups, is a far healthier choice. Studies have repeatedly shown that vegetarians who don't supplement their diets with Vitamin D, B12, and iron are prone to becoming anemic. And I know we're just talking about non-meat eaters, but vegetarians who don't eat fish either also typically miss out on Omega-3 fatty acids that are essential, not just for our physical well-being, but also potentially help with depression and some personality disorders. And I'd also like to mention that research at Oxford University recently followed 35,000 individuals from the ages of 20 to 89 for a period of five years and discovered that vegans are 30% more likely to break a bone than meat eaters.

Now, as for the environmental argument, yes, many vegetarians argue that meat production harms the environment. But what they don't tell you—and of course they must know this—is that fruit and vegetable farming has just as severe environmental implications. The vast majority of non-organic farms still use pesticides and insecticides that kill off just as many beneficial predators as pests, and so have a negative effect on our ecosystems. These dangerous chemicals also frequently get into water supplies…and speaking of water, you need vast amounts of it to grow vegetables commercially, and this can cause water shortages and, in extreme cases, drought. And one final point—bear in mind that vegetarians also produce more gas than meat-eaters. The problem lies in the human body's inability to fully digest the complex carbohydrates in the vegetarian diet, which results in higher production of gases like hydrogen, carbon dioxide, and methane. People may laugh, but it's no laughing matter, I assure you.

Finally, the argument about cost. Well, I have to say that this argument really doesn't hold water. I'm not sure where Ms. ... Abby got her statistics from, but it's a well-known fact that one of the reasons why people in the US don't eat enough fruit and vegetables, by which I mean at least five servings a day, is because of the cost of fresh fruit and vegetables in this country. Meat and poultry prices have hardly gone up at all during the last few years, whereas the price of fruit and vegetables has skyrocketed, and many people say they simply can't afford to eat their five servings a day. So the argument that going vegetarian will save you money—well, it's just not an argument at all.

I'd like to sum up by saying that of course the main reason why we should all eat meat in moderation is that human beings are omnivores, and that means that we eat everything. Carnivores, like lions and tigers, don't suddenly start eating grass, and herbivores like sheep or goats, don't suddenly start eating meat. Omnivores should continue to have a balanced diet, which, as I said earlier, should cover all the main food groups.

J Thanks very much, Mark. Now, Abby, I'm sure you have more to say and react to what Mark has just said…

9.15

How to eat out

Tip 1 *Always order the fish.*
Really good fresh fish is very hard to find, very hard to store and keep fresh—you've got to really cook it as soon as you buy it or there's no point. It's often fiddly to prepare and very smelly to cook. It's what restaurants are FOR! It just amazes me that people will go into a restaurant and order the steak. A thing you can buy almost anywhere, keep for weeks, and cook however you like without doing anything to it and it'll always basically be OK.

Tip 2 *Never eat the bread.*
An ex-girlfriend of mine eats nothing all day. She claims she doesn't get hungry. So, whenever we meet for dinner, she is utterly starving and gobbles up the entire bread basket and three pats of butter without pausing for breath. Then halfway through her main course she starts poking about and saying, "I don't know why they give you such large portions, I'll never eat all this!" I just don't know why people eat the bread. You shouldn't be that hungry. Ever. Bread is not a first course. It's a breakfast food, an accompaniment to certain terrines. But in an expensive place with a TV chef and a whole range of exciting things to chew on for the next couple of hours, why would anyone want to fill up with bread? I always tell them, as soon as I arrive, to bring no bread. But sometimes they do and you must tell them to take it away.

Tip 3 *Have the vegetarian option—but not in a vegetarian restaurant.*
As a rule, the best vegetarian food is cooked by meat-eating chefs who know how to cook, rather than by bearded hippies. For this reason, if you want good vegetarian food, go to a normal, that is, omnivorous, restaurant. There may not be much choice, but personally I would much rather restaurants focused on doing one or two things brilliantly than offered a whole load of stuff that was just about OK.

Tip 4 *Never sit at a table outside.*
Why on earth would you want to eat outside? I suppose in a hot country where there's no air conditioning, it might be nice to sit outside in the shade overlooking the sea. But on a busy London street? Crazy. Go indoors. Also, in most restaurants the outside tables are ruined by smokers. If you want to eat outside in London, take sandwiches and eat them in one of the wonderful parks.

Tip 5 *Insist on tap water.*
We have invested years and years and vast amounts of money into an ingenious system which cleans water and delivers it very cheaply to our homes and workplaces through a tap. And yet last year we bought three billion liters of bottled water. That's just free money for the restaurant, so don't order mineral water! Ask for a jug of tap.

Tip 6 *How to complain—and get a result.*
Complain nicely, politely, apologetically. But firmly, and at the very moment of disappointment. "I'm awfully sorry to make a fuss," you might say, "but this fish really isn't as fresh as I'd hoped. I really can't eat this. What else might I have as a replacement that can come quickly?" There's simply no way you can lose with that. The end result is likely to be free main courses, a jolly time, and an amicable departure.

Tip 7 *Be nice to the staff.*
Just be nice to them, that's all. You should always be nice to everybody, obviously, but if you're not, make being nice to staff in restaurants your only exception. Don't flirt with waitresses, and don't ask foreign staff where they're from. Just smile, and say *please* and *thank you*, and look at them when you're ordering. And then shut up and eat.

9.17 Part 1

Interviewer Professor McGavin, you're an expert in arthropods. Could you start by telling us what arthropods are?

George Well, arthropods are, are this really enormous group of animals; I mean they're, they're much bigger than any other animal group on Earth. They comprise about, you know, three quarters of, of all animals and they're the, they're the animals that have lots of hinged legs: so crustacea, spiders, insects, that sort of thing. Hard outsides, lots of hinged legs.

I And what is it about them that interests you?

G Arthropods have got to interest everybody because they are, to all intents and purposes, the, the major animal group on Earth. So if you call yourself a zoologist and you don't know anything about arthropods, you really don't know anything about anything, because they are the majority! Everybody gets very excited about, uh, backboned animals, things with a spine: uh, bats, cats, rats, mammals, amphibians, fish, birds, they only comprise 2.9% of all species, whereas arthropods comprise about 66% of all species. So, you know in terms of, of species, they are immensely important. In terms of what they do, they are immensely important.

I Were you interested in them right from the start, from when you were a child?

G When I was very young, I, I knew that the natural world was the most interesting thing around. So I wanted to be outside, and you don't have to be outside very long before you find, you know, insects and spiders and things, you know, doing interesting things. But I was interested more generally as a kid, and it was only when I got to Edinburgh for my first degree that I realized that actually insects were the major player in any habitat. And we were on a field trip to the west coast of Scotland, when all my classmates were looking for badgers and owls and eagles, and failing to find them, but at our feet were hundreds of thousands of ants doing very interesting things, and I thought, "Well, the– surely this is easier to work on?"

I I understand that there are several species that are named after you. Could you tell us a little about them?

G One of the great things about being in a field for long enough is that people will eventually describe a new species and think, "Oh, what on earth am I going to call this?" you know, and normally they're named after the country or how they look or something like that. But five people around the world have named, uh, an insect in my honor, and a spider, I think, so I have a plant hopper in Africa, I've got a shield bug from Borneo, uh, I think an ant from Africa as well, a cockroach from southeast Asia, which is, is great, and they have my name, uh, attached to them! What's making me slightly depressed is the fact that, uh, these things may not survive. Uh, even though they've been named in my, my honor, we're losing species at a quite alarming rate now, because of habitat loss. And the sad truth is that although we are pretty sure there are eight million species of arthropods out there unknown, our chances of ever finding them and naming them are probably pretty slim, because they will come and they will go without us ever knowing they were there.

9.18 Part 2

Interviewer Quite a lot of people have phobias of insects and spiders. Why do you think that is?

George I sometimes wonder why people have a phobia. I mean, they, they say it's because they're unpredictable, they, they move in a strange way, they've got lots of legs, well, you know, I don't know. It, it– I think it's passed on. I think if you're a kid growing up, you have a fascination with the thing arou– all the animals around you, and I think adults sometimes pass their fears on by, by going, "Oh, what's that? Oh, it's a spider," you know. In some parts of the world it, it's perfectly justifiable to, to have a fear of spiders, because there are many places in the world where, you know, spiders can injure you severely. In the UK, however, there are no spiders which can injure you at all. You might get a slight irritation or, you know, a swelling, but, but still there are something like seven million people in the United Kingdom who are terrified of spiders, and, and moths.

I Do you think it's possible for them to be cured of their phobia?

G It is possible to, to train people out of fears, uh, by, by simply exposing them to something you know on a regular basis, and perhaps if they have a spider phobia, you start with a very small spider and you say, well, "Have it on your hand, examine it, you know, it's fine." And I've, I've actually cured a girl who had a spider phobia in a, in a day and by the end of the day she was able to hold a tarantula. Um, and I, I think it's– you know, if people look at the natural world, if they look at insects or spiders, and they understand them, then you begin to, to really enjoy them. But, but if you just cut yourself off, which is what most people do, they say, you know, "I'm going to have an insect-free zone around me," it, it's not possible.

I I'm assuming you're not afraid of any insects or spiders, but have you ever been in a situation where you were genuinely frightened of an animal?

G We were filming in the Amazon after dark, because it was a program about animals after dark, and I saw a, a head of a snake poking out from under a leaf, and of course I thought, well, "This is great, you know, quick, the camera! Come on, let's get down and have a look at this thing." You know, I'm not stupid, so I, I got a stick and I, I lifted this leaf up gingerly, and of course it was a fer de lance, which is one of the most dangerous snakes in the whole of South America, responsible for more human deaths than probably any other snake. And as I lifted it up sort of looked at me, you know, and they don't like head torches, so I'm wearing a head torch shining right in its face! It does this, you know! And then I realize that it's four feet long, it's twice as long as my stick, which means that it could get me very easily indeed. So I, I just sort of froze, I could feel my heart pounding, and I just gent– gingerly put the leaf down and said, "We'll just leave this one, I think!" That could have been very nasty.

🔊 9.19 Part 3

Interviewer Would you ever just kill an insect that was in your house?

George Well, in my career I have killed millions of insects. As part of my work is, you have to collect them, uh, because you can't name them or describe them or work on them unless you kill them. In my home, that's a different thing. If it's a, if it's a bee that has come in by accident, or a wasp or something like that, I will catch it and outside it goes. Fleas, however, if you have a cat and you don't control the fleas, are a bit of a pest and I will definitely get rid of the fleas.

I Eating insects has recently become quite fashionable. Is it a realistic solution to the problem of world nutrition, or is it just a flash in the pan, for want of a better phrase?

G I don't think it's a flash in the pan because you can farm them in, in, in a very easy way. And as long as you can make the food available in a palatable form, uh, I mean, I've, I've eaten insects for, for years and years, fry them up and grind them into flour and make, you know, bread out of it. No, it, it isn't a flash in the pan, um, we will have to, to address this quite seriously in the next, you know, hundred or so years.

I Why do we not eat insects in Europe?

G In the West we, we tend to not eat insects and, and lots of people say it's because insects are dirty or they look funny or whatever. It's actually not anything to do with those things, it's, it's about ecology, it's about a thing called "optimal foraging theory," which simply says if you use up more energy collecting food to feed yourself and your family than you get back from eating it, it won't happen, it's, it's not a thing that will, will occur in that area of the world. So in the West, where it's cold and insects are relatively small, it's, it's not a very sensible idea. However, in hot countries where insects are larger and swarm and can be collected very, very easily, and that's anywhere from Mexico, Japan, South America, you know, any of these countries, it makes sense. It's very easy to harvest enough food, uh, in a relatively short time, half an hour, an hour, which will provide a, a sizeable meal. And it's, it's a thing that we've been doing as a species for a million years.

I If you were trying to convert someone to insect-eating, what would be the first thing you would cook them?

G Well, you, you would have to make the food appealing and interesting and, uh, you know, attractive, so I would start with a, with a mealworm, uh, in a snack! Roasted mealworms are awfully good!

I How often do you cook insects?

G As often as I can! I cook insects as often as I can! I like to open audiences' eyes to the possibility of eating insects. We eat prawns, we eat lots of things, you know, snails, but I mean, insects are essentially flying prawns. OK, they, they tend to be smaller. But I, I had an audience once in, in Oxford of 200 eight-, eight- to twelve-year-olds and at, at the end of my lecture I cooked up a big wok of, of crickets, fried them up with some garlic and a bit of salt and pepper, handed them round, and the kids went wild! They, they ate the whole lot. From the back of the audience came a mum with a face like thunder, and she came down to the front of the of the auditorium and said, "My son's just eaten six crickets!" I went, "Yeah, and your point is?" She was like, "At home he doesn't even eat broccoli." And I just went… I said, "Well, clearly it's the way you cook your broccoli."

🔊 9.21

Interviewer What's the most interesting animal that you've ever seen in the wild?

Jenny I think the most interesting animal I've ever seen in the wild is an elephant. It was in Thailand, actually, at an elephant sanctuary where we got to bathe them and pet them.

I Why did it make such an impression on you?

J Uh, the sanctuary, uh, was for rehabilitating elephants that were injured in the wild, um, but they actually allowed them to just roam around free, uh, so it was really impressive.

I Is there anywhere you would particularly like to go to see animals or the natural world?

J Yes. I would love to go to Japan to see the snow monkeys.

Interviewer What's the most interesting animal that you've ever seen in the wild?

Alex Um, an orangutan. Yeah, an orangutan. Certainly.

I Where was that?

A In Borneo. In the Malaysian part of Borneo.

I Why did it make such an impression on you?

A Uh, simply because we'd gone there specially to see them. It was one of my favorite animals. But, we'd been told the chances of seeing them in the wild were very slim, uh, and so I'd kind of lowered my expectations and when we did actually get to see one, it was very, very exciting and unexpected.

I Is there anywhere you would particularly like to go to see animals or the natural world?

A Oh, um, yes. Uh, I'd, I'd really like to go to, uh, East Africa. Uh, to see the kind of, the mountains, around there. Uh, it's a part of the world I've not been to and I'd really like to go and explore that.

Interviewer What's the most interesting animal that you've ever seen in the wild?

Sarah Uh, the most interesting animals I've seen are giant sea turtles. It was in Hawaii.

I Why did it make such an impression on you?

S They're just so big! They're huge! You see them on TV but never in real life.

I Is there anywhere you would particularly like to go to see animals or the natural world?

S Hmm, I think I'd like to go to South Africa and go on a safari.

Interviewer What's the most interesting animal that you've ever seen in the wild?

James Um, I saw a giraffe once. I mean, it's not that interesting, I suppose, but I did see it in the wild.

I Where was that?

J That was in Ethiopia, in northern Ethiopia.

I Why did it make such an impression on you?

J I think because I wasn't expecting to see it. I was, uh, hitchhiking on the back of a, a truck, uh, and we were driving just through, um, the countryside, and suddenly we saw a giraffe running along the side of the truck and it was, it was kind of amazing, um, so I suppose that's why it was, you know, pretty good to see.

I Is there anywhere you would particularly like to go to see animals or the natural world?

J Um, I've always wanted to see whales in the wild. Um, I've never, I've never had the chance to do it, but it looks just so amazing, the, the size of them. Um so I'd like to do that, yeah.

Interviewer What's the most interesting animal that you've ever seen in the wild?

Karen The most interesting animal I've seen in the wild? Um, that would be a tiger in a national park in India, so, um, it's very rare that you can actually, um, spot them, so I was very fortunate enough to, um, just to see one and just the grace of the movement and the awareness of, you know, everything around him or her, um, was extraordinary.

I Is there anywhere you would particularly like to go to see animals or the natural world?

K Madagascar. I'd love to see, um, animals in the natural world there. I've seen, um, a few David Attenborough documentaries, um, it's like, I want to go there now.

🔊 10.1

Interviewer Why did you decide to leave the UK and live abroad?

Emma Well, actually it was David who convinced me it was a good idea. A long time ago, going back, I was studying at the, my final year at the University of Warwick and David was working at that time in Majorca and we met in England and then he returned to work in Majorca. And then it was, it was very– we kept in touch by letters and it was very easy to be seduced by the, the lifestyle he had there, the lovely swimming, the barbecues in the mountains, the, the fishing for octopus, so I was sitting finishing my le–, my essays in the– the library windows covered with rain and, yes, so when I graduated I, I went very happily out to, to Spain to be with him and we both got jobs in Vigo in, in Spain working as language teachers in a private school and we had a lovely time, we just– we worked, and when we weren't working we spent the time discovering the area, going out on our bikes and learned to windsurf, yes, that was a great year.

I So a very happy introduction to Spain for you. And how did you both end up in Mairena?

David Well, it was by chance, really, we'd, we'd been working as English teachers for, for several years, ten years perhaps in my case, and we realized that we had the opportunity to, to take a year off, a sabbatical year as it were, with a view to then going back to, to teaching again and we had a friend who had a, a small house in the, in, in a village in the mountains south of Granada and he'd agreed to, to let us rent this house for, for next to nothing, for a year, so that's what we did, but whilst we were there we wandered around and cycled around and finally stumbled on this little village of Mairena where we live now and fell in love with the village, fell in love with the house that we, we lived in for a while at first and realized at the end of the year that we were, we were having a ball and enjoying it too much, really to, to want to go back, so at that point we realized that we had to, to find a way of, of earning a living because we didn't have any money and so we, I, I got a job in Granada in fact just teaching for a year or so and then we opened what's now *Las Chimeneas*, our little hotel and restaurant.

I How integrated do you feel in the local community?

D Well, one of the things that made me feel very integrated and indeed very, very proud in fact was, was being invited to, to join the local council and I worked for six years as the the deputy mayor and not necessarily a very good deputy mayor, but I kind of enjoyed it, and it was, you know, I consider it as an honor to be, to be involved and asked to get involved in in local politics and it's, it's a useful thing as well, rather than just being on the outside protesting at decisions taken after the event it's quite useful to be part of the decision-making process as well. And…

E I think for me the, the thing that really made a difference was when we had children, because especially, as being, being, you know a mother in the village it meant that you met other mothers and people felt that it was a reason to talk, and our children are friends with the other kids, they come round to play now, so yeah, that was a big difference for me.

D And having the business as well because we, you know people can see that we're, we're actually working, and we're working alongside our neighbors, because, you know, we're lucky, we're– enough to be in a position where we've been able to employ quite a lot of the local villagers as, you know, as cooks, and chefs, and taxi drivers, and so on.

I What do you like most about living in Mairena?

E The obvious thing and almost a cliché is the weather, but you can't underestimate that, I mean, the weather does affect your everyday life and also simple things like the incredible clear skies and the light. But I think it's something more than that, as long as I can remember I always had a hankering, I really wanted to live in a very small community, I remember even as a child it was something that I always had an ambition to do. And I think something about living in a very small village, everything seems very kind of human, very manageable, you, you know everybody, you literally know everybody in the village, and what's also been great the last few years is that we bought some land which is filled with, almonds, and olive and fruit trees, so we spend a lot of tr– time down there and learning how to farm like the locals do, because they have very complicated watering techniques, so we've had to speak to locals and learn how to farm the land.

I Are there any downsides to living there?

E It's the traveling, isn't it, we have to spend probably more time than we would like in a car to, to buy something simple. On, on the one hand it's great being away from shops, it's like a kind of a, real kind of consumer detox, but on the other hand when you actually have to buy something it means you have a long journey, which I could do without.

D And there's lots of paperwork as well, Spain is a very heavily bureaucratic country as well, and so there's lots of certification and permits and so on that we've got to, we've got to get together and that always means a drive of a couple of hours to, to get to, to Granada, the local center to, to get paperwork sorted out.

I Is there anything you miss about the UK?

D Well, obviously we miss friends and family, I mean that's the, the big thing, but we're lucky we live in a, a nice part of the world and so we, we get lots of visitors, who come out and, and stay with us which is nice and then, you know, often it's very trite, silly little things that you miss, I mean I miss pubs with carpets and soft lighting and, you know, polite dog walkers, that kind of thing.

E The fact that actually when we come back we often come back to London so, what I really like about the UK is, is that sense of cultural diversity, just traveling on public transport in London, you're very aware of the, the, the very wide range of people living here which obviously you wouldn't get in a, a small rural community. And, of course, the, the great thing about that is being in London is, yeah, you can choose, the, the– you know, rest– any kind of restaurant, that's a big treat to come back and be able to choose what kind of food you want to eat.

I Do you think you'll come back to the UK one day?

D Well, you never know, I mean, we, we, we never took a, a decision that we would stay in Spain forever, so it was kind of by chance, by accident that we've been in Spain so long, so we, we've never really ruled it out, it would be tricky I think to come back, largely for economic or financial reasons, Britain is a very expensive place to buy a house at the moment, and then of course there's the boys, the boys, our two sons are now aged 7 and 13, so they were born and brought up in Spain, so it would be, they would be really uprooted for them to take them back to the UK, I think now, that would be perhaps a, a bigger hurdle.

E Yeah, for sure, that's the main reason why, why I can't see us going back is definitely Dan and Tom, but of course, I think once you've spent 15 years building up a business then also that's something you don't want to to easily turn your back on.

🔊 10.9

Interviewer There's a deeply held belief that sports teach us valuable lessons about life and ultimately make us better people. In your opinion, is that true?

Kantowski Call me old-fashioned, but I actually do believe that, having played sports myself when I was younger. There are some things that sports can teach you. Just in general terms, it teaches you to respect authority—for example, when there's a referee in the game, there's an authority figure. And it teaches you how to get along with others and cooperate. When I was a kid, we would play ball sometimes without supervision, and we'd have to get along by choosing up sides for the teams. When there was an issue with the rules, we'd have to get together and come up with a compromise. So, yes, I think there's a lot of lessons to be learned, especially when you're young, that help you later on in life. Now, when it comes to individual sports, the effect is even more evident than in team sports. It takes an incredible amount of discipline, for example, with tennis and golf and track, which aren't team sports. It's a matter of getting up early, training on your own, and all the repetition that you need to do, sometimes without supervision. A lot of people who aspire to be professional athletes can't afford a trainer or a coach, especially when they're young. So the discipline involved in individual sports is a valuable lesson in life as well.

I OK. On the whole, would you say that sports bring about more happiness or unhappiness in the world?

K Well, as long as there's some perspective there, and you look at sports as a sort of a temporary escape from real life, as entertainment—like going to a movie—if you have that kind of perspective, then I think sports can enhance your life. And life is better with diversions. With sports, a lot of people look forward to following their teams: it gives them a sense of family, a sense of community, and some wonderful memories. And as entertainment, sports have tremendous value. But again, there has to be some perspective. When you go past the level of sports as entertainment, as diversion, as pastime, when it gets into the obsession area, then it's probably not a good thing. People who get too carried away by whether their team wins or loses are not in a healthy situation. As long as you can look at sports as a diversion, it's fine. Part of the secret of life, and this certainly applies to sports, is to do it in moderation, and being a sports fan is no different. But overall, I would say sports create a great deal of happiness.

I So, do you think there's a sense that sports have replaced religion in modern society?

K That's a great question. Probably for a lot of people, it has. I'm thinking of some of these major sporting events that draw worldwide interest, like the World Cup, for instance. You see the passion of the fans, and I think that passion is wonderful, as long as it doesn't carry over into fanatical levels. Again, we get back to that obsession thing, and once you've crossed that line where sports are no longer just entertainment, diversion, and pastime—when it crosses the line, then yes, it can border on religion for a lot of people.

I OK. Do you think there's any difference between using technology to gain an advantage (I don't know, for example, high-tech swimsuits) and doping - I mean taking performance-enhancing drugs?

K That's a profound question. I think if you're really honest about it, it's hard to see the difference. I mean, if you think about a sport like tennis or maybe golf, and you consider the advances in technology in the equipment, and if you go back to the 1930s and 1940s and think about the small wooden tennis racquets and the wooden golf clubs. If those players had had today's equipment in their hands, it would have made a huge difference in their game, a bigger impact on their game than performance-enhancing drugs! The advances in technology have really done more to increase performance than drugs have. We're all quick to criticize, and there's a stigma attached to using drugs that doesn't exist with the equipment, but in a lot of ways they're similar. I think equipment, technology, diet, and education—all those things have done more to enhance athletic prowess and performance than drugs.

I We expect athletes to be positive role models. Is there any reason why we should?

K Years ago, people looked up to athletes, and they were our heroes. But there's no reason why they should be role models—they're in the public eye more than others, but they're human, like everyone else. All the money and adulation is difficult for these athletes to handle, paradoxically. Money and fame tend to bring down a lot of celebrities, like actors and rock stars, not just athletes. There's a lot of temptation and money involved that you don't see in other professions. Also, there's more pressure nowadays, with the way the media has changed, and with social media. Everyone is looking for a sensational story, and athletes are more prone to being caught in scandals than ever before. If it were up to me, parents and teachers, people like that, they would be the real role models.

I Right. Do sports occupy a disproportionately high place in the media and have we lost all sense of proportion when it comes to sports?

K There is a disproportionate amount of interest in sports. There's an insane amount of hype around some of these big events, like the Super Bowl and the World Cup. The media knows that there's a captive audience, and more is better! You know, the first Super Bowl didn't even sell out, yet in today's world it's considered the most important event you can imagine, so it just shows how perspectives have shifted. But the media reflects interest more than they create it—they're giving the public what they want. I'm not sure the media is totally to blame, either; it's just a form of economics.

have as a main verb

1 We **have** a large extended family.
   Do you **have** any money on you?
   She **has** a really bad cold right now.
2 He **doesn't have** lunch at home.
   I'm having problems with my Wi-fi.
3 **Do** we really **have to** spend Thanksgiving with your parents again?
4 We're going to **have** the kitchen **repainted** next week.
   I **had** my eyes **tested** when I got my new glasses.
   Where do you **have** your hair **cut**?

When *have* is a **main verb**, we use auxiliary verbs, e.g., *be* or *do*, to make questions and negatives. We don't usually contract *have* when it is a main verb.

1 We use *have* as a main verb for possession.
   have with this meaning is a stative (non-action) verb and is not used in continuous tenses.
• *have* is also a stative verb when used to talk about relationships or sicknesses.
2 We use *have* + object as a main verb for actions and experiences, e.g., *have lunch, a snack, a conversation, a problem*, etc., *have* with this meaning is a dynamic (action) verb and can be used in continuous tenses.
3 We use *have to* as a main verb to express obligation, especially obligation imposed by others, and rules and regulations.
4 We use *have* as a main verb + object + past participle to say that you ask or pay another person to do something for you.

have as an auxiliary verb

1 How many children **have** you **got**? **I've got** three, two boys and a girl.
   They **haven't got** much money.
2 I **haven't** the time to go to the bank.
3 **I've got to** go now—I'm meeting my girlfriend for lunch.
4 They**'ve been** married for 15 years.
   How long **has** Anna **been going** out with James?
5 She'll **have** finished lunch in a few minutes so you can call her then.
   I want to **have** started a family by the time I'm 30.
   If I **hadn't** taken a taxi, I wouldn't **have** arrived in time.

When *have* is an auxiliary verb, we make questions by inverting *have* and the subject, and negatives with *haven't / hasn't*. *have* as an auxiliary verb is often contracted to *'ve / 's*; *had* is contracted to *'d*.

1 We often use *have got* for possession. The meaning is exactly the same as *have*.
• *have* here is an auxiliary verb.
• *have got* has a present meaning. We usually use *had* for the past, not *had got*.
• *have got* is very common in informal English.
2 In negative sentences, we occasionally leave out *got*, especially in fixed expressions like *I haven't time., I haven't a clue.*
3 We use *have got to* to express obligation, especially in informal English.
• *have got to* is usually used for a specific obligation rather than a general or repeated obligation. Compare:
   I've got to make a quick phone call. (= specific)
   I have to wear a suit to work. (= general)
4 We use *have* as an auxiliary verb to form the present perfect simple and continuous.
5 We also use *have* for other perfect forms, e.g., the future perfect, the perfect infinitive, the past perfect, etc.

---

a Right (✓) or wrong (✗)? Correct the mistakes in the highlighted phrases.
   A You look exhausted.
   B Yes, I've been looking after my sister's kids all day. ✓
1 I don't think you should drive until you've had your brakes fixed.
2 A Why don't you want to come?
   B I haven't got any money.
3 Has your husband to work tomorrow or is he taking the day off?
4 The staff members don't have to dress formally in this company—they can wear what they like.
5 How long have you been having your apartment in Denver?
6 What time are we having dinner tonight?
7 My parents had got a lot of problems with my sister when she was a teenager.
8 I don't have a vacation for 18 months. I really need a break.
9 Have we got to do this exercise now, or can we do it later for homework?

b Rewrite the sentences using a form of *have* or *have got*.
   Her brother moved to Canada in 2016 and he still lives there.
   Her brother*'s been living in Canada since 2016*.
1 She's an only child.
   She _____.
2 We used to pay someone to take a family photograph every year.
   We used _____.
3 Buying car insurance is obligatory for all drivers.
   All _____.
4 He last saw his father in 2017.
   He _____.
5 He lacks the right qualifications for this job.
   He _____.
6 It's not necessary for us to do it now; we can do it later.
   We _____.
7 We knew almost everyone at the party—it was really enjoyable.
   We knew almost everyone at the party—
   we _____.
8 When did you start having problems at school?
   How long _____ at school?
9 I need someone to fix the heater. I think the thermostat is broken.
   I need _____.
   I think the thermostat is broken.

 p.7

result

> 1 I have a job interview next week, **so** I bought myself a suit!
> 2 It had snowed hard all night. **As a result**, the airport was closed until 11:00 a.m.
>   We regret that you do not have the necessary qualifications, and **therefore** / **consequently** we are unable to offer you the job.

1 *so* is the most common way of introducing a result or a logical connection.
2 *as a result*, *therefore*, and *consequently* (more formal than *so*) are often used at the beginning of a sentence or clause.
* *therefore* and *consequently* can also be used before a main verb, e.g., *We have therefore / consequently decided not to offer you the job.*

reason

> 1 I have stopped writing to her **because** / **as** / **since** she never answers me.
>   Why did your boss resign? **Because** his wife was sick.
> 2 The plane was late **because of** the fog.
>   Flight 341 has been delayed **due to** / **owing to** adverse weather conditions.

1 *because*, *as*, and *since* (more formal) are synonyms and are used to introduce clauses giving a reason. *as* and *since* are often used at the beginning of a sentence, e.g., *As / Since the rain hasn't stopped, we've decided not to go out.*
* We use *because* (not *as* or *since*) to answer a *Why…?* question.
2 *because of*, *due to*, and *owing to* also express the reason for something. They are usually followed by a noun, a gerund, or *the fact that* + clause.
* *due to* and *owing to* are more formal than *because of*.

purpose

> 1 I took a language course **to** / **in order to** / **so as to** improve my English.
> 2 She closed the door quietly **so as not to** / **in order not to** wake the baby.
> 3 They moved to Quito **so** (**that**) they could see their grandchildren more often.
> 4 I'm not going to tell Ann **in case** she tells everyone else.

1 *to*, *in order to*, and *so as to* introduce a clause of purpose and are all followed by an infinitive. *to* is the most informal.
2 For negative purpose we use *so as not to* or *in order not to*.
3 You can also use *so* (*that*) + *can* / *could* + verb or *will* / *would* + verb to express purpose. You can leave out *that* in informal English.
* Use *so* (*that*) when there is a change of subject in the clause of purpose, e.g., *She put a blanket over the baby so* (*that*) *he wouldn't be cold.*
4 We use *in case* + a clause when we do something in order to be ready for future situations / problems or to avoid them.

contrast

> 1 We enjoyed the concert, **but** we didn't have very good seats.
>   Agnes was attracted to the stranger, **yet** something in her head was telling her not to get close to him.
>   It's a really good idea. **However**, it may be too expensive.
>   The moon shone brightly. **Nevertheless**, it was hard to find our way.
> 2 We enjoyed the movie **although** / **even though** / **though** it was long.
> 3 **In spite of** being 85, she still travels all over the world.
>   **Despite** her age…
>   **Despite** the fact that she's 85…

1 *but* is the most common and informal way of introducing contrast and is usually used to link two contrasting points within a sentence.
   yet is used in the same way, but is more formal / literary.
   however and *nevertheless* are usually used at the beginning of a sentence to connect it to the previous one and are usually followed by a comma.
* *nevertheless* (or *nonetheless*) is more formal / literary than *however*.
2 *even though* is more emphatic than *although*. *though* is more common in informal speech.
* *Though* can also be used at the end of a phrase as a comment adverb, e.g., *He's very friendly—a little stingy, though.*
3 After *in spite of* and *despite* use a gerund, a noun, or *the fact that* + clause.

---

a Circle the right linker.
   ⟨**Even though**⟩/ *Despite* she's working really hard, I don't think she'll be able to catch up.
   1 We can't afford to take a vacation this year *as* / *so* we are broke.
   2 Could we rearrange my schedule *so that* / *in case* I don't have so many classes on Fridays?
   3 I got to the interview on time *due to* / *in spite of* the fact that my train was late.
   4 The restaurant chain has had a very difficult year. *Nevertheless* / *As a result*, they haven't had to close any of their restaurants.
   5 He gets a good salary *though* / *since* the job itself is very monotonous.

b Circle the better option according to register.
   Sales have increased over the last three months. *So* / ⟨**Therefore**⟩ we will be hiring five new employees.
   1 I've been home for the last three days *because of* / *owing to* this nasty cough I have.
   2 The organization has severe financial problems, and *so* / *consequently* half the staff have been laid off.
   3 The company has reported declining sales this year. *Nevertheless* / *But* they have so far managed to avoid any workforce cuts.
   4 I stopped at a gas station *to* / *in order to* fill up the tank.
   5 I thought it was an amazing movie. It was really depressing, *though* / *however*.
   6 It has been announced that the last game of the season has been canceled *due to* / *because of* the severe weather.

c Join the sentences using the **bold** word(s), making any necessary changes.
   We only use energy-efficient light bulbs. We don't want to waste electricity. **so as**
   We only use energy-efficient light bulbs so as not to waste electricity.
   1 Our seats were a long way from the stage. We enjoyed the play. **In spite**
      We _____
   2 It took us a long time to get there. The traffic was heavy. **because of**
      It _____
   3 I took the price tag off the bag. I didn't want Becky to know how much it had cost. **so**
      I _____
   4 Keep the receipt for the sweater. Your dad might not like it. **in case**
      Keep _____
   5 Susanna is an only child. She isn't at all spoiled. **Even though**
      Susanna _____
   6 Prices have risen because production costs have increased. **due to**
      Prices _____

← p.13

1 **You** can learn a language faster if you go to live in a country where it is spoken.
2 **One** tends to have problems understanding very strong accents.
3 When **we** talk about an accent, **we** must not confuse this with pronunciation.
4 **They** always say that it's never too late to learn a new language.
  They should make it a requirement for people to learn two foreign languages at school.
5 If someone goes to live in a foreign country, **they** will have to get used to a different way of life.
  Could the person who left **their** bag in the library please come and see me?

1 We often use *you* to mean people in general.
2 We can also use *one* + third person singular of the verb to mean people in general. *one* is much more formal than *you* and rarely used in spoken English.
• We can also use *one's* as a possessive adjective, e.g., *When confronted with danger, one's first reaction is often to freeze.*
3 *we* can also be used to make a general statement of opinion that includes the reader / listener.
4 In informal English, we often use *they* to talk about other people in general, or people in authority, e.g., **They** *always say…* (They = people in general); **They** *should make it compulsory…* (They = the government).
5 We use *they*, *them*, and *their* to refer to one person who may be male or female, instead of using *he or she*, *his or her*, etc.

reflexive and reciprocal pronouns

1 You need to take care of **yourself** with that cold.
  He's very egocentric. He always talks about **himself**.
2 I managed to complete the crossword puzzle! I was really proud of **myself**.
3 We decorated the house **ourselves**.
  There's no way I'm going to do it for you. Do it **yourself**!
4 I don't feel very comfortable going to the movies **by myself**.
5 My ex-husband and I don't talk to **each other** anymore.
  My mother and sister don't understand **one another** at all.

1 We often use reflexive pronouns when the subject and object of a verb are the same person.
• We don't usually use reflexive pronouns with some verbs that may be reflexive in other languages, e.g., *wash*, *shave*, etc. NOT *He got up, shaved himself, and …*
• *enjoy* is always used with a reflexive pronoun when not followed by another object, e.g., *Enjoy your meal!* BUT *Did you enjoy* ***yourself*** *last night?*
2 We can also use reflexive pronouns after most prepositions when the complement is the same as the subject.

> 🔍 **Object pronouns after prepositions of place**
> After prepositions of place, we use object pronouns, not reflexive pronouns, e.g., *She put the bag next to her on the seat.* NOT *next to herself*

3 We can use reflexive pronouns to emphasize the subject, e.g., *We decorated the house ourselves.* (= we did it, not professional decorators)
4 *by* + reflexive pronoun = alone, on your / her, etc., own.
5 We use *each other* or *one another* for reciprocal actions, i.e., A does the action to B and B does the action to A.

it and *there*

1 **It's** 10 o'clock. **It's** 30 degrees today. **It's** five miles to the coast.
2 **It was** great to hear that you and Martina are getting married!
  It used to be difficult to buy fresh pasta here, but now you can get it everywhere.
3 **There have been** a lot of storms recently.
  There used to be a movie theater on that street.

1 We use *it* + *be* to talk about time, temperature, and distance.
2 We also use, e.g., *it* + *be* as a "preparatory" subject before adjectives. *It was great to hear from you.* NOT *To hear from you was great.*
3 We use *there* + *be* + noun to say if people and things are present or exist (or not). You cannot use *It…* here. NOT *It used to be a movie theater on that street.*

a Circle the right pronoun. Check (✓) if both are possible.
  They helped **one** another / *themselves* to prepare for the exam.
  1 *One / You* can often tell where people are from by the way they speak.
  2 Can you put my suitcase on the rack above *yourself / you*?
  3 Emma and her sister look incredibly like *each other / one another*. Are they twins?
  4 Steve's a really private person and he rarely talks about *him / himself*.
  5 Either Suzie or Mark has left *her / their* bag behind, because there's only one in the back of the car.
  6 When a person goes to live abroad, it may take *them / him* a while to pick up the language.
  7 *They / One* say that eating tomatoes can help protect the body against certain diseases.

b Complete with a pronoun.
  Don't tell him how to spell it. Let him figure it out by *himself*.
  1 If anyone has not yet paid _____ tuition, _____ should go to registration immediately.
  2 Isabel is very hot-tempered. She finds it very hard to control _____.
  3 I wouldn't stay in that hotel—_____ say the rooms are tiny and the service is awful.
  4 There is a total lack of communication between them. They don't understand _____ at all.
  5 Did they enjoy _____ at the festival?
  6 Are you going to have the apartment repainted or will you and Jo do it _____?
  7 It's always the same with taxis. _____ can never find one when _____ need one!

c Complete with *it* or *there*.
  There was a very interesting article about language learning in **The Times** yesterday.
  1 _____'s illegal to to text while you're driving. _____ used to be a lot of accidents caused by that.
  2 Look. _____'s a spelling mistake in this word. _____ should be *j*, not *g*.
  3 How many miles is _____ to San Diego from here?
  4 _____'s scorching today. _____ must be at least 95 degrees.
  5 _____'s no need to hurry. The train doesn't leave for a while.
  6 _____'s not worth buying the paper today. _____'s absolutely nothing interesting in it.

 p.17

narrative tenses: describing specific incidents in the past

> This **happened** when I **was** about five years old. My father **had gone away** on business for a few days and my brother and I **were sleeping** in my parents' bedroom. Before we **went** to bed that night, I **had been reading** a very scary story about a wicked witch. In the middle of the night, I **woke up** suddenly and **saw** that a figure in a dark coat **was standing** at the end of my bed. I **screamed** at the top of my lungs.

When we describe specific incidents in the past, we use **narrative tenses**, i.e., the simple past, past continuous, and past perfect or past perfect continuous.

- We use the simple past to talk about the main actions in a story (*We went to bed… I woke up… I screamed*).
- We use the past continuous to set the scene (*We were sleeping in my parents' bedroom*) and to describe actions in progress in the past (*Somebody was standing at the end of my bed*).
- We use the past perfect and the past perfect continuous to talk about the earlier past, i.e., things that happened before the main event (*My father had gone away… I had been reading a story*).

used to and *would*: describing habitual events and repeated actions in the past

> 1 Every summer, my family **used to rent** an old house in Maine. My sister and I **often walked** to the harbor in the morning, where we **used to watch** the fishermen cleaning their nets.
> 2 Every night before we went to bed, my mother **would tell** us stories, but she **would never read** them from a book—she **would always make them up** herself.
> 3 When I was a teenager, my friends **were always teasing** me because of my red hair.

1 We often use *used to* + the base form of the verb as an alternative to the simple past to talk about things that we did repeatedly in the past.

- We can also use *used to* + the base form of the verb to talk about situations or states that have changed, e.g., *I used to have much longer hair when I was younger.*

2 We use *would* + the base form of the verb as an alternative to *used to* to talk about things that we did repeatedly in the past.

- We <u>don't</u> use *would* with stative verbs, i.e., to talk about situations or states that have changed. NOT ~~I would have much longer hair when I was younger.~~
- We don't use *would* without a time reference, e.g., *I used to play the violin.* NOT ~~I would play the violin.~~

3 We can also use *always* + past continuous for things that happened repeatedly, especially when they were irritating habits.

> 🔍 **Variety in descriptions of past events**
> When we describe past habits or repeated past actions we tend, for reasons of variety, to alternate between *used to*, *would*, or the simple past (with adverbs of frequency).

a Circle the right verb form. Check (✓) if both are possible.
Corinne and I *used to be* / *would be* very close, but recently we've grown apart.
1 When I came into the room, my aunt *sat* / *was sitting* with her back to me. When she turned around, I could see that she *had been crying* / *had cried.*
2 Our grandmother *always used to have* / *would always have* a surprise waiting for us when we visited.
3 My sister *used to live* / *would live* on her own, but then she *used to buy* / *bought* a house with her boyfriend.
4 My brother *didn't use to look* / *wouldn't look* at all like my father, but now he does.
5 When I was small, I *was always getting* / *always used to get* into trouble at school and my parents *used to punish* / *would punish* me by not letting me play with my friends on the weekend.
6 Suddenly we heard a tremendous crash and we saw that a car *crashed* / *had crashed* into a tree and gas *poured* / *was pouring* onto the road.

b Complete with the verb in parentheses, using a narrative tense or *would* / *used to*.
My earliest memory
When I was about four or five, my grandmother, who was Mexican, *was living* (live) in Los Angeles, and we children often ¹_____ (spend) weekends at her apartment. My grandfather ²_____ (die) a couple of years earlier, so I suppose she was in need of company. We loved going there, as my grandmother ³_____ (cook) special meals for us and ⁴_____ (take) us for beautiful walks along Venice Beach, which wasn't far at all. One occasion that I remember really well was when I ⁵_____ (invite) to stay with her on my own, without my brothers and sisters. On the first day, after lunch, my grandmother ⁶_____ (go) into her bedroom for a nap. I ⁷_____ (try) to sleep, but I couldn't, so after a while I ⁸_____ (get up) and ⁹_____ (decide) to explore her apartment. Everything was very quiet, so I was convinced that my grandmother ¹⁰_____ (sleep). The room I most ¹¹_____ (want) to explore was my grandfather's study, I imagine, exactly because I ¹²_____ (tell) not to go in there. I opened the door and went in, and was immediately drawn to his large old desk. I ¹³_____ (climb) onto the chair and ¹⁴_____ (see) on the desk a green pen in a kind of stand, with a bottle of ink. I ¹⁵_____ (ask) my parents for a real pen for a long time, but they ¹⁶_____ (refuse), foreseeing the mess that I was almost bound to make with the ink. I picked up the pen and then tried to open the bottle of ink. At that moment I ¹⁷_____ (hear) my grandmother's voice saying, "Christina? Where are you? What are you doing?" To my horror, I ¹⁸_____ (realize) that my grandmother ¹⁹_____ (get up) out of bed and ²⁰_____ (come) towards the study. Two seconds later, she ²¹_____ (open) the door. I will never forget the awful feeling of shame that she ²²_____ (catch) me doing something that she ²³_____ (forbid) me to do.

 p.21

1 I **got** an email from Marc today saying that he was leaving me!
 If you're going to the post office, could you **get** me some stamps?
 Let's not bother with a taxi—we can **get** the bus.
 When do you think we'll **get to** Beijing?
2 We'd better go home. It's **getting dark**.
 I seem to have **gotten** very **forgetful** recently.
 The traffic **gets worse** on the local roads every day.
 I don't think my mother will ever **get used to** living on her own.
3 Did you know Dan **got fired** last week?
 My husband **got caught** on the freeway driving 80 miles per hour.
4 I'm going to **get my hair cut** next week.
 I need to **get my passport renewed**—it expires in a couple of months.
5 We need to **get someone to fix** the heater—it's not working well.
 Could you **get Jane to finish** the report? I'm too busy to do it this afternoon.

get is one of the most common verbs in English and can be used in many different ways.
1 *get* + noun / pronoun usually means "receive," "bring," "fetch," "obtain," "buy," or "catch;" with *to* + a place it means "arrive at / in."
2 We use *get* + adjective or comparative adjective to mean "become."
• Compare *be* + adjective and *get* + adjective:
 It's dark. It's getting dark.
 I'm used to the climate in California now. I'm getting used to the climate in California.
3 We can use *get* + past participle instead of *be* to make a passive structure. This is more informal than using *be* and is often used to talk about bad or unexpected things that have happened.
4 In informal spoken English, we sometimes use *get* + object + past participle instead of *have* + object + past participle to say that you ask or pay another person to do something for you.

◄ See 1A p.142

5 We can use *get* + object + infinitive to mean "make," "tell," "persuade," or "ask" somebody (to) do something.

a Replace *get* with another verb in the correct form so that the sentences mean the same.
 He **got** blamed for the break-up of their marriage. *was*
 1 My father **is getting** increasingly forgetful in his old age. _____
 2 Do you know anywhere near here where I can **get** a newspaper? _____
 3 Could you **get** your brother to lend you the money? _____
 4 We had to **get** the roof repaired, as it was damaged in the storm. _____
 5 I **got** an email out of the blue today from an old school friend. _____
 6 If I **get** the 7:30 train, would you be able to pick me up at the train station? _____
 7 Do you think they'll **get** here in time for lunch? _____
 8 If you're going upstairs, could you **get** me my jacket? It's on the bed. _____
 9 She's going to **get** caught if she's not careful. _____
 10 How can I **get** you to change your mind? _____

b Complete with the right forms of *get* and the words in parentheses.
 I think we should stop playing now. It*'s getting dark*. (dark)
 1 I _____ in time. It was about to run out. (my passport / renew)
 2 My husband has only been in the UK for two months and he just can't _____ on the left. (used / drive)
 3 Monica's fiancé _____ in a car crash. He was lucky to survive. (almost / kill)
 4 I can _____ tomorrow night so we can go out. (my sister / babysit)
 5 If you can't find your keys, we'll have to _____. (all the locks / change)
 6 We _____ by the police today. They were looking for a stolen car. (stop)
 7 I went to the eye doctor yesterday to _____. (eyes / test)
 8 **A** What happened to your hand?
 B I _____ by our neighbor's dog yesterday. (bite)

◄ p.29

Expression	Use
A I really like your shirt. Doesn't Ahmet have one just like it? **B** Yes he does. **Speaking of** Ahmet, did he get the job he applied for?	To change the direction of a conversation, but making a link with what has just been said.
So let's meet at five o'clock then. **By the way** / **Incidentally**, could you lend me some money until the weekend?	To introduce something you have just thought of, or to change the subject completely.
A Did you see the game last night? **B** No, I didn't. **Actually** / **In fact** / **As a matter of fact,** I don't really like basketball.	To introduce additional surprising or unexpected information.
We didn't go away for the weekend because I had too much work. **In any case** / **Anyway** the weather was awful, so we didn't miss anything.	To introduce the idea that what you said before is less important than what you are going to say now, or to return to the main topic after a digression.
Yes, it was a bad accident. **At least** nobody was killed, though. Tom's coming to the meeting, or **at least** he said he was.	To introduce a positive point after some negative information, or to qualify what you have just said or to make it less definite.
As I was saying, if Mark gets the job we'll have to reorganize the department.	To return to a previous subject, often after you have been interrupted.
On the whole, I think that women make better journalists than men.	To generalize.
I like both houses, but **all in all**, I think I prefer the one next to the train station.	To say that you are taking everything into consideration.
I think we should buy them. **After all**, we'll never find them anywhere cheaper than this.	To introduce a strong argument that the other person may not have taken into consideration.
I don't think I'll go to Nick's party. It will finish very late. **Besides**, I won't know many people there.	To add additional information or arguments.
Basically, my job involves computer skills and people skills.	To introduce the most important or fundamental point.
Obviously, it is easier to live in Japan if you can speak the language.	To introduce a fact that is very clear to see or understand.
She's very selfish. **I mean**, she never thinks about other people at all.	To make things clearer or give more details.
A lot of people booed, and some people even left early. **In other words**, it was a complete disaster.	To say something again in another way.
Please try not to make a mess when you make the cake. **Otherwise** I'm going to have to clean the kitchen again.	To say what the result would be if something did not happen or if the situation were different.
As far as accommodations **are concerned**, … **As regards** / **Regarding** the accommodations, the options are living with a family or living in a dormitory.	To introduce a new topic or to announce a change of subject.
The government is going to help first-time buyers. **That is to say**, it is going to make mortgages more easily available.	To introduce an explanation or clarification of a point you have just made.
On the one hand, more young people today carry knives. **On the other hand**, the total number of violent crimes has dropped.	To balance contrasting facts or points. *On the other hand* is also used alone to introduce a contrasting fact or point.

a Circle the right discourse marker.

A What a good movie! I really enjoyed it. Didn't you?
B *Actually* / *Incidentally*, I didn't like it very much.
A Why not?
B [1]*Basically* / *After all*, I thought the plot was completely unbelievable.
A I wouldn't call it unbelievable. [2]*In other words* / *In any case*, it wasn't supposed to be a true story.
B I know, but it was set in a specific historical period. [3]*Otherwise* / *Obviously* you can't expect the dialogue to be totally authentic, [4]*I mean* / *on the other hand*, nobody knows exactly how people spoke in Roman times, but [5]*besides* / *at least* the details should be right. There were cannons in the battle scene and they weren't invented till a thousand years later! [6]*All in all* / *That is to say*, I thought it was a pretty awful movie.
A We'll have to agree to disagree then. [7]*By the way* / *As a matter of fact*, do you know what time the last train leaves? I don't want to miss it. [8]*Otherwise* / *In any case*, I'll have to get a taxi home.
B At 11:40. Don't worry, we have plenty of time. [9]*In fact* / *Besides*, I think we even have time to get something to eat. There's a good Italian restaurant just around the corner.
A Good idea. [10]*As I was saying* / *Speaking of* Italian food, I made a wonderful risotto with mushrooms last night…

b Complete with a discourse marker. Sometimes more than one answer may be possible.

The movie was a box office disaster. *That is to say*, it cost more to produce than it made in receipts.

1 Jason is an excellent teacher, although _____ I think younger teachers are usually better with five-year-olds.
2 **A** Did end up buying the shoes?
  B No, they were too expensive. And _____ I decided that I didn't really like them that much.
3 I really think you should apply for the manager position. _____ you have nothing to lose.
4 **A** I've just read a great book that Manuel lent me.
  B _____ Manuel, did you know he's moving to New York?
5 **A** How was your day?
  B Fine. I finished work earlier than usual. _____, did you remember to get a birthday present for your mom?
6 _____ salary, you will be paid on the last day of each month, with a bonus in December.
7 It was a very overcast day, but _____ it didn't rain.
8 **A** Do your wife's parents live near you, then?
  B _____, they live in the apartment below us. It's not ideal, but it does have some advantages.
9 They've hired me as a kind of troubleshooter— _____, somebody who resolves problems when they occur.
10 The food was delicious and the service was excellent. _____, the meal was a great success.
11 You'd better hurry up with your homework, _____ you won't be able to watch TV tonight.
12 I'm not sure what the best solution is. _____, buying our own place would mean not paying rent, but _____, I'm not sure we can afford a mortgage.

p.33

 Go online to review the grammar for each lesson

modal verbs: *must, may, might, can't, should, ought*

1 Ariana **must be** very well off—she has an enormous house.
You **must have seen** him—he was standing right in front of you!
2 They **can't be playing** very well—they're losing 3–0.
You **can't / couldn't have spent** very long on this essay—you've only written 100 words.
3 I haven't seen the sales manager today. He **may / might / could be** out of the office.
The keys of the storage cabinet have disappeared. Do you think someone **may / might / could have taken** them?
He **may / might not have heard** the message I left.
4 If I mail the letter today, it **should / ought to arrive** on Friday.
I mailed the letter a week ago. It **should / ought to have arrived** by now.

1 As well as using *must* for obligation, we also use *must* + base form to say that we are almost sure something is true about the present and *must have* + past participle to say that we are almost sure something was true or happened in the past.
2 We use *can't* + base form to say that we are almost sure that something isn't true in the present and *can't have / couldn't have* + past participle to say that we are almost sure that something didn't happen / wasn't true in the past.
• We don't use *must not / must not have* with this meaning.
3 We use *may / might / could* + base form and *may have / might have / could have* + past participle to say that we think it's possible that something is true in the present, or was true / happened in the past.
• We only use *may not* or *might not* to talk about a negative possibility. NOT ~~couldn't~~
4 We use *should / ought to* + base form to describe a situation we expect to happen. We use *should have / ought to have* + past participle to describe a situation we would expect to have happened in the past.

> 🔍 **Base form or continuous base form after modals?**
> *He must work really hard. He never gets home before 9:00 p.m.*
> (= deduction about a habitual action)
> *There's a light on in his office. He must still be working.*
> (= deduction about an action in progress at the moment of speaking)

adjectives and adverbs for speculation

1 He's **bound / sure to** be here in a minute. He left an hour ago.
She's **sure / bound to** know. She's an expert on the subject.
2 I think she's **likely / unlikely to** agree to our proposal.
It is likely / unlikely that the government will raise interest rates this year.
3 She'll **definitely pass** the exam. She's worked really hard.
She **definitely won't** pass the exam. She hasn't done any work at all.
He'll **probably be** here around 8:00. He usually leaves work at 7:30.
He **probably won't be** here until about 8:15. He's stuck in a traffic jam.

1 *bound* and *sure* are adjectives. We use *be bound* or *be sure* + infinitive to say that we think something is certain to be true or to happen.
2 *likely* and *unlikely* are also adjectives (not adverbs). We can use subject + *be likely / unlikely* + infinitive, or *it is likely / unlikely* + *that* + clause.
3 *definitely* and *probably* are adverbs. They go before a main verb and after the auxiliary if there is one in ⊞ sentences and before the auxiliary in ⊟ sentences.
• With *be* they go after the verb in ⊞ sentences and before the verb in ⊟ sentences, e.g., *He's probably Canadian. The painting definitely isn't genuine.*

---

a Right (✓) or wrong (✗)? Correct the mistakes in the **highlighted phrases**.
Jim didn't leave work until 6:00, so <mark>he won't likely be here</mark> before 7:00. ✗
Jim didn't leave work until 6:00, so he isn't likely to be here before 7:00.
1 My glasses aren't in their usual place. <mark>Someone must move them</mark>.
2 **A** Do you know where Ann is?
B <mark>She should be in the library</mark>. That's where she said she was going.
3 **A** What's that noise in the garage?
B <mark>I think it can be</mark> the neighbor's cat.
4 I'm sure Brazil will win tonight. <mark>They're unlikely to lose</mark> three times in a row.
5 I think you should delete that photo of Tina. <mark>She won't definitely like</mark> it.
6 <mark>Julian is bound be late</mark>—he always is.
7 No one's answering the phone at the store. <mark>I'd say they've probably gone home</mark>.
8 I don't think Marta has gone to bed yet. <mark>I think she must still study</mark>.
9 <mark>It's very likely that the boss will retire</mark> in a year or two.

b Rewrite the sentences using the **bold** word.
Perhaps Luke has gotten lost. He has no sense of direction. **might**
Luke *might have gotten lost*. He has no sense of direction.
1 I don't think he'll have time to stop by and see us. He has a very tight schedule. **probably**
He _____. He has a very tight schedule.
2 I'm not sure she'll ever get over the breakup. **may**
She _____ the breakup.
3 They will probably have heard the news by now. **ought**
They _____ now.
4 I didn't leave my credit card in the restaurant. I remember putting it in my wallet. **can't**
I _____. I remember putting it in my wallet.
5 I'm sure your sister will like the scarf—it's just her style. **bound**
Your sister _____. It's just her style.
6 The company director probably won't resign, despite the disastrous sales figures. **unlikely**
The company director _____, despite the disastrous sales figures.
7 I'm sure he was in love with her, otherwise he wouldn't have married her. **must**
He _____, otherwise he wouldn't have married her.
8 Are you sure you locked the back door? **definitely**
Did _____ lock the back door?
9 According to press reports, the couple will probably get divorced soon. **likely**
According to press reports, it's _____ soon.

 p.38

1. **Not only is the plot** great, (but) it's also very well written.
   Not until you can behave like an adult **will we treat** you like an adult.
   Never have I heard such a ridiculous argument.
   No sooner had the soccer game started than it began to snow heavily.
2. **Not only did you forget** to shut the window, (but) you also forgot to lock the door!
   Not until you become a parent yourself **do you understand** what it really means.
3. The train began to move. **Only then was I able** to relax.
   Only when you leave home **do you realize** how expensive everything is.
   Hardly had I sat down when / before the train began to move.
   Rarely have I met a more irritating person.

In formal English, especially in writing, we sometimes change the usual word order to make the sentence more emphatic or dramatic.

1. This structure is common with negative adverbial expressions such as *Not only…, Not until…, Never…,* and *No sooner…than* (= a formal way of saying *as soon as*).
- When we use inversion after the above expressions, we change the order of the subject and (auxiliary) verb. NOT ~~Not only the plot is great,…~~
  Compare:
  I have never heard such a ridiculous argument. (= usual word order)
  Never have I *heard such a ridiculous argument.* (= inversion to make the sentence more emphatic)
2. In the simple present and simple past tense, rather than simply inverting the subject and verb, we use *do / does / did* + subject + main verb. NOT ~~Not only forgot you to shut the window…~~
3. Inversion is also used after the expressions *Only then…, Only when…, Hardly / Scarcely…, Rarely…*

> 🔍 **Overuse of inversion**
> Inversion should only be used occasionally for dramatic effect. Overusing it will make your English sound unnatural.

Rewrite the sentences to make them more emphatic.

I had just started reading when all the lights went out.
No sooner *had I started reading than all the lights went out*.

1. I didn't realize my mistake until years later.
   Not until _____.
2. We had never seen such magnificent scenery.
   Never _____.
3. They not only disliked her, but they also hated her family.
   Not only _____.
4. We only understood what he had really suffered when we read his autobiography.
   Only when _____.
5. We had just started to eat when we heard someone knocking at the door.
   Hardly _____.
6. I have rarely read such a badly written novel.
   Rarely _____.
7. Until you've tried to write a novel yourself, you don't realize how hard it is.
   Not until _____.
8. The hotel room was depressing, and it was cold as well.
   Not only _____.
9. We only light the fire when it is unusually cold.
   Only when _____.
10. Shortly after he had gone to sleep the phone rang.
    No sooner _____.
11. I only realized the full scale of the disaster when I watched the six o'clock news.
    I watched the six o'clock news. Only then
    _____.
12. He has never regretted the decision he took on that day.
    Never _____.
13. I spoke to the manager and the problem was taken seriously.
    Only when _____.
14. He had scarcely had time to destroy the evidence before the police arrived.
    Scarcely _____

 p.41

seem / appear

1 **It seems / appears that** when people multitask, they in fact do one thing after another in quick succession.
The new marketing manager **seems / appears to be** very friendly.
Excuse me. **There seems to be** a mistake with my order.
2 **It would seem / appear that** Mr. Young had been using the company's assets to pay off his private debts.

1 We often use *seem* and *appear* to give information without stating that we definitely know it is true, in this way distancing ourselves from the information.
We can use *It seems / appears + that* + clause, or subject + *seem / appear* + infinitive.
2 We use *It would seem / appear + that* + clause to distance ourselves even further from the information, making it sound even less sure. This is more formal than *It seems / appears…*

the passive with verbs of saying and reporting

1 **It is said that** using a washing machine saves people on average 47 minutes a day.
It has been announced by a White House spokesperson **that** the president has been taken to the hospital.
2 The company director **is expected to resign** in the next few days.
The missing couple **is understood to have been living** in Panama for the last five years.
3 There **are thought to be** over a thousand species in danger of extinction.

Another way of distancing ourselves from the facts, especially in formal written English, is to use the passive form of verbs like *say*, *think*, etc., to introduce them. We can use:
1 *It* + passive verb + *that* + clause.
• Verbs commonly used in this pattern are: *agree, announce, believe, expect, hope, say, suggest,* and *think.*
2 subject + passive verb + infinitive.
• Verbs commonly used in this pattern are: *believe, expect, report, say, think,* and *understand.*
3 *There* can also be used + passive verb + infinitive. Compare:
It is said that there are more than five million people living in poverty in this country.
There are said to be more than five million people living in poverty in this country.

other distancing expressions: *apparently, according to, may / might*

1 **Apparently,** Jeff and Katie have separated.
2 **According to** new research, the idea that we have to drink two liters of water a day is a myth.
3 Dinosaurs **may have died out** due to extremely rapid climate change.
There are rumors that the band, who broke up ten years ago, **might be planning** to reform and record a new album.

1 We use *apparently* (usually either at the beginning or the end of a phrase) to mean that we have heard / read something, but that it may not be true. This is very common in informal conversation.
2 We use *according to* to specify where information has come from. We use it to attribute opinions to somebody else. NOT *According to me….*
3 Using *may / might* also suggests that something is a possibility, but not necessarily true.

---

a Complete the sentences with *one* word to distance the speaker from the information. Sometimes more than one answer may be possible.
Apparently, people who multitask often have concentration problems.
1 It _____ that the less children sleep, the more likely they are to behave badly.
2 It _____ appear that someone has been stealing personal items from the changing rooms.
3 Mark _____ to have aged a lot over the last year.
4 He may not look it, but he is _____ to be one of the wealthiest people in the country.
5 _____ to some sources, the latest research is seriously flawed.
6 Despite the fact that there will be an autopsy, his death is _____ to have been from natural causes.
7 _____ are thought to be several reasons why the species died out.
8 The missing couple is believed _____ have had financial difficulties.
9 It is understood _____ the senator will be resigning in the near future.

b Rewrite the second sentence so that it means the same as the first.
People say that mindfulness helps people to deal with stressful work environments.
It is *said that mindfulness helps people to deal with stressful work environments.*
1 Apparently, people who work night shifts die younger.
It would _____.
2 It is possible that the prisoners escaped to Canada.
The prisoners may _____.
3 We expect that the mayor will make a statement this afternoon.
The mayor is _____.
4 The company has announced that the new drug will go on sale shortly.
It _____.
5 People believe that stress is responsible for many common skin complaints.
Stress _____.
6 The instructions say you have to charge the phone for at least 12 hours.
According _____.
7 It appears that the government is intending to lower the the interest rate.
The government _____.
8 People have suggested that birth order has a strong influence on children's personality.
It _____.
9 It seems that there are more bike riders on the road than there used to be.
There _____.

◀ p.47

1 It's so expensive! I **wish** I **could** afford it!
  I **wish** (that) you **hadn't spoken** to Jane like that—you know how sensitive she is.
2 **If only** he **were** less stubborn! Then we wouldn't have so many arguments!
  If only you **hadn't forgotten** the map, we'd be there by now.
3 I **wish** she **were** more generous.
  If only the weather **were** warmer, we could walk there.
4 **I'd rather** you **left** your dog outside—I'm allergic to animals.
  Are you sure this is a good time to talk? **Would you rather** I **called** back later?
5 Don't you think **it's time** you **found** a job? It's been months since you graduated from college.

1 We use *wish* + simple past to talk about things we would like to be different in the present / future (but which are impossible or unlikely).
  We use *wish* + past perfect to talk about things that happened / didn't happen in the past and that we now regret.
• We sometimes use *that* after *wish*.
2 You can also use *If only...* instead of *wish* with the simple past and past perfect. This can be used by itself (*If only I knew!*) or with another clause.
• *If only* is slightly more emphatic than *wish*.
• When we want to talk about things we want to happen or stop happening because they annoy us, we use *wish* or *If only* + person / thing + *would* + base form, e.g., *I wish the bus would come! If only he wouldn't keep whistling when I'm working!*
3 We can use *were* instead of *was* for *I / he / she / it* after *wish* and *if only*.
4 We use *would rather* + subject + past tense to express a preference.
• We can also use *would rather* + base form when there is no change of subject, e.g., *I'd rather not talk about it.* However, we cannot use this structure when the subject changes after *would rather*, e.g., *I'd rather you didn't talk about it.* NOT *I'd rather you not talk about it.*
5 We use the simple past after *It's (high) time* + subject to say that something has to be done now or in the near future.
• We can also use *It's time* + infinitive when we don't want to specify the subject, e.g., *It's time to go now.*

a Complete with the correct form of the verb in parentheses.
  I wish I <u>hadn't lent</u> Gary that money now. Who knows when he'll pay it back? (not lend)
1 It's time the government _____ that most people disagree with their environmental policy. (realize)
2 My wife would rather we _____ an apartment in the city, but it was too expensive. (rent)
3 I wish you _____ to stay a little longer last night— we were having such a good time! (be able)
4 Would you rather we _____ the subject now? (not discuss)
5 I think it's time the company _____ expecting us to put in so much overtime for no extra pay. (stop)
6 If only I _____ a little more when I was earning a regular salary, I wouldn't be so hard up now. (save)
7 I'd rather you _____ me in cash, please. (pay)
8 If only we _____ the name of the store, we could Google it and see where it is. (know)
9 Do you wish you _____ to college or are you glad you left school and started work? (go)

b Rewrite the sentences using the **bold** word or phrase.
  The children ought to go to bed. It's nearly nine o'clock. **time**
  It's time the children went to bed. It's nearly nine o'clock.
1 I'd prefer you not to wear shoes in the living room, if you don't mind. **rather**
  _____, if you don't mind.
2 I would like to be able to afford to travel more. **wish**
  _____
  travel more.
3 We shouldn't have painted the room blue—it looks awful. **if only**
  _____—it looks awful.
4 Don't you think you should start looking for a job? **time**
  Don't you think _____
  for a job?
5 He should be more positive. Then he'd enjoy life more. **if only**
  _____. He'd enjoy life more.
6 Would you prefer us to come another day? **rather**
  _____
  another day?
7 I should have bought the tickets last week. They would have been cheaper then. **wish**
  _____ last week. They would have been cheaper then.

 p.51

verb + object + infinitive

> 1 She **advised him not to travel** by train.
> We **expect the flight to arrive** at 7:50.
> It **took us forever to get** there.
> 2 I'm **waiting for my friend to arrive.**
> We've **arranged for a taxi to come** at 6:30.
> 3 I **want the Lakers to win.**
> I **would hate you to think** that I don't appreciate your offer of help.
> I'**d like you to send** me the bill.

1 We often use the following verbs + object + (*not*) infinitive:
advise, allow, ask, beg, cause, enable, encourage, expect, force, help, intend, invite, mean, order, persuade, recommend, remind, take (time), teach, tell, warn.
- After *advise, persuade, remind, teach, tell,* and *warn* you can also use an object + *that* clause, e.g., *The airline advises that you carry your passport at all times.*

> 🔍 **Other patterns with infinitive or gerund**
> After *recommend* you can use object + infinitive OR a *that* clause, e.g., *He recommended me to take some cash.* OR *He recommended that I took some cash.*
> After *advise, allow, encourage,* or *recommend,* if you want to use another verb, but <u>not</u> a subject, a gerund is needed, e.g., *We don't allow eating and drinking on the premises. I recommend visiting the museum.*

2 After some verbs including *arrange, ask, plan,* and *wait* we put *for* immediately after the verb before the object + infinitive.
3 We also often use this structure with *want, would like, would love, would prefer,* and *would hate.*
- After these verbs a *that* clause is impossible.
NOT *I want that the Lakers wins. I would hate that you think …*

verb + object + base form

> Please **let me explain**!
> He **made me feel** really guilty.
> Can you **help me do** the dishes?

We can use object + base form after *let, make,* and *help.*
- *help* can be followed by object + base form or infinitive e.g., *She helped me (to) make the dinner.*

> 🔍 **Passive form of *make somebody do something***
> When *make somebody do something* is used in the passive, it is followed by the infinitive, e.g., *We were made to clean our rooms every morning.*

verb + object + gerund

> Please don't **keep me waiting**!
> I **dislike people telling** me what to do.
> I **don't mind you running** in the yard, but please don't run in the house.

We often use the following verbs + object + gerund: *dislike, hate, imagine, involve, keep, mind, prevent, remember, risk, stop.*

Complete the second sentence so that it means the same as the first.

"Be especially careful because of the snow and ice," the police told drivers.

The police warned drivers <u>to be</u> *especially* <u>*careful*</u> ~~care~~ because of the snow and ice.

1 You sit down—I'll make the coffee.
You sit down. Let _____ _____ the coffee.
2 I felt uncomfortable because of the situation at work.
The situation at work made _____ _____ _____.
3 You are going to stay with an American family. We have made the arrangements.
We have arranged _____ _____ _____ _____ with an American family.
4 I don't have a problem if Jane comes, but I'd prefer that her boyfriend didn't.
I don't mind _____ _____, but I'd prefer that her boyfriend didn't.
5 Please don't think that I didn't enjoy myself, because I did!
I would hate for _____ _____ _____ that I didn't enjoy myself, because I did!
6 You paid for everything, which wasn't what I expected.
I didn't expect _____ _____ _____ _____ everything.
7 It would be wonderful if you stayed for a few days.
I would love for _____ _____ _____ for a few days.
8 If you want to live at home again, your younger sisters will have to share a bedroom.
Living at home again will involve _____ _____ _____ _____ to share a bedroom.
9 I told Hannah not to forget to do the dishes.
I reminded _____ _____ _____ the dishes.
10 Did you really use to be shy? I can't imagine it!
I can't imagine _____ _____ shy!
11 We were able to buy a bigger house thanks to the money my uncle left me.
The money my uncle left me enabled _____ _____ _____ a bigger house.
12 The guards wouldn't let us cross the border.
The guards prevented _____ _____ _____ the border.
13 I could call back later if you're busy now.
Would you prefer _____ _____ _____ _____ later?
14 The car might break down on vacation. We don't want to take the risk.
We don't want to risk _____ _____ _____ _____ while we're on vacation.
15 I don't like it when people answer their smartphones in restaurants.
I dislike people _____ _____ _____ in restaurants.
16 When I was an intern, the secretaries made me do all the photocopying.
When I was an intern, I _____ _____ _____ _____ all the photocopying.
17 I think you should get a tablet. They're easier to carry.
I recommend _____ _____ _____ a tablet. They're easier to carry.

⬅ p.57

real and unreal

1. They **won't get** a table unless they**'ve** already **made a reservation**.
   Can I **borrow** your dictionary for a minute if you**'re not using** it?
   If it **stops** raining, **I'm going to** walk into town.
2. How **would** you **know** if he **wasn't telling** the truth?
   If we **had** a little more time here, we **could go** to the museum.
3. I **would have bought** it if they**'d had** it in my size.
   If you**'d been looking** where you were going, you **wouldn't have tripped**.

1. First conditional sentences are used to talk about a possible present or future situation and its result.
   We use any present tense in the *if* clause and any form of the future or a modal verb in the other clause.
2. Second conditional sentences are used to talk about hypothetical or improbable situations in the present or future.
   We use the past tense (simple or continuous) in the *if* clause and *would* (or *could / might*) + base form in the other clause.

> 🔍 ***was* or *were* in the *if* clause?**
> We can use *were* instead of *was* after *I / he / she / it* in the *if* clause and we always use *were* in the expression *If I were you…*

3. Third conditional sentences are used to talk about a hypothetical situation in the past.
   We use the past perfect (simple or continuous) in the *if* clause and *would have* (or *could / might have*) + past participle in the other clause.

mixed conditionals

> I **wouldn't be** in this mess if I **had listened** to your advice.
> If she **didn't** still **love** him, Jane **would have left** Mike by now.

If we want to refer to the present and the past in the same sentence, we can mix tenses from two different types of conditional, e.g.,
I wouldn't be in this mess (second conditional) *if I had listened to your advice* (third conditional).
Jane would have left Mike by now (third conditional) *if she didn't still love him* (second conditional).

alternatives to *if* in conditional sentences

1. I'll tell you what happened **as long as / so long as** you promise not to tell anyone else.
   Provided / Providing (that) the bank lends us all the money we need, we're going to buy that house we liked.
   They agreed to lend us the car **on the condition (that)** we returned it by the weekend.
2. I'm going to sell the car **whether** you agree with me **or not**.
3. **Even if** I get the job, I'm going to continue living with my parents for a while.
4. **Supposing / Suppose** you lost your job, what would you do?
5. **Had I seen** the sign, I would have stopped.

1. We often use *as long as / so long as*, *provided / providing (that)*, and *on the condition (that)* instead of *if* to emphasize what must happen or be done for something else to happen.
   - *that* is often omitted in spoken English. *on condition that* is slightly more formal than the other expressions.
2. We can use *whether* + subject + verb + *or not* instead of *if* to emphasize something is true in either of two cases.
   - The word order can also be: *I'm going to sell the car **whether or not** you agree with me.*
3. We can use *even if* instead of *if* for extra emphasis.
4. We can use *supposing / suppose* when we ask someone to imagine that something is true or might happen. It is usually used at the beginning of a sentence.
5. In third conditionals, we can invert *had* and the subject and leave out *if*.
   Had I known… = If I had known…

---

a. Right (✓) or wrong (✗)? Correct the mistakes in the highlighted phrases.
   If you hadn't been here last night, I don't know what I would do. ✗
   If you hadn't been here last night, I don't know what I would have done.
   1. They wouldn't have made you marketing manager if they didn't think you were right for the job.
   2. The government would accept more refugees if the camp isn't so crowded.
   3. If you've done all your homework, you can go out this evening.
   4. We wouldn't be living in Singapore now if my company hadn't been taken over by a multinational.
   5. Hannah would be on the varsity team if she didn't get injured last month.
   6. If you've ever been to New York, you will know exactly what I'm talking about.
   7. They would get divorced a long time ago if they didn't have young children.
   8. If the storm wasn't at night, more people would have died.
   9. If their flight hasn't been delayed, they will have arrived by now.
   10. I wouldn't have bought the house if I knew I was going to have so many problems with it.

b. Complete the sentences with *one* word. Don't use *if*.
   <u>Supposing</u> we can't find a taxi, how will we get home?
   1. My father has agreed to lend me the money _____ I pay it back by the end of the year.
   2. _____ if I had played my best, I still wouldn't have beaten him.
   3. I'll tell you exactly what happened as _____ as you promise not to tell anyone.
   4. _____ the rebels not surrendered, there would have been a lot more casualties.
   5. The company will only employ me _____ the condition that I sign a two-year contract.
   6. We've decided we're going to go ahead with the event _____ we sell all the tickets or not.
   7. I'm convinced Amy won't get back together with her boyfriend, _____ if he apologizes.
   8. _____ we do buy a dog, who's going to take it for walks?
   9. I'm going to make an appointment for you at the doctor's _____ you like it or not.
   10. _____ the plane not caught fire, there would have been more survivors.

 p.61

can, must, should, ought to, had better

1 I **couldn't** take any photos in the gallery, so I bought some postcards.
 If you want to apply for this job, you **must** be able to speak Spanish.
 We **should** / **ought to** go on the freeway—it's much quicker.
2 We **should have** / **ought to have gone** on the freeway—it would have been quicker.
3 You**'d better** mail the packages today or they won't get there in time.

1 The most common modal verbs for talking about permission and obligation are *can* / *could*, *must*, and *should* / *ought to*.
• We can also use *May I…?* to ask for permission, e.g., *May I use your phone?*
2 We can use *should have* or *ought to have* + past participle to talk about past events that did not happen and that we regret.
3 *had better* is stronger and more urgent than *should* / *ought to* and is often used to give strong advice or a warning. It usually refers to the immediate future.
• The negative is *had better not*. NOT ~~hadn't better~~.

must not / don't have to

You **must not** bring children under 12 into this restaurant.
You **don't have to** tip here unless you think the service was especially good.

must not and *don't have to* are completely different.
– *must not* is used to express an obligation not to do something.
– *don't* / *doesn't have to* is used to express an absence of obligation.

⬅ See 1A p.142 for information about *have to* and *have got to* to express obligation.

need

1 You usually **need to** check in at least two hours before a flight leaves.
 You **don't need to** take a jacket. It's going to be hot today.
2 We **needn't** lock the car. Nobody will steal it in this parking lot.
3 We **needn't have booked** / **didn't need to book**. The restaurant is empty!
4 We had plenty of gas so we **didn't need to stop**, which saved time.

1 We use *need* / *don't need* + *to* + base form to say that something is necessary / unnecessary. You can use these forms for habitual, general, and specific necessity.
2 When we want to say that something is unnecessary on a specific occasion, we can also use *needn't* + base form.

🔍 **don't need to or needn't?**
We use *don't need to* (NOT *needn't*) for habitual or general necessity, e.g., *I don't need to wear glasses. My eyesight is still good.* NOT ~~I needn't wear glasses~~.

3 When something was not necessary, but you did it, you can use either *needn't have* + past participle or *didn't need to* + base form.
4 When something was not necessary, so you did not do it, you must use *didn't need to*. NOT ~~We had plenty of gas so we needn't have stopped, which saved time.~~
• Compare:
 We didn't need to book. (= It wasn't necessary. We may have booked or we may not.)
 We needn't have booked. (= We booked, but it wasn't necessary.)

be able to, be allowed to, be permitted to, be supposed / meant to

1 Starting tomorrow we **won't be able to** park on this street.
 You**'re not allowed to** smoke in any public buildings in our country.
2 It **is not permitted to** take cell phones into the exam room.
3 We **are supposed** / **meant to** check in at 3:30. What time is it now?
 You **aren't supposed** / **meant to** park here—it's a hospital entrance.

1 We often use person + *be able to* or *be allowed to* + base form instead of *can* to talk about what is possible or permitted.
• We **don't** use *it isn't allowed to…* NOT ~~It isn't allowed to take cell phones into the exam room.~~
2 *it* + *be permitted to* + base form is used in formal situations, e.g., notices and announcements, to say what can / can't be done according to the law or to rules and regulations.
3 We can also use *be supposed to* / *be meant to* + base form to say what people should or shouldn't do, often because of rules. There is often a suggestion that the rules are not necessarily obeyed, e.g., *Students are not supposed / meant to have guests after 12:00, but everyone does.*

a (Circle) the right form. Check (✓) if both are possible.
We *couldn't* / *weren't allowed to* go out at night when we were growing up. ✓
1 You *aren't supposed to* / *aren't meant to* park here, but everyone does.
2 You*'d better not* / *don't have to* use his computer. He hates other people touching it.
3 I *shouldn't have* / *must not have* lost my temper last night. I feel really guilty about it now.
4 It is *not permitted* / *not allowed* to take flash photographs in this museum.
5 You *can* / *need to* pay cash here because they don't accept credit cards.
6 You are *allowed to* / *able to* drive in the US when you are 16.
7 We *didn't need to get* / *needn't have gotten* a visa, which was lucky, as we only booked our vacation at the last minute.
8 You really *ought to have* / *should have* gotten advice from a specialist about your back problem.
9 You *better* / *'d better* be on time tomorrow or you may be kicked out of class!
10 You *don't have to* / *needn't* bring your car—we can go in mine.

b Complete the sentences with *three words*.
If you don't finish your homework, you won't be <u>able to watch</u> TV.
1 You don't _____ _____ _____ to go into the art gallery. Entrance is free.
2 We remind you that this is a non-smoking flight. Smoking _____ _____ _____ anywhere on the aircraft.
3 You'd _____ _____ _____ late—you know what Kim is like about punctuality!
4 You _____ _____ _____ back until next month. I don't need the money right away.
5 You _____ _____ _____ you didn't like the pasta. You know how sensitive he is about his cooking.
6 It was a difficult trip because we _____ _____ _____ trains three times.
7 A lot of people think that governments _____ _____ _____ more to protect young people's health.
8 You aren't _____ _____ _____ a motorcycle in New York if you don't wear a helmet.
9 We didn't _____ _____ _____ sweaters after all—it's really warm!
10 Am I _____ _____ _____ a suit to the wedding, or is it quite informal?

⬅ p.67

hear, see, smell, feel, taste

I **can hear** a noise downstairs.
Can you **see** the blue circle at the top of the painting?
I **can smell** burning. Are you sure you turned the gas off?
I **can feel** a draft—is there a window open?
I **can't taste** the garlic in the soup.

The five basic verbs of the senses, *hear*, *see*, *smell*, *feel*, and *taste* are stative (non-action) verbs and are not usually used in the continuous form.

• We usually use *can* with these verbs to refer to something happening right now, instead of the present continuous, e.g., *I can smell gas.* NOT ~~I'm smelling gas.~~ *I can't see the board.* NOT ~~I'm not seeing the board.~~

• *hear* and *see* can also be dynamic verbs and can be used in the continuous form, but with a different meaning. Compare:
I've been hearing good things about you recently. (= been receiving information)
I'm seeing James tonight. (= have arranged to meet him)

hear / see + base form or gerund

1 I **heard** the girl **play** a piece by Chopin.
    I **saw** the man **enter** the bank.
2 I **heard** the girl **playing** a piece by Chopin.
    I **saw** the man **entering** the bank.

1 We often use *hear / see* + object + base form verb. This means you heard or saw the whole action.
2 We can also use *hear / see* + object + gerund. In this case the meaning is slightly different, meaning you heard / saw an action in progress or a repeated action.
• The distinction above also applies to verbs after *watch*, *notice*, *listen*, and *feel*.

look, feel, smell, sound, taste + adjective / noun

1 She **looks** athletic. These shoes **feel** uncomfortable. That **smells** delicious.
    This music **sounds** awful. The soup **tastes** salty.
2 You **look like** your mother. It **sounds like** thunder. This **tastes like** tea, not coffee.
3 She looked **as if** / **as though** she had been crying.
    It sounds **as if** / **as though** someone is trying to open the door.
4 This smells / tastes **of** garlic. This smells / tastes **like** garlic.

When we talk about the impression something or someone gives us through the senses, we use *look, feel, smell, sound,* and *taste.*
After these verbs we can use:
1 an adjective.
2 *like* + noun (but see 4 below for *like* or *of* after *taste / smell*).
3 *as if / as though* + a clause.
4 Compare *smell / taste of* and *smell / taste like*:
    It tastes / smells *of* garlic. (= it has the taste / smell of garlic)
    It tastes / smells *like* garlic. (= it has a similar taste / smell to garlic, but it probably isn't garlic)

seem

1 You **seem** worried. Is something wrong?
2 You **seem to be** a bit down today. Are you OK?
    The waiter **seems to have made** a mistake with the bill.
3 It **seemed like** a good idea at the time, but in fact it wasn't.
    It **seems as if** / **as though** every time I clean the car it rains.

We can use *seem* and *look* to talk about the impression something gives us. Compare:
You seem worried. (= I get this impression from the way you are behaving in general—voice, actions, etc.)
You look worried. (= I get this impression from your face.)
After *seem* we can use:
1 an adjective.
2 a base form verb (simple or perfect or continuous).
3 *like* + noun or *as if / as though* + a verb phrase.
• *seem* is not used in the continuous form.

a Right (✓) or wrong (✗)? Correct the mistakes in the highlighted phrases.
    I'm smelling something funny in here. What on earth is it? ✗
    I can smell something funny in here. What on earth is it?
    1 Kerry says she hasn't been feeling very well recently—do you know what's the matter with her?
    2 We could hardly sleep at all, as we could hear the wind howling in the trees all night.
    3 I was close when it happened. I actually heard the bomb exploding.
    4 Do you know what this piece is? It sounds of Beethoven's 7th, but I'm not quite sure.
    5 I think we should send the juice back. It tastes like vinegar.
    6 They said this bag was leather, but it's feeling more like plastic.
    7 Raquel and you seemed to be getting along well last night. What did you think of her?

b (Circle) the right verb form. Check (✓) if both are possible.
    The waiter *looks* /(*seems*) to have forgotten about us.
    1 He *looked / seemed* very angry about something.
    2 It *looks / seems* as if it's going to rain very soon.
    3 It doesn't *look / seem* possible that ten years have passed since we last met.
    4 Jane *is looking / is seeming* very tired, don't you think?
    5 You *look / seem* much more like your father than your mother. You have his eyes.

c Complete the sentences with *one* word.
    The clouds are very low. It looks *as* if it's going to snow.
    1 This tastes a little _____ a soup my mother used to make. What's in it?
    2 I haven't met the boss yet, I've only spoken to him on the phone. He _____ nice though.
    3 I assume she's gone out because I heard the door _____ about five minutes ago.
    4 The engine sounds as _____ there's something wrong with it. I think we should stop.
    5 My mother's favorite perfume is one that smells _____ roses. Apparently it's made from thousands of petals.
    6 As we walked through the streets we saw lots of young children _____ tourists for money.
    7 Could you possibly speak up a little? I _____ hear you very well.

 p.71

complex gerunds and infinitives

1. She hates **being told** she should exercise more.
   I'm tired of **being lied to**. I want the truth.
   It's very difficult **to get promoted** in this company.
   My car needs **to be serviced**.
2. He thanked them for **having helped** him.
   Having studied one language previously makes it easier to learn another.
   How wonderful **to have finished** all our final exams!
   By the time I'm 30 I hope **to have started** a family.
3. I would like **to have seen** your face when they told you you'd won the competition!
   We would rather **have stayed** in a more central hotel, but they were all full.
4. I'd like **to be lying** on the beach right now.
   She seems **to be coughing** a lot—do you think she's OK?

1. We use a passive gerund (*being done*) or a passive infinitive (*to be done*) to describe actions that are done to the subject.
2. We use a perfect gerund (*having done*) or a perfect infinitive (*to have done*) if we want to emphasize that an action is completed or in the past.
   - Often there is no difference between using a simple gerund or infinitive and a perfect gerund or infinitive, e.g.,
   He denied stealing / having stolen the money.
   It was our fault. It was foolish of us not to lock / not to have locked the car.
3. We use the perfect infinitive after *would like, would love, would hate, would prefer,* and *would rather* to talk about an earlier action. Compare:
   I would like to see the Eiffel Tower. (= when I go to Paris in the future)
   I would like to have seen the Eiffel Tower. (= I was in Paris, but I didn't see it)
4. We use a continuous infinitive (*to be* + verb + *-ing*) to say that an action / event is in progress around the time we are talking about.

other uses of gerunds and infinitives

1. **It's no use worrying**. There's nothing you can do.
   Is there any point (in) asking him? He never has anything useful to say.
   It's no good talking to my dad because he doesn't listen to me.
2. We had **an agreement to share** the costs.
   Our **plan** is **to leave** on Saturday.
3. You can't visit the Palacio de Bellas Artes in a day—there's **too much to see**.
   There wasn't **enough** snow for us **to ski**.
4. Is there **anything to eat**? There's **nowhere to go** at night.
5. I don't know **where to go** or **what to do**.
6. He's the **youngest** player ever **to play** for Peru.

1. We use the gerund after certain expressions with *it* or *there*, e.g., *It's no use, There's no point, It's no good*, etc.
We use the infinitive:
2. after nouns formed from verbs that take the infinitive, e.g., *agree, plan, hope*, etc.
3. after expressions with quantifiers, e.g., *enough, too much, a lot, plenty of,* etc.
   - When we want to refer to the subject of the infinitive verb we use *for* + person or object pronoun before the infinitive. This can be used before any infinitive structure, e.g., after adjectives: *It's very difficult **for me to decide**.*
4. after *something, anywhere*, etc.
5. after question words (except *why*).
6. after superlatives and *first, second, last*, etc., e.g., *Who was the first person to walk on the moon?*

> 🔍 **and + verb**
> We often use *and* + verb instead of infinitive after *try, wait, come,* and *go,* e.g., *Come and see me when you're next in New York. I'm not sure what's going to happen—we need to wait and see.*

a Complete with the right gerund or infinitive form of the verb in parentheses.
I don't like *being prescribed* (prescribe) sleeping pills, even if I'm having problems sleeping.
1. I was smart _____ (follow) my mother's advice. She was exactly right.
2. I'd love _____ (be) there when you told him you were leaving.
3. If I had a serious illness, I would prefer _____ (tell) the truth by my doctor.
4. It's no use _____ (run). The train will have left by now.
5. Mark seems _____ (work) too hard. He looks very tired.
6. By the time I'm 55, I expect _____ (save) enough to be able to just work part-time.
7. The man denied _____ (commit) the crime.
8. There will be plenty of time to have something _____ (eat) at the airport.
9. It's no good _____ (call) him because he's bound to have put it in airplane mode.
10. Who was the second man _____ (walk) on the moon?

b Rewrite the sentences using the **bold** word.
Don't get angry with the doctor. That won't help. **point**
There's no point getting angry with the doctor.
1. We don't have much time so we can't do any more shopping. **enough**
   We _____ do anymore shopping.
2. I hate it when people wake me up from a siesta. **woken**
   I _____ from a siesta.
3. Are you sorry you didn't study harder at school? **regret**
   _____ harder at school?
4. I love it when people help me in the kitchen even when I don't ask them. **without**
   I love it when people help me in the kitchen _____.
5. I really wish I'd been able to go to your birthday party. **love**
   I _____ your birthday party.
6. The children look as if they're having a good time, don't you think? **seem**
   _____, don't you think?
7. I'm not planning to have an operation until I've tried all the other alternatives. **plan**
   My _____ until I've tried all the other alternatives.

⬅ **p.78**

present and future forms

1 **I'm seeing** Sarah tomorrow. We**'re having** lunch together.
2 **I'm going to** have my hair cut tomorrow. She**'s going to** get the last train home.
3 **I'll be going** to the supermarket later—do you want anything? **Will** we **be having** dinner at the usual time? I'm going to see a movie and it starts at 8:00.
4 The train **leaves** in five minutes. Our classes **start** next Tuesday.

1 The present continuous is the most common way to talk about arrangements, i.e., fixed plans for the future, when the time and place have been decided.
2 *be going to* is the most common way to express future plans and intentions and to imply that a decision has been made.

> ### 🔍 *be going to* or the present continuous?
> In most cases you can use either *going to* or the present continuous without much difference in meaning. However, the present continuous emphasizes that a time and place to do something has been decided, while *going to* emphasizes the intention. Compare:
> *I'm seeing Sarah tomorrow.* (= it's our arrangement)
> *I'm going to give her a birthday present.* (= it's my intention)
> We do not use the present continuous when it is clear that something is only an intention, but no arrangements have been made, e.g., *I'm going to talk to Mike about it when I see him next.* NOT *I'm talking to Mike about it…*

3 The future continuous can often be used instead of the present continuous to refer to future arrangements.
• We sometimes use it to emphasize that we are talking about something that will happen anyway rather than something we have arranged. Compare:
I'm seeing Sarah tomorrow. (= I have arranged it)
I'll be seeing Sarah at the party tomorrow. (= it will happen anyway, but I didn't arrange it)
• It is often used to make polite inquiries about arrangements, e.g., *Will you be meeting us at the airport?*
4 We can use the simple present to talk about future events that are part of a timetable or a regular schedule.

other ways of expressing future arrangements

1 My sister **is due to** arrive at 7:30. Can you meet her at the train station?
2 My sister **is about to** have a baby, so I need to keep my phone turned on.
3 It has been announced that the president **is to visit** Brazil next month.

1 *be due to* + base form can be used to say that something is arranged or expected at a certain time.
• We also use *due* on its own to mean "expected," e.g., *The next train is due in five minutes.*
2 We use *be about to* + base form to say that something is going to happen very soon.
• We can also use *be on the verge of* + gerund with a similar meaning, but this is slightly more formal and implies something is more imminent, e.g., *It is believed that the senator is on the verge of resigning.*
3 We can use *be* + infinitive in a formal style to talk about official plans and arrangements.

---

a (Circle) the right verb form. Check (✓) if both are possible.
I see / (I'm seeing) some friends after class tonight.
1 Don't call me between 5:00 and 6:00 because I'll *be having / have* a massage.
2 **A** What are you going to do this evening?
   B I'm not sure. I'm probably *going to watch / watching* the game.
3 When I see my brother next I'm *going to ask / asking* him to pay me back the money I lent him.
4 My dad *is retiring / will be retiring* at the end of this year.
5 My flight *is due to arrive / arrives* at 6:00.
6 It'll be easy to recognize me when I arrive on Saturday. *I'll be wearing / I'm wearing* a white suit.
7 The new exhibition *is to open / is going to open* next month.
8 *I'll be seeing / I'm going to see* John at work tomorrow. I can give him your message then.
9 The train *is going to leave very soon / is about to leave*.

b Look at the sentences you have checked. Is there any difference in meaning or register between the two forms?

c Rewrite the sentences using the **bold** word.
I'm meeting Myriam tonight. **going**
I'm _____*going to meet*_____ Myriam tonight.
1 We're going to leave in a minute. Could you call me back later? **about**
_____. Could you call me back later?
2 Our second-line manager is going to be promoted in the next few months. **due**
_____ in the next few months.
3 Are you going to the cafeteria at lunchtime? If so, could you get me a sandwich? **will**
_____? If so, could you get me a sandwich?
4 The board of directors are about to sign a new agreement. **point**
_____ a new agreement.
5 The manager intends to respond to your complaint in the near future. **responding**
_____ in the near future.

🔴⬅ p.82

ellipsis after linkers

1 He got up **and** (he) **took** a shower.
   She came to the meeting, **but** (she) **didn't say** anything.
   We should call him **or** (we should) **send** him an email.
   We usually have dinner at 7:00 and **then** (we) **watch** TV.
2 They locked the doors and windows **before they left**.
   We'll look at the photos **after we finish** dinner.
   He's stressed **because he has** too much work.
   She was horrified **when she saw** the mess he had left.
   I met Sam **while he was working** in Seoul.

1 After *and*, *but*, and *or* we often leave out a repeated subject or subject and auxiliary verb, especially when the clauses are short.
• After *then* we can also leave out a repeated subject pronoun.
2 We cannot leave out the subject pronoun after *before*, *after*, *because*, *when*, and *while*.

ellipsis after auxiliaries or with infinitives

1 Laura has never been to Brazil, but her sister **has**.
   Gary thinks he's right, but he **isn't**.
   They said I would love the movie, but I don't think I **would**.
   I didn't like the movie, but Mike **did**.
2 I thought I **would be able to** come tonight, but in fact I **can't**.
   I know you**'ve** never **learned** to drive, but I really think you **should have**.
   A You **must** see his latest movie!
   B I already **have**.
3 I've never ridden a motorcycle, but I**'d love to**.
   The students cheated on the exam, even though I **told** them **not to**.

1 We often leave out a repeated verb phrase or adjective and just repeat the auxiliary or modal verb, or the verb *be*, e.g., *Laura has never been to Brazil, but her sister has been there. Gary thinks he's right, but he isn't right.*
• If the verb we don't want to repeat is the present or simple past, we use *do / does / did* in the ellipsis.
2 We can use a different auxiliary or modal verb from that used in the first part of the sentence.
3 We can also leave out a repeated verb phrase after the infinitive. This is called a reduced infinitive, e.g., *I've never ridden a motorcycle, but I'd love to ride one.*

ellipsis with *so* and *not*

1 I'll have finished the work by Friday, or at least I **hope so**.
   A Will you be working on Saturday?
   B I **imagine so**, unless we get everything done tomorrow.
   A You do know it wasn't my fault, don't you?
   B If you **say so**.
2 A Do you think it'll rain tonight?   B I **hope not**.
   A She's not going to pass, is she?   B I**'m afraid not**.
   The children may be back, but I **don't think so**.

1 With positive clauses we often use *so* instead of repeating a whole ⊞ clause after verbs of thinking (*assume, believe, expect, guess, hope, imagine, presume, reckon, suppose, think*) and also after *be afraid, appear / seem,* and *say*.
• *I hope so.* = I hope I'll have finished the work by Friday.
2 With negative clauses we can use either a ⊞ verb + *not* or a ⊟ verb + *so*.
• We usually use a ⊞ verb + *not* with *be afraid, assume, guess, hope, presume,* and *suspect*, e.g., *I hope not.*
• We usually use a ⊟ verb + *so* with *think*, e.g., *I don't think so.*
• With other verbs (*appear, believe, expect, imagine, seem,* and *suppose*) we can use either form, e.g.,
   A *I don't think they'll come now. It's very late.*
   B *No, I suppose not. / I don't suppose so.*

a Cross out the words / phrases that could be left out.
   They look happy, but they aren't really ~~happy~~.
   1 Everyone else loved the hotel we stayed in, but I didn't like it.
   2 Nobody expects us to win, but we might win.
   3 I didn't end up taking the job, but now I think I should have taken it.
   4 I got into the car and I turned the radio on.
   5 A Would you like to come for dinner tomorrow?
      B I'd love to come to dinner, but I'm afraid I can't come.
   6 We don't go to the theater very often, but we used to go before we had children.
   7 I won't be able to go to the concert, but my wife will be able to go.
   8 We didn't enjoy the movie because we arrived late and we missed the beginning.

b Complete with the right modal or auxiliary form.
   I'd like to help you this week but I *can't*.
   1 I'm not vegetarian but my wife _____.
   2 I would love to fly a plane, but I know that I never _____.
   3 Nobody believes me when I say that I'm going to resign, but I _____.
   4 We thought that Karen would get the job, but she _____.
   5 In the end they didn't come, even though they had promised that they _____.
   6 If you haven't seen the movie yet, you _____. It's absolutely fantastic!
   7 If I could help you I would, but I'm afraid I _____.
   8 I don't speak Arabic, but my friend _____.

c Respond to the first sentence using the right form of the verb in parentheses and **either** a reduced infinitive **or** *so / not*.
   A Would you like to come over for dinner?
   B I *'d love to*. (love)
   1 A The weather forecast said it would rain this weekend.
      B I _____. I was planning to do some gardening. (hope)
   2 A Do you drink diet soda?
      B I _____, but I gave it up last year. (use)
   3 A If you think she's coming down with the flu, you shouldn't send her to school.
      B I _____. She might give it to the other children. (suppose)
   4 A Have you spoken to Martin yet?
      B No, but I _____ after the meeting. (try)
   5 A Do you think we should leave early to miss the traffic?
      B I _____, although I'm really enjoying myself. (guess)
   6 A Why are you going to try skydiving?
      B I don't know. I _____. (always / want)
   7 A Did Amira go out again?
      B Yes she did, even though I _____. (tell / not)
   8 A The bank's open until 5:00 p.m. today, isn't it?
      B Yes, I _____. (imagine)

← p.88

9B nouns: compound and possessive forms

apostrophe s

1 I borrowed my **father's** car. I accidentally stepped on the **cat's** tail.
The **company's** main office is in New York.
2 It's my **friends'** wedding. That's the **children's** room.
The blond girl is **Alex and Maria's** daughter.
3 We had dinner at **Tom's** last night. My mother is at the **doctor's**.
4 They played terribly in last **Saturday's** game. She spent a **month's** pay for those shoes!

Possessive forms express the idea of "having" (in a very general sense) that exists between two nouns.
1 We usually use a possessive noun (+ 's) when something belongs to or is a characteristic of a particular person or thing.
• If a name (or singular noun) finishes in s, we either put an apostrophe at the end of the word or add 's, e.g., *Chris' book* or *Chris's book*.
2 With plural nouns we put the apostrophe after the s, e.g., *friends'*. With irregular plurals that don't end in s (*people, children, men*, etc.) we add 's.
• If there are two people, we put the 's on the second name.
3 When 's refers to premises, e.g., "the house of" or "the store of," we often omit, e.g., *house* or *store*.
4 We often use 's or s' with time expressions, e.g., *yesterday's news, a week's vacation*.

using *of* (instead of apostrophe s)

1 Can you remember the name **of** the movie?
My brother lives at the end **of** the road.
The problems **of** old age are many and varied.
2 Tarik is the brother **of** my cousin in Turkey I told you about.
3 Laura is a friend **of** my sister's.

1 We usually use an *of* phrase, not 's, with things or abstract nouns.
2 We tend to use *of* and not 's to express possession with a long phrase, e.g., NOT ~~my cousin in Turkey I told you about's brother.~~
3 With *friend, colleague*, etc., we often say, e.g., *a friend of* + name / noun + 's (= one of my sister's friends).

compound nouns

1 I need the **can opener**. Do you know where it is?
I bought a huge **flowerpot** at a **garden center** near my house.
My brother is a **company director** and my sister is a **history teacher**.
I opened the **car door**, got in, and put on my **seat belt**.
2 I bought my son a new **story book**.
What does that **road sign** mean?
3 There was a **carton of milk** on the table and two **soda cans**.

1 We use compound nouns to express many common ideas in English. The first noun modifies or describes the second noun. *can opener* = an opener for cans, *history teacher* = a teacher of history. The first noun is usually singular, unless it has no singular form, e.g., *clothes*, but the second noun can be singular or plural.

> 🔍 **One word, two words, or hyphenated?**
> Compound nouns are usually two separate words, but they are sometimes joined together as one word, e.g., *sunglasses, bathroom*, or occasionally hyphenated, e.g., *house-hunter, fortune-teller*.

2 We use compound nouns to describe a common class of object or person. Compare:
a story book BUT *a book about house decoration*
a road sign BUT *a sign of the times*
3 With containers, a compound noun (e.g., *a milk carton*) focuses on the container (usually empty), whereas the container + possessive noun (*a carton of milk*) focuses on the contents (the container is usually full).
• Other common examples are *a soda can / a can of soda, a jam jar / a jar of jam, a tuna can / a can of tuna, a matchbox / a box of matches*, etc.

---

a **Circle** the right option. Check (✓) if both are possible.
Let's make (**chicken soup**) / *soup of chicken* for dinner tonight.
1 I enjoy spending time with *my friend's children / my friends' children*.
2 Didn't I meet you *at Jenny's / at Jenny's house* one night?
3 The hero dies at *the end of the movie / the movie's end*.
4 She's *the wife of my friend who lives in Australia / my friend who lives in Australia's wife*.
5 I want to introduce you to Jake. He's *a colleague of my sister's / a my sister's colleague*.
6 When you go to the supermarket, can you buy me *a milk carton / a carton of milk*?
7 The *photo of the house / house's photo* made me want to buy it.
8 I'm looking for a *stories book / story book* that would be good for an eight-year-old.
9 We found *an old photograph box / a box of old photographs* in the attic.
10 The Tower of London is one of *London's most popular tourist attractions / the most popular tourist attractions in London*.
11 There's *a soda can / a can of soda* on the table. Did you leave it there?

b Look at the sentences you have checked. Is there any difference between the two phrases?

c Complete with a compound or possessive noun using a word from each list and 's or ' where necessary.

| Alice and James | bottle | cats | ~~children~~ | dessert |
| garage | government | marketing | ocean | today |

| ~~bedroom~~ | bowls | door | list | menu | manager |
| opener | proposal | view | wedding | | |

I always leave the light on in the *children's bedroom*—my youngest child is scared of the dark.
1 I can't find the _____. It's usually in this drawer, but it's not there now.
2 It's _____ next week and I don't have anything to wear yet.
3 I'm in the mood for something sweet. Could I see the _____, please?
4 **A** There's avocado toast on _____.
   B Great—my favorite!
5 Can I introduce you to Jenny White, our _____? She's been with our company for six years.
6 Don't forget to lock the _____ when you take the car out.
7 We would like a room with an _____, if that's possible.
8 Fraud and abuse have been discovered in the _____ providing relief funds for storm victims.
9 Make sure you fill the _____ with water every day.

← p.92

---

1 beginning with *What...* or *All...*

I need a coffee.	**What I need is** a coffee.
We don't like the weather here.	**What we don't like is** the weather here.
I just want to travel.	**All I want is** to travel.
I only touched it!	**All I did was** touch it!

2 beginning with *What happens is... / What happened was...*

You take a test and then you have an interview.	**What happens is (that)** you take a test and then you have an interview.
We left our passports at home.	**What happened was (that)** we left our passports at home.

3 beginning with *The person who / that..., The thing that / which ..., The place where..., The first / last time..., The reason why...,* etc.

I spoke to the manager.	**The person (who / that) I spoke to was** the manager.
I was irritated by his attitude.	**The thing that / which irritated me was** his attitude.
We stayed in a five-star hotel.	**The place where we stayed was** a five-star hotel.
I last saw him on Saturday.	**The last time I saw him was** on Saturday.
I bought it because it was cheap.	**The reason (why) I bought it was** because / that it was cheap.

4 beginning with *It*

A boy in my class won the prize.	**It was a boy in my class who** won the prize.
We had the meeting last Friday.	**It was last Friday when** we had the meeting.
They charged us extra for the bread.	**It was the bread (that)** they charged us extra for.

When we want to focus attention on or emphasize one part of a sentence, we can do this by adding certain words or phrases to the beginning of the sentence. This is sometimes called a "cleft sentence."

1 We can make some kinds of sentences more emphatic by beginning with *What* (= the thing) or *All* (= the only thing) + clause + *be* and then the part of the sentence we want to emphasize.

2 To emphasize an event or sequence of events, we can begin with *What happens is (that)... / What happened was (that)...*

3 We can make part of a sentence more emphatic by beginning with an expression like *The person who, The place where, The first / last time, The reason why,* etc. + clause + *be,* with the emphasized part of the sentence at the end.

4 We can also use *It is / was* + the emphasized part of the sentence + a relative clause.

🔍 ***It was me who...* or *It was I who...?***
In informal spoken English, if the emphasized part is a pronoun, we usually use the object pronoun after *It is / was,* e.g., *I paid the bill.—It was me who paid the bill.* Compare: *It was I who paid the bill.* (= very formal)

a Complete the sentences with *one* word.
The *last* time I saw my brother was on his birthday.
1 _____ was my father who told me not to marry him.
2 _____ I hate about Sundays is knowing you have to work the next day.
3 The _____ why I want you to come early is so that we can have some time to chat.
4 After you've submitted your résumé, what _____ next is that you get called for an interview.
5 It's not my fault you can't find the papers! _____ I did was clean up your desk a little.
6 The _____ where we're going to have lunch is a sort of artists' café near the theater.
7 _____ happened was that I lost the piece of paper with my flight information on it.
8 It was _____ who told Angela about the party. I didn't realize it was a surprise.

b Rewrite the sentences using the **bold** word.
I only need a small piece of paper. **all**
All I need is a small piece of paper.
1 She left her husband because he cheated on her. **reason**
_____ because he cheated on her.
2 We stopped in an absolutely beautiful place for lunch. **place**
_____ was absolutely beautiful.
3 We got stuck in an enormous traffic jam. **happened**
_____ we got stuck in an enormous traffic jam.
4 They didn't apologize for arriving late, which really annoyed me. **what**
_____ they didn't apologize for arriving late.
5 Your brother broke the laptop. **it**
_____ broke the laptop.
6 I only said that I didn't like her dress. **all**
_____ that I didn't like her dress.
7 I like my Aunt Emily best of all my relatives. **person**
_____ is my Aunt Emily.
8 You pick up your tickets at the box office. **happens**
_____ you pick up your tickets at the box office.
9 Right now you need to sit down and put your feet up. **what**
_____ to sit down and put your feet up.
10 I first met Serena at a conference in Taiwan. **time**
_____ at a conference in Taiwan.

 p.97

defining relative clauses

1 She's the woman **who / that won the marathon**.
   That's the stadium **which / that is going to be used** for the World Cup final.
2 That's the neighbor **whose dog never stops barking**.
3 James is the man **(who) I met at the party**.
   That's the store **(which / that) I told you about**.
4 My sister's the only person **to whom I can talk**. My sister's the only person **(who) I can talk to**.
   This is the hospital **in which** I was born. This is the hospital **(that) I was born in**.
5 She told me **what she had seen**.
   What I like best about New York is the tall buildings.

We use *who, which, whose, whom*, and *what* to introduce a defining relative clause, i.e., a clause that gives essential information about somebody or something.

1 We can use *that* instead of *who / which*. This is very common in conversation.
2 We use *whose* to mean "of who" or "of which."
3 When *who* or *which / that* are the <u>object</u> of the verb in the relative clause, you can leave them out.
4 In formal English, after a preposition, use *whom* for a person and *which* for a thing. In informal English it is more common to leave out the relative pronoun and put the preposition after the verb.
5 We use *what* as a relative pronoun to mean "the thing" or "things which."

See Writing A review p.118 for the rules for reduced relative clauses.

non-defining relative clauses

1 My brother, **who doesn't like sports**, was given a tennis racket for his birthday!
   The palace, **which was built in the 12th century**, is visited by thousands of tourists.
2 Adriana hasn't come to class for two weeks, **which is a little worrying**.
3 They have three children, **all of whom** are good at sports.
   My favorite foods are bread, cookies, and cakes, **none of which** are very good for me.
   A lot of parents, **many of whose** children go to the local school, are protesting today about plans for the new road.

1 A non-defining relative clause gives extra, non-essential information about a person or thing.
   In written English, this kind of clause is separated by commas, or between a comma and a period.
   You can't use *that* instead of *who / which*. NOT *My brother, that doesn't like sports,...*
2 *which* can be used to refer to the whole of the preceding clause.
3 We sometimes use *of which / of whom / of whose* after *some, any, none, all, both, either, neither, several, enough, many*, and *few*.
   We can also use *of which / of whom / of whose* after expressions of quantity and superlatives.

---

a Right (✓) or wrong (✗)? Correct the mistakes in the highlighted phrases.
   She's the neighbor that her daughter has just had a baby. ✗
   She's the neighbor whose daughter has just had a baby.
1 This is the program I was telling you about.
2 Is this the train that it goes to Beacon?
3 She told her boss she'd overslept, that was absolutely true.
4 My son, that is very bright, is applying to Stanford University.
5 The employee to who I spoke gave me some inaccurate information.
6 The woman whose suitcase didn't arrive never got it back.
7 The Canary Islands, which are situated off the coast of Africa, are a popular tourist destination.
8 Everyone in my family always eats that I cook.
9 That's the painting for which we paid over a thousand dollars.
10 The baseball team which fans yell the loudest is usually considered to be the New York Yankees.
11 Which we love about living in Paris is the street cafés.
12 My doctor told me to go jogging, play tennis, or do Pilates, none of what I enjoy.

b Join the sentences using a relative pronoun and the right punctuation.
   I failed my driver's test. It's a pity.
   I failed my driver's test, which is a pity.
1 They gave us a present. This was a complete surprise.
   They...
2 My girlfriend is very intelligent. She's an architect.
   My girlfriend...
3 It's too hot in my apartment. This makes it impossible to sleep.
   It's...
4 A car crashed into mine. It was a Honda.
   The car...
5 I spoke to a police officer. She was driving a police car.
   The police officer...
6 We only bought our computer two months ago. It keeps on crashing.
   Our computer...
7 I left some things on the table. They aren't there anymore.
   The things...
8 That's the electrician. He did some work for my mother.
   That's...
9 I have two brothers. Neither of them can swim.
   I have two brothers...
10 The houses are still in very good condition. Many of them were built in 1870.
   The houses...

 p.102

Personality

1 ADJECTIVES

a Complete the sentences with the adjectives in the list.

bright /braɪt/   conscientious /ˌkɑnʃiˈɛnʃəs/
determined /dɪˈtərmənd/   gentle /ˈdʒɛntl/
resourceful /rɪˈsɔrsfl/   sarcastic /sɑrˈkæstɪk/
self-sufficient /sɛlf-səˈfɪʃnt/   spontaneous /spɑnˈteɪniəs/
steady /ˈstɛdi/   straightforward /ˌstreɪtˈfɔrwərd/
sympathetic /ˌsɪmpəˈθɛtɪk/   thorough /ˈθɜroʊ/

1 He's very _thorough_. Whatever part of a job he's doing, he does it with great attention to detail.
2 He's very _____. He can usually figure out how to solve a problem.
3 He's really _____. He never needs anyone else's help.
4 His girlfriend is a _____ woman. She's sensible and he can really rely on her—just what he needs!
5 She's very _____. Once she's decided to do something, nothing will stop her.
6 My nieces are both really _____. They get good grades at school in all their subjects.
7 He's not very _____. When I was sick last week he didn't even call me.
8 She is so _____! She worked all weekend to make sure she got everything done.
9 My sister's a very _____ person. She's calm and kind and she never gets angry.
10 She's such a _____ person. She's honest and open and says what she thinks.
11 He's very _____. He can suddenly decide to go to Paris in the morning and in the evening he's there!
12 Our math teacher used to be so _____. She loved making comments that were the opposite of what she really meant.

b 🔊 1.6 Listen and check.

> 🔍 **False friends**
> Beware false friends—a word from a foreign language that looks similar to a word in your own language, but has a different meaning. One such example is *sympathetic*. Many languages have a similar adjective—*sympathique* (French), *simpático* (Spanish and Portuguese), *sympatyczny* (Polish)—which means *friendly*.

2 PHRASES

a Complete the phrases with the verbs from the list in the right form.

change   refuse   seem   take (x2)   tend

1 My father _tends_ **to** avoid conflict. He never argues with my mother—he just leaves the room.
2 I don't really like _____ **risks**, especially with money.
3 She makes life hard for herself because she _____ **to compromise**. Everything has to be perfect.
4 She's very stubborn. She rarely _____ **her mind** even when she knows she's probably wrong.
5 I worry about my grandmother. She's so trusting that it would be easy for people to _____ **advantage of** her.
6 **On the <u>surface</u> he** _____ **self-confident, but deep down** he's really insecure.

b 🔊 1.7 Listen and check.

3 IDIOMS

a Match the **bold** idioms 1–6 to their meanings A–F.

1 F My brother-in-law is very **down to earth**.
2 ☐ My mom has **a heart of gold**.
3 ☐ My boss is kind of **a cold fish**.
4 ☐ My brother's **a real pain in the neck**.
5 ☐ Dad's **a soft touch**.
6 ☐ My uncle has **a very short <u>temper</u>**.

A He's unfriendly and he never shows his emotions.
B She's incredibly kind to everyone she meets.
C He's so annoying—he's always taking my things.
D I can always persuade him to lend me his car on weekends.
E He gets angry very easily.
F He's very sensible and practical.

b 🔊 1.8 Listen and check.

> 🔍 **Being negative about people**
> We often use *a bit / a little bit of / kind of a* before negative adjectives or idioms to "soften" them, e.g., *She can be a little sarcastic. He's a little bit of a pain in the neck. He's kind of a cold fish.* We also often use *not very* + positive adjectives rather than using negative ones, e.g., *He's not very bright*, rather than *He's stupid.*

ACTIVATION Think of people you know for two adjectives from **1**, a phrase from **2**, and an idiom from **3**. Tell your partner about them and why they suit the description.

 p.8

Work

1 ADJECTIVES DESCRIBING A JOB

a Match sentences 1–6 with A–F.

1 C My boss has a deep, **authoritative** /əˈθɒrəteɪtɪv/ voice.
2 ⬜ I'm a cashier at a supermarket. I really enjoy my job, but it can be a little **monotonous** /məˈnɒtnəs/ and **repetitive** /rɪˈpɛtətɪv/.
3 ⬜ I'm an elementary school teacher. I find working with young children very **rewarding** /rɪˈwɔːdɪŋ/.
4 ⬜ I work for a small graphic design company and my job's really **motivating** /ˈmoʊtəˌveɪtɪŋ/.
5 ⬜ Being a surgeon is very **demanding** /dɪˈmændɪŋ/.
6 ⬜ I work at an accounting firm. My job is incredibly **tedious** /ˈtiːdiəs/.

A I have to do exactly the same thing every day.
B It makes me happy because it's useful and important.
C When he speaks, we all stop what we're doing and listen to him carefully.
D It's very high pressure and you have to work long hours.
E It's really boring and it makes me feel impatient all the time.
F The kind of work I do and the people I work with make me want to work harder (do better).

b 🔊 **1.10** Listen and check.

ACTIVATION Think of a job you could describe with each adjective in **1**.

2 COLLOCATIONS

a Complete the text with the words in the list.

career challenge clocking experience for full job management permanent positions qualifications unpaid

What I'm really thinking—THE INTERN

I've just started my third internship. At the end of it, I will have been an [1]**unpaid worker** for over a year. It feels as though I'm not in control of my own life, that I'm helpless. [2]**Academic** _____ and [3]**work** _____ are almost irrelevant when you're competing against people who have years of experience, many of whom are taking a step down the [4]_____ **ladder**. I'm not picky—I've spent time in a children's charity, [5]**events** _____, a press office—but they haven't gotten me a [6]_____ **job**. It's demoralizing. And exhausting—[7]_____**-hunting** is a [8]_____**-time occupation**. I [9]_____ anyone who disagrees with me about this. After [10]_____ **out**, most people can be free for the night. For the intern, it's time to go home and look for work. I have no idea how many [11]_____ I've [12]**applied** _____ since graduating, but it's more than 100.

b 🔊 **1.11** Listen and check.

c Complete the two words that collocate with the groups below. What do the phrases mean?

maternity paternity sick	I_____	freelance permanent (opp temporary / fixed-term) full-time (opp part-time)	j_____

3 THE SAME OR DIFFERENT?

a Look at the pairs of words or phrases. Write **S** if they have the same or a very similar meaning and **D** if they are different.

1 colleagues — co-workers — S
2 quit (a job) — resign — ⬜
3 staff — workforce — ⬜
4 be laid off — be downsized — ⬜
5 be out of work — be on leave — ⬜
6 be fired — be sacked — ⬜
7 get promoted — get a raise — ⬜
8 skills — qualifications — ⬜
9 hire somebody — employ somebody — ⬜
10 perks — benefits — ⬜

b 🔊 **1.12** Listen and check.

ACTIVATION Can you explain the difference between the **D** words in meaning or register?

← p.11

 Go online to review the vocabulary for each lesson

Phrases with *get*

1 EXPRESSIONS WITH *GET*

a Complete the sentences with the expressions in the list.

a hold of	a shock	back at	into <u>trouble</u> with	out of the way
rid of	the chance	~~the impression~~	the joke	to know

1 I get *the impression* you're a little annoyed with me.
2 You'll get _____ when you see him. He looks awful.
3 Since we stopped working together, we hardly ever get _____ to see each other.
4 Everyone else laughed, but I didn't get _____.
5 When you get _____ him, I think you'll really like him.
6 I need to speak to Martina urgently, but I just can't get _____ her.
7 I want to get _____ that awful painting, but I can't because it was a wedding present from my mother-in-law.
8 I'm going to get _____ my brother for telling my parents I got home late. Now I won't lend him my bike.
9 He's going to get _____ his wife if he's late again.
10 I tried to walk past him, but he wouldn't get _____.

b 🔊 3.3 Listen and check. What do the expressions mean?

2 IDIOMS WITH *GET*

a Match sentences 1–10 to A–J.

1 *I* **Get real**!
2 ☐ **Get a life**!
3 ☐ I'm **not getting <u>anywhere</u>** with this crossword puzzle.
4 ☐ She really **gets on my nerves**.
5 ☐ She really needs to **get her act together**.
6 ☐ They **get along like a house on fire**.
7 ☐ You should **get a move on**.
8 ☐ Your grandfather must be **getting on** in age.
9 ☐ My boyfriend just never **gets the <u>message</u>**.
10 ☐ She always **gets her own way**.

A It's just too difficult for me.
B Is he in his eighties now?
C They have exactly the same tastes and interests.
D Her exam is in two weeks and she hasn't even started studying.
E If you don't leave soon, you'll miss the train.
F Everything about her irritates me, her voice, her smile—everything!
G He just does whatever she tells him to.
H I keep dropping hints about us getting engaged, but he doesn't seem to notice.
I There's no way you can afford that car!
J You're 40 and you're still living with your parents!

b 🔊 3.4 Listen and check. What do the idioms mean?

ACTIVATION Make personal sentences with two expressions from 1 and two idioms from 2, and tell a partner.

3 PHRASAL VERBS WITH *GET*

a Match the **bold** phrasal verbs to A–L.

1 *J* How often do you **get together with** your extended family?
2 ☐ How long do you think it usually takes people to **get over** a breakup?
3 ☐ How do you react if somebody interrupts you when you're trying to **get on with** some work?
4 ☐ Do you have any friends who you find it difficult to **get through to** in spite of trying to talk to them honestly?
5 ☐ What are the best subjects to study in your country if you want to **get into** politics?
6 ☐ What's the best way to **get around** your city, on foot or by public transportation?
7 ☐ Have you ever cheated on an exam and **gotten away with** it?
8 ☐ What's the minimum amount of money you would need to **get by** if you were living alone in your town?
9 ☐ If you **get** a little **behind** with your work or studies during the week, do you make up for it on the weekend?
10 ☐ Does bad weather ever **get you down**?
11 ☐ In your family, who is best at **getting out of** doing their share of the housework?
12 ☐ If you leave people a message, does it annoy you if they don't **get back to** you immediately?

A recover from
B start a career or profession
C move from place to place
D make somebody understand
E manage with what you have
F fail to make enough progress
G depress you
H respond to somebody by speaking or writing
I avoid a responsibility or obligation
J meet socially
K continue doing
L do something wrong without getting caught

b 🔊 3.5 Listen and check.

ACTIVATION Ask and answer the questions in **3** with a partner.
🔙 p.27

Conflict and warfare

1 WEAPONS

a Match the words and pictures.

arrow /ˈærou/	shield /ʃild/
bow /bou/	spear /spɪr/
1 cannon /ˈkænən/	sword /sɔrd/
helmet /ˈhɛlmət/	

b ▶️ 3.8 Listen and check.

2 PEOPLE & EVENTS

a Match the people and definitions.

ally /ˈælaɪ/   casualties /ˈkæʒəltiz/   civilians /səˈvɪlyənz/
commander /kəˈmændər/   forces /ˈfɔrsɪz/   refugees /ˌrɛfyuˈdʒiz/
snipers /ˈsnaɪpərz/   survivors /sərˈvaɪvərz/   troops /trupz/
the wounded /ˈwundəd/

1 *casualties* : people who have been killed or injured in a war
2 _____ : people who are forced to leave their country or home because there is a war, or for political or religious reasons
3 _____ : a group of people who have been trained to protect others, usually with weapons, e.g., *armed ~*, *security ~*, *peace-keeping ~*.
4 _____ : soldiers in large groups
5 _____ : an officer in charge of a group of soldiers
6 _____ : people who have been injured by weapons
7 _____ : people who are not members of the armed forces
8 _____ : people who shoot at others from a hidden position
9 _____ : people who have managed to stay alive in a war
10 _____ : in time of war, a country that has agreed to help and support another country

b Match the events and definitions.

ceasefire /ˈsisˌfaɪər/   civil war /ˈsɪvl wɔr/   coup /ku/
rebellion /rɪˈbɛlyən/   revolution /ˌrɛvəˈluʃn/   siege /sidʒ/   treaty /ˈtriti/

1 *rebellion* : an attempt by some of the people in a country to change their government, using violence
2 _____ : a sudden change of government that is illegal and often violent
3 _____ : an attempt by a large number of people in a country to change their government
4 _____ : when two armies agree to stop fighting temporarily
5 _____ : a war between groups of people in the same country
6 _____ : when an army tries to take a city or building by surrounding it and stopping the food supply
7 _____ : a formal agreement between two or more countries.

c ▶️ 3.9 Listen and check your answers to **a** and **b**.

3 VERBS

a Complete the sentences with the verbs in the list in the correct form.

blow up   break out   capture   declare
defeat   execute   loot   overthrow
release   retreat   shell   surrender

1 The rebels *overthrew* the government. (= removed them from power using force)
2 Fighting _____ between the rebels and the army. (= started)
3 The army _____ the rebel positions. (= fired missiles at)
4 The rebels _____ . (= moved back, away from the army)
5 Some of the rebels _____ . (= admitted they had lost and wanted to stop fighting)
6 The rebels _____ the airport runway. (= made it explode)
7 The government _____ war on the rebels. (= announced their intention to go to war with them)
8 Some rebels _____ the city. (= stole things from stores and buildings)
9 The army _____ over 300 rebels. (= took them prisoner)
10 They finally _____ the rebels. (= beat them)
11 The army _____ most of the rebel prisoners. (= let them go)
12 They _____ the rebel leader. (= killed him as a punishment)

b ▶️ 3.10 Listen and check.

ACTIVATION Are there any current news stories related to conflict or warfare? What are they about?

↩ p.31

Go online to review the vocabulary for each lesson

Sounds and the human voice

1 SOUNDS

a 🔊 **4.1** All the words in the list can be both nouns and regular verbs. Many of them are onomatopoeic (they sound like the sound they describe). Listen to the sounds and the words.

bang /bæŋ/   buzz /bʌz/   click /klɪk/   crash /kræʃ/
creak /krik/   crunch /krʌntʃ/   drip /drɪp/   hiss /hɪs/
honk /hɑŋk/   hum /hʌm/   rattle /ˈrætl/   roar /rɔr/
screech /skritʃ/   slam /slæm/   slurp /slɜrp/   sniff /snɪf/
snore /snɔr/   splash /splæʃ/   tap /tæp/   tick /tɪk/
whistle /ˈwɪsl/

b Complete the **Sounds** column with the words in the list.

		Sounds
1	This clock has a very loud ____.	tick
2	Don't ____! Get a tissue and blow your nose.	____
3	To get the new software, just ____ on the "download" icon.	____
4	There was a ____ as he jumped into the swimming pool.	____
5	Did you hear that ____? It sounded like a gun.	____
6	I heard a floorboard ____ and I knew somebody had come into the room.	____
7	I could hear the ____ of a fly, but I couldn't see it anywhere.	____
8	I hate people who ____ at me when I slow down at a yellow light.	____
9	When I'm nervous, I often ____ my fingers on the table.	____
10	Don't ____ your soup! Eat it quietly.	____
11	The snake reared its head and gave an angry ____.	____
12	Please turn the faucet off all the way, otherwise it'll ____.	____
13	We could hear the ____ of the crowd in the soccer stadium from our hotel.	____
14	Some of the players continued playing because they hadn't heard the ____.	____
15	I don't remember the words of the song, but I can ____ the tune.	____
16	Please don't ____ the door. Close it gently.	____
17	I heard the ____ of their feet walking through the crisp snow.	____
18	I can't share a room with you if you ____ — I won't be able to sleep.	____
19	Every time a bus or truck goes by, the windows ____.	____
20	I heard the ____ of brakes as the driver tried to stop and then a loud ____.	____

c 🔊 **4.2** Listen and check.

2 THE HUMAN VOICE

a Match the verbs and definitions.

giggle /ˈgɪgl/   groan /groʊn/   mumble /ˈmʌmbl/
scream /skrim/   sigh /saɪ/   sob /sɑb/
stutter /ˈstʌtər/   whisper /ˈwɪspər/   yell /yɛl/

1 *scream* to make a loud, high cry because you are hurt, frightened, or excited
2 _____ (*at somebody*) to shout loudly, e.g., because you are angry
3 _____ (*at something*) to laugh in a silly way
4 _____ (*to somebody*) to speak very quietly, so that other people can't hear what you're saying
5 _____ to speak or say something in a quiet voice in a way that is not clear
6 _____ to make a long deep sound because you are in pain or annoyed
7 _____ (or stammer) to speak with difficulty, often repeating sounds or words
8 _____ to cry noisily, taking sudden sharp breaths
9 _____ to take in and then let out a long deep breath, e.g., to show that you are disappointed or tired

b 🔊 **4.3** Listen and check.

c Answer the questions using one of the verbs in **a**.

What do people do…?
- when they are nervous
- when they are terrified
- when they lose their temper
- when they are not supposed to be making any noise
- when they are amused or embarrassed
- when they speak without opening their mouth enough
- when they are relieved
- when their team misses a penalty
- when they are very unhappy about something

ACTIVATION Choose five sounds from **1** and two verbs from **2**. Make the sounds for your partner to identify.

⬅ **p.36**

Expressions with *time*

1 VERBS

a Complete the sentences with the verbs in the list.

give   have   kill   make up for   run out of   save
spare   spend   take (x2)   take up   ~~waste~~

1 I _waste_ **a lot of time** playing games and messaging on my computer instead of studying.
2 If you take the freeway, you'll _____ **time**—it's much quicker than the local roads.
3 I had three hours to wait for my flight, so I sat there doing *sudoku* puzzles to _____ **time**.
4 There's no hurry, so _____ **your time**.
5 When my mother was young, she never had the chance to travel. Now she's retired and wants to _____ **lost time**, so she's booked a trip around the world.
6 The novel is 700 pages long and I'm a slow reader. It's going to _____ **me a long time** to finish it.
7 I'd better go home now. If I'm late again, my dad will _____ **me a hard time**.
8 I would like to go camping this weekend, but my final exams are next week, so I can't _____ **the time**.
9 My children _____ **all my time**—I never seem to get to read a book or watch a movie!
10 New York's such a fantastic city! You're going to _____ **the time of your life** there.
11 Let's not _____ **too long** at the museum or we'll _____ **time**.

b ◗ 5.4 Listen and check.

2 PREPOSITIONAL PHRASES

a Complete the **Prepositions** column with the prepositions in the list.

at (x3)   before   behind   by   from (x2)   in   off   ~~on~~   to (x2)

	Prepositions
1 I'm really punctual, so I hate it when other people aren't ▨ **time**.	_on_
2 I've never heard of that singer. He must have been ▨ **my time**.	_____
3 ▨ **the time** we got to our hotel, it was nearly midnight.	_____
4 I missed the birth of my first child. I was on a plane ▨ **the time**.	_____
5 He's been working too hard recently. He needs some **time** ▨.	_____
6 If we don't take a taxi, we won't get to the airport ▨ **time** for the flight.	_____
7 I don't eat out very often, but I get takeout ▨ **time to time**.	_____

8 He suffers from back pain and it makes him a little irritable ▨ **times**. _____
9 You can come **anytime** ▨ **10:00** ▨ **2:00**. _____
10 He's a little ▨ **the times**—he still thinks men should wear a suit and tie at work. _____
11 Don't try to multitask. Just do **one** thing ▨ **a time**. _____

b ◗ 5.5 Listen and check.

3 EXPRESSIONS

a Match sentences 1–12 to A–L.

1 ▨ I   The referee's looking at his watch.
2 ▨   He hardly spoke to me at lunch.
3 ▨   I'm really looking forward to my vacation.
4 ▨   I'm sorry, I can't help you this week.
5 ▨   I can't afford a new computer.
6 ▨   She's sure to find a job eventually.
7 ▨   I think I need to take up a hobby.
8 ▨   Stop writing, please.
9 ▨   I thought I was going to be late.
10 ▨   You look very young in that photo.
11 ▨   I hate doing my taxes.
12 ▨   You've had that computer for years.

A But in the end I got to the airport **with time to spare**.
B He spent **the whole time** talking on his cell phone.
C **Time's up.** The exam is over.
D **I'm** a little **short on time**.
E **I've got time on my hands** since I retired.
F I'll have to make do with this one **for the time being**.
G It's only **a matter of time**.
H It must have been taken **a long time ago**.
I **There isn't much time left.**
J **This time next week** I'll be lying on the beach.
K **It's about time** you got a new one.
L They're incredibly tedious and **time-consuming**.

b ◗ 5.6 Listen and check.

ACTIVATION Choose six of the **bold** time expressions and write a synonym or a phrase with the same meaning, e.g., **save time** = spend less time, **on time** = punctual.

◀ p.48

◗ **Go online** to review the vocabulary for each lesson

Money

1 NOUNS

a Match the nouns and definitions.

> ~~budget~~ deposit do<u>na</u>tion fare fee fine grant
> in<u>sta</u>llment loan lump sum <u>sa</u>vings will

1. _budget_ the money that is available to a person or organization and a plan as to how it will be spent over a period of time, *have a limited ~*
2. _____ money that is given by the government or another organization for a particular purpose, e.g., education, *give / receive a ~*
3. _____ money that a bank lends and somebody borrows, *take out a ~*
4. _____ an amount of money that you pay for professional advice or services, e.g., to a lawyer, *charge / pay a ~*
5. _____ the money you pay to travel by bus, plane, taxi, etc., *pay a ~*
6. _____ money that you keep, e.g., in the bank, and don't spend, *have a ~ account*
7. _____ money that you give to an organization such as a charity in order to help them, *make a ~*
8. _____ money paid as punishment for breaking a law, *pay a ~*
9. _____ one of a number of payments that are made regularly until something has been paid for, *pay an ~*
10. _____ the first part of a larger payment, *make / pay a ~*
11. _____ a legal document that says what is to happen to somebody's money and property after they die, *make a ~*
12. _____ an amount of money that is paid at one time and not on separate occasions, *pay a ~*

b 🔊 5.9 Listen and check.

2 MONEY IN TODAY'S SOCIETY

a 🔊 5.10 Listen to the sentences. With a partner, say what you think the **bold** phrases mean.

1. We live in **a consumer society**, which is dominated by spending money on material possessions.
2. The **standard of living** has risen a lot over the past ten years.
3. People's **income** has gone up, but **inflation** is high, so the **cost of living** has also risen.
4. House prices are rising and many **can't afford** to buy a home.
5. Online banking allows people to **manage their accounts**, e.g., check their **balance** and **make transfers** and **payments**.
6. People who have loans have to pay high **interest rates**.
7. A lot of people are **in debt** and have problems getting a **mortgage** to buy their first home.
8. Some people make money by buying and selling **shares of stock** on the **stock market**.
9. Our **currency** is unstable and **exchange rates** fluctuate a lot.
10. A lot of small businesses **went bankrupt** during **the recession**.

b Which aspects of the sentences above are true in your country?

3 ADJECTIVES

a Look at the *Oxford Learner's Thesaurus* entries for *rich* and *poor*. Match the synonyms and definitions.

> **rich** *adj.* rich, <u>a</u>ffluent, <u>loa</u>ded, <u>wea</u>lthy, well-off
>
> 1 _rich_ / _____ having a lot of money, property, or valuable possessions
> 2 _____ (rather formal) rich and with a good standard of living: The ~ Western countries are better equipped to face the problems of climate change.
> 3 _____ (often used in negative sentences) rich: His parents are not very ~ .
> 4 _____ [*not before noun*] (very informal) very rich: Let her pay. She's ~ .
>
> **poor** *adj.* poor, broke, hard up, <u>penn</u>iless
>
> 5 _____ having very little money; not having enough money for basic needs
> 6 _____ (literary) having no money, very poor: She arrived in 1998 as a virtually ~ refugee.
> 7 _____ (informal) having very little money, especially for a short period of time: After he lost his job, he was so ~ he couldn't afford to eat out at all.
> 8 _____ [*not before noun*] (informal) having no money: I'm always ~ by the end of the month.

b 🔊 5.11 Listen and check.

4 SLANG WORDS

> 🔍 **Slang**
> Slang refers to very informal words and expressions that are more common in spoken language. Some slang words (though none of the ones below) can be offensive or taboo.

🔊 5.12 Read and listen to the dialogues. What do the **bold** slang words mean?

1. **A** Nice car! How much are you going to ask for it?
   B **Five grand**. What do you think?

2. **A** I need **five bucks** for a sandwich.
   B Sure, here you are.

3. **A** Great hat! Was it expensive?
   B No, only a **five spot**. I got it at a thrift shop.

4. **A** What's the building work going to cost you?
   B About **50K**. We're redoing the kitchen.

ACTIVATION Make sentences about your country with two words from each section **1**, **2**, and **3**.

⬅ p.52

Phones and technology

1 COLLOCATIONS

a **(Circle)** the right word. Check (✓) if both are possible.

1 I need to **(charge)** / *unplug* my phone—the battery's very low.
2 Can you *give* / *make* me a call this afternoon?
3 I need to *make* / *do* a few calls now. I'll get back to you later.
4 Do you want my cell phone number or my *landline* / *home phone*?
5 I've been calling Tom on his cell phone, but it's *occupied* / *busy* all the time.
6 I know he's been trying to call me all day because I have three *lost* / *missed* calls from him.
7 You have reached the voicemail for 555–4890. Please leave a message after the *tone* / *beep*.
8 In some American towns, the *reception* / *coverage* isn't very good and people can't get a good *sign* / *signal* for their cell phones.

b 🔊 **6.4** Listen and check.

2 PHRASAL VERBS

a **Complete the sentences with the phrasal verbs in the list.**

cut off	free up	get through	~~hang up~~	log in
put through	run out	scroll down	speak up	top out

1 I have to _hang up_ now. My flight's about to board.
2 We were Skyping, but then we were suddenly _____ in the middle of the conversation.
3 The memory limits for many cell phones _____ at 64 gigabytes.
4 I'm not sure if I'll be able to print the whole document because the black ink is about to _____.
5 I tried calling her office, but I couldn't _____. The lines were permanently busy.
6 I can't hear you very well. Could you _____ a little?
7 If you hold, I'll _____ you _____ to the accounts department.
8 If you already have an account with us, _____ with your username and password.
9 I need to delete some files to _____ more space on the hard drive.
10 If you _____ the page, you'll see the attachment at the bottom.

b 🔊 **6.5** Listen and check.

3 SIMILAR BUT DIFFERENT

Talk to a partner. How would you explain the difference between…?

1 a screen and a touch screen
2 a keypad and a keyboard
3 a password and a passcode
4 your contacts and your settings
5 broadband and Wi-fi
6 a laptop and a tablet
7 an update and a pop-up
8 a cookie and a virus
9 streaming and downloading

TIP Change the language on your phone, tablet, or laptop to English. You will very quickly reinforce your phone and technology vocabulary!

⬅ **p.60**

Prefixes

1 NEGATIVE PREFIXES

a Put the words in the list in the right column to make negatives.

agree   appropriate   attractive   capable   coherent   competent   continue   do   easy
embark   honest   hospitable   legal   legitimate   literate   logical   mobile   moral
official   personal   practical   rational   regular   relevant   replaceable

im-	il-	ir-	in-	un-	dis-
					disagree

b 🔊7.4 Listen and check. What letters do the words begin with after **im-**, **il-**, and **ir-**?

2 PREFIXES THAT ADD OTHER MEANINGS

a Read the sentences carefully and match the highlighted prefixes to their meanings A–T.

1 D My daughter has outgrown most of her clothes—she needs a bigger size.
2   A lot of common English verbs are monosyllables, like *get, have, give*, etc.
3   After being proven innocent, he was reinstated at his old job.
4   After the operation, I'll have to go to the hospital once a week as an outpatient.
5   As a child, she was ill-treated* by her stepmother and this had serious repercussions.
6   I haven't been feeling very well recently. The doctor told me to take multivitamins.
7   I must have misunderstood you. I thought you said you didn't want to come tonight.
8   I need to install a new antivirus program on my computer.
9   I was incredibly lucky on my flight to New York—I was upgraded to business class!
10   The police are trying to defuse the situation between the politicians and the protesters.
11   My brother took postgraduate classes in translation and interpreting.
12   A ceasefire is an essential precondition for any negotiation.
13   My sister is overweight—she goes through periods of compulsive overeating.
14   The committee has biannual meetings in October and March.
15   Several different species now coexist peacefully side by side.
16   This work is totally substandard. It's just not acceptable.
17   There will be an intergovernmental conference to look at climate change.
18   They're really understaffed right now because a lot of their workers are sick.
19   When he lifted her up, he seemed to have almost superhuman strength.
20   I'm not very good with my camera. I almost always use the autofocus setting.
      *The prefix *ill* is always followed by a hyphen.

A not enough
B too much
C more than one, many
D further, better, bigger
E wrongly
F below
G two, twice
H against
I one
J by yourself, by itself
K after
L outside, not inside
M before
N remove or reduce
O higher, towards the top
P together
Q badly
R between
S above average
T again

b 🔊7.5 Listen and check.

🔍 **Prefixes with more than one meaning**
Some prefixes have more than one meaning, e.g., *out-, de-*. Compare:

out- + verb usually means further, greater, etc., (than), e.g., *outnumber*
out- + noun / adjective means outside, e.g., *outbuilding*
de- often means remove or take away, e.g., *demystify* = remove the mystery
de- can also mean reduce, e.g., *devalue* = reduce the value of something

ACTIVATION Which prefixes from **2** could you use before each of these words?

-cook (v)   -lingual   - war
-national   -place (v)

🔵 p.67

Travel and tourism

1 VERBS & VERB PHRASES

a Complete the collocations with the verbs in the list.

cancel   chill out   ex**tend**   get a**way**   go
go on   hit   post**pone**   re**charge**   **sample**
~~set off~~   soak up   wander a**round**

1   _set off_____(set out) on a journey / early / late
2   _____ a trip / a visit (= finish later than planned)
3   _____ camping / backpacking / sightseeing / for a stroll
4   _____ vacation / an outing / a trip / a safari / a trek / a cruise / a journey
5   _____ a trip / a flight / a visit (= decide not to go)
6   _____ (or put off) a trip / a visit (= reschedule it for a later time)
7   _____ the old town (= explore in a leisurely way)
8   _____ (unwind) (*informal*) after a tiring day
9   _____ (immerse yourself in) the atmosphere / the culture
10 _____ the local cuisine
11 _____ the stores IDM
12 _____ from it all IDM
13 _____ your batteries IDM

b   🔊 **8.7** Listen and check. What do you think the three idioms mean?

2 DESCRIBING PLACES

a Complete the sentences with the words or phrases in the list.

breathtaking /ˈbrɛθteɪkɪŋ/   dull /dʌl/   **lively** /ˈlaɪvli/
off the **bea**ten track /ɔf ðə ˈbiːtn træk/   over**crow**ded /oʊvərˈkraʊdəd/
~~over**ra**ted~~ /oʊvərˈreɪtəd/   pictu**resque** /pɪktʃəˈrɛsk/   re**mote** /rɪˈmoʊt/
spoiled /spɔɪld/   **tack**y /ˈtæki/   **tour**isty /ˈtʊrɪsti/   un**spoiled** /ˌʌnˈspɔɪld/

1   I think that restaurant's _overrated__ . (= with a better reputation than it really deserves)
2   The museum's pretty _____, but the café's good. (= boring)
3   The stores are very _____, but we bought some nice things. (= designed to attract a lot of tourists)
4   The oceanfront has been _____ by all the new hotels. (= changed for the worse)
5   It's a really _____ area at night. (= full of life and energy)
6   We found a great coffee shop on a side street in Los Angeles, _____. (= away from where people usually go)
7   The hotel pool is always _____. (= with too many people)
8   The view is absolutely _____. (= very impressive, spectacular)
9   We went to a very _____ little fishing village yesterday. (= pretty, especially in a way that looks old-fashioned)
10 The souvenirs were all plastic Eiffel Towers and key rings, really _____ stuff. (= cheap, badly made, and / or lacking in taste)
11 The site of the temple is extremely _____—you can only get there on foot and it takes four hours. (far away from places where other people live)
12 It's a lovely city, almost completely _____ by tourism. (beautiful because it has not been changed)

b   🔊 **8.8** Listen and check.

ACTIVATION Talk about your last vacation using some of the collocations in **1**.

Can you think of a place in your country that you could describe with each of the adjectives in **2**?

🔴 p.80

🟢 **Go online** to review the vocabulary for each lesson

Animal matters

1 ANIMALS, BIRDS, & INSECTS

Young ones

a Match the animals and their young.

calf (*pl* -ves) /kɑf/
chick /tʃɪk/   foal /foʊl/
kitten /ˈkɪtn/   lamb /læm/
~~puppy~~ /ˈpʌpi/

1	dog	*puppy*
2	cat	_____
3	horse	_____
4	cow	_____
5	sheep	_____
6	hen	_____

b 🔊 **9.1** Listen and check.

Where they live

c Match the animals, birds, and insects and the places where they live.

~~bee~~ ca**n**ary dog
goldfish horse **black**bird

1	a hive /haɪv/	*bee*
2	a **stable** /ˈsteɪbl/	_____
3	a **cage** /keɪdʒ/	_____
4	a **kennel** /ˈkɛnl/	_____
5	a tank /tæŋk/	_____
6	a nest /nɛst/	_____

d 🔊 **9.2** Listen and check. What other animals might live in these places?

The noises they make

e Match the animals and the noises they make.

bird cat dog horse lion pig
~~mouse~~

1	squeak /skwik/	*mouse*
2	bark /bɑrk/	_____
3	neigh /neɪ/	_____
4	me**ow** /miˈaʊ/	_____
5	roar /rɔr/	_____
6	grunt /grʌnt/	_____
7	**twit**ter /ˈtwɪtər/	_____

f 🔊 **9.3** Listen and check.

Animal parts

g Match the words and pictures.

☐	a beak /bik/	☐	horns /hɔrnz/
☐	claws /klɔz/	☐	paws /pɔz/
☐	a fin /fɪn/	1	a shell /ʃɛl/
☐	fur /fər/	☐	a tail /teɪl/
☐	hooves (s. hoof) /huvz/	☐	wings /wɪŋz/

h 🔊 **9.4** Listen and check.

ACTIVATION Make "mind maps" for the animals below.

dog   bird   cat   horse

kennel (n)   bark (v)   puppy (n)
fur (n)   **dog**   tail (n)
paws (n pl)   claws (n pl)

2 ANIMAL ISSUES

🔊 **9.5** Listen to the questions below and focus on the meaning and pronunciation of the **bold** words and phrases. With a partner, say what they mean.

In your country, are there any…?
1 organizations that **protect** animals and their **environment**, or **animal charities**
2 **animal rights activists** who organize protests against the use of animals for entertainment, product testing, or in medical research
3 national or regional celebrations where animals are **treated cruelly**
4 national parks or conservation areas where animals **live in the wild**
5 **endangered species** /ɪnˈdeɪndʒərd ˈspiʃiz/
6 animals that are **hunted for sport**
7 animals that are being **bred in captivity** in order to reintroduce them into the wild
8 animals that are kept or transported in **inhumane conditions**, e.g., **veal calves**

ACTIVATION Answer the questions in **2**. Give examples.

⬅ p.87

Preparing food

1 HOW FOOD IS PREPARED

a Match the words and pictures.

- ☐ baked figs
- ☐ barbecued ribs
- ☐ boiled rice
- 1 chopped parsley
- ☐ deep-fried onion rings
- ☐ grated cheese
- ☐ grilled fillet of fish
- ☐ ground beef
- ☐ mashed potatoes
- ☐ melted chocolate
- ☐ peeled shrimp
- ☐ poached egg
- ☐ roasted lamb
- ☐ scrambled eggs
- ☐ sliced bread
- ☐ steamed mussels
- ☐ stewed plums
- ☐ stuffed chicken breast
- ☐ toasted bagel
- ☐ whipped cream

b 🔊 9.11 Listen and check.

2 UTENSILS

a Match the words and pictures.

- ☐ a baking tray /ˈbeɪkɪŋ treɪ/
- 1 a colander /ˈkɑləndər/
- ☐ a cutting board /ˈkʌtɪŋ bɔrd/
- ☐ a frying pan /ˈfraɪŋ pæn/
- ☐ a food processor /fud ˈprɑsɛsər/
- ☐ a kettle /ˈketl/
- ☐ a (mixing) bowl /ˈmɪksɪŋ boʊl/
- ☐ a saucepan /ˈsɔspæn/ (or pot) /pɑt/
- ☐ a sieve /sɪv/
- ☐ a whisk /wɪsk/

> 🔍 **pots and pans**
> This phrase is often used to refer to a mixture of cooking utensils. A pot is any kind of deep round container used for cooking.

b 🔊 9.12 Listen and check.

🔙 p.90

ACTIVATION Have you had any food recently that was prepared in any of the ways in **1**?

Which of the utensils in 2 might you need to make…?

an omelet   spaghetti   cookies

Are there any of the other utensils you'd use?

		usual spelling		! but also
	tree	ee	screech fee	routine suite
		ea	creak treaty	siege key people
		e	even tedious	receipt
	fish	i	kill drip	message
			risk idiom	repetitive
			stick quit	business building
				synonym
	ear	eer	career	period serious
			engineer	weird
		ere	adhere	
			atmosphere	
		ear	fear spear	
	cat	a	bang crash	
			slam tap	
			balance salary	
	egg	e	gentle debt	wealthy
			neck tense	breathtaking
			benefit	steady friendly
			temporary	many said says
	chair	air	aircraft fair	scary bear
			repair	wherever there
		are	spare fare	their
	clock	o	occupation	squash want
			obviously	calm knowledge
			shock sob	
			contract	
			deposit	
	saw	a	bald wall	caught fought
		aw	paw claws	audience
		al	walk talk	
	horse	(o)or	forces snore	war roar pour
			outdoor	board
		ore	bore score	
	boot	oo	loot troops	moving coup
		u*	due flu	wounded through
		ew	view blew	bruise suit
				beauty shoe

* especially before consonant + *e*

☐ vowels   ☐ vowels followed by /r/   ☐ diphthongs

		usual spelling		! but also
	bull	u	bullet pushed	should would
		oo	cooking	woman
			goodness	
			stood wood	
	tourist	A very unusual sound.		
		ur	curious during plural	
		ure	mature endure secure	
		eur	Euro Europe	
	up	u	hum hunt	blood flood
			gut stuck	tough enough
			mussels	couple trouble
			discuss	
		o	above oven	
	computer	Many different spellings—always unstressed.		
		assertive relative challenging		
		complain opinion profession		
		successful		
	bird	er	herbs nerves	earth learner
		ir	circuit birth	world worse
		ur	slurp fur	picture journey
	owl	ou	around	plough drought
			amount	
			profoundly	
		ow	powerful	
			overcrowded	
			meow	
	phone	o*	totally joke	soulmate
			bonus post	although
		oa	groan loaded	shoulders
		ow	arrow below	
	car	ar	bark smart	heart
			sarcastic	
	train	a*	wages hatred	great steak
		ai	tail training	neighbor weight
		ay	away tray	survey obey
	boy	oi	point spoiled	
			voice choice	
		oy	loyal	
			employer	
	bike	i*	sniper wild	eye neither
			Wifi	aisle guy
		y	deny ally	
		igh	sigh bright	

Consonant sounds

		usual spelling	! but also
parrot	p / pp	perks poached recipe deep / apparently gripping	
bag	b / bb	breed bite tablet grab / scribble bubble	
key	c / k / ck / qu	screen economic / skill bankrupt / click trick / quick picturesque	chorus chiropractic technician accurate
girl	g / gg	grunt guided arguably drug / giggle aggressive	ghost colleague
flower	f / ph / ff	fire refugee / photography metaphor / affluent sniff	laugh rough
vase	v	vast voicemail survive review government hive	of
tie	t / tt	track touristy strength retreat / rattle settings	mashed chopped debt receipt
dog	d / dd	defeat declare update crowd / add middle	steamed bored
snake	s / ss / c before e, i, y	stranger responsible / hiss across / ceasefire civilians fancy	scenery psychoanalyst
zebra	z / zz / s	zip zone / buzz dizzy drizzle / misery refuses avoids	dessert
shower	sh / ti (+ vowel) / ci (+ vowel)	shocked sheet shellfish rash / addiction operation / species crucial	sugar sure chef cliché anxious pressure
television		invasion conclusion pleasure casualties massage	

		usual spelling	! but also
thumb	th	thorough thriller thick sympathetic breath death	
mother	th	though therefore either nevertheless smooth	
chess	ch / tch / t (+ure)	change crunch / switched match / capture sculpture	
jazz	j / g / dge	juggle enjoyable / cage besiege / edgy gadget	soldier suggest
leg	l / ll	legal lively landline deal / colleague scroll	
right	r / rr	revolution ribs grand scrambled / surrender overrated	wrist wrinkled
witch	w / wh	wings waist willing towards / whistle whisper	one once
yacht	y / before u mule	yell yoga yogurt yourselves	
monkey	m / mm	mumble motivated temper consumer / stammer recommend	limb dumb
nose	n / nn	nightmare internet monotonous / penniless cannon	knowledge design foreigner
singer	ng / before k	length strong wing / ankle blink	
house	h	heat horns history inherit behave unhelpful	whoever whom whole

☐ voiced ☐ unvoiced

Go online to watch the Sound Bank videos

OXFORD
UNIVERSITY PRESS

198 Madison Avenue

New York, NY 10016 USA

Great Clarendon Street, Oxford, ox2 6dp,
United Kingdom

Oxford University Press is a department of the
University of Oxford. It furthers the University's
objective of excellence in research, scholarship,
and education by publishing worldwide. Oxford is a
registered trade mark of Oxford University Press in the
UK and in certain other countries

ISBN: 978 0 19 490709 5 STUDENT BOOK (PACK
COMPONENT)

ISBN: 978 0 19 490708 8 STUDENT BOOK (PACK)

ISBN: 978 0 19 490700 2 ONLINE PRACTICE ACCESS
CARD (PACK COMPONENT)

ISBN: 978 0 19 490707 1 ONLINE PRACTICE (PACK
COMPONENT)

Printed in China

This book is printed on paper from certified and well-
managed sources

ACKNOWLEDGMENTS

Back cover photograph: Oxford University Press building/David Fisher

The authors would like to thank all the teachers and students around the world whose feedback has helped us to shape this series. The authors would also like to thank: all those at Oxford University Press (both in Oxford and around the world) and the design team who have contributed their skills and ideas to producing this course. A very special thanks from Clive to Maria Angeles, Lucia, and Eric, and from Christina to Cristina, for all their support and encouragement. Christina would also like to thank her children Joaquin, Marco, and Krysia for their constant inspiration.

The publisher and authors would also like to thank the following for their invaluable feedback on the materials: Adam Szynal, Beatriz Martín García, Brian Brennan, Danny Fernandez, Elif Barbaros, Federico Alonso, Freia Layfield, Isidro Almendarez, Jane Hudson, Janet Whitfield, Joanna Sosnowska, John Bolton, Juliana Sluszter, Katarzyna Bielawska, Lesley Pouland, Magda Miszczak-Berbeć, Magda Muszyńska, Morgan Ormond, Pavlina Zoss, Philip Drury, Rachael Smith, Robert Anderson, Sandy Millin, Sinead O'Dea, Tim Weatherhead, Wayne Rimmer.

The Publisher and Authors are very grateful to the following who have provided information, personal stories, and/or photographs: Ghislaine Kenyon, Lisa Imlach (and Skyscanner), Cristina Zurawski, Adrian Hodges, Polly Akhurst (and 'Talk to me London'), Daniel Hahn and Free Word, who published his blog, Beverly Johnson, The School of Life, David and Emma Illsley, Angela Masajo, Eliza Carthy, Professor Mary Beard, Jordan Friedman, Quentin Blake, George McGavin.

The publisher is grateful to those who have given permission to reproduce the following extracts and adaptations of copyright material: p.9 Adapted extracts from the Myers Briggs Test included in the BBC program "What's your personality type?". Reproduced courtesy of Mentorn Media; p.10 Extract from "What I'm really thinking: the female boxer", www.theguardian.com, 30 January 2016. Copyright Guardian News & Media Ltd 2016. Reproduced by permission; pp.10–11 Extract from "What I'm really thinking: the university lecturer", www.theguardian.com, 21 December 2012. Copyright Guardian News & Media Ltd 2012. Reproduced by permission; p.9 Extract from "What I'm really thinking: the 999 operator", www.theguardian.com, 24 August 2013. Copyright Guardian News & Media Ltd 2013. Reproduced by permission; p.12 Adapted extract from "The Sunday Times 100 Best Companies", www.thesundaytimes.co.uk, 2014. Reproduced by permission of News Syndication; p.17 Adapted extract from "Spell It Out: The Singular Story of English Spelling" by David Crystal by Daisy Goodwin, www.thesundaytimes.co.uk, 19 August 2012. Reproduced by permission of News Syndication; pp.20–21 Extract from *Boy: Tales of Childhood* by Roald Dahl, published by Penguin Books Ltd (2008) and Jonathan Cape Ltd (2012). © 1984 by Roald Dahl. Reproduced by permission of David Higham and Farrar Straus and Giroux. All rights reserved; p.25 Adapted extract from "Speaking Two Languages May Slow Brain Aging" by Shelley Emling, www.huffpost.com, 2 June 2014. ©2019 Verizon Media. Reproduced by permission; pp.26–27 Extracts from *Take Care of Yourself* by Sophie Calle, (Actes Sud, 2007). © ADAGP, Paris 2015. Reproduced by permission; p.28 Adapted extract from "Blind date", The Guardian, 19 December 2009. Copyright Guardian News & Media Ltd 2009. Reproduced by permission; p.28 Adapted extract from "The Inside Out Dating Guide 2 – 10 tips for a first date" by Sarah Abell,

www.telegraph.co.uk, 23 July 2010. © Telegraph Media Group Limited. Reproduced by permission; p.37 Adapted extract from "Experience: I have a phobia of sound" by Vicky Rhodes, www.theguardian.com, 22 February 2014. Copyright Guardian News & Media Ltd 2014. Reproduced by permission; p.39 Extracts from www.talktome.global. Reproduced by permission; p.39 Adapted extracts from the comments under "Yes, London is an unfriendly city – and long may it stay that way" by Stuart Heritage, www.theguardian.com, 6 April 2014. Copyright Guardian News & Media Ltd 2014. Reproduced by permission; p.40 Adapted extracts from "Time to Rename the Spoiler: Knowing How Something Ends May Actually Make It More Enjoyable" by Maria Konnikova, http://bigthink.com, 8 September 2011. Reproduced by permission of The Big Think Inc.; p.40 Adapted extract from "Do Not Read This Post: The 10 Biggest Book Spoilers, Ever" by Lauren Passell, barnesandnoble.com, 22 August 2013. Reproduced by permission of barnesandnoble.com LLC; p.42 Adapted extracts from "Translation diary: 1 – An Introduction" (28 October 2013) and "Translation diary: 7 - Try, try again" (10 December 2013) by Daniel Hahn, www.freewordcentre. com. Copyright © Daniel Hahn 2013. Reproduced by permission; p.45 Adapted extract from "Experience: I've been to the quietest place on Earth" by George Michelson Foy, www.theguardian.com, 18 May 2012. Copyright Guardian News & Media Ltd 2012. Reproduced by permission; p.47 "The Chocolate Meditation" by Dr. Danny Penman and Professor Mark Williams from http://franticworld.com/. © 2015 Danny Penman. Reproduced by permission; p.47 Adapted extract from "Working With Mindfulness: Overcoming the Drive to Multitask" by Jacqueline Carter, www.huffingtonpost.com, 26 February 2014. Reproduced by permission of Jacqueline Carter; pp.50–51 Adapted extract from "Do women really want to marry for money?" by Judith Woods, www.telegraph.co.uk, 5 January 2011. © Telegraph Media Group Limited. Reproduced by permission. p.56 Adapted extract from "Living with your parents as an adult: a survival guide" by Tom Meltzer, www.theguardian.com, 21 January 2014. Copyright Guardian News & Media Ltd 2014. Reproduced by permission; p.58 Adapted text from The School of Life presentation "Why small pleasures are a big deal", www.theschooloflife.com/bookshop/, 5 December 2016. Reproduced by permission; pp.60–61 Adapted extract from "How to quit your tech: a beginner's guide to divorcing your phone" by Martha Hayes, www.theguardian.com, 13 January 2018. Copyright Guardian News & Media Ltd 2018. Reproduced by permission; p.62 Adapted extract from "Common Behavioral Addictions" by Chris Iliades, www.everydayhealth.com, accessed 30 October 2014. Reproduced by permission of Everyday Health; p.65 Adapted extract from "How I stay calm, by people with very stressful jobs", Interview by Anita Chaudhuri, www.theguardian.com, 1 March 2014. Copyright Guardian News & Media Ltd 2014. Reproduced by permission; pp.66–67 Extracts from *1,227 Quite Interesting Facts To Blow Your Socks Off* by John Lloyd, John Mitchinson and James Harkin (Faber and Faber Ltd, 2012). Copyright © 2013, 2012 by QI Ltd. Used by permission of Faber and Faber Ltd and W. W. Norton & Company, Inc.; p.68 Adapted extract from "In the Interests of Safety review – it's health and safety gone mad!" by Steven Poole, www.theguardian.com, 25 June 2014. Copyright Guardian News & Media Ltd 2014. Reproduced by permission.; pp.72–73 Adapted extract from "Wolfgang Beltracchi: a real con artist" by Christopher Goodwin, The Times, 10 May 2014. Reproduced by permission of News Syndication; p.77 Adapted extract from "What doctors won't do", www.theguardian. com, 19 January 2013. Copyright Guardian News & Media Ltd 2013. Reproduced by permission; p.78 Adapted extract from "Do the maths: the science behind the numbers that govern our lives" by Rosie Ifould, www. theguardian.com, 16 November 2013. Copyright Guardian News & Media Ltd 2013. Reproduced by permission. p.80 Adapted from "What kind of traveller are you?", Virgin Money Traveller Type Infographic. © Virgin Money PLC. Reproduced by permission; p.81 Adapted extract from "Why I'm Absolutely Sick Of The Traveler Vs Tourist Debate" by Courtney Jones, www.thoughtcatalog.com, 11 April 2016. © The Thought & Expression Company, LLC 2016; p.85 Adapted extract from "4 times you can skip travel insurance—and 3 times you should buy it" by Megan Leonhardt, www. cnbc.com, 15 June 2018. © 2019 CNBC LLC. Reproduced by permission; p.86 Adapted extract from "In defence of not liking animals" by Tim Lott, www.theguardian.com, 3 May 2013. Copyright Guardian News & Media Ltd 2013. Reproduced by permission; p.91 Adapted extract from *How to Eat Out: Lessons from a Life Lived Mostly in Restaurants* by Giles Coren, (Hodder & Stoughton, 2012). Reproduced by permission of Curtis Brown Group Ltd, London, on behalf of Giles Coren Copyright © Giles Coren 2013; pp.92–93 Adapted extract from "Happy eaters Azealia Banks, Goldie, Beth Ditto, Anthony Bourdain: my favourite comfort food" by Jay Rayner with interviews by Eleanor Morgan, www.theguardian.com, 24 November 2013. Copyright Guardian News & Media Ltd 2013. Reproduced by permission; p.98 Adapted extract from "Why I became a U.S. citizen" by Angela Masajo, www.stories.marquette.edu, 10 December 2018. Reproduced by permission of Angela Masajo; p.100 Adapted extract from "G2: Wellbeing: Running or aerobics? Yoga or Pilates? Making the decision to get fit is the easy part – choosing how to go about it is the difficult bit. Petra Bee offers some advice" by Petra Bee, The Guardian, 6 March 2007. Copyright Guardian News & Media Ltd 2007. Reproduced by permission; p.103 Adapted extract from "How Technology is Affecting Sports" by Lewis Howes, www.sportsnetworker.com, 12 May 2010. Reproduced by permission of Sports Networker

Illustrations by: Agnes Bicocchi p. 47; Mark Duffin p.100; Lo Cole: pp.10, 11, 50; Olivier Latyk pp.18, 66, 67, 108, 109, 110, 112, 169; Helen Musselwhite pp.78, 79; The Project Twins pp.9, 162; Roger Penwill pp.68, 69; Sean Sims pp.80 (shoes), 108.

Pronunciation chart artwork: by Ellis Nadler

The publisher would like to thank the following for their kind permission to reproduce photographs: Cover: Hobbit/Shutterstock. Polly Akhurst p.38 (Talk to me London); Alamy Images pp.6 (© Banco de México Diego Rivera Frida Kahlo Museums Trust, Mexico, D.F. / DACS 2019), 14 (Martin & Eliza Carthy/Lebrecht Music and Arts Photo Library), 15 (Eliza Carthy/WENN Ltd), 16 (letterpress alphabet/Tetra Images), 21 (film scene from Charlie and the Chocolate Factory/Pictorial Press Ltd), 26 (modern art gallery/Forray Didier/Sagaphoto.com), 30 (The Great Escape/AF archive), 30 (video still of Gladiator/Photo 12), 31 (video still of 12 Years a Slave/ PictureLux / The Hollywood Archive), 32 (Sophie Marceau/AF archive), 32/33 (Mel Gibson in Braveheart/ ScreenProd / Photononstop), 33 (Braveheart movie poster/World History Archive), 34 (Fresco Detail, Young Girl Reading, 1st Century BC. Artist: Unknown/The Print Collector), 40 (girl reading in front of oversized book display/Andrew Fox), 45 (anechoic chamber/ZUMA Press, Inc), 46 (man eating and talking on phone/Cultura Creative (RF), 56 (mother and daughter/Catchlight Visual Services), 57 (teenager leaving home/Catchlight Visual Services), 57 (frustrated father shouting/Juice Images), 58 (old photo album/csm), 62 (women with many shopping bags/Big Cheese Photo LLC), 70 (wooden cabinet/Folio Images), 74 (childrens book/Sunshine), 88 (steak/Zoonar GmbH), 89 (sheep in truck/Eye Ubiquitous), 89 (giraffe in zoo/Stephen Dorey ABIPP), 96 (terraced houses/Michael Jenner), 96 (inside of inn/Richard Wayman), 116 (children paying hopscotch, 1970s/Heritage Image Partnership Ltd), 118 (Gone Girl book/sjbooks), 124 (Phnom Bakheng temple, Cambodia/Sasha Stowe), 126 (tagliatelle with summer truffle/Zoonar GmbH), 165 (Indian spear/Valentyna Chukhlyebova), 166 (tap/Witold Krasowski), 171 (hiking/ Hero Images Inc.), 172 (horse's legs/Image Source); Jay Brooks p.113 (Stef and Graham wedding day); CartoonStock Ltd p.163 (Ikea Interview/Canary Pete); Companhia das Letras p.42 (Kiko Farkas / Máquina Estúdio e Thiago Lacaz / Máquina Estúdio/ Companhia das Letras); Corbis p. 93 (91 (raw monkfish tail/Lawton/SoFood); Dansie p.19 (4); Digital Learning Associates p.45 (video still from Comic Book Writer video); Eyevine Ltd p. 61 (Anisah Osman Britton/ David Vintiner/Guardian); Faber and Faber Ltd pp.66 ('QI The Book of General Ignorance The Noticeably Stouter Edition' by John Lloyd and John Mitchinson © QI Ltd), 108 ('QI The Book of General Ignorance The Noticeably Stouter Edition' by John Lloyd and John Mitchinson © QI Ltd); Getty Images pp.6 (Frida Kahlo Portrait/Bettmann), 19 (young businessman/Shannon Fagan), 21 (chocolate bar/Tom Grill), 23 (headshot of Jean Piaget/Patrick Grehan), 23 (nanny and child 1890s/ KGPA Ltd), 23 (boy looking in mirror/Constance Bannister Corp), 23 (children playing on swings/David Leahy), 28 (women with gifts/JGI/Jamie Grill), 29 (child painting car/Erik

Dreyer), 29 (hair cut/Peathegee Inc), 29 (paint swatches/Witthaya Prasongsin), 32 (Adrian Hodges/Frederick M. Brown), 33 (poster for Spartacus/Silver Screen Collection), 38 (Miao People Celebrate Manggao Festival In Liuzho/VCG), 51 (Jojo Moyes/J. Quinton), 52 (Mohammad Yunus, Chairman of Grameen Bank/Thomas Samson), 54 (subway/Don Emmert/AFP), 57 (dentist/shapecharge), 57 (boy with grandfather/Paul Burns), 58 (beach in Dominican Republic/Marco Bottigelli), 58 (man playing violin/ Hill Street Studios), 58 (fresh figs/Taras Lisovych), 58 (wedidng day/ fabio Cardoso), 62 (couple using digital devices/Tetra Images), 62 (woman eating doughnuts/Wade), 62 (woman having injections/Vincent Besnault), 62 (skydiving/Kevin Elvis King), 62 (man cycling/adamkaz), 63 (Dr. Travis Stork/Mark Davis), 66 (Ronaldo/Angel Martinez/Real Madrid), 70 (slinky toy/Savushkin), 70 (pirate lego/mattjeacock), 72 (Max Ernst/Berenice Abbott), 73 (Helene and Wolfgang Beltracchi/Baptiste Giroudon/Paris Match), 81 (traveling person/MStudioImages), 83 (woman sat on plane two men asleep on her shoulders/Peter Cade), 83 (cramped tube/Chris Turner), 89 (pit bull terrier/John Wayne Lucia III), 89 (dog jumping through hoop/GK Hart/Vikki Hart), 91 (cafe/Maisant Ludovic), 92 (Goldie the DJ/Pal Hansen), 93 (Cornelia Parker/Pal Hansen), 93 (Yotam Ottolenghi/Levon Biss/Contour by Getty Images), 102 (stadium crowd cheering/GDT), 103 (spectators watching football match/simonkr), 103 (Suarez biting Chiellini/Daniel Garcia), 103 (Matt Wel/David Hancock), 103 (arguing with referee/Attila Kisbenedek), 105 (Wimbledon/Oli Scarff), 108 (Miao People Celebrate Manggao Festival In Liuzho/VCG), 116 (boy with tablet computer/Stephen Simpson), 120 (hands using smartphone/Tetra Images), 122 (students on laptop/damircudic), 171 (tourists/Hinterhaus Productions), 171 (museum/Tim Grist Photography), 173 (poached egg/Diana Miller), (damsons being cooked for jam/David Marsden); Daniel Hahn p.42; Mairi Hamilton p.19 (1); Mona Hatoum p.70 'Incommunicado', 1999, mild steel and wire 50 x 191/2 x 37 5/8 in (127 x 49.5 x 95.5 cm) © Mona Hatoum; Edward Woodman, courtesy White Cube; Damien Hirst p.70 Damien Hirst and Science Ltd. All rights reserved, DACS/Artimage 2019. Photo: Prudence Cuming Associates Ltd; Stephanie Hodges pp.28 (blind date), 113 (blind date/wedding day); Hodder & Stoughton p.91 ('How to eat out' by Giles Coren). Florentijn Hofman p.70 'Kobe Frog', © Florentijn Hofman; David and Emma Illsley p.96; Lisa Imlach/Skyscanner p.13; iStockphoto p. 49 (time spiral/mipan); Beverly Johnson p.43; Frida Kahlo p.6: © Banco de México Diego Rivera Frida Kahlo Museums Trust, Mexico, D.F. / DACS 2019; Jeremy Lambert p.19 (3); Las Vegas Review Journal p.103 (Ron Kantowski). Richard Long pp. 70 © Richard Long. All Rights Reserved, DACS 2019; Angela Masajo p.98; Oxford University Press pp. 19 (Cristina Zurawski/OUP), 63 (portrait of woman/Cecilie_Arcurs), 63 (teen boy portrait/Photodisc), 63 (girl with purple hair/Ingram), 63 (lifebuoy/Corbis), 63 (senior man portrait/Photodisc), 63 (top of man's head/izusek), 100 (weight trainer/ostill); Oxford University Press Video Stills pp. 14, 15, 19, 25, 34 (Mary Beard), 35 (Surita Gupta), 53, 54 (Jordan Friedman and Stressbuster), 55, 65, 74 (Quentin Blake), 75 (headshots), 94 (George McGavin), 95 (headshots), 105; Clive Oxenden p.82; Press Association Images, 72 (Helene Beltracchi/HO/AP); Profile Books/Spell It Out by David Crystal p.17; The Random House Group p.20 (Boy by Roald Dahl/Boy Cover Artwork © Quentin Blake/Used by arrangement with The Random House Group Limited); National Museum and Galleries of Wales Enterprises Ltd: p.70 Blaenau Ffestiniog Circle by Richard Long, credited as: © Richard Long. All Rights Reserved, DACS 2019; Newscom pp.27 (Sophie Calle/BISSON/JDD/SIPA), 38 (polar bear crossing Millennium Bridge/Parry David/PA Photos/ABACA), 93 (Azealia Banks/Lionel Urman), 103 (Serena Williams/Vantagenews); Lily Sadeghi-Nejad p.19 (5); Shutterstock pp.8 (desert with chess figures/Bruce Rolff), 22 (earth/Anton Balazh), 29 (boy throwing out trash/TinnaPong), 34 (Gladiator 2000/Snap Stills), 37 (woman covering ears/file404), 38 (ALAIN ROBERT/Shutterstock), 38 (Play-Doh/Chevrolet), 39 (people icons/Macrovector), 39 (smiling young man/Terry Schmidbauer), 40 (surprise/angellodeco), 48 (frustrated man at airport/Tyler Olson), 54 (hammock/Filip Fuxa), 57 (stressed student/ESB Professional), 58 (grilled cheese sandwich/Olga Miltsova), 58 (hanglider/DCornelius), 58 (Uffizi Museum Gallery/muratart), 58 (black caviar/Tatyana Berkovich), 58 (lily/Laszlo Szelenczey), 60 (hands holding phone/Akhenaton Images), 62 (man playing video games/Cody Wheeler), 68 (stop sign/Andrii_M), 70 (blue agate/Yuri Megel), 75 (feather/Galushko Sergey), 75 (pen nib/koosen), 76 (pills/Triff), 76 (syringe/Yanas), 76 (capsules/Richard M Lee), 76 (medicines/kaarsten), 77 (doctor/DimaP), 86 (kitten/Andrey_Kuzmin), 88 (vegetables/Africa Studio), 91 (couple having lunch/Trendsetter Images), 92 (Lorraine TV show/Ken McKay/ITV), 92 (chilli peppers/Edward Westmacott), 92 (biscuits and gravy/Martha Graham), 93 (oysters/Olga Popova), 93 (gummy bears/Viktor1), 94 (ant/Andrey Pavlov), 94 (lanternfly/Mr. Suttipon Yakham), 94 (moth/Coprid), 94 (shield bugs/Eric Isselee), 94 (cockroach/smuay), 94 (bumblebee/Allocricetulus), 94 (flea/Cosmin Manci), 95 (meal worm/Michiel de Wit), 95 (cricket/Eric Isselee), 95 (wasp/irin-k), 96 (rain outside window/Coffeemill), 165 (wooden arrow/Andrey Burmakin), 165 (bow and arrows/Christian Weber), 165 (ancient Greek helmet/Vartanov Anatoly), 165 (ancient bronze shield/Tatiana Popova), 165 (sword/oksana2010), 166 (water splash/Serg64), 171 (cruise/ NAN728), 172 (Labrador puppy/Nikolai Tsvetkov), 172 (calf/Eric Isselee), 172 (chick/yevgeniy11), 172 (foal/Eric Isselee), 172 (grey kitten/absolutimages), 172 (lamb/Erik Lam), 172 (canary/xpixel), 172 (goldfish/Gunnar Pippel), 172 (bumblebee/Allocricetulus), 172 (blackbird/xpixel), 172 (turtle shell/Pearl Media), 172 (fish fin/Kondor83), 172 (cat's tail/schankz), 172 (cormoran/Suzanna Ruby), 172 (desert horned sheep/Chris Gardiner), 172 (toucan/holbox), 172 (dog paws/tim elliott), 172 (animal fur/ We.photography), 172 (eagle claws/Nomad_Soul), 173 (parsley/optimarc), 173 (raw mince/Elena Elisseeva), 173 (grilled fish/svry), 173 (prawns/Bildagentur Zoonar GmbH), 173 (baked figs/zi3000), 173 (sliced bread/graham oakes), 173 (onion rings/Brent Hofacker), 173 (stuffed chicken breast/Robyn Mackenzie), 173 (whipped cream/Tamara Kulikova), 173 (mashed potato/Volosina), 173 (boiled rice/highviews), 173 (barbecue pork ribs/Everything), 173 (grated cheese/Gayvoronskaya_Yana), 173 (toasted bagels/Christopher WIlans), 173 (scrambled egg on toast/Robyn Mackenzie), 173 (mussels/Nadezda Cruzova), 173 (roast leg of lamb/Joe Gough), 173 (melted chocolate/kaband), 173 (colander/Gavran333), 173 (frying pan/Evgeny Karandaev), 173 (whisk/Jiri Hera), 173 (sifting flour/Africa Studio), 173 (chopping board/Evlakhov Valeriy), 173 (biscuits on tray/Elena Elisseeva), 173 (metal bowl/Andrey Starostin), 173 (food processor/Sean van Tonder), 173 (boiling kettle/Petr Malyshev), 173 (metal saucepan/goutam kr. sen); Skyscanner/Mary Porter pp.12, 114; Telegraph Media Group Limited p. 51 (Jemima Lewis/Andrew Crowley); Paul de Villiers p.19 (6); Women's World Banking, p. 53 (3 photos of women/Julie Slama).

Commissioned photography by: Dean Ryan pp. 20 (book), 41, 90 (menu), 91 (book).

Although every effort has been made to trace and contact copyright holders before publication, this has not been possible in some cases. We apologise for any apparent infringement of copyright and, if notified, the publisher will be pleased to rectify any errors or omissions at the earliest possible opportunity.